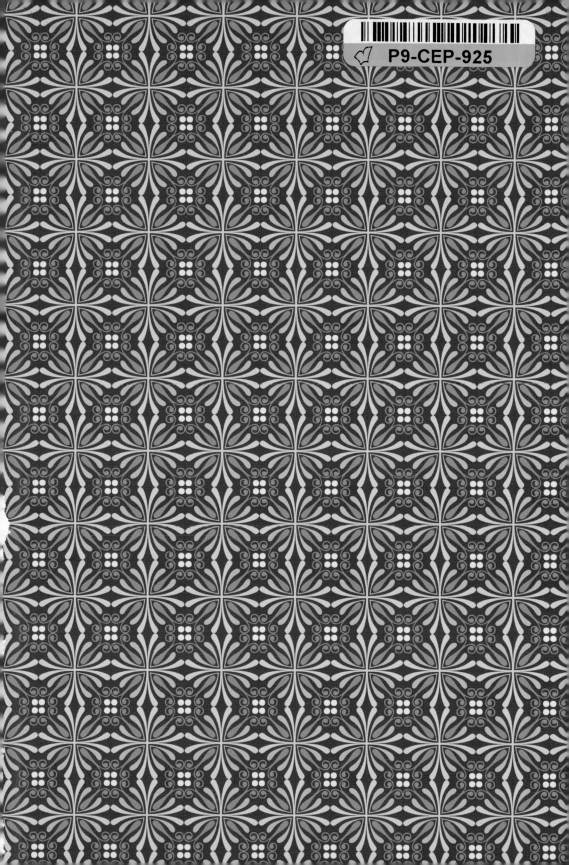

The Book of

Answers

Publications International, Ltd.

Contents

❋ ❋ ❋ ❋

What Was the Boston Tea Party All About? ✦ Why Are We Supposed to Remember the Alamo? ✦ What Did Custer Stand For in His Last Stand? ✦ What Happened to Russia's Imperial Family? ✦ How Did American Women Get the Vote? ✦ What Was World War I Called Before World War II? ✦ Who Betrayed Anne Frank? ✦ Why Did the Nazis Keep a Record of the Holocaust? ✦ How Did the United Nations Start? ✦ What Was Project MKULTRA? ✦ What Were History's Shortest Wars?

Highlights include: Were the Ancient Egyptians the First to Practice Mummification? ✦ If the Maya Were So Brilliant, Why Aren't They Still Around? ✦ Who Are the Aborigines? ✦ Why Did the Romans Sell Urine? ✦ Were There Female Druids? ✦ What Happened to the Anasazi? ✦ Who Were the Goths? ✦ Were the Viking Berserkers Really Berserk? ✦ What Happened to the Knights Templar? ✦ Who Were the Incas? ✦ Are There Cultures in Which Women Have Multiple Husbands? ✦ How Are Weddings Celebrated Around the World? ✦ Do Dutch Couples Always Split the Bill? ✦ Do Ekimos Really Have a Thousand Words for Snow? ✦ What's the Difference Between Cajun and Creole? ✦ What Was the Iroquois League? ✦ Are Good Manners the Same Around the World?

Highlights include: What Are the All-Time Deadliest Disasters? ✦ Can You Outrun Lava? ✦ How Do You Survive a Sinking Car? ✦ How Far Do You Have to Dive Underwater to Escape Gunfire? ✦ What Was the Year Without a Summer? ✦ What Happened to the Donner Party? ✦ What Was America's Deadliest Natural Disaster? ✦ How Many Were Killed in the Triangle Shirtwaist Fire? ✦ What Happened to the Hindenburg? ✦ What Was the Munich Air Disaster? ✦ Has Anyone Survived a Fall from the Golden Gate Bridge? ✦ Who Has Survived Being Stranded at Sea? ✦ How Do You Escape Quicksand? ✦ Can People Get Sucked Out of Planes?

Highlights include: Who Are the Non-Suspects in Police Lineups? ✦ What Was the Cadaver Synod? ✦ Who Was the Bloody Countess? ✦ What's the Difference Between Mass Murders and Serial Killers? ✦ How Many Tools Do You Need to Pick a Lock? ✦ What Is North America's Oldest Law Enforcement Agency? ✦ Who Founded the Mafia? ✦ What Did Lizzie Borden Do? ✦ Who Was Jack the Ripper? ✦ How Did Prohibition Get Started? ✦ Why Do Judges Wear Black Robes? ✦ Who Was H. H. Holmes? ✦ How Do You Make a Citizen's Arrest? ✦ What's the Point of Multiple Life

Sentences? ✦ How Are a Copyright, a Patent, and a Trademark Different? ✦ What Are the Finer Points of an Insanity Plea? ✦ Who Murdered the Clutters? ✦ Why Do Cops Say You Have the Right to Remain Silent? ✦ Who Are Some of the 20th Century's Worst Criminals?

Chapter 1

Animal Kingdom

How Do Worms Breathe?

Worms spend most of their lives underground. But unlike most "underground" creatures, worms don't make tunnel systems and dens—instead, they squish, slide, and squirm through the soil, leaving nary a trace of their presence. Since they don't create any more room than they need for themselves in the earth, how is it possible for them to breathe?

✳　✳　✳　✳

A WORM LACKS THE accoutrements typically associated with breathing (i.e., a mouth, a nose, lungs). It breathes by taking in oxygen through the pores in its skin. To make this possible, the worm's skin must be moist. (This is why, after it rains, worms that are stranded on the sidewalk perish before they can get back into the soil—the sun dries them right out, suffocating them.) Oxygen is absorbed by the capillaries that line the surface of a worm's slimy skin; from there, it goes straight into the bloodstream. In mammals, this process is longer by one step: They take oxygen into their lungs, where it is then transferred to the bloodstream.

Worms can survive underwater for a sustained period of time, but their pores don't function the same way a fish's gills do, so a submerged worm will eventually drown. Some scientists believe that this is why worms come to the surface during a rainstorm: The soil becomes too wet and threatens to drown them. Of course, as we mentioned, this pilgrimage to the surface can lead to a different set of problems.

It seems that the key to a worm's longevity is successfully squirming the fine line between too little and too much moisture. That, and avoiding the pinching fingers of anglers and curious children.

Why Do Cats Purr?

Felines are forever mysterious to mere humans. One of our favorite ponderings is the act of purring.

✳   ✳   ✳   ✳

Don't cats purr because they're content? When cats purr, people are happy. But cats aren't always happy when they purr. There are actually several reasons why cats purr, and happiness is only one of them. Purring begins at birth and is a vital form of communication between mother and kitten. The kitten purrs to let its mother know it's getting enough milk, and the mother cat purrs back to reassure her kitten.

What's the significance of purring? Cats purr throughout their lives and often at times you wouldn't expect. Cats purr when they are frightened, ill, or injured, and they even purr while giving birth. Animal behaviorists believe that cats purr under stressful conditions to comfort themselves and to signal their feelings to other cats. A frightened cat may purr to indicate that it is being submissive or non-threatening, and an aggressive cat may purr to let other cats know that it will not attack. Some cats purr even when they're dying.

Interestingly, domestic cats aren't the only felines that purr. Some of the big cats—lions, cougars, and cheetahs—also exhibit this endearing behavior. But it's much more soothing—not to mention safer—to stroke a purring pet cat than the king of the jungle.

What Animals Keep Harems?

When we hear the word harem, we envision an exotic den that housed the concubines of a wealthy sultan. In the animal kingdom, however, harems are so common that some scientists believe monogamy to be unusual. Here are a few animals that keep harems.

✳ ✳ ✳ ✳

Elephant Seals

MALE ELEPHANT SEALS, found in the Antarctic and along the California coast, are enormous creatures that can reach up to 18 feet long. Their harems start off as a form of female bonding; toward the end of their 11-month pregnancies, females go ashore to give birth in groups. The males follow, fighting among themselves for the right to mate with the females once they've given birth.

Elk

Elk live in the Rocky Mountain region of the western United States and Canada, as well as in the Appalachian region of the eastern United States. Each fall, male elk fight with one another to win the females that will form their harems, which usually consist of six females. The females leave the harems in the spring and form small groups to care for their young before rejoining other elk in herds of up to 400 for the summer. This time, however, the tables are turned, with herds structured as a matriarchy, with one female leader.

Hamadryas Baboons

Most species of baboon form harems, though these are generally informal groupings. By contrast, male hamadryas baboons, which live in Africa, guard their harems fiercely and will attack any female that appears to be wandering away from the group. Males will also attempt to raid another male's harem to capture his females.

Shrimp

These crustaceans are found in most seas of the world, and they all form harems, usually consisting of one male and as many as ten females. The interesting thing about shrimp harems is that when the male leader dies, he may be replaced by a young female shrimp that is able to change her gender in order to take his place.

American Buffalo

American buffalo, or bison, live on plains and prairies, in river valleys, and sometimes in forests. During breeding season—between July and October—males will fight for control of harems by charging at each other until one of them gives up. Harems generally include only three or four females, but during breeding season they keep the males so busy that they have little time to even eat.

Sperm Whales

A harem is just one option for the sperm whale, which will take part in a number of social groupings over its lifetime. Young whales often form coed schools that gradually split up as dominant males drive off smaller ones until just one male is left with as many as 25 females.

Lions

All species of lion form harems (commonly known as prides), usually consisting of one or two adult males, plus six to eight females and their cubs. Because they are smaller, quicker, and more agile than males, females do the hunting. While the lionesses are at work, the males patrol the area and protect the pride from predators.

Bats

Depending on the species, a male bat may have as many as 30 females in its harem. Female bats seek out males, drawn by their scents or, in some cases, their mating calls. Male African hammer-headed fruit bats can produce a symphony of loud, low-frequency honks by banding together in groups. When a female approaches, the calls become more frantic as each male battles to outdo the others.

Wild Horses

American feral horses, found on the East Coast and in the western part of the country, form harems that typically consist of one or two dominant males with five or six mares. A dominant male horse can be dictatorial, keeping his females in line by biting their necks and flanks. Adult mares will rarely leave a harem, and the groups tend to stay together even if the dominant male dies or is replaced.

When Do Fish Sleep?

It's hard to tell whether fish are sleeping because they don't have eyelids. That's why you'll never win a staring contest with your pet guppy—its eyes are always open.

* * * *

SINCE FISH CAN'T close their eyes, how do they get their beauty sleep? They don't, at least not in the way we humans do. Their body functions slow down and they get a bit dozy, but they're generally still alert enough to scatter when danger arises. You could say that they're having a relaxing daydream, but they never actually fall into a deep sleep.

Some fish simply float motionless in the water as they doze; others, such as grouper and rockfish, rest against rocks or plants. The craftier varieties, like bass and perch, hole up underneath rocks and logs or hide in crevices. Others stay on the move while in a daze, recharging without ever stopping.

In the 1930s, biologist David Graham watched a fish sleeping upright on its tail for an hour or so. Then Graham turned on the lights, and the fish jerked back into a swimming position and darted around. It was the aquatic equivalent of being caught napping in school.

When exactly do fish rest? It varies from species to species. Most fish rely on the weak light from the surface to see, and since that light pretty much disappears at night, it's thought that a lot of fish do their resting then. However, some fish rest during the day, while others do so randomly. There are, it seems, no set bedtimes in the fish world.

What Eats Sharks?

The shark has a reputation for being a people killer, ruthlessly nibbling on a leg or an arm just to see how it tastes. But we eat way more of them than they do of us. And we aren't the only ones partaking in their sharkliciousness.

✳   ✳   ✳   ✳

FOR THE MOST part, the big predator sharks are in a pretty cushy position ecologically. As apex predators, they get to do the eating without all that pesky struggle to keep from being eaten. They are important to the ecosystem because they keep everything below them in check so there are no detrimental population booms. For example, sharks eat sea lions, which eat mollusks. If no one ate sea lions, they'd thrive and eat all the mollusks. So if sharks are apex predators (so are humans, by the way), they aren't ever eaten, right? Wrong. Sometimes a shark gets a hankering for an extra-special treat: another shark.

Tiger sharks start eating other sharks in the womb: Embryonic tiger sharks will eat their less-developed brothers and sisters. This practice of eating fellow tiger sharks continues through adulthood. And great white sharks have been found with four- to seven-foot-long sharks in their stomachs, eaten whole.

There's also what is called a feeding frenzy. What generally happens is that an unusual prey (shipwreck survivors, for example) presents itself and attracts local sharks, which devour the unexpected meal. The sharks get so worked up while partaking, they might turn on each other.

Orcas and crocodiles have also been known to snack on shark when the opportunity presents itself. Note that both orcas and crocodiles are also apex predators. So while there are no seafaring animals that live on shark and shark alone, sharks aren't totally safe.

Finally, there's that irksome group of animals known as humans. Many people who reside in Asia regularly partake of shark fin soup, among other dishes prepared with shark ingredients. Shark meat is also eaten in Australia and European countries including Italy, France, Spain, Germany, and Iceland.

Even with all this crazy shark-eating, it's a good bet that a sea lion or mackerel would happily trade places with the apex predator any day of the week.

Why Do Zebras Have Stripes?

The zebra is among the flashy few of the animal world.

✳   ✳   ✳   ✳

LIKE THE BUTTERFLY, the tiger, and the peacock, the zebra looks like it treated itself to a vanity paint job. Which is why one of the theories explaining the evolutionary advantage of those flamboyant stripes sounds counterintuitive: The stripes may actually help zebras blend in.

For one thing, vertical stripes can mesh pretty well with the vertical lines made by the tall grass that covers the ground in much of the zebra's natural habitat. There's a noticeable color difference, of course—tall grass comes in shades of yellow, green, and brown that don't exactly match the zebra's stark black-and-white coat. But this probably doesn't matter much, since the zebra's primary predators—the lion and hyena—seem to be colorblind.

The stripes may also provide the zebras with another way to visually confuse their predators. Zebras usually stick together in herds, where the clusters of vertical stripes can make it tricky for predators to figure out where one zebra ends and another zebra begins. A lion, for example, might have difficulty homing in on any specific zebra, especially the more vulnerable foals. And once the herd starts to move, it's just a blur of stripes.

Some zoologists don't put much stock in the camouflage theory and suggest that the real evolutionary advantage of stripes has to do with a zebra's social life. Every zebra has a unique stripe pattern that can allow the animal to easily identify a friend (or perhaps a mortal enemy). Each zebra's stripe pattern serves as a sort of name tag, a way to be identified within a massive herd. Stripes may also help zebras stick together when predators attack, even at night. In case of emergency, zebra logic may say, follow the stripes.

Another theory suggests that zebra stripes are really a type of bug repellent. Tsetse flies, like other parasitic biting arthropods, seem to be drawn to large, one-colored surfaces—after all, that's how most large animals can be identified. But zebra stripes defy the norm, which may cause the tsetse flies to overlook the beasts when they're hunting for a free meal. There's strong evidence to support this theory: First, tsetse flies bite zebras much less frequently than they do other big animals. Second, there are more tsetse flies in the regions of Africa where zebras sport more pronounced patterns of stripes.

Of course, it's possible that the stripes may serve all of these purposes, at least to some degree. Or perhaps zebras are simply showing off.

What Animals Are Cannibals?

Cannibalism, the act of consuming one's own species, is more common in the natural world than you might think. Read on for examples of animals that take a bite out of their own kind.

✳ ✳ ✳ ✳

Rats and Mice—When populations of mice and rats rise rapidly, there's less food to go around. And when this happens, the hungry and stressed survivors sometimes kill and eat their young. What's particularly interesting about rat cannibalism is that a lot of the time, it's the mama rat that does the eating. When a baby rat is sick or deformed, the mother may eat it because she knows it won't survive, and it will give her strength after labor.

Lions—An adult lion that wants to take over a pride will often kill the group's lion cubs. Basically, it's a way to ensure that there's no rivalry between the preexisting cubs and any that he may father. Sometimes the lions will also eat the cubs. An odd side benefit (for the lion, anyway): If her cubs are dead, a lioness will usually go into heat after two or three weeks, allowing the lion to mate with her sooner. Nice way to woo a lady.

Chickens—Chickens will eat a lot of funky stuff—including their own kin. Cannibalism occurs in chickens most often when they are kept in close captivity and mistake pecking their brethren for typical food foraging. It's also been suggested that some laying hens crave more protein and, er, get by with a little help from their friends.

Caterpillars—Before monarch and queen butterflies become beautiful winged creatures, they're less-than-adorable caterpillars that often eat the eggs of their own species. Hey, it takes a lot of energy to turn from a wormy-looking grub into a lovely butterfly, and they need the calories.

Baboons—The males of several primate species practice infanticide. Baboons have been known to kill and occasionally eat their young. Bands of male primates will attack a rival group and drive off any males. Like the lions, they then kill the offspring so they can mate with the females.

Seagulls—Perhaps a response to overcrowding and food scarcity, male gulls often make a lunch (or breakfast or dinner) of gull eggs and hatchlings.

Crows—It's not pretty, but it's effective: Sometimes a crow will eat the eggs and chicks of his rivals to ensure his own successful breeding.

Spiders—If you're going on any dates with a black widow spider in the near future, watch your back: These and other female arachnids are known to kill and eat their mates either before, during, or after intercourse. But why? There are many theories as to why the female does this, including nourishment or biological habit. As to why the males continue to let it happen, that's a mystery.

Mantid—Perhaps the most well-known cannibal in nature is the Chinese mantid, or praying mantis. The female eats her mate immediately after mating. In fact, it has been studied that more than 63 percent of a female mantis's diet is made up of her paramours.

Hippos—Hippos are one of the largest mammals in the world, able to grow 11 feet long and almost 5 feet tall. These animals eat grass for the most part, but there have been cases when, faced with starvation, hippos have committed cannibalism. Considering the average male hippo weighs between 3,500 and 9,920 pounds, that's a big meal.

Sand Gobies—There are a lot of fish in the sea—and some of them eat their own species. The male sand goby tends the eggs, while the female goes off to mate again. If the eggs still haven't hatched after a long breeding season, sometimes the male goby will eat them.

Does the Color Red Anger Bulls?

A bullfight brings a certain image to mind: a magnificently attired matador waving a crimson cloak at a snorting, stampeding bull. Most observers would turn red-faced upon learning that the color of the cape does not cause the animal to charge.

✳   ✳   ✳   ✳

I F YOU QUESTIONED the average person about what transforms a bull from a passive, pasture-loving bovine into a rip-roaring lethal ton of bolting beef, the answer you'd receive would probably revolve around the rotating red cape brandished by the sartorially splendid matador. If it could offer a retort, the bull would tell you that it isn't the color of the cloak that causes it to snort and stomp; rather, it's the matador's tormenting and provoking mannerisms that raises its ire. The constant furling and unfurling of the red cape by a skilled matador unleashes an aggressive streak in the bull, which has been specially bred and trained to be belligerent and hostile. The exaggerated movements cause the animal to charge at full speed with the intent of doing harm to the manipulator of the muleta. To further anger (and weaken) the bull, a horseman called a picador stabs the animal in the neck and shoulders repeatedly with a sword.

Seeing Red

Cape color has never been a factor, because bulls are colorblind. They are charging at the movement of the matador and his cape, which they perceive to be gray in color. The traditional bullfighter's cape is crimson for two reasons: Red is a color that can be easily seen by the onlookers who enjoy watching this type of spectacle, and it also camouflages the blood that is inevitably spilled by the slowly butchered bull.

What Happened to the Passenger Pigeon?

When Europeans first visited North America, the passenger pigeon was easily the most numerous bird on the continent. But by the early 1900s, it was extinct. What led to this incredible change in fortune?

✳ ✳ ✳ ✳

Pigeons on the Wing

FROM THE FIRST written description of the passenger pigeon in 1534, eyewitnesses struggled with how to describe what they saw. Flights of the 16-inch-long birds were staggeringly, almost mind-numbingly big; flocks were measured in the millions, if not billions, and could be heard coming for miles. When passing overhead, a flight could block out the sun to the point that chickens would come in to roost. Passenger pigeons flew at around 60 miles an hour—one nickname dubbed the bird the "blue meteor"—but even so, a group sighted by Cotton Mather was a mile long and took hours to pass overhead. At least one explorer hesitated to detail what he had seen, for fear that the entirety of his report would be dismissed as mere exaggeration.

Settlers viewed the pigeons with trepidation. A passing flock could wreak havoc on crops, stripping fields bare and leading to famine. A flight passing overhead or roosting on your land would leave everything covered with noxious bird droppings— a situation that would lead to more fertile soil in following years but did little to endear the creatures to farmers at that moment.

Pigeons on the Table

With such vast numbers, what could possibly have led to the extinction of the passenger pigeon? There are a number of theories, but the most likely answer seems to be the most obvious: People hunted them out of existence. Native Americans had long used the pigeons as a food source, and the Europeans followed suit, developing a systematic approach to harvesting the birds that simply outstripped their ability to reproduce. At first, the practice was an exercise in survival—a case of explorers feeding themselves on the frontier or settlers eating pigeon meat in place of the crops the birds had destroyed. However, necessity soon evolved into a matter of convenience and simple economy—the birds were cheap to put on the table.

Killing the birds in bulk was almost a trivial exercise. Initially, settlers could walk up under trees of nesting birds and simply knock them down using oars. As the birds became more wary, firearms were a natural choice for hunters; flocks were so dense, one report gives a count of 132 birds blasted out of the sky with a single shot. Nets were strung across fields, easily yanking the birds from the air as they flew. Perhaps most infamously, a captive bird would be tied to a platform that was raised and then suddenly dropped; as the pigeon fluttered to the ground, other pigeons would think the decoy was alighting to feed and would fly down to join him—a practice that became the origin for the English term "stool pigeon." Hunters would catch the birds in nets, then kill them by crushing their heads between thumb and forefinger.

Pigeons on Display

By 1860, flocks had declined noticeably, and by the 1890s calls went out for a moratorium on hunting the animals—but to no avail. Conservation experts tried breeding the birds in captivity to little effect; it seemed the pigeons longed for the company of their enormous flocks and could not reproduce reliably without them. By the time experts realized this, the flocks no longer existed.

Sightings of passenger pigeons in the wild stopped by the early 1900s. A few survivors remained in captivity, dying one by one as ornithologists looked on helplessly. The last surviving pigeon, a female named Martha, died at the Cincinnati Zoological Garden on September 1, 1914. Her body was frozen in ice and shipped to the Smithsonian Institution, a testament to the downfall of a species.

Can Chickens Fly?

Anyone who has watched a chicken attempt to fly can't help but feel sorry for the creature. It's a combination of a hop, a lunge, and a spasm.

✳ ✳ ✳ ✳

WHY CAN'T CHICKENS fly? After all, they're birds, which means that they have wings. Why not spread those wings and follow their feathered brothers and sisters into the sky?

The problem is that because it's bred to provide humans with jumbo eggs, meaty thighs, and voluptuous breasts, the domestic chicken just isn't very aerodynamic. Furthermore, most domestic chickens are raised in cages on poultry farms and have scarcely enough room to move, let alone fly.

Chickens weren't always grounded. Though they would never have been confused with soaring eagles, chickens did fly at one time in their evolutionary history. The wild red jungle fowl of India, from which chickens are descended, is still able to flap its way up to the tops of trees to escape predators. But for today's domestic chickens, flight is just a distant memory stored deep within their genetic makeup. Besides, these dim-witted animals are far more interested in what's on the ground (seed) than what's above them (sky).

There are a few breeds of chicken that you may still spot in trees or on the tops of fence posts, such as bantams or other smaller varieties. Free-range chickens, which get to run around the farmer's barnyard instead of growing fat and lazy on a roost all day, can also approximate flight—which is the reason that many have their wings clipped. We suspect that these clipped free-rangers aren't the chickens you'll be chowing down during your neighborhood bar's next ten-cent wing night.

What Are the World's Most Dangerous Animals?

The world's most dangerous animal has a legacy of death that stains history. What is this ravenous, bloodthirsty beast? A human, of course. After humans, here are the most dangerous animals in the world.

✳   ✳   ✳   ✳

Mosquitoes

ABOUT 500 MILLION cases of mosquito-borne diseases occur each year, killing as many as 2.7 million. The seemingly innocuous mosquito is in fact the deadliest non-human on the planet, spreading up to a dozen diseases, including malaria, dengue, Zika, and West Nile virus. With more than 3,500 different species, mosquitoes inhabit every corner of the globe, but only a handful carry diseases. The species that live in Africa, Asia, and the Americas are the deadliest.

Venomous Snakes

Snake attacks account for close to 100,000 deaths per year, making these reptiles the deadliest on the planet. Only about 450 of the 3,000 snake species are venomous, and the deadliest live in Africa, Asia, and Australia. Depending on the species of snake and the severity of the bite, death can ensue in a matter of hours if no treatment is given.

Scorpions

The scorpion is a highly compact killing machine that takes more than 3,000 human lives every year. Just 25 of the 1,500 species of scorpions are deadly to humans, and the most venomous live in Africa, the Americas, and Central Asia. The most lethal is the fat-tailed scorpion of North Africa.

Crocodiles

The Nile crocodile is the most dangerous crocodile to humans, followed by the crocs that inhabit Australia. With more than 60 teeth of various sizes, crocodiles are active, vicious, and treacherous brutes that kill approximately 1,000 people each year. But crocs don't just capture prey with their lethal teeth; with an incredibly swift twist of the tail, a croc can capture prey by swatting it from the shore and into the water where it is seized and devoured.

Elephants

We generally think of elephants as friendly, approachable, sometimes cute animals. But don't let that image fool you—each year they crush some 500 humans. Most elephant attacks occur in Africa and India, but attacks in zoos and circuses around the world are becoming more common. Elephants can be very unpredictable, and even so-called tame elephants have turned on and attacked trainers who have known them for years. The number of elephant attacks continues to rise as humans decimate the habitat of this majestic beast. Although elephants are herbivores, when humans get in the way of their food supply, they will use their six tons of bulk, not to mention their menacing tusks, to trample and gore a person to death in a matter of seconds.

Hippos

Found around rivers and lakes throughout Africa, no animal exudes more raw power than the mighty hippo. They might appear lazy and slow, but a hippo can run faster than a person and can maneuver its bulky head and jaws with deadly efficiency. The hippopotamus is an herbivore, but it won't hesitate to attack a human if it feels threatened. Hippos are responsible for approximately 500 human deaths per year, and, like elephants, they charge, trample, and gore their victims to death.

Box Jellyfish

Nearly a hundred swimmers and sunbathers are fatally stung

every year by box jellyfish, which live in the tropical waters of Australia, the Philippines, Papua New Guinea, Malaysia, Indonesia, and Vietnam. A few people have died within a minute of being touched by the cluster of long tentacles, which can number between 40 and 60 in large specimens. When the tentacles come into contact with human skin, they react immediately—clinging to the skin and releasing their venom. If the victim runs or thrashes about, absorption of the venom quickens. And if the victim attempts to remove the tentacles, even more venom is released. Fortunately, the sting from the box jellyfish is usually not fatal, but death by cardiac arrest can occur if antivenin is not given immediately.

Cape Buffalo

Found in Africa south of the Sahara, Cape buffalo are imposing creatures, standing about five feet at the shoulder and weighing nearly a ton. Tip to tip, their horns can measure as much as 58 inches across. Although they are herbivores, Cape buffalo consider humans viable predators, and they won't hesitate to charge and put those horns to work. It's been estimated that each year, Cape buffalo are responsible for about 100 human fatalities.

Leopards

The most adaptable of the big cats, leopards can be found in deserts and forests, on mountains, at sea level, and in lands as diverse as China, India, and Kenya. Leopards have been described as the most physically perfect of the big cats. Weighing 125 pounds or more and averaging two feet tall at the shoulder and seven feet long from nose to tail, they are one of the most powerful animals in the world. Left unchallenged, leopards tend to be shy and retiring, and they will avoid a confrontation with humans. But when challenged, an angry leopard is ferocious, capable of concentrating all its energy into a short-range attack of lightning speed, resulting in about 30 human deaths each year.

Do Cats Always Land on Their Feet?

Cats are curious creatures: Many people believe that a dropped kitty will right itself and land safely on it feet, only to step away aloof and unaffected.

✳ ✳ ✳ ✳

A BELGIAN LEGEND HAS it that in A.D. 962, Baldwin III, Count of Ypres, threw several cats from a tower. It must have been a slow news year, because the residents of Ypres named the last day of their annual town fair "Cat Wednesday" and commemorated it by having the village jester throw live cats from a belfry tower—a height of almost 230 feet. But there's no need to call PETA: The last time live cats were used for this ceremony was in 1817, and since then stuffed animals have been thrown in their place.

As cruel as this custom was, it is unclear whether the cat toss was meant to kill cats or to demonstrate their resilience. After that last live toss in 1817, the village record keeper wrote the following: "In spite of the height of the fall, the animal ran off quickly so that it might never be caught again in a similar ceremony." How could the cat have survived such a tumble?

Twist and Meow

Cats have an uncanny knack for righting themselves in midair. Even if a cat starts falling head first, it almost always hits the ground on its paws. The people of Ypres weren't the only ones amazed and amused by this feline feat. In 1894, French physiologist Etienne-Jules Marey decided to get to the bottom of the mechanics of cat-righting by taking a series of rapid photographs of a cat in midfall. Marey held a cat upside down by its paws and then dropped it several feet onto a cushion.

The resulting 60 sequential photos demonstrated that as the cat fell, it initiated a complex maneuver, rotating the front of its body clockwise and then the rear part counterclockwise. This motion conserved energy and prevented the cat from spinning in the air. It then pulled in its legs, reversed the twist again, and extended its legs slightly to land with minimal impact.

High-Rise Syndrome

The story gets even more interesting. In 1987, two New York City veterinarians examined 132 cases involving cats that had fallen out of the windows of high-rise buildings (the average fall was five and a half stories). Ninety percent of the cats survived, though some sustained serious injuries. When the vets analyzed the data, they found that, predictably, the cats suffered progressively greater injuries as the height from which they fell increased. But this pattern continued only up to seven stories; above that, the farther the cat fell, the greater chance it had of surviving relatively unharmed.

The researchers named this peculiar phenomenon High-Rise Syndrome and explained it this way: A cat that fell about five stories reached its terminal velocity—that is, maximum downward speed—of 60 miles per hour. If it fell any distance beyond that, it had the time not only to right itself in midair but also to relax and spread itself out to slow down its fall, much like a flying squirrel or a parachute.

What's Stored in a Camel's Hump?

The amazingly adaptable camel can plod through the desert for a week without fluids—but don't attribute this water-conservation ability to that big hump.

✳   ✳   ✳   ✳

WITH AN UNWIELDY body that defies its life's mission and a disposition that often has it spitting at its owner, a camel's value as a "desert horse" seems questionable. Then there's that outsized hump, or humps in the case of the Bactrian camel. Hideous so far as aesthetics go, this natural canteen is the camel's true claim to fame. Because of it, the ungainly beast can travel with impunity in temperatures hot enough to fry an egg or kill a person. Or so many people believe.

In truth, this assertion is all wet. A camel does not store water in its hump. That bulge is composed primarily of fatty tissue that, when metabolized, serves as a source of energy. When this energy supply runs low because of a lack of nourishment, the hump shrinks considerably, sometimes to the point of flopping over to one side. On a healthy camel, however, the hump can weigh as much as 80 pounds.

A camel has a unique way of carrying and storing water—through its bloodstream. For this reason, it can go as many as eight days without a drink and can lose as much as 40 percent of its body weight before it feels ill effects. The amount it drinks when water is available—as much as 21 gallons in about ten minutes—would cause severe problems in most animals. What's more, a camel isn't too particular about the water it drinks. A muddy puddle that another animal might wrinkle its nose at would be slurped dry by a thirsty camel.

Do Elephant Graveyards Really Exist?

Do dying elephants actually separate themselves from their herd to meet their maker among the bones of their predecessors?

✳   ✳   ✳   ✳

JUST AS SEARCHING for the Holy Grail was a popular pastime for crusading medieval knights, 19th-century adventurers felt the call to seek out a mythical elephant graveyard. According to legend, when elephants sense their impending deaths, they leave their herds and travel to a barren, bone-filled wasteland. Although explorers have spent centuries searching for proof of these elephant ossuaries, not one has ever been found.

Elephants Never Forget

Unlike most mammals, elephants have a special relationship with their dead. Researchers from the United Kingdom and Kenya have revealed that elephants show marked emotion—from actual crying to profound agitation—when they encounter the remains of other elephants, particularly the skulls and tusks. They treat the bones with unusual tenderness and will cradle and carry them for long periods of time and over great distances. When they come across the bones of other animals, they show no interest whatsoever. Not only can elephants distinguish the bones of other elephants from those of rhinoceroses or buffalo, but they appear to recognize the bones of elephants they were once familiar with. While an elephant graveyard would be a good way to ensure that surviving elephants wouldn't be upset by walking among their dead on a daily basis, it does not fit with the elephants' seeming sentiment toward their ancestors.

Honor Your Elders

The biggest argument against an elephant burial ground can be found in elephants' treatment of their elders. An elephant would not want to separate itself from the comfort and protection of its herd during illness or infirmity, nor would a herd allow such behavior. Elephants accord great respect to older members of a herd, turning to them as guiding leaders. They usually refuse to leave sick or dying older elephants alone, even if it means risking their own health and safety.

But What About the Bones?

Although there is no foundation for the idea that the elephant graveyard is a preordained site that animals voluntarily enter, the legend likely began as a way to explain the occasional discovery of large groupings of elephant carcasses. These have been found near water sources, where older and sickly elephants live and die in close proximity. Elephants are also quite susceptible to fatal malnutrition, which progresses quickly from extreme lethargy to death. When an entire herd is wiped out by drought or disease, the remaining bones are often found en masse at the herd's final watering hole.

There are other explanations for large collections of elephant bones. Pits of quicksand or bogs can trap a number of elephants; flash floods often wash all debris (not just elephant bones) from the valley floor into a common area; and poachers have been known to slay entire herds of elephants for their ivory, leaving the carcasses behind.

In parts of East Africa, however, groups of elephant corpses are thought to be the work of the *mazuku*, the Swahili word for "evil wind." Scientists have found volcanic vents in the earth's crust that emit carbon monoxide and other toxic gases. The noxious air released from these vents is forceful enough to blow out a candle's flame, and the remains of small mammals and birds are frequently found nearby. Although these vents have not proved to be powerful enough to kill groups of elephants, tales of the *mazuku* persist.

The Term Trudges On

Although no longer considered a destination for elephants, the elephant graveyard still exists as a geologic term and as a figure of speech that refers to a repository of useless or outdated items. Given how prominent the legend remains in popular culture, it will be a long time before the elephant graveyard joins other such myths in a burial ground of its own.

What Are the World's Biggest Insects?

Although most people consider insects to be one of life's little annoyances, the following species are more like something out of a science-fiction movie. Don't try to swat one of these.

✳   ✳   ✳   ✳

South American male acteon beetle (*Megasoma acteon*): Not only is the acteon beetle regarded as the bulkiest insect on the planet, but it also has an impressive frame. Males can grow to be three and a half inches long by two inches wide and an inch and a half thick, with three sets of menacing tarsal claws. Its thick, smooth armor and robust thoracic horns make it look like a miniature cross between a rhinoceros and an elephant. It's commonly found in the South American tropics, where it likes to consume tree sap and fruit.

Hercules beetle (*Dynastes hercules*): This beast can grow to be seven inches long. About half of that length is consumed by a threatening, sword-shape horn and a second smaller horn that  curves back toward the head. The male Hercules is smooth and shiny with attractive green-and-black wing cases. This beetle feeds on tree sap and lives in North America.

Giant New Zealand weta (*Deinacrida heteracantha*): The Maori people of New Zealand call this insect "the God of the ugly things," an appropriate observation. It looks like a thwarted attempt to cross a cockroach with a cricket. The weta's body typically measures three inches in length, excluding its protruding legs and antennae, which can more than double its size. It eats leaves, other insects, fungi, dead animals, and fruit.

Borneo stick insect (*Pharnacia kirbyi*): At close to 13 inches in length (20 inches when it stretches its legs), this is the longest

insect on the planet. It is also known as the bent twig insect, for its amazing ability to bend its body at an acute angle and stay that way for hours. The female feeds primarily on bramble during the night, and during the day she keeps very still to avoid being spotted by predators. Males are not quite as big.

Giant Brazilian ant (*Dinoponera gigantea*): The heavyweight champ of ants measures in at more than one inch, and its ability to lift 20 times its body weight makes it one of the strongest creatures in the world. It also displays amazing memory and learning skills, as well as the ability to correct mistakes. It lives in the wetlands and woodlands of the Brazilian jungle and feeds primarily on lowland plants.

South American longhorn beetle (*Titanus giganteus*): This species, also known as the titan beetle, can grow up to six inches long and has extremely powerful legs. The beetle's most prominent—and most menacing—feature is its huge mandible, which can allegedly snap pencils in half. This bug's diet consists of plants, shrubbery, and decaying organic matter.

Giant Fijian longhorn beetle (*Xixuthrus heros*): This intimidating native of the Fijian island of Viti Levu has a body length of five and a half inches and emits a frightful hissing noise when challenged. Ounce for ounce, its jaws are as powerful as those of a killer shark. Luckily for humans, it prefers tropical plants.

South American giant cockroach (*Blaberus giganteus*): The baddest of the cockroach clan lives in dark caves and can reach lengths up to four inches. It discourages predators by mimicking the color of noxious beetles and emitting a foul odor. This cockroach will eat anything but prefers fruit and vegetation.

What Makes a Firefly's Butt Glow?

Fireflies are nature's night pilots, diving and swooping like tiny prop planes, communicating their location and intent with a series of flashing lights.

✳   ✳   ✳   ✳

To POTENTIAL PREDATORS, these lights say, "Stay away." To potential mates, they say, "Come hither." To a child running around the yard with a Mason jar, they can mean a lamp that will grow brighter and more fascinating with each bug caught.

Like all animals possessing bioluminescent traits, fireflies produce their light by means of chemical reaction. The bugs manufacture a chemical known as luciferin. Through a reaction powered by adenosine triphosphate and an enzyme called luciferase, luciferin is transformed into oxyluciferin. In the firefly, this reaction takes place in the abdomen, an area perforated by tubes that allow oxygen to enter, feed the chemical reaction, and become bonded to the luciferin and luciferase produced by the insect. Oxyluciferin is a chemical that contains charged electrons; these electrons release their charge immediately, and the product of this release is light.

All fireflies emit light in the larvae stage. This is thought to be a warning sign to animals looking for snacks: Chemicals in the firefly's (and the firefly larvae's) body have a bitter taste that is undesirable to predators. Studies have shown that laboratory mice quickly learn to associate the bioluminescent glow with a bad taste, and they avoid food that radiates this light.

In adult fireflies, bioluminescence has a second purpose: Some species of firefly use their glow—and distinctive patterns made by dipping and swooping, in which they draw simple patterns against the black of night—to attract a mate. Each firefly species, of which there are 1,900 worldwide, has its own pattern. Male fireflies flit about and show off, while the females sit in a tree or in the grass. The females will not give off light until they see a male displaying the wattage and sprightliness they're looking for in an attractive mate.

They must choose carefully, however, as there are certain adult firefly species that are unable to manufacture luciferin on their own. These species obtain the chemical by attracting unwitting members of other species and consuming them. They do this because without the chemical, they appear to predators much as any other night-flying insects; they need the chemical to advertise their bitter taste.

In the end, this effort might be for naught. The flavor particular to the firefly has that special something that some frogs cannot get enough of. For these frogs, the blinking lights are not so much a warning as a sign reading, "Come and get it!"

Why Don't Animals Need Glasses?

Humans are so quick to jump to conclusions. Just because you've never sat next to an orangutan at the optometrist's office or seen a cat adjust its contact lenses, you assume that animals don't need corrective eyewear.

✳   ✳   ✳   ✳

ANIMALS DO DEVELOP myopia (nearsightedness), though it seems less widespread in nature than among humans. For one thing, nearsighted animals—especially carnivores— would have an extremely difficult time hunting in the wild. As dictated by the rules of natural selection, animals carrying the myopia gene would die out and, thus, wouldn't pass on the defective gene.

For years, nearsightedness was thought to be mainly hereditary, but relatively recent studies have shown that other factors may also contribute to the development of myopia. Some researchers have suggested that myopia is rare in illiterate societies and that it increases as societies become more educated. This doesn't mean that education causes nearsightedness, but some scientists have speculated that reading and other "close work" can play a role in the development of the condition.

In accordance with this theory, a study of the Inuit in Barrow, Alaska, conducted in the 1960s found that myopia was much more common in younger people than in older generations, perhaps coinciding with the introduction of schooling and mass literacy in Inuit culture that had recently occurred. But schooling was just one component of a larger shift—from the harsh, traditional lifestyle of hunting and fishing at the edge of the world to a more modern, Western lifestyle. Some scientists believe that the increase of myopia was actually due to other changes that went along with this shift, such as the switch from eating primarily fish and seal meat to a more Western diet. This diet is heavier on processed grains, which, some experts believe, can have a bad influence on eye development.

And this brings us back to animals. Your beloved Fido subsists on ready-made kibble that's heavy on processed grains, but its ancient ancestors ate raw flesh. If this switch to processed grains might have a negative effect on the eyesight of humans, why not in animals, too?

Unfortunately, there's not much we can do for a nearsighted animal. Corrective lenses are impractical, glasses would fall off, and laser surgery is just too darn expensive. Sorry, Fido!

Are Cats the Only Animals That Bury Their Waste?

If you think a cat isn't smart, consider that it's the only animal with enough sense to bury its waste.

✳ ✳ ✳ ✳

Don't Forget About Humans

Technically, CATS AREN'T the only animals that bury their waste. We humans have been burying our bodily waste for thousands of years, and all signs point toward the continuance of this habit. Civilizations would be overrun by stink if we didn't.

But in terms of "lower" animals, cats are indeed the only animals that have the courtesy to dispose of their droppings. The only other animal that possesses an inclination to do something special with its feces is the chimpanzee, which will sometimes chuck turds at rival chimps in fits of anger. Every other animal just lets the turds fall where they will.

Uncovering the Origins

The house cat's habit of covering its feces probably goes back to its ancestors in the wild. In nature, cats sometimes bury their waste in an effort to hide it from predators and rival cats. In effect, it's the opposite of using urine to mark territory; in an effort to remain incognito, cats do their best to hide any trace of their presence.

By the same token, a dominant cat will leave its poop anywhere it pleases within its territory in order to scare off trespassing felines. A pile of fly-covered waste, and the distinctive smell that wafts from that pile, functions like a BEWARE OF CAT sign. For another cat to ignore this warning would be to invite trouble in the form of teeth and claws.

Your house cat's tendency to bury its feces in a litter box may be a sign that it recognizes your dominance in the house. And if it uses the litter box but neglects to cover its leavings—as some cats do—it may be your tabby's way of acknowledging a kind of shared dominance over the abode.

You needn't worry about your place in the pecking order until you come home and find urine stains in the corners of the room and feces in the middle of the floor. At that point, you are trespassing on your cat's territory—sitting on *its* couch, watching *its* television, popping *its* popcorn—and you'd better start paying rent . . . or prepare to face its terrible wrath.

Are Koalas and Pandas Really Bears?

Although bearlike in appearance, with their rounded ears, plush fur, and black noses, koalas aren't actual bruins. Pandas, on the other hand, are true to form.

✳ ✳ ✳ ✳

Cute as an Opossum?

THERE ARE FEW animals on Earth cuter than the cuddly koala. They're sometimes called Australia's teddy bears, but koalas are in fact related more closely to the ratlike American opossum than the impressive American grizzly.

Koalas are marsupials, which means they raise their young in special pouches, just like kangaroos, wallabies, and wombats (which are also indigenous to Australia). Their young, called joeys, are about the size of a large jelly bean when born and must make their way through their mother's fur to the protection of the pouch if they are to survive. As a baby grows, it starts making trips outside the pouch, clinging to its mother's stomach or back but returning to the pouch when scared, sleepy, or hungry. When a koala reaches a year old, it's usually large enough to live on its own.

Unlike real bears, koalas spend almost their entire lives roosting in trees, traveling on the ground only to find a new tree to call home. Koalas dine exclusively on eucalyptus leaves, of which there are more than 600 varieties in Australia. Eucalyptus leaves are poisonous to most other animals, but koalas have special bacteria in their stomachs that break down dangerous oils in the leaves.

The Case for Pandas

Until recently, the giant panda, despite its appearance, was also considered a non-bear. Some scientists believed pandas were more closely related to the raccoon, whereas others speculated that they were in a group all their own. However, by studying the animals' DNA, scientists were able to confirm that the giant panda is a closer relative to Yogi Bear than it is to Rocky Raccoon.

How Fast Is a Snail's Pace?

The word "slow" hardly begins to cover it. These animals make all others look like Speedy Gonzales. Next to the snail, tortoises look like hares, and hares look like bolts of furry brown lightning.

✳   ✳   ✳   ✳

ALL OF THIS snail talk brings to mind a bad joke: What did the snail riding on the tortoise's back say? *Whee!* But enough of the bad jokes—you want to know just how fast a snail travels.

Garden snails have a top speed of about 0.03 mile per hour, according to *The World Almanac and Book of Facts*. However, snails observed in a championship race in London took the 13-inch course at a much slower rate—presumably because snails lack ambition when it comes to competition. To really get a snail moving, one would have to make the snail think its life was in jeopardy. Maybe the racing snails' owners should be wearing feathered wings and beaks, cawing instead of cheering.

The current record holder of the London race, the Guinness Gastropod Championship, is a snail named Archie, who made the trek in two minutes, 20 seconds in 1995. This calculates to 0.0053 mile per hour. At that rate, a snail might cover a yard in 6.4 minutes. If he kept going, he might make a mile in a little less than eight days.

In the time it takes you to watch a movie, your pet snail might travel about 56 feet. You could watch a complete trilogy, and your snail might not even make it out of the house. Put your pet snail on the ground and forget about him—he'll be right around where you left him when you get back. So long as no one steps on him, that is.

What Are the World's Braniest Animals?

It's notoriously difficult to gauge intelligence, both in humans and animals. Comparing animal IQs is especially tricky, since different species may be wired in completely different ways. But when you look broadly at problem-solving and learning ability, several animal brainiacs do stand out from the crowd.

✳ ✳ ✳ ✳

Great Apes

SCIENTISTS GENERALLY AGREE that after humans, the smartest animals are our closest relatives: chimpanzees, gorillas, orangutans, and bonobos (close cousins to the common chimpanzee). All of the great apes can solve puzzles, communicate using sign language and keyboards, and use tools. Chimpanzees even make their own sharpened spears for hunting bush babies, and orangutans can craft hats and roofs out of leaves. One bonobo named Kanzi has developed the language skills of a three-year-old child—and with very little training. Using a computer system, Kanzi can "speak" around 250 words and can understand 3,000 more.

Dolphins and Whales

Dolphins are right up there with apes on the intelligence scale. They come up with clever solutions to complex problems, follow detailed instructions, and learn new information quickly—even by watching television. They also seem to talk to each other, though we don't understand their language. Scientists believe some species use individual "names"—a unique whistle to represent an individual—and that they even refer to other dolphins in "conversation" with each other. Researchers have also observed dolphins using tools. Bottlenose dolphins off the coast of Australia will slip their snouts into sponges to protect themselves from stinging animals and abrasion while foraging for food on the ocean floor. Marine biologists believe whales exhibit similar intelligence levels as well as rich emotional lives.

Elephants

In addition to their famous long memories, elephants appear to establish deep relationships, form detailed mental maps of where their herd members are, and communicate extensively over long distances through low-frequency noises. They also make simple tools, fashioning fans from branches to shoo away flies. Researchers have observed that elephants in a Kenyan national park can even distinguish between local tribes based on smell and clothing. The elephants are fine with one tribe but wary of the other, and for good reason: That tribe sometimes spears elephants.

Parrots

People see intelligence in parrots more readily than in other smart animals because they have the ability to speak human words. But in addition to their famed verbal abilities, the birds really do seem to have significant brain power. The most famous brainy bird, an African gray parrot named Alex, who died in 2007, exhibited many of the intellectual capabilities of a five-year-old. He had only a 150-word vocabulary, but he knew basic addition, subtraction, spelling, and colors, and had mastered such concepts as "same," "different," and "none."

Monkeys

They're not as smart as apes, but monkeys are no intellectual slouches. For example, macaque monkeys can understand basic math and will come up with specific cooing noises to refer to individual objects. Scientists have also trained them to learn new skills by imitating human actions, including using tools to accomplish specific tasks. They have a knack for politics, too, expertly establishing and navigating complex monkey societies.

Dogs

If you're looking for animal brilliance, you might find it right next to you on the couch. Dogs are good at learning tricks, and they also demonstrate incredible problem-solving abilities, an understanding of basic arithmetic, and mastery of navigating complex social relationships. A 2009 study found that the average dog can learn 165 words, which is on par with a two-year-old child. And dogs in the top 20 percent of intelligence can learn 250 words. Border collies are generally considered the smartest breed, followed by poodles and German shepherds. One border collie, named Rico, actually knows the names of 200 different toys and objects. When his owners ask for a toy by name, he'll go to the next room and retrieve it for them.

What Are Periodical Cicadas?

Periodical cicadas are a specific set of seven species of the Magicicada *genus that emerge every 13 or 17 years. What is astounding about them, aside from their unmistakable buzzing sound, is their highly synchronized life cycles. Periodical cicadas are native to eastern North America and exist nowhere else in the world. The 17-year species are found in northern states, while 13-year cicadas appear in southern and midwestern states.*

✳ ✳ ✳ ✳

AFTER LIVING UNDERGROUND for 13–17 years, feeding on the fluids of plant roots, periodical cicada nymphs emerge when soil temperatures reach 64 degrees (typically in May).

They usually emerge in the evening, often after a warm rain. Once above ground the cicada nymphs climb a tree where they shed their skins, expand their wings, and change to their adult coloring. Periodical cicadas are black with orange wing veins and red eyes. In fact, they have five eyes.

Adult periodical cicadas live for only three to four weeks, and as such, they are all gone by mid-July. As adults, the sole objective of the periodical cicada is to reproduce. This is where that signature sound comes into play. Male cicadas will call females using a species-specific mating call created by vibrating their tymbals, the corrugated exoskeleton on their torso. This sound has been described as a "weeeeeee-whoa" sound or a tiny maraca shaken at a high-speed fading into an electric buzz sound. What gets really jarring is when there is a chorus of males "singing." This group of males can reach a volume ranging as high as 85–100 decibels, equivalent to the sound of a diesel train passing or a lawn mower at full bore.

After mating, females climb tree branches and split the bark depositing 24–48 eggs, and as many as 600 eggs over their life span. Six to ten weeks after the eggs are laid, the eggs hatch and newborn nymphs drop to the ground to burrow underground as nymphs starting a new 13- or 17-year cycle.

Periodical cicadas are harmless to humans and do not sting or bite. They are edible and considered a delicacy in some locales.

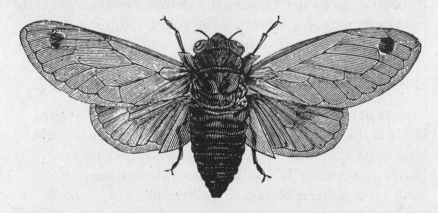

Chapter 2

Earth and Space

Does Sound Travel Quicker Through Water or Air?

When you came across this question in the table of contents, you probably thought, "Everyone knows the answer to that one. It's so obvious." This, of course, is exactly why we chose to include it. It is our honored duty to inform you that you are 100 percent wrong.

✳ ✳ ✳ ✳

SOUND ACTUALLY TRAVELS much faster through water than air. We'll get to the hows and whys in a moment, but let's start with the reason that you and everyone who is not an engineer were so sure that you knew the correct answer.

The confusion probably stems from the fact that we humans are designed to process sound waves that are transmitted through air, not water. Perhaps you learned this as a child at the local swimming pool, when you and your buddy dipped your heads beneath the surface and then attempted to communicate. Although you may have heard something, it was most likely an unintelligible gurgle.

The act of turning vibrations into sounds involves a series of bones in the inner ear—the malleus, incus, and stapes—and bone conductivity is 40 percent less effective underwater. Furthermore, when the auditory canal fills with water, the eardrum (another major aspect involved in the sensation of hearing) doesn't vibrate properly. As a result, many people just assume that sound travels less efficiently through water.

But the truth is, sound travels approximately five times faster through water than air. We say "approximately" because there are several variables to consider, such as temperature, altitude, and humidity. But whether you are talking about cold air or warm water, there must be some sort of medium in order to facilitate the transmission of sound waves. (There is no sound in the vacuum of space.)

Essentially, sound waves are just molecules bouncing off of other molecules until they reach your ears and are processed as sound. Because water is denser than air, these molecules are packed closer together and sound waves are able to travel at a greater velocity. For the same reason, sound can travel farther through water than air before dissipating. (Sound, in fact, travels fastest through solids such as metal. That's why people have been known to put an ear to a rail to hear if a train is approaching.)

Gases such as air are relatively poor conductors of sound— they just happen to be the right environment for the human auditory system. So, yes, we kind of set you up with this one— and for that, we apologize. It was all in the name of providing you with a nugget of valuable knowledge.

Which Way Is North?

If you, like most people, think the topmost symbol on a compass always points north, take care not to get lost in the Southern Hemisphere.

✳ ✳ ✳ ✳

NORTH, SOUTH, EAST, and west: These directions are meant to be set in stone, the unchangeable points of reference that lead sailors through treacherous seas and intrepid adventurers through dark and unknown lands. Yet even these directions, such stalwarts of clarity and precision, come with a medley of misconceptions.

The North Magnetic Pole

One misconception is that a compass points to the North Pole. In reality, a compass points toward Earth's North Magnetic Pole, which is different from the geographic pole that you'll find on a map. Earth has a magnetic field, which is created by the swirling motion of molten lava that resides in its core. This magnetic field makes an angle with Earth's spin axis. The geographic poles, in contrast, are the places that Earth's imaginary spin axis pass straight through. So while the geographic and magnetic poles are close to each other, they are never in the exact same place. If you're heading "due north" as the compass reads, you're heading to the North Magnetic Pole, not the North Pole. But compasses don't work close to a magnetic pole, so if you're going to the North Pole, a compass will take you only so far.

To complicate matters further, the North Magnetic Pole is always moving, because the motion of the swirling lava changes. Today, the North Magnetic Pole is about 500 miles from the geographic North Pole. Over the last 150 years, the North Magnetic Pole has crept north over 620 miles. Meanwhile, the South Magnetic Pole was 1,776 miles from the geographic South Pole, in Antarctica just south of Australia. The rates of change of the magnetic poles vary, but lately they've been moving at approximately 25 miles per year. Scientists project that the North Magnetic Pole could reach Siberia in the next few decades.

The South Magnetic Pole

That moves us right along to misconception number two, which is that the "N" on a compass always points north.

Assuming that the designation "north" always coincides with the notion of "up," the runaway North Magnetic Pole reminds us that "up" is relative. Earth is a sphere, so logically any single point could be designated as the top, making whatever lies opposite this arbitrary top the arbitrary bottom. It made sense for early mapmakers to draw the North Pole at the top of a map, because this was their approximation of where that handy compass pointed. As the North Magnetic Pole continues to wander from the point cartographers deemed the "North Pole," the designation of this geographic location as due north may eventually become obsolete.

Meanwhile, in the Southern Hemisphere, a compass points toward the South Magnetic Pole and more or less toward the corresponding yet inevitably inaccurate location that is deemed the geographic South Pole. Early mapmakers hailed from the Northern Hemisphere, so the North Pole is logically represented as being at the top of the map and the top of the world. Yet in the Southern Hemisphere, it would be equally logical to place the South Pole at the top of the map.

Why Is the Sky Blue?

What if the sky were some other color? Would a verdant green inspire the same placid happiness that a brilliant blue sky does? Would a pink sky be tedious for everyone except girls under the age of fifteen? What would poets and songwriters make of a sky that was an un-rhymable orange?

✳   ✳   ✳   ✳

WE'LL NEVER HAVE to answer these questions, thanks to a serendipitous combination of factors: the nature of sunlight, the makeup of Earth's atmosphere, and the sensitivity of our eyes.

If you have seen sunlight pass through a prism, you know that light, which to the naked eye appears to be white, is actually made up of a rainbow-like spectrum of colors: red, orange, yellow, green, blue, and violet. Light energy travels in waves, and each of these colors has its own wavelength. The red end of the spectrum has the longest wavelength, and the violet end has the shortest.

The waves are scattered when they hit particles, and the size of the particles determines which waves get scattered most effectively. As it happens, the particles that make up the nitrogen and oxygen in the atmosphere scatter shorter wavelengths of light much more effectively than longer wavelengths. The violets and the blues in sunlight are scattered most prominently, and reds and oranges are scattered less prominently.

However, since violet waves are shorter than blue waves, it would seem that violet light would be more prolifically scattered by the atmosphere. So why isn't the sky violet? Because there are variations among colors that make up the spectrum of sunlight—there isn't as much violet as there is blue. And because our eyes are more sensitive to blue light than to violet light, blue is easier for our eyes to detect.

That's why, to us, the sky is blue. And we wouldn't want it any other way.

Are the Colors of the Rainbow Always in the Same Order?

The order of the colors—red, orange, yellow, green, blue, indigo, and violet, from the top to the bottom—never changes. You may see a rainbow missing a color or two at its borders, but the visible colors always will be in the exact same order.

✳   ✳   ✳   ✳

RAINBOWS ARE CAUSED by the refraction of white light through a prism. Water droplets in the air act as prisms. When light enters a prism, it is bent slightly. The different wavelengths of light bend at different angles, so when white light hits a prism, it fans out. When the wavelengths are separated, the visible wavelengths appear as a rainbow.

The colors of a rainbow always appear in the same order because the wavelengths of the visible color spectrum always bend in the same way. They are ordered by the length of their waves. Red has the longest wavelength, about 650 nanometers. Violet has the shortest, about 400 nanometers. The other colors have wavelengths that fall between red and violet.

The human eye is incapable of seeing light that falls outside of these wavelengths. Light with a wavelength shorter than 400 nanometers is invisible; we refer to it as ultraviolet light. Likewise, light with a wavelength longer than 650 nanometers cannot be seen; we call it infrared light.

Now, about that pot of gold at the end of a rainbow—how do you get to it? If we knew that, we'd have better things to do than answer these silly questions.

Why Are You Colder on a Mountain, Even Though You're Closer to the Sun?

This question assumes you might think that the only factor influencing temperature is proximity to that fireball in the sky. In other words, this question assumes you might be an idiot. It's much more complicated than proximity.

✳   ✳   ✳   ✳

IT HAS TO be, or else the lowest nighttime temperatures on Mercury, which is two-and-a-half times closer to the sun than Earth is, wouldn't be −297 degrees Fahrenheit. And the moon, which is sometimes 240,000 miles closer to the sun than Earth is, wouldn't get as cold as −280 degrees Fahrenheit.

The reason it's colder on a mountaintop is because at that altitude, the atmosphere is different. Specifically, the air pressure is lower. The pressure at the top of Mount Everest, which is five-and-a-half miles above sea level, is less than a third of what it is at sea level.

During July—the warmest month on Everest—the average temperature hovers around –2 degrees Fahrenheit. It doesn't get above freezing up there, ever.

In simplest terms, when air is put under more pressure, it gets warmer. When the pressure lessens, it gets colder. That's why a bicycle pump warms up when you pump up a tire—in addition to the friction that's caused by the piston inside, the pump creates air pressure. It's also why an aerosol can gets downright cold if you spray it too long—air pressure escapes from the can.

When you think about all this, you realize how many scientific factors combine to make Earth hospitable for life. The moon has no atmosphere whatsoever; Mercury has a minute amount of it. The precise combination of gases that make up our atmosphere accounts for the air we breathe, the way the sun warms it, the color of the sky, and myriad other factors that explain life as we know it.

In fact, the cold temperatures at the top of a mountain are pretty minor when it comes to the miraculous—but scientifically logical—realities that are related to atmosphere.

How Much Rain Does It Take to Make a Rain Forest?

It takes 80 inches of rain per year to make a rain forest, but the scientists who categorize these things aren't picky.

✳   ✳   ✳   ✳

THERE SHOULD BE no feelings of inadequacy among forests whose drops per annum don't quite make the 80-inch cut. If a wooded area has a rate of precipitation that comes close to that mark, it will most likely be taken into the fold.

Rain falls about 90 days per year in a rain forest. As much as 50 percent of this precipitation evaporates, meaning that rain forests recycle their water supply. In non-rain forest areas, water evaporates and is transported (via clouds) to different regions. In a rain forest, however, the unique climate and weather patterns often cause the precipitation to fall over the same area from which it evaporated.

A rain forest is comprised of evergreen trees, either broadleaf or coniferous, and other types of intense vegetation. These regions collectively contain more than two-thirds of the plant species on the planet. There are two types of rain forests: tropical and temperate. Tropical rain forests are located near the equator; temperate rain forests crop up near oceanic coastlines, particularly where mountain ranges focus rainfall on a particular region.

Rain forests can be found on every continent except Antarctica. The largest tropical rain forest is the Amazon in South America; the largest temperate rain forest is in the Pacific Northwest, stretching from northern California all the way up to Alaska.

At one time, rain forests covered as much as 14 percent of the earth, but that number is now down to about 3 percent.

Scientists estimate that an acre and a half of rain forest—the equivalent of a little more than a football field—is lost every second. The trees are taken for lumber, and the land is tilled for farming.

Where Does Dew Come From?

You wake up on a cool spring morning to find the sunrise glittering over the grass, refracted in a million tiny droplets of dew. It didn't rain, but everything is wet. If it didn't rain, where did all the water come from?

✳ ✳ ✳ ✳

DEW GATHERS PRIMARILY on cool mornings, particularly during spring and fall, when the temperature is much lower than it was the previous evening. During the heat of the day, the air is filled with water vapor. As the air cools, the land (along with the grass, trees, flowers, and objects left outdoors) cools with it.

Water vapor becomes heavier as the temperature falls. As the weight increases, the air becomes oversaturated, and when that oversaturated air comes into contact with something cool—such as a blade of grass—water molecules cling together and form a dew droplet. Grass and plants are usually the first to collect dew because they lose water vapor themselves, making the air above them highly saturated with water. (Oversaturated air is also what gives us clouds, mist, fog, and rain. Small droplets of condensation form mist or fog. Larger droplets form rain.)

Dew will only gather on material that has cooled, however, which is why your driveway isn't wet in the morning—a concrete slab holds heat much longer than a blade of grass. The air above the driveway is warmed by the concrete, and thus not as heavily saturated as the air over bare ground.

Why Are Most Plants Green?

Maybe they're envious of our ability to walk over to the sink and get a drink of water.

✳   ✳   ✳   ✳

WHILE THAT THEORY is certainly compelling, plants aren't green with envy. The green comes from a pigment called chlorophyll. Pigments are substances that absorb certain wavelengths of light and reflect others. In other words, pigments determine color—you see the wavelength of light that the pigment reflects. A plant is green because the chlorophyll in it is really good at absorbing red and blue light but lousy at absorbing green light.

You find a heaping helping of chlorophyll in plants because chlorophyll's job is to absorb sunlight for use in photosynthesis, which is the process of converting sunlight and carbon dioxide into food (carbohydrates) that plants need to survive. So, since a plant wouldn't get too far without delicious carbs, just about every plant is partially green. This isn't true across the board, though. Some plants use different pigments for photosynthesis,

and there are a few hundred parasitic plant species that don't need chlorophyll because they mooch carbohydrates that are produced by other plants. But for the most part, land plants depend on chlorophyll to maintain their active plant lifestyle. And by extension, so do we, since animal life depends on plants to survive.

But why reflect green and absorb red and blue rather than the other way around? The short answer is that the red and the blue light are the good stuff. The sun emits more red photons than any other color, and blue photons carry more energy than other colors. Sunlight is abundant enough that it wouldn't be efficient to absorb all light, so plants evolved to absorb the areas of the light spectrum that offer the best bang for the buck. And it's a good thing, too: If plants needed to absorb the full spectrum of sunlight to get by, they'd be black—and the outdoors would have a gloomy tint.

What Are Some of the World's Strangest Plants?

When the first Western explorers returned from the Congo, they told tall tales of monstrous plants that demanded human flesh. Although we now know that no such plants exist, there are plenty of weird and scary plants in the world—enough for a little shop of horrors.

✳   ✳   ✳   ✳

Kudzu—When this vine, native to China and Japan, was brought to the United States in 1876, its ability to grow a foot per day quickly made it a nuisance. With 400-pound roots, 4-inch-diameter stems, and a resistance to herbicides, it is nearly impossible to eliminate.

Cow's Udder—This shrub is known alternately as Nipple Fruit, Titty Fruit, and Apple of Sodom. (Did a group of 4th graders name it?) A relative of the tomato, it sports poisonous orange fruit that look like inflated udders.

King Monkey Cup—The largest of carnivorous pitcher plants traps its prey in pitchers up to 14 inches long and 6 inches wide. It then digests them in a half gallon of enzymatic fluid. The plant has been known to catch scorpions, mice, rats, and birds.

Titan Arum—Known in Indonesia as a "corpse flower," this plant blooms in captivity only once every three years. The six-foot-tall bloom weighs more than 140 pounds and looks, as its Latin name says, like a "giant shapeless penis." Even less appealingly, it secretes cadaverene and putrescine, odor compounds that are responsible for its smell of rotting flesh.

Resurrection fern—This epiphyte (that is, air plant) gets its nutrients and moisture from the air. Although other plants die if they lose 8–12 percent of their water content, the resurrection fern simply dries up and appears dead. In fact, it can survive despite losing 97 percent of its water content.

Wollemi pine—Previously known only through 90 million-year-old fossils, the Wollemi pine tree was rediscovered in Australia in 1994. Fewer than 100 adult trees exist today. Although propagated trees are being sold around the world, the original grove's location is a well-guarded secret, disclosed to only a few researchers.

Rafflesia arnoldii—Also known as a "meat flower," this parasitic plant has the largest single bloom of any plant, measuring three feet across. It can hold several gallons of nectar, and its smell has been compared to "buffalo carcass in an advanced stage of decomposition."

Hydnora africana—This parasitic plant is found in Namibia and South Africa growing on the roots of the Euphorbia succulent. Most of the plant is underground, but the upper part of the flower looks like a gaping, fang-filled mouth. And, because smelling like rotting flesh is de rigueur in the weird-plant world, it emits a putrid scent to attract dung or carrion beetles.

Aquatic duckweed—Also known as watermeal because it resembles cornmeal floating on the surface of water, this is the smallest flowering plant on Earth. The plant is only .61 millimeter long, and the edible fruit, similar to a (very tiny) fig, is about the size of a grain of salt.

Spanish moss—Although it is a necessary prop in Southern Gothic horror tales, Spanish moss is neither moss nor Spanish. Also known as Florida moss, long moss, or graybeard, it is an air plant (epiphyte) that takes nutrients from the air. It's also related to the pineapple and has been used to stuff furniture, car seats, and mattresses.

Baobab tree—The baobab is the world's largest succulent,  reaching heights of 75 feet. It can also live for several thousand years. Their strange, root-like branches gave rise to the legend that they grow upside down. Their enormous trunks are often hollowed out and used as shelter, including a storage barn, an Australian prison, a South African pub, bus stops, and in Zambia, a public toilet (with flushing water, no less).

Why Aren't There Southern Lights?

There are! We just hear more about their northern counterparts.

✳   ✳   ✳   ✳

THE SOUTHERN LIGHTS are called the "aurora australis," and according to those who've seen them (including famed explorer Captain James Cook, who named the lights in 1773), they are just as bright and alluring as the aurora borealis in the north. We don't hear about them because the viewing area—around the geomagnetic South Pole—is mostly unpopulated.

Northern or southern, the lights are the result of solar storms that emit high-energy particles. These particles travel from the sun as a solar wind until they encounter and interact with the earth's magnetic field. They then energize oxygen atoms in the upper atmosphere, causing light emissions that can appear to us as an arc, a curtain, or a green glow. If these oxygen atoms get really excited, they turn red.

There are other atoms in the ionosphere, and they produce different colors when they're titillated by those solar winds. Neutral nitrogen will produce pink lights, and nitrogen radicals glow blue and violet.

Usually, the lights are visible only in latitudes between ninety degrees (at the poles) and thirty degrees. In the north, that large swath includes most of Europe, Asia (excluding India, except for its northernmost tip, and southern countries such as Myanmar, Thailand, and Cambodia), the United States, and Canada. In the south, though, only the southernmost tips of Australia and Africa and the countries of Chile, Argentina, and Uruguay in South America are within that zone.

So in reality the question is this: If a light shines in the south and there is no one there to see it, does it still dazzle?

Is the North Star Always in the North?

The answer is yes, but it's not quite that simple. Although the North Star is always in the north, it isn't always the same star.

✳   ✳   ✳   ✳

THE NORTH STAR is also called the Pole Star because it is the star most directly above Earth's North Pole. It appears due north of the observer, and the angle between it and the horizon tells the latitude of the observer. Consequently, the North Star has been used for navigation for thousands of years.

However, the North Star has limited capability as a navigational tool. Because it is only visible in the Northern Hemisphere, it is of no help south of the equator. There is no precise Southern Hemisphere equivalent to the North Star, although the constellation Crux, or the Southern Cross, points to the South Pole.

But back to the North Star and why its identity changes: Due to the precession of the equinoxes (which is a fancy astronomer's term for "Earth wobbles when it turns"), the axis upon which our planet rotates shifts ever so slightly. As the shift occurs over many centuries, another star in the distance elbows its way in as the useful North Star. Currently, it's Polaris, a middling bright star at the end of the Little Dipper's handle, about 430 light-years from Earth.

Time is running out for Polaris, just as it did for its predecessors. In 3000 B.C., the star Thuban in the constellation Draco served as the North Star. In A.D. 3000, Gamma Cephei, or Alrai, will get the call. Iota Cephei will have its turn in A.D. 5200, followed by Vega in A.D. 14000.

For now, though, Polaris will guide you if you are lost. Unless you happen to be adrift off the coast of, say, Peru. Then you're pretty much screwed.

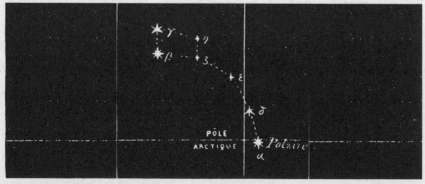

How Are Stars and Planets Different?

Even astronomers quibble over this one. In the most general terms, stars and planets can be differentiated by two characteristics: what they're made of and whether they produce their own light. According to the Space Telescope Science Institute, a star is "a huge ball of gas held together by gravity." At its core, this huge ball of gas is super-hot. It's so hot that a star produces enough energy to twinkle and glow from light-years away. You know, "like a diamond in the sky."

✳   ✳   ✳   ✳

IN CASE YOU didn't know, our own sun is a star. The light and energy it produces are enough to sustain life on Earth. But compared to other stars, the sun is only average in terms of temperature and size. Talk about star power! It's no wonder that crazed teenage girls and planets revolve around stars. In fact, the word "planet" is derived from the Greek *plan te* ("wanderer"). By definition, planets are objects that orbit around stars. As for composition, planets are made up mostly of rock (Earth, Mercury, Venus, and Mars) or gas (Jupiter, Saturn, Neptune, and Uranus).

Now hold your horoscopes! If planets can be gaseous, then just what makes Uranus different from the stars that form Ursa Major? Well, unlike stars, planets are built around solid cores. They're cooler in temperature, and some are even home to water and ice. Remember what the planet Krypton looked like in the *Superman* movies? All right, so glacial Krypton is not a real planet, but you get the point: Gaseous planets aren't hot enough to produce their own light. They may appear to be shining, but they're actually only reflecting starlight.

So back to the astronomers: Just what are they quibbling about? Well, it's tough agreeing on exact definitions for stars and planets when there are a few celestial objects that fall somewhere in between the two. Case in point: brown dwarfs.

Brown dwarfs are too small and cool to produce their own light, so they can't be considered stars. Yet they seem to form in the same way stars do, and since they have gaseous cores, they can't be considered planets either. So what to call brown dwarfs? Some say "failed stars," "substars," or even "planetars." In our vast universe, there's plenty of room for ambiguity.

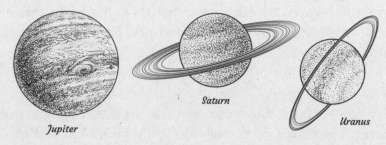

Jupiter

Saturn

Uranus

Where Does Tektite Come From?

The origin of strangely shaped bits of glass called tektites *has been debated for decades—do they come from the moon? From somewhere else in outer space? It seems the answer is more down-to-earth.*

❋   ❋   ❋   ❋

THE FIRST TEKTITES were found in 1787 in the Moldau River in the Czech Republic, giving them their original name, "Moldavites." They come in many shapes (button, teardrop, dumbbell, and blobs), have little or no water content, and range from dark green to black to colorless.

Originally, many geologists believed tektites were extraterrestrial in origin, specifically from the moon. They theorized that impacts from comets and asteroids—or even volcanic eruptions—on the moon ejected huge amounts of material. As the moon circled in its orbit around our planet, the material eventually worked its way to Earth, through the atmosphere, and onto the surface.

One of the first scientists to debate the tektite-lunar origin idea was Texas geologist Virgil E. Barnes, who contended that tektites were actually created from Earth-bound soil and rock. Many scientists now agree with Barnes, theorizing that when a comet or asteroid collided with the earth, it sent massive amounts of material high into the atmosphere at hypervelocities. The energy from such a strike easily melted the terrestrial rock and burned off much of the material's water. And because of the earth's gravitational pull, what goes up must come down—causing the melted material to rain down on the planet in specific locations. Most of the resulting tektites have been exposed to the elements for millions of years, causing many to be etched and/or eroded over time.

Unlike most extraterrestrial rocks—such as meteorites and micrometeorites, which are found everywhere on Earth—tektites are generally found in four major regions of the world called *strewn* (or splash) fields. The almost 15-million-year-old Moldavites are mainly found in the Czech Republic, but the strewn field extends into Austria; these tektites are derived from the Nordlinger Ries impact crater in southern Germany. The *Australites, Indochinites,* and *Chinites* of the huge Australasian strewn field extend around Australia, Indochina, and the Philippines; so far, no one has agreed on its source crater. The *Georgiaites* (Georgia) and *Bediasites* (Texas) are North American tektites formed by the asteroid impact that created the Chesapeake Crater around 35 million years ago. And finally, the 1.3-million-year-old *Ivorites* of the Ivory Coast strewn field originate from the Bosumtwi crater in neighboring Ghana. Other tektites have been discovered in various places around the world but in very limited quantities compared to the major strewn fields.

How Do Astronauts Go to the Bathroom?

Weightlessness sure seems fun. You see those astronauts effortlessly floating around, mugging for the camera, and magically spinning their pens in midair. But what you don't get to see is what happens when nature calls.

✳ ✳ ✳ ✳

The Final Frontier

YOU CAN BE sure that as much as astronauts enjoy swimming through the air like waterless fish, there's one place on Earth where all astronauts thank their lucky stars for gravity: the bathroom.

During shuttle flights, astronauts sat on a commode with a hole in it, not unlike a normal toilet—except for the restraints that fit over the feet and thighs to prevent bodies from floating away. Suction replaced gravity, so the seat was cushioned, allowing the astronaut's posterior to form an airtight seal around the hole. If everything was situated properly, the solid waste went down the main hole: A separate tube with a funnel on the end took care of the liquids. With so much going on, relaxing with a newspaper was not really an option.

But it was worse in the early days of the Apollo missions (1961–1975). When an Apollo astronaut had to go number two, he attached a specially designed plastic bag to his rear end. The bag had an adhesive flange at its opening to ensure a proper seal.

But if you think that this procedure couldn't have been any more undignified, consider this: There was no privacy. The astronauts would usually carry on with their duties while they were, you know, doing their duty. In the words of Apollo astronaut Rusty Schweickart, "You just float around for a while doing things with a bag on your butt." With no gravity and no suction, getting the feces to separate from the body was, generally, an hour-long process. It began with removing the bag—very carefully—and ended with lots and lots of wiping.

Waste Management

Where does all this stuff go? In the past, fecal material was dried, compressed, and stored until the ship returned to Earth. The International Space Station periodically shoots collections of poop at Earth, to burn up in the atmosphere. And spaceships have been leaving trails of urine in the sky for rather a long time. The memory of this procedure caused Schweickart to wax darn-near poetic, calling a urine dump at sunset, "one of the most beautiful sights" he saw in space.

"As the stuff comes out and hits the exit nozzle," Schweickart went on, "it instantly flashes into ten million little ice crystals, which go out almost in a hemisphere. The stuff goes in every direction, all radially out from the spacecraft at relatively high velocity. It's surprising, and it's an incredible stream of . . . just a spray of sparklers almost. It's really a spectacular sight."

And you thought stars looked cool.

What Happens to the Stuff We Launch Into Space and Don't Bring Back?

No one gives much thought to all the stuff we launch into space and don't bring back, but it creates a major hazard.

* * * *

Steer Clear of That Satellite

I F YOU THINK it's nerve-wracking when you have to swerve around a huge pothole as you cruise down the highway, just imagine how it would feel if you were hundreds of miles above the surface of Earth, where the stakes couldn't be higher. That's what the crew of the International Space Station (ISS) faced in 2008, when it had to perform evasive maneuvers to avoid debris from a Russian satellite.

And that was just one piece of orbital trash—all in all, there are tens of millions of junky objects that are larger than a millimeter and are in orbit. If you don't find this worrisome, imagine the little buggers zipping along at up to 17,000 miles per hour. Worse, these bits of flotsam and jetsam constantly crash into each other and shatter into even more pieces.

The junk largely comes from satellites that explode or disintegrate; it also includes the upper stages of launch vehicles,  burnt-out rocket casings, old payloads and experiments, bolts, wire clusters, slag and dust from solid rocket motors, batteries, droplets of leftover fuel and high-pressure fluids, and even a space suit. (No, there wasn't an astronaut who came home naked—the suit was packed with batteries and sensors and was set adrift in 2006 so that scientists could find out how quickly a spacesuit deteriorates in the intense conditions of space.)

The U.S. and Russia: Space's Big Polluters

So who's responsible for all this orbiting garbage? The two biggest offenders are Russia—including the former Soviet Union—and the United States. Other litterers include China, France, Japan, India, Portugal, Egypt, and Chile. Each of the last three countries has launched one satellite during the past twenty years.

Most of the junk orbits Earth at between 525 and 930 miles from the surface. The ISS operate a little closer to Earth—at an altitude of about 250 miles—so it doesn't see the worst of it. Still, the ISS's emergency maneuver in 2008 was a sign that the situation is getting worse.

NASA and other agencies use radar to track the junk and are studying ways to get rid of it for good. Ideas such as shooting at objects with lasers or attaching tethers to some pieces to force them back to Earth have been discarded because of cost considerations and the potential danger to people on the ground. Until an answer is found, NASA practices constant vigilance, monitoring the junk and watching for collisions with working satellites and vehicles as they careen through space. Hazardous driving conditions, it seems, extend well beyond Earth's atmosphere.

Is the Red Sea Blue?

How do intensely blue-green waters get identified as red? Read on to find out.

✳   ✳   ✳   ✳

STANDING ON THE shore of the Red Sea, you might wonder how its waters, clearly blue-green, could be so obviously mislabeled with the moniker "Red." Did the person who named this 1,200-mile strip of sea, located between Africa and Asia, suffer from an acute case of colorblindness? No, it's more likely he or she saw the Red Sea while the *Trichodesmium erythracum* was in full bloom. Before you get all excited, *Trichodesmium erythraeum* is not some kind of wildly exotic orchid indigenous to Egypt. It's simply a type of cyanobacteria, aka marine algae.

You've seen how an overgrowth of algae can turn your favorite pond or motel pool a murky shade of opaque green, right? In the case of the Red Sea, the alga is rich in a red-colored protein called phycoerythrin. During the occasional bloom, groups of red- and pink-hued *Trichodesmium erythraeum* blanket the surface of the sea. When they die off, they appear to transform the waters from a heavenly shade of blue to a rustier reddish-brown.

While this algae-induced color change is a widely accepted derivation for the Red Sea's name, there is another theory: Some say mariners of antiquity were inspired by the region's mineral-rich red mountain ranges and coral reefs, so they named the body of water *Mare Rostrum* (Latin for "Red Sea"). In 1923, English author E. M. Forster agreed, describing the Red Sea as an "exquisite corridor of tinted mountains and radiant water."

However you choose to color it, one fact still remains: Beneath a ruddy exterior, there lies a deep Red Sea that is true blue.

Does Anything Live in the Dead Sea?

The Red Sea isn't really red, and the Black Sea isn't really black—so what are the odds that the Dead Sea is really dead?

✳ ✳ ✳ ✳

IF YOU'VE EVER gone for a dip in the Dead Sea, you'll know that there is at least a shred of truth to the name. The Dead Sea's otherworldly qualities make swimmers buoyant—everyone's doing the "dead man's float."

Located between Israel and Jordan, the Dead Sea is, at 1,300 feet below sea level, the lowest surface point on Earth. The very bottom is 2,300 feet below sea level. Water flows into the Dead Sea from the Jordan River, but then it has no place to go, since it's already reached the lowest possible surface point on the planet. The fresh water that flows into the Dead Sea evaporates quickly because of the high temperatures in the desert, and it leaves behind a deposit of minerals.

These minerals have accumulated to make the Dead Sea the pungent stew that it is today. Slightly more than 30 percent of the Dead Sea is comprised of minerals, including sodium chloride, iodine, calcium, potassium, and sulfur. These minerals have been marketed as therapeutic healing products for people with skin conditions; many cosmetic companies have their own line of Dead Sea products.

The Dead Sea is reported to be six times saltier than an ocean, and salt provides buoyancy for swimmers. No form of life could survive in these conditions, right? Not exactly. It's true that every species of fish introduced into this body of water has promptly died, but in 1936, an Israeli scientist found that microscopic pieces of green algae and a few types of bacteria were living in the Dead Sea. So the Dead Sea can't technically be considered dead.

Why Don't Underwater Tunnels Collapse?

Ever dig a hole at the beach? Just when you think you're finally going to get all the way to China, the walls collapse and your whole hole disappears. (Which, incidentally, is why you should never let children dig at the beach unsupervised.) The length of time your walls will hold up before caving in is known to sandhogs as the "stand-up" time.

✳ ✳ ✳ ✳

WHO ARE SANDHOGS? They're not little animals burrowing into the sand; they're the men and women who earn their livings in tunnel construction, and they wear the name proudly. Tunnel digging is a high-risk job, and sandhogs obviously have a vested interest in the stand-up time of mud walls, especially when they're digging an underwater tunnel. How exactly can you dig a tunnel through the wet, soggy mud at the bottom of a river without courting certain disaster?

English engineer Marc Isambard Brunel asked this same question in 1818. While strolling on the London docks one day, he noticed a shipworm, aka *teredo navalis*, boring through some rotting timbers. How did the tiny worm make a tunnel without getting crushed? Close inspection revealed that the worm used its hard, shell-like head as a shield. As the worm ate into the wood like an excavating shovel, its head moved forward, making a tunnel large enough for its body to pass through.

Brunel built himself a cast-iron shield shaped like the head of the worm, only his was two stories high and had several doors for mouths. A worker standing behind the shield would excavate earth through a door. As a hollow space was created in front of the shield, a set of jacks pressed the iron frame forward a few inches at a time, leaving a smooth section of earth where the rim of shield had been. Instantly, bricklayers would get to work, reinforcing this mud wall before it caved in.

As you may guess, this was a slow process. It took Brunel eighteen years to complete a 1,506-foot tunnel beneath London's River Thames. His shield method worked, however, and parts of his tunnel, which opened in 1843, are still in use today.

Do Rivers Always Flow North to South?

No, rivers are not subject to any natural laws that compel them to flow north to south. Only one thing governs the direction of a river's flow: gravity.

✳ ✳ ✳ ✳

QUITE SIMPLY, EVERY river travels from points of higher elevation to points of lower elevation. Most rivers originate in mountains, hills, or other highlands. From there, it's always a long and winding journey to sea level.

Many prominent rivers flow from north to south, which perhaps creates the misconception that all waterways do so. The Mississippi River and its tributaries flow in a southerly direction as they make their way to the Gulf of Mexico. The Colorado River runs south toward the Gulf of California, and the Rio Grande follows a mostly southerly path.

But there are many major rivers that do not flow north to south. The Amazon flows northeast, and both the Nile and the Rhine head north. The Congo River flaunts convention entirely by flowing almost due north, then cutting a wide corner and going south toward the Atlantic Ocean.

There's a tendency to think of north and south as up and down. This comes from the mapmaking convention of sketching the world with the North Pole at the top of the illustration and the South Pole at the bottom.

But rivers don't follow the conventions of mapmakers. They're downhill racers that will go anywhere gravity takes them.

Chapter 3

Quantum Leaps

Was Math Discovered or Invented?

This question has been kicked around by just about every serious philosopher over the past 2,500 years or so. In that light, it might seem somewhat curious to find it discussed in the same book that brings you questions like "Why does Swiss cheese have holes?" But, hey, we're not afraid to tackle the tough ones.

✳　✳　✳　✳

INVENTED THINGS DIDN'T exist before they were invented. They may meet a pressing, timeless human need—such as, you know, the electric foot-callus sander—but they weren't around until a light bulb went off in someone's head.

Discovered things always have existed, such as the element strontium. It's been around forever, but nobody knew it until 1787 when Scottish miners near the village of Strontian found it in the mineral strontianite.

Where does math fit in? To many folks, math is simply a symbolic representation of the real, physical world. You can call the number two "two" or you can call it "Shirley," but the concept underlying 2 + 2 = 4 has always been there. When man figured out that concept, he discovered math. This is what Plato felt.

But others question this belief on fairly abstract philosophical grounds, essentially saying that if math "existed" before we conceived of it or discovered it, then we have to accept the existence of an abstract notion even without human brains there to be aware of it. Philosophers call this "theism," and apparently it makes some of them nervous.

To us it makes sense that math was discovered. Math is a specific, precise, rigorous way of describing the physical world, involving hard-and-fast rules. There are different ways of expressing or arriving at the concept of "four," but that concept is always distinct from "five" in precisely the same way; you can't say that four things are five things. This reality was there as soon as there were four things in the universe, even though people weren't around to understand it.

We're getting into metaphysics here—"If a tree falls in the forest..." stuff—but that's the way philosophy is. Makes your high school geometry seem pretty straightforward in comparison, doesn't it?

Where Did Indoor Plumbing Originate?

A "civilized" life would not be possible without water pipes.

✳ ✳ ✳ ✳

HUMBLE HOLLOW TUBES have been improving our quality of life for thousands of years. As it turns out, the piping of water in and out of living spaces originated in many different ancient civilizations. Plumbing technology was often developed only to be lost until it was reinvented from scratch. Lead pipes have been found in Mesopotamian ruins, and clay knee joint piping has been traced to Babylonia. The Egyptians used copper piping. But the most sophisticated ancient waterworks flourished at the hands of the Harappan Civilization (circa 3300–1600 B.C.) in present-day India and Pakistan.

The Harappans boasted of a network of earthenware pipes that would carry water from people's homes into municipal drains and cesspools. Archeological excavation in the 1920s uncovered highly planned cities with living quarters featuring individual indoor baths and even toilets. Thanks to the Harappans' advanced ceramic techniques, they were able to build ritual baths up to 29 feet long and 10 feet deep—as big as modern-day swimming pools.

While the Romans can't be credited with the invention of water pipes, their mastery of pipe-making influenced plumbing up to the 20th century. (The word *plumbing* comes from the Latin word for lead, *plumbum.*) Pipes were made by shaping sheets of the easily malleable (and highly toxic) molten lead around a wooden core. Plumbers then soldered the joints together with hot lead. It could be said that they were largely responsible for "civilizing" Rome, making it a place where homes had bathtubs as well as indoor toilets that flushed into underground sewage systems. Fresh water was piped directly into kitchens, and there were even ways of "metering" how much water was being used by the width of the pipe installed. (Even then, convenience had its price!)

Which Ancient Greek First Drew a Map of the World?

The Greek philosopher Anaximander is one of the greatest thinkers of all time. With his wide range of interests and brilliant mind, Anaximander fits the mold of a "Renaissance Man." Of course, he was born 2,000 years before the Renaissance.

✳   ✳   ✳   ✳

ANAXIMANDER WAS THE first philosopher in history to have written down his work—perhaps that is also why he's known as such a groundbreaker. Unfortunately, even though he produced and recorded the work, for the most part it has not survived. We mostly know of Anaximander through doxographers, or writers who document the beliefs, thoughts, and theories of their predecessors. In Anaximander's case, Aristotle and Plato have told us most of what we know about his work.

A Long Time Ago in a Land Far Away...

Born in the seventh century B.C. in ancient Greece, Anaximander came from Miletus, a city in Ionia, which is now the western coast of Turkey. This area was a cultural enclave known for its progressive views on philosophy and art—it paved the way for the brilliant artistic development of Athens in the fifth century B.C.

A true rationalist, Anaximander boldly questioned the myths, the heavens, and the existence of the gods themselves. He wanted to devise natural explanations for phenomena that had previously been assumed to be supernatural. As founder of the science of astronomy, he was credited with building the first *gnomon*, or perpendicular sundial, which he based on the early work of the Babylonians and their divisions of the days.

The First Map of the World

Breaking new ground in geography as well, Anaximander has also been credited as being the first cartographer to draw the entire inhabited world known to the Greeks. The map was likely circular, and a river called Ocean surrounded the land. The Mediterranean Sea appeared in the middle of the map, and the land was divided into two halves, one called Europe and the other, Southern Asia. What was assumed to be the habitable world consisted of two small strips of land to the north and south of the Mediterranean Sea.

The accomplishment of this map is far more significant than it might originally appear. Firstly, it could be used to improve navigation and trade. But secondly, and perhaps more importantly, Anaximander thought that by displaying the lay of the land, so to speak, and demonstrating which nations and people were where, he might be able to convince the Ionic city-states to form a federation to push away outside threats.

Earth Is a Tabletop

Watching the horizon, Anaximander concluded that Earth was cylindrical, its diameter being three times its height, with man living on the top. He also thought that Earth floated free in the center of the universe, unsupported by pillars or water, as was commonly believed at the time. "Earth didn't fall," Aristotle recounted, "because it was at equal distances from the extremes and needed not move in any particular direction since it is impossible to move in opposite directions at the same time."

These were amazing and progressive ideas primarily for one simple reason: They were not based on things that Anaximander could have observed but, instead, were the result of conclusions he reached through rational thought. This is the first known example of an argument based on the principle of sufficient reason, rather than one of myth.

By boldly speculating about the universe, Anaximander molded the direction of science, physics, and philosophy. The idea that nature is ruled by laws just like those in human societies, and anything that disturbs the balance of nature does not last long, should make us pause and think...just as Anaximander did.

Who Invented the Printing Press?

Sure, Johannes Gutenberg's development of the printing press in 15th-century Germany led to mass-market publishing. But innovations in printing technology were around long before Gutenberg revolutionized the industry.

✳ ✳ ✳ ✳

The Stamp of Uniformity

ALTHOUGH PRINTING IS usually associated with reading materials, the original impetus behind printing technology was the need to create identical copies of the same thing. Printing actually began with coining, when centralized states branded their coins with uniform numbers and symbols. In those days, written manuscripts were copied the old-fashioned way, letter by letter, by hand. Only the upper echelons of society were literate, books were costly, and the laborious and artistic method of copying matched the rarity of books.

The first major innovation in printing came with the Chinese invention of block printing by the eighth century A.D. Block printing involved carving letters or images into a surface, inking that surface, and pressing it on to paper, parchment, or cloth. The method was used for a variety of purposes, from decorating clothes to copying religious scrolls. The blocks were usually made of wood, which posed a problem as the wood eventually decayed or cracked. Oftentimes entire pages of a manuscript, complete with illustrations, were carved into a single block that could be used again and again.

The Chinese also invented movable type, which would prove to be the prerequisite to efficient printing presses. Movable type is faster than block printing because individual characters, usually letters or punctuation, are created by being cast into molds. Once this grab bag of individual characters is made, they can then be reused and rearranged in infinite combinations by changing the typeset. Movable type characters are also more uniform than the carved letters of block printing. Pi-Sheng invented this method in 1045 using clay molds. The method spread to Korea and Japan, and metal movable type was created in Korea by 1230.

Supply and Demand

The Chinese didn't use movable type extensively because their language consists of thousands of characters, and movable type makes printing efficient only in a language with fewer letters, like the English alphabet's 26. Meanwhile, Europeans used the imported concept of block printing to make popular objects like playing cards or illustrated children's books. During the Middle Ages, serious secular scholarship had all but disappeared in Europe, and the reproduction of new and classical texts was mostly confined to the Asian and Arab worlds.

That is, until literacy began to spread among the middle classes, and lay people, especially in Germany, showed an interest in reading religious texts for themselves. Thus, German entrepreneur Johannes Gutenberg, the son of a coin minter, began to experiment with metal movable type pieces. It's believed Gutenberg was unfamiliar with the previously invented Chinese method, but at any rate, several other Europeans were experimenting with similar methods at the same time as Gutenberg.

By the 1440s, Gutenberg had set up a printing shop in Mainz, Germany, and in 1450, he set out to produce a Bible. Gutenberg perfected several printing methods, such as right justification, and preferred alloys in the production of metal types. By 1455, Gutenberg's press had produced 200 copies of his Bible—quite the feat at the time, considering one Bible could take years to copy by hand. These Bibles were sold for less than hand-copied ones yet were still expensive enough for profit margins equivalent to modern-day millions.

Presses soon popped up all across Europe. By 1499, an estimated 15 million books had been produced by at least 1,000 printing presses, mostly in Germany and then throughout Italy. For the first time ever, ideas were not only dreamed up and written down—they were efficiently reproduced and spread over long distances. The proliferation of these first German printing presses is commonly credited with the end of the Middle Ages and the dawn of the Renaissance.

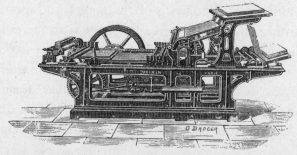

What's the Theory of Relativity?

The greatest theory of all time was a group effort.

✳ ✳ ✳ ✳

THERE IS AN oft-repeated story about the 17th century astronomer Isaac Newton that describes how he was sitting under an apple tree one day, when a piece of fruit fell from the tree and hit him on the head. That knock on the noggin suddenly prompted Newton to come up with the law of gravity, inspired by the apple's painful fall toward the earth.

Newton did propose his theory after spending time in an apple orchard, but he was simply observing the fact that apples occasionally fell to the ground. Newton published his law of gravity in 1687, which stated that every body in the universe is attracted to every other body with a force directly proportional to the product of their masses and inversely proportional to the square of the distance between them.

Although it was a groundbreaking hypothesis at the time, even Newton himself was never quite sure that it was a complete explanation. While most of the time his ideas worked perfectly throughout the solar system, there were anomalies and paradoxes that never fit in with his theory. It took centuries before scientists began to come up with new ideas about the forces at work in the universe.

Some of these scientists included Dutch physicist Hendrik Lorentz, French mathematician Henri Poincare, and German theoretical physicist Max Planck, all of whom helped to change the way scientists looked at the universe. Two other scientists, Americans Albert A. Michelson and Edward W. Morley, would make a significant discovery in 1887 that at first seemed to be a failed experiment, but would soon open the door to one of the most famous theories in science.

Moving Through the Aether

Michelson and Morley set out to find the presence and measure the properties of a substance called "aether," which, at the time, was believed to fill empty space. The assumption was that since on Earth, waves in water must move in water and sound waves must move through air, wavelengths of light must also require a substance in which to move. Scientists named this theoretical substance "aether," after the Greek god of light.

So, using a device called an interferometer, which measures the interference properties of light waves, Michelson and Morley set out to prove that aether existed. They theorized that if it existed, it would seem like a moving substance to those on Earth, the same way air feels like a moving substance if you hold your hand out of a moving car's window. The Michelson-Morley experiment aimed to detect this "aether wind" by measuring the speed of light in different directions. A mirror would split a beam of light into two directions, and then recombine them, after which the scientists would measure changes in speed that could be attributed to aether. But to their surprise, Michelson and Morley found no significant differences whatsoever, and their experiment was considered a failure.

A Special Theory

But just because an experiment fails doesn't mean you don't keep researching. After the Michelson-Morley experiment, scientists continued looking for answers about what makes up the universe. And by 1905, Albert Einstein debuted his theory of special relativity, which was based on two statements: One, that the laws of physics appear the same to all observers, and two, that the speed of light, which clocks in at 186,000 miles per second, is unchanging, contrary to what Michelson and Morley originally believed. However, the theory of special relativity only applied when there was an absence of gravity; gravity itself was another puzzle to be solved.

Einstein theorized that the speed of light was the absolute

boundary for motion, meaning that nothing can travel faster than the speed of light. According to Newton's law, if the sun were to start wobbling in space, Earth would immediately wobble as well, instantaneously affected by the gravity. Einstein didn't accept this idea, since the influence of the sun's gravity would have to travel much faster than the speed of light in order to instantaneously affect Earth. But Einstein also realized that the sun does somehow have the ability to reach out across millions of miles of space and pull on Earth with its gravity. So after he formed his theory of special relativity, he kept searching, knowing there was still more to the story.

A Strange Conundrum

It's easy to see gravity at work here on Earth, where knocking a book off a desk will cause it to fall to the floor. But the sun somehow exerts a pull of gravity across empty space. Perhaps, Einstein thought, empty space itself was the answer. By 1912, the scientist was working on the question full-time, and in 1915, after a decade of what he considered some of the most intellectually challenging years of his life, Einstein published his theory of general relativity, which expanded on his original theory of special relativity.

Matter, Einstein theorized, such as the sun and planets, causes the space around it to warp and curve, which then influences how other matter reacts. Gravity, then, is not a force, but rather a curved field that is created by the presence of mass. But that's not all: even time, the scientist believed, could be warped, with time moving more slowly near massive bodies like Earth. Acceleration causes time to move more slowly, as well, in a phenomenon called time dilation. It may sound like science fiction (and the idea has, in fact, been used in plenty of science fiction books and films), but it's actually science fact!

General relativity predicted that the light from distant stars would warp as it passed by the sun on its way to Earth. But the only way scientists could observe such a phenomenon would be during a total eclipse, as the sun's light is much too bright otherwise. So on the date of the next solar eclipse, May 29, 1919, astronomers gathered in Sobral, Brazil, and on the island of Principe off the west coast of Africa, where the eclipse would be most noticeable. They took photographs as the moon passed in front of the sun, and then spent the next several months analyzing them.

On September 22, 1919, Einstein got the news that the photographs had confirmed his theory. Einstein had guessed that the light deflection of the starlight near the sun would be twice what would be expected from Newton's laws, and the photographs proved him correct. The theory of relativity was also used to predict the rate at which two neutron stars orbiting each other will move toward one another. When Einstein's theory was applied to this phenomenon, it was accurate to within a trillionth of a percent, once again confirming his hypothesis.

In fact, the theory of relativity is one of the most oft-tested and subsequently confirmed theories in science, but there is still one test researchers would love to carry out. If Einstein was correct in his theory that space warps and bends due to the mass of objects, then if two objects collide in space, they must cause a sort of "ripple effect" in the fabric of space, not unlike two boats colliding on a lake. So far, scientists have been unable to observe such a phenomenon, as by the time a ripple from any distant colliding stars or black holes reached Earth, the wave would be infinitesimally small and extremely difficult to detect. But new sensors and devices are being developed that can sense the slightest difference in gravitational waves, so it may not be long before one more piece of the relativity puzzle falls into place. In the meantime, those of us who aren't scientists can continue enjoying science fiction films, but perhaps with a new appreciation. Some of that fiction isn't so far from fact, after all.

Did Ben Franklin Really Discover Electricity?

As it turns out, Benjamin Franklin did not discover electricity. What's more, the kite he famously flew in 1752 while conducting an experiment was not struck by lightning. If it had been, Franklin would be remembered as a colonial publisher and assemblyman killed by his own curiosity.

✳   ✳   ✳   ✳

Before Ben

BLESSED WITH ONE of the keenest minds in history, Benjamin Franklin was a scientific genius who made groundbreaking discoveries in the basic nature and properties of electricity. Electrical science, however, dates to 1600, when Dr. William Gilbert, physician to Queen Elizabeth, published a treatise about his research on electricity and magnetism. European inventors who later expanded on Gilbert's knowledge included Otto von Guericke of Germany, Charles Francois Du Fay of France, and Stephen Gray of England.

The Science of Electricity

Franklin became fascinated with electricity after seeing a demonstration by an itinerant showman (and doctor) named Archibald Spencer in Boston in 1743. Two years later, he bought a Leyden jar—a contraption invented by a Dutch scientist that used a glass container wrapped in foil to create a crude battery. Other researchers had demonstrated the properties of the device, and Franklin set about to increase its capacity to generate electricity while testing his own scientific hypotheses. Among the

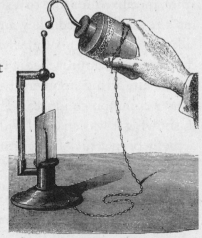

principles he established was the conservation of charge, one of the most important laws of physics. In a paper published in 1750, he announced the discovery of the induced charge and broadly outlined the existence of the electron. His experiments led him to coin many of the terms currently used in the science of electricity, such as battery, conductor, condenser, charge, discharge, uncharged, negative, minus, plus, electric shock, and electrician.

As Franklin came to understand the nature of electricity, he began to theorize about the electrical nature of lightning. In 1751, he outlined in a British scientific journal his idea for an experiment that involved placing a long metal rod on a high tower or steeple to draw an electric charge from passing thunder clouds, which would throw off visible electric sparks. A year later, French scientist Georges-Louis Leclerc successfully conducted such an experiment.

The Kite Runner

Franklin had not heard of Leclerc's success when he undertook his own experiment in June 1752. Instead of a church spire, he affixed his kite to a sharp, pointed wire. To the end of his kite string he tied a key, and to the key a ribbon made of silk (for insulation). While flying his kite on a cloudy day as a thunderstorm approached, Franklin noticed that loose threads on the kite string stood erect, as if they had been suspended from a common conductor. The key sparked when he touched it, showing it was charged with electricity. But had the kite actually been struck by lightning, Franklin would likely have been killed, as was Professor Georg Wilhelm Richmann of St. Petersburg, Russia, when he attempted the same experiment a few months later.

The Lightning Rod

Although Franklin did not discover electricity, he did uncover many of its fundamental principles and proved that lightning is, in fact, electricity. He used his knowledge to create the lightning rod, an invention that today protects land structures and ships at sea. He never patented the lightning rod but instead generously promoted it as a boon to humankind. In 21st-century classrooms, the lightning rod is still cited as a classic example of the way fundamental science can produce practical inventions.

How Was Oxygen Discovered?

We tend to take oxygen for granted. If fact, we didn't even know it existed until the 18th century.

✳   ✳   ✳   ✳

THIS ELEMENT IS absolutely necessary for almost all life on Earth, with the exception of some anaerobic microorganisms and tiny creatures that live at the bottom of the sea. But for the vast majority of us, oxygen is what feeds our cells and provides us with energy. And breathing is so automatic that we rarely think about it, unless it becomes difficult. But there may be a good reason we hardly ever think about oxygen; after all, it is the third most abundant element in the universe, so it's never hard to find.

Surprisingly, however, oxygen only makes up about 21 percent of the air we breathe. The rest is mostly nitrogen, at around 78 percent, with trace amounts of carbon dioxide, neon, and helium thrown in. The combination of nitrogen and oxygen is interesting, because while our bodies need oxygen, they can't process too much of the gas: breathing pure oxygen for too long would cause irreversible lung damage and eventually death. But the presence of nitrogen, which is a non-reactive, inert gas, allows us to breathe in just the right amount of oxygen. Oxygen, on the other hand, is a very reactive gas, which is exactly what we need to provide our cells with energy. But too much oxygen in the atmosphere would result in a very combustible planet.

Combustible Air

In fact, the combustion of air was one of the first characteristics noticed by early scientists, including Leonardo da Vinci, who noted that a portion of air is consumed not only during respiration, but during combustion, as well. By the late 17th century, scientists like Robert Boyle and John Mayow proved that air was necessary for fire to burn. But around the same time, a theory was developed by German alchemist Johann Becher called the "phlogiston theory." This theory stated that matter contained a substance called "phlogiston" which was released when the matter was burned. This "dephlogisticating" released the phlogiston into the air, where it was absorbed by plants, which then became highly combustible. Though scientists had noticed that fire eventually burns out in an enclosed space, they took this as proof that air was only able to absorb a certain amount of phlogiston. This mysterious phlogiston, which could never seem to be observed or contained, nevertheless was assumed to permeate all things.

Because of the phlogiston theory, even scientists who managed to produce oxygen, including Robert Hooke, Ole Borch, Mikhail Lomonosov, and Pierre Bayen, didn't understand the significance of their findings. It wasn't until the 1770s that two scientists, Swedish pharmacist Carl Wilhelm Scheele and British chemist Joseph Priestley, independently and definitively discovered oxygen.

In 1771, Scheele began experimenting with mercuric oxide, silver carbonate, and magnesium nitrate, heating them to obtain oxygen, which he called "fire air." Familiar with the phlogiston theory, he suggested that this "fire air" combined with phlogiston when materials were burned. But Scheele made another important discovery about air: not only was it composed of "fire air," but something he called "foul air," as well. Scheele's description of fire air and foul air, now known to be oxygen and nitrogen, debunked the long-held assumption that air was a singular element.

Around the same time, Priestley was running his own experiments, heating up mercuric oxide until it produced oxygen. He made note of the gas's ability to feed bright flames, and called it "dephlogisticated air." He even trapped a mouse in a container filled with the gas, and was amazed to find that not only did it live four times longer than it would have if it had been breathing regular air, but it seemed to have extra energy once it was released.

Although Scheele made his observations first, his findings weren't published until 1777; Priestley, however, published a paper in 1775 titled "An Account of Further Discoveries in Air," so he is most often credited with the discovery of the element. But there was one more scientist, French chemist Antoine Lavoisier, who made important contributions in the discovery of oxygen. Lavoisier finally discredited the phlogiston theory, by proving that the gas discovered by Scheele and Priestley was a chemical element and being the first to correctly explain how combustion works. He also made a lasting contribution by naming the gas *oxygène*, from the Greek "oxys," meaning acid, and "genes" meaning producer, because he believed the gas was found in all acids. While this was eventually determined to not be the case, the name oxygen stuck for good.

The discoveries that these scientists made helped to finally bring an end to the ancient Greek theories about "classical elements," which suggested that earth, water, fire, and air were elements themselves. This belief persisted for centuries, which Priestley noted when he said that there are few ideas that "have laid firmer hold upon the mind." Fortunately, there are also few things scientists love more than to expand the knowledge we have of the world around us.

Who Invented the Guillotine?

One of the great ironies in history is that Dr. Joseph-Ignace Guillotin was an opponent of capital punishment. But despite the fact that he was the guillotine's namesake, he did not invent the device.

* * * *

How the Guillotine Came to Be

THE INFAMOUS DEATH machine's true creators were Antoine Louis, the French doctor who drew up the initial design around 1792, and Tobias Schmidt, the German piano maker who executed it. (Pun intended.)

Joseph-Ignace Guillotin's contribution came a bit earlier. As a delegate to France's National Assembly of 1789, he proposed the novel idea that if executions could not be banned entirely, the condemned should at least be entitled to a swift and relatively merciful death. What's more, he argued that all criminals, regardless of whether they were rich or poor, should be executed by the same method.

This last point may seem obvious, but prior to the French Revolution, wealthy miscreants who were up to be offed could slip executioners a few coins to guarantee speedy dispatches. Poorer ones often went "coach class"—they got to be the coach while horses tied to their arms and legs pulled them in four different directions. What a way to go!

In April 1792, the Assembly used its new guillotine for the first time on a platform in Paris' Place de Grève. Two vertical wooden beams served as runners for the slanted steel blade and stood about fifteen feet high. At the bottom, two boards with a round hole, called the *lunette*, locked the victim's head in place. The blade was hoisted to the top with pulleys and released with a lever. After a few grisly mishaps, executioners learned to grease the grooves on the beams with tallow in order to ensure that no one was left with half a head, which in this case was definitely not better than having none at all.

The Reign of Terror

The first head to roll was that of Nicolas Jacques-Pelletier, a common thief. During the Reign of Terror, from January 1793 to July 1794, more than ten thousand people had an exit interview with "Madame Guillotine," including King Louis XVI and his wife, Marie Antoinette. The daily parade of victims drew crowds of gawkers. Journalists printed programs, vendors sold refreshments, and nearby merchants rented out seats with unobstructed views. This bloody period ended with the execution of Robespierre, one of the Revolution's leaders and an early advocate of the guillotine. France continued to use the guillotine in cases of capital punishment throughout the 19th and 20th centuries. The last official guillotine execution took place on September 10, 1977.

Because they were embarrassed by their association with this instrument of terror, the descendants of Joseph Guillotin petitioned the government to change the name of the machine. The government declined to comply, so the family changed its name instead and passed into obscurity. Not so for the guillotine itself: Though it is now relegated to museums, it remains a grim symbol of power, punishment, and sudden death.

When Did Fire Hydrants First Appear?

A device first conceived in the 1600s saves countless lives and millions of dollars in property every year.

✳ ✳ ✳ ✳

FIRE HYDRANTS ARE one of the most ubiquitous fixtures in U.S. cities. Squat, brightly painted, and immediately recognizable, two or three of them adorn virtually every city block in the United States. New York City alone has more than 100,000 hydrants within city limits.

Fire hydrants as we know them today have been around for more than 200 years, but their predecessors first appeared in London in the 1600s. At that time, Britain's capital had an impressive municipal water system that consisted of networks of wooden pipes—essentially hollowed-out tree trunks—that snaked beneath the cobblestone streets. During large blazes, firefighters would dig through the street and cut into the pipe, allowing the hole they had dug to fill with water, creating an instant cistern that provided a supply of water for the bucket brigade. After extinguishing the blaze, they would drain the hole and plug the wooden pipe—which is the origin of the term *fireplug*—and then mark the spot for the next time a fire broke out in the vicinity.

Fanning the Flames of Invention

In 1666, a terrible fire raged through nearly three-quarters of London. As the city underwent rebuilding, the wooden pipes beneath the streets were redesigned to include predrilled plugs that rose to ground level. The following century, these crude fireplugs were improved with the addition of valves that allowed firefighters to insert portable standpipes that reached down to the mains. Many European countries use systems of a similar design today.

With the advent of metal piping, it became possible to install valve-controlled pipes that rose above street level. Frederick Graff Sr., the chief engineer of the Philadelphia Water Works department, is generally credited with designing the first hydrant of this type in 1801, as part of the city's effort to revamp its water system. A scant two years later, pumping systems became available, and Graff retrofitted Philly's hydrants with nozzles to accommodate the new fire hoses, giving hydrants essentially the same appearance that they have today. By 1811, the city boasted 185 cast-iron hydrants along with 230 wooden ones.

Hydrants Spread Like Wildfire

Over the next 50 years, hydrants became commonplace in all major American cities. But many communities in the north faced a serious fire safety problem during the bitter winters. The mains were usually placed well below the frost line, allowing the free-flow of water year-round, but the aboveground hydrants were prone to freezing, rendering them useless. Some cities tried putting wooden casings filled with sawdust or other insulating material, such as manure, around the hydrants, but this wasn't enough to stave off the cold. Others sent out armies of workers on the worst winter nights to turn the hydrants on for a few minutes each hour and let the water flow.

The freezing problem wasn't fully solved until the 1850s, with the development of dry-barrel hydrants. These use a dual-valve system that keeps water out of the hydrant until it is needed. Firefighters turn a nut on the top of the hydrant that opens a valve where the hydrant meets the main, letting the water rise to street level. When this main valve is closed, a drainage valve automatically opens so that any water remaining in the hydrant can flow out. Very little else about the design of fire hydrants has changed since. In fact, some cities are still using hydrants that were installed in the early 1900s.

Who Invented the Match?

For thousands of years, "keep the home fires burning" wasn't a cute saying—it was a major undertaking. Once your fire went out, there was no way to start it again except with good old-fashioned friction (i.e., rubbing two sticks together or striking a flint against a rock until you got a light).

✳ ✳ ✳ ✳

AROUND 1680, ROBERT Boyle, a chemist from Ireland, discovered that a stick coated with sulfur would ignite instantly when rubbed against a piece of paper coated with phosphorous. But prior to the Industrial Revolution, both sulfur and phosphorous were expensive and hard to produce, so Boyle's discovery had no practical application for nearly one hundred fifty years.

Real matches appeared on the market in 1827 after John Walker, an English chemist and apothecary, stirred up a mixture of potassium chlorate and antimony sulfide. He coated the end of a stick with this mixture, let it dry, scraped it against sandpaper, and—just like that—fire. Walker named his match-sticks Congreves, after the weaponry rockets that were developed by Sir William Congreve around 1804. Like rockets, Walker's Congreves often did more harm than good, sending showers of sparks that lit not just lamps and stoves, but also rugs, ladies' dresses, and gentlemen's wigs.

But such calamities didn't deter Samuel Jones, another Englishman. Jones modified Walker's process to make it less explosive, patented the result, and called his products Lucifers, a playful reference to the devilish odor given off by burning sulfide. Despite their nasty stench, Lucifers proved to be a big hit among gentlemen who liked to indulge in the new pastime of smoking cigars.

In an effort to produce an odor-free match, French chemist

Charles Sauria added white phosphorous to the sulfur mixture in 1830. Unfortunately, white phosphorous not only killed the smell, but it also those who made the matches. Thousands of the young women and children who worked in match factories began to suffer from phossy jaw, a painful and fatal bone disease caused by chronic exposure to the fumes of white phosphorous. (Once white phosphorous was understood to be poisonous, reformers worked to ban it from matches, finally succeeding with the Berne Convention of 1906, an international treaty that prohibited its use in manufacture and trade.)

In the 1850s, Swedish brothers John "Johan" and Carl Lundstrom created a match that was coated with red instead of white phosphorous on the striking surface. Red phosphorous was more expensive, but unlike its pale cousin, it was not toxic when inhaled.

Over the next sixty years, inventors experimented with many types of red phosphorous matches, the best being the "safety" matches that were patented by the Diamond Match Company of the United States in 1910. President William Howard Taft was so impressed by the company's new matches that he asked Diamond to make its patent available to everyone "for the good of all mankind." On January 28, 1911, Diamond complied, and ever since, the match business has been booming. You might say it's spread like wildfire.

Did Thomas Edison Invent the Light Bulb?

Although Thomas Alva Edison was one of the most prolific inventors in history, the light bulb was not one of his brainstorms.

✳ ✳ ✳ ✳

EDISON REPORTEDLY CONDUCTED more than 3,000 experiments in an attempt to perfect the filament for a light bulb, but his research was based on the work of diligent inventors before him. Historians cite at least 22 people who had presented various forms of the incandescent lamp prior to Edison. They include Englishman Humphry Davy, who in 1802 demonstrated the world's first incandescent light. In 1835, Scotsman James Lindsay demonstrated a constant electric light, and in 1841, Frederick de Moleyns of England was granted the first patent for an incandescent lamp. In 1845, American John W. Starr acquired a patent for an incandescent bulb that used carbon filaments.

These early inventors were followed by Joseph Wilson Swan, an English physicist who in 1850 demonstrated a workable, though short-lived, vacuum bulb. As Swan turned his attention to producing a better carbon filament, Edison began his own research. In 1879, he successfully demonstrated a carbon filament bulb that lasted 13 hours. When he began commercializing his invention in Great Britain, however, Swan sued him. Eventually, their two companies merged, as Ediswan. In America, Edison lost his patent in 1883 when the U.S. Patent Office ruled that his work was based on the prior research of inventor William Sawyer. After a number of court hearings, that ruling was overturned in 1889.

Slowly Lit

Although Edison's light bulb became the first commercially viable electric lamp in the United States, the technology took decades to become widely used. In 1925, 46 years after Edison patented his light bulb, only 25 percent of the U.S. population used electric lighting.

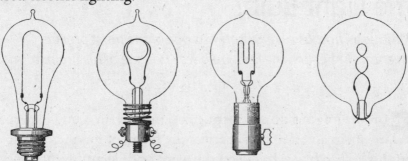

How Was Braille Developed?

How do you make up your own language? Louis Braille did it with equal parts perseverance and creativity.

✳ ✳ ✳ ✳

Ingredients

TAKE LOUIS BRAILLE, an inquisitive, creative boy who lost his sight after stabbing himself in the eye with an awl. Send him on scholarship to the National Institute for Blind Youth in Paris. Expose him to a cumbersome and slow method of reading. Now add a soldier from the French army by the name of Charles Barbier and his system, sonography, which used raised dots to represent sound. He developed this language to help soldiers communicate in the field without drawing attention to their positions, but the army eventually nixed it for being too complex.

The Mixture

These ingredients laid the basis for Braille's work. Over time, Braille developed a system that could be recognized and understood by passing the fingers over characters made up of an arrangement of one to six embossed points. Braille is a system made up of rectangles; each rectangle, or cell, has two columns and three rows. Each position has a particular number assigned to it—in the left column, moving down, the positions are numbered one, two, and three; in the right column, moving down, the positions are four, five, and six. Raised points at particular positions have particular meanings. For example, points raised at positions one, three, and four represent the letter m.

Because this system can be written with a stylus and a slate, the visually impaired have a means by which they can both read and write. Not only is that a recipe for further learning and efficient communication, but it's also a method by which they can increase their independence.

Who Was the First to Use Anesthesia?

In the middle of the 19th century, three intoxicating solvents with bad reputations became the first crude "switches" that could turn consciousness off and on—paving the way for the revolution of painless surgical medicine.

* * * *

ON MARCH 30, 1842, a doctor from rural Georgia laid an ether-soaked towel across the mouth and nose of a young patient with two cysts on the back of his neck. The physician, Crawford Williamson Long, excised one of the growths while his patient was under. In the process, he made medical and scientific history. Long was perhaps the first doctor to use what is today called a "general anesthetic"—a substance that reduces or eliminates conscious awareness in a patient, allowing a doctor to perform incisions, sutures, and all other surgical procedures in between.

The "general"—which means complete or near-complete unconsciousness—is quite different from the targeted "local" anesthetic, an invention with origins shrouded in mystery. (Some ancient Inca trepanation rituals involved drilling a hole in the patient's skull to allow evil spirits to escape; to reduce the literally mind-numbing pain, the Incan shaman chewed leaves of the narcotic coca plant and spat the paste into the subject's wound.)

Unfortunately for Georgia's Dr. Long, the awards and acclaim that should have accompanied his medical milestone went to a dentist from Boston, who used ether four years later to knock out a patient in order to remove a tooth. Because this procedure was performed at the world-renowned Massachusetts General Hospital—and not at a backwoods country practice in the Deep South—the fame of the Massachusetts innovator,

William T. G. Morton, was practically assured. Within two months of Morton's tooth extraction, doctors across Europe were toasting the Yankee who had invented pain-free surgery.

The story of the stolen spotlight, however, can't entirely be blamed on the prejudice of urban versus rural or North versus South. Long, who was known to enjoy the occasional "ether frolic," didn't publicize his use of ether as a general anesthetic until 1849, seven years after his initial use of it, and three years after Morton's world-acclaimed surgery.

Wake Up, Mr. Green. Mr. Green?

By 1849, a London physician, John Snow, had invented a specialized ether inhaler to better administer a safe but effective dose of the painless surgical gas. Snow was responding to the need for more scientific care in the fledgling field of anesthesiology. Lethal doses of ether had already been administered in some botched surgeries, and Snow eventually championed chloroform, which, he would later write, is "almost impossible ... [to cause] a death ... in the hands of a medical man who is applying it with ordinary intelligence and attention."

Chloroform and ether each had their downsides, though. Chloroform could damage the liver and occasionally even cause cardiac arrest, but ether required more time for the patient to both enter and exit the anesthetized state.

Nothing To Laugh About

Some American practitioners championed a third popular early anesthetic: nitrous oxide or "laughing gas," although its reputation suffered when not enough of it was administered in an early demonstration during a tooth extraction at Harvard Medical School. When the patient cried out in pain, the dentist, Horace Wells, was booed out of the room. In a turn of tragic irony, Wells later became a chloroform addict and committed suicide in 1848, just three years after the Harvard fiasco.

By the 1860s and '70s, many surgeons had given up advocating

one gas over another, preferring instead to use a mixture—
either chloroform or nitrous oxide to induce anesthesia, followed by ether to keep the patient in an unconscious state.

Who Invented Air Conditioning?

*If you've ever been to a state like Arizona, where temperatures
in July in Phoenix average over 100 degrees, you've probably
wondered how humans could've lived in such a place in the days
before air conditioning.*

✳ ✳ ✳ ✳

WHILE MANY OFTEN joke that the soaring temperatures
in states like Arizona and Nevada are a "dry heat," the
same can't be said for other sweltering locations, like humid
Houston, Texas, or Savannah, Georgia. And even northern locations like Boston, New York, and Chicago can reach
uncomfortably warm temperatures in the middle of summer,
hitting at least 90 degrees several times a year.

Before air conditioning, people dealt with the heat in many
different ways. Homes were often built with air flow in mind,
with high ceilings to allow the warmer air to rise, and windows
placed on opposite sides of a room so opening them would
create a cross-breeze. Homes in New Orleans were commonly
built "shotgun" style: rooms were lined up in a single row,
with doors at each end of the house to allow a breeze to flow
through. Families would spend time on porches outdoors to
escape the stifling interior of their house, sometimes snoozing
on screened-in "sleeping porches." In big cities like New York,
residents could lounge, and even sleep, on fire escapes. And
some people got even more imaginative, hanging wet laundry
just outside doorways so the breeze would carry cooled air into
the home.

While these methods may have provided some relief from
relentless heat and humidity, one physician in 1800's Florida

felt that they weren't enough. John Gorrie, who attended the College of Physicians and Surgeons in Fairfield, New York, moved to the warm Gulf Coast town of Apalachicola, Florida, in 1833. The 30-year-old doctor was studying tropical diseases, and embraced the popular theory of the time that warm, humid air contributed to the spread of illnesses like malaria. In fact, this theory was so commonplace that the name "malaria" was derived from the medieval Italian for "bad air."

Gorrie felt that cooling the air in hospital rooms would help prevent the spread of disease, so he came up with the idea of suspending buckets of ice from the ceiling. But in warm Florida, the only way to obtain ice was to have it shipped from northern states, an expensive and complicated endeavor. In an attempt to cut down on costs and time, Gorrie designed a machine to create ice, using a compressor that could be powered by water, steam, wind-driven sails, or even a horse. Gorrie was granted a patent for his invention in 1851, but it never really caught on as a marketable device. Still, it was the first attempt anyone had ever made to find a mechanical way to artificially cool an indoor space. It would take another half century of hot, humid, sweaty summers before the idea of mechanical cooling would come to the forefront again.

In the summer of 1902, the Sackett-Wilhelms Lithographing and Publishing Company in Brooklyn, New York, had a problem. Magazine pages that were printed by the company kept wrinkling, due to the high humidity in the plant. They sought the help of the Buffalo Forge Company, an equipment manufacturing business. The task of solving this problem fell to engineer Willis Carrier.

Coils That Cool

Carrier developed a mechanical system that used coils that could both cool and remove moisture from the air by cooling water, becoming the world's first modern air conditioner. Carrier continued to refine and improve his invention, and his

"Apparatus for Treating Air" was granted a U.S. patent in 1906. Carrier was the first to recognize the relationship between dew point—the temperature at which air must be cooled to create water vapor—and humidity, helping engineers design more efficient air conditioning systems.

But the first air conditioners were still much too big, bulky, and loud to be used in homes, so most people got their first taste of indoor cooling in public buildings. In 1904, an air conditioning system was used to cool the 1,000-seat auditorium in the Missouri State Building at the St. Louis World's Fair, marking the first time air conditioning was used for the general public, and providing hot attendees with a much-needed cooldown. By the 1930s, with the advent of Hollywood movies, Americans had a new refuge for escaping summer heat: movie theaters. Carrier, who founded the heating, ventilating, and air conditioning (HVAC) company Carrier Corporation in 1915, developed an air conditioning system for movie theaters that became popular with the general public, especially during the struggles of the Great Depression.

Greatest Contribution of the Century

In the late 1930s, air conditioning technology was improving, resulting in smaller, quieter systems, and the first window air conditioner made its debut. Still too expensive for anyone but the rich, window units were seen as a luxury, found mostly in fancy hotels. But over the next decade, improvements in manufacturing made window air conditioners more and more affordable, and by the late 1940s, many American homes were enjoying the comfort of indoor cooling. The technology was beginning to catch on in other countries, as well, with British politician Sir Sydney Frank Markham writing in 1947, "The greatest contribution to civilization in this century may well be air conditioning—and America leads the way."

This "great contribution" eventually became popular in the corporate world in the 1940s and '50s. Originally hesitant to spend money on air conditioning, employers soon changed their minds when studies began proving that employees worked more efficiently in comfortable temperatures. By the end of the 1950s, nearly 90 percent of employers believed that air conditioning created a positive effect on employee productivity, with one study showing that typists were 24 percent more efficient in a cooled space.

Nation of Addicts

By the 1960s and '70s, air conditioner use was soaring in the United States, with southern states like Florida and Arizona seeing huge population increases. But the road to cool air wasn't always smooth; surprisingly, the life-changing technology had critics as well as converts. In 1979, *TIME* magazine writer Frank Trippett lamented that Americans were "all but addicted" to the refreshing technology, and his point wasn't without merit: with only 5 percent of the world's population at the time, the United States was consuming more air conditioning than all other countries combined. When the 1979 energy crisis hit, lawmakers realized that American energy consumption needed to be dialed back. The Energy Department established the Appliance and Equipment Standards Program, which implemented minimum energy conservation standards for appliances such as refrigerators, washing machines, and air conditioners.

Air conditioners were struck with another blow in the 1990s, when chlorofluorocarbon coolants, which had been used as air conditioner refrigerating fluid since the 1930s, were linked to the depletion of the ozone in Earth's stratosphere. Although the fluids were safe and non-flammable, they were eventually phased out in favor of hydrofluorocarbons (HFCs), which do not deplete ozone; unfortunately, HFCs are a greenhouse gas that can affect climate change. But don't worry about ditching your central AC just yet: recent research is discovering new, non-toxic, energy efficient coolants, and these will one day replace HFCs and make air conditioning much more environmentally friendly.

Today, air conditioning is extremely common in the United States, with around 88 percent of all new homes constructed including central air conditioners. In the Southern states, the stats are even higher, with 99 percent of new homes including the much-appreciated feature. Even Canadians enjoy air conditioning in their cooler locale, with 55 percent of homes including one. While Frank Trippett may have been correct in his assumption that Americans are "addicted" to air conditioning, it's hard to imagine choosing to sleep on the fire escape.

What Did Louis Pasteur Discover?

"No, a thousand times no; there does not exist a category of science to which one can give the name applied science. There are science and the applications of science, bound together as the fruit to the tree which bears it."

✳ ✳ ✳ ✳

LOUIS PASTEUR'S CONTRIBUTIONS to modern biology are immense: he discovered pasteurization, vaccinations for anthrax and rabies, and microbial fermentation. His discoveries advanced the germ theory of disease, disproved the theory of spontaneous generation, and helped to found the study of bacteriology.

Pasteur was born in Dole, France, in 1822. Although he was an average student, he obtained a Bachelor of Arts in 1840, a Bachelor of Science in 1842, and a Doctorate at the École Normale in Paris in 1847. He spent the first several years of his career as a teacher and researcher in Dijon Lycée before becoming a chemistry professor at the University of Strasbourg. He married Marie Laurent, the daughter of the university's director, and together they had five children. Three survived to adulthood.

Chirality and Isomerism

In 1849, Pasteur was studying the chemical properties of

tartaric acid, a crystal found in wine sediments, and comparing them to paratartaric acid, a synthetic compound which had the same chemical composition. The two behaved differently, however, and he determined to discover why. He passed polarized light through each crystal, and found that while tartaric acid rotated the light, paratartaric acid did not. In doing so he discovered the principles of molecular chirality and isomerism; the former describes compounds that are mirror images, and the latter the fact that compounds can have identical molecular formulas and different chemical structures.

Fermentation and Germ Theory

In 1856, a winemaker asked Pasteur his advice on preventing stored alcohol from going bad. Pasteur surmised that fermentation and spoiling are caused by microorganisms, and demonstrated that the presence of oxygen was not necessary for this to occur. He showed experimentally that wine soured when lactic acid was produced by bacterial contamination. Having established this, he then realized that heating liquids could kill the majority of microorganisms that were present, preventing them from spoiling. He patented the process in 1865, calling it pasteurization.

His discovery that bacteria were responsible for fermentation and spoiling led him to suggest that the same microorganisms also caused human and animal diseases—now called the germ theory of disease. He proposed that protecting humans from bacteria could reduce disease, leading to the development of antiseptics.

Disproving Spontaneous Generation

For centuries, the prevailing wisdom held that living organisms arose spontaneously from nonliving matter; fleas were believed to appear from dust and maggots from dead flesh. Pasteur suspected that this was not the case when he observed that yeast did not grow on sterilized grapes. His assertion that spontaneous generation was incorrect sparked a furious debate, and the French Academy of Sciences proposed a cash prize for anyone who could prove or disprove the theory. Pasteur devised an experiment in which he boiled broth in swan-necked flasks. The necks of the flasks prevented airborne particles from reaching the broth. He also exposed a control set of boiled broth to the air. Nothing grew in the swan-necked flasks, but microorganisms did grow in the control set, demonstrating that spontaneous generation was incorrect.

Vaccination

Pasteur discovered the principle of vaccination almost by accident. While he was studying chicken cholera, his assistant inoculated a group of chickens with a culture of the disease that had spoiled. While the chickens became ill, they did not die. Pasteur attempted to re-infect the chickens, but discovered that the weakened culture had made them immune to cholera. Pasteur would go on to apply this principle to developing vaccinations for anthrax and rabies.

He founded the Pasteur Institute in 1887. In 1894, he suffered a stroke, and died the following year. He was buried at Notre Dame Cathedral.

"Louis Pasteur's theory of germs is ridiculous fiction."

—TOULOUSE PHYSIOLOGY PROFESSOR PIERRE PACHET, 1872

Who Invented Dynamite?

It may be surprising to learn that Alfred Nobel—the creator of the Nobel Prize—also created dynamite.

✳ ✳ ✳ ✳

BORN IN 1833, Alfred Nobel had science and technology in his blood. He was a descendant of medical professor Olof Rudbeck the Elder, who discovered the lymphatic system. Alfred's father Immanuel, an architect and engineer, was the inventor of plywood. His brothers founded Russia's oil industry.

The Swedish chemist, engineer, and inventor was no stranger to explosives, being the son of a machine and weapons manufacturer. As a teenager, Nobel traveled to Paris to study chemistry. While there he met Italian chemist Ascanio Sobrero, who had invented nitroglycerin in 1847. Although Sobrero strongly objected to the study of nitroglycerin, due to its tendency to explode when subjected to heat or pressure, Nobel was fascinated by the idea of an explosive that could rival the less-powerful gunpowder of the day. After returning to Sweden, Nobel grew determined to find a way to safely handle the dangerous substance.

Devising a Double-Edged Sword

Nobel's father had turned over his manufacturing business to one of his older sons, Ludvig, and Nobel set up some space in a shed at the family factory where he could create nitroglycerin. He invented a detonator and a blasting cap, which made it possible to detonate the mixture from a distance. But it didn't solve the problem of its instability. Nobel's quest to find a safe way to handle the substance turned tragic on September 3, 1864, when his research shed exploded, killing five people, including his younger brother, Emil. But instead of allowing this loss to halt his work, Nobel grew even more determined to find a safe way to handle nitroglycerin, moving his work to an isolated part of Germany in the hopes of avoiding any more casualties.

Over the next several years, Nobel built more factories to manufacture and distribute the explosive, experimenting with different ways to handle and transport it. He became well-known for his volatile product, which was in demand despite its dangerous nature. In 1866, he expanded business outside of Europe, founding the United States Blasting Oil Company in New Jersey. But it didn't take long before the factory was destroyed by explosions. It seemed that Nobel would never find the secret to stabilizing the unpredictable nitroglycerin.

Then, in 1867, Nobel finally stumbled upon the solution he'd been looking for. He had already had the idea to combine the nitroglycerin with another substance in the hopes of making it more stable, but his experiments with sawdust, cement, and coal had all been unsuccessful. His final experiment was to add diatomaceous earth, a powdery white substance that contains the fossilized remains of algae, to the nitroglycerin. To his excitement, the combination resulted in a malleable paste that stabilized the nitroglycerin and made the substance safely portable.

Nobel called the mixture "dynamite," after the Greek word *dunamis*, which can mean power, strength, or force, and is also the root of words like "dynamic" and "dynamo." He invented an improved blasting cap for the mixture, and patented his dynamite in the United States and the U.K. A few years later, Nobel also created gelignite, a very stable, easily moldable, jelly-like explosive popularly used in quarries and mines.

Nobel earned great wealth thanks to his explosive creations, a fact that many found objectionable. And it was this reputation, along with an accidental obituary, that ultimately led to the creation of the most famous scientific prizes in the world. In 1888, Nobel's older brother Ludvig passed away while in France. But a French newspaper erroneously assumed that Alfred was the Nobel who had died, and it printed a scathing obituary in which it referred to him as "the merchant of death." Nobel was greatly dismayed to think that he would be remembered in such a way, so he came up with an idea: In his last will and testament, he stipulated that 94 percent of his vast wealth should be used to establish an annual international award honoring achievements in physical science, chemistry, medical science, literature, and furthering peace.

Nobel's plan certainly worked: Today, we are much more likely to associate the scientist with the Nobel Prize than with dynamite. As for Sobrero, he was reportedly "horrified" that his discovery of nitroglycerin led to the creation of such a destructive invention. But both Sobrero and Nobel would be comforted to know that nitroglycerin—in safe, diluted amounts—is now one of the most-commonly prescribed drugs in the country, with more than four million prescriptions written every year. For all of its destructive potential, it's safe to say that nitroglycerin has now saved far more lives than it has ever taken.

Who Discovered DNA?

Swiss physician and biologist Friedrich Miescher's amazing discovery began in 1869.

✳   ✳   ✳   ✳

ALTHOUGH HE'D EARNED his medical degree the year before, Friedrich Miescher was hearing impaired due to a bout with typhoid fever and felt his deafness would be a hindrance when dealing with patients. So instead, he focused on research, studying white blood cells called neutrophils.

The scientist obtained used bandages from a nearby hospital, carefully washing them with sodium sulfate to remove cells without damaging them. His plan was to then isolate and identify the various proteins within the blood cells.

A Substance with Unique Properties

Miescher experimented with different salt solutions to study the cells, and then tried adding an acid. When he did so, he noticed a substance that separated from the solution, but its properties were unlike those of the proteins he'd been studying. This substance, which he dubbed "nuclein," contained phosphorus and nitrogen, and dissolved when he added an alkali solution. Miescher knew he'd stumbled upon something important, but the tools and methods available to him at the time limited much further research. It would take decades before his discovery, which was later called "nucleic acid" and finally "deoxyribonucleic acid" and "ribonucleic acid," or DNA and RNA, was appreciated as a major scientific breakthrough.

In 1881, German biochemist Albrecht Kossel began to further Miescher's research, isolating the organic compounds found in the nearly identical molecules of DNA and RNA: adenine, cytosine, guanine, thymine, and uracil. Kossel was awarded a Nobel Prize for his work in 1910, just a year after another scientist, Russian biochemist Phoebus Levene, identified some fundamental differences between DNA and RNA when he discovered the phosphate-sugar-base components of the molecules. DNA has a thymine base and deoxyribose sugar; RNA has a uracil base and ribose sugar.

Although other scientists had proposed that these molecules might have something to do with heredity, it was still widely believed that proteins served to carry genetic information. But British bacteriologist Frederick Griffith was the first to demonstrate that DNA could be responsible for this property. In 1928, Griffith mixed two forms of the *Pneumococcus* bacteria, a "smooth" form and a "rough" form, transferring the properties of the "smooth" bacteria to the "rough" bacteria. Fifteen years later, Canadian-American physician Oswald Avery and his coworkers, Colin MacLeod and Maclyn McCarty, identified DNA as the substance that causes genetic transformation, verifying Griffith's findings.

Crick and Watson

Almost ten years later, in May 1952, a PhD student at King's College London, Raymond Gosling, working under the supervision of his instructor, Rosalind Franklin, was studying samples of DNA by hydrating the substance and using x-ray diffraction photography to take images. One of these images, called Photo 51, drew the attention of two scientists, Francis Crick and James Watson, who were working together at the Cavendish Laboratory at the University of Cambridge. The photo displays a fuzzy, X-shaped image, with each leg of the "X" appearing like the rung of a ladder. After studying the blurry photograph and consulting many other sources of information, Crick and Watson proposed the three-dimensional, double-helix model of DNA structure. Although slight changes have been made to Crick and Watson's initial suggestions, the main features of their model turned out to be correct.

The pair's theory was that DNA was a double-stranded helix, connected by hydrogen bonds. Adenine bases were always paired with thymine, and cytosine paired with guanine. Now that they understood more about the structure, Crick and Watson proposed another theory about DNA replication. They believed that when DNA replicated, it would be "semiconservative," meaning that the two strands of DNA would separate during replication, with each strand acting as a template for the synthesis of a new strand.

In 1958, molecular biologists Matthew Meselson and Franklin Stahl ran an experiment to test this theory. In what has been called "the most beautiful experiment in biology," the Meselson-Stahl experiment extracted DNA from *E. coli* bacteria and allowed it to replicate. The resulting DNA strands were studied and found to be consistent with Crick and Watson's semiconservative replication hypothesis.

While Crick and Watson are often credited with "discovering" DNA, it is clear that the pair had plenty of help along the way. Thanks to the discoveries and research of everyone from Miescher to Meselson and Stahl, the study of DNA has led to a myriad of practical uses. DNA profiling can now be used to convict or exonerate an individual accused of a crime; genetic genealogy can use DNA to help us find ancestors we never knew we had; and we may even one day be able to genetically modify DNA to eradicate certain diseases or conditions. With barely 150 years of research behind us, the science behind DNA is still fairly new; no doubt more discoveries are just over the horizon.

Who Invented the Car?

The car as we know it today was invented by Karl Benz, who distilled centuries of accumulated wisdom, added a dose of original thinking, and unleashed upon the world the 1886 Benz Patent Motorwagen.

UNLEASHED IS A strong word to describe the debut of a three-wheel contraption with nine-tenths of a horsepower and a top speed of 9.3 miles per hour. But the machine that trundled over the cobblestones of Mannheim, Germany, on July 3, 1886, was the first self-propelled vehicle to employ a gasoline-powered internal combustion engine as part of a purpose-built chassis—the basic definition of the modern automobile.

Something so momentous seldom occurs without a qualifier, however—and so it is with the Benz Patent Motorwagen. For Karl Benz, the qualifier was another vehicle that first ran under its own power in 1886, just 60 miles away in Cannstatt, Germany. It was the inventive handiwork of partners Gottlieb Daimler and Wilhelm Maybach. Their machine also used a gas-burning single-cylinder engine, but it was mounted on a horse-type carriage. Daimler's carriage was specially constructed by a Stuttgart coachbuilder for this purpose, and had the four-wheel layout that eventually became standard practice.

But when forced to decide, historians give the edge to Benz as the "inventor" of the automobile. His patent was issued first (in January 1886); his Motorwagen was in operation at least a month before Daimler and Maybach's; and, vitally, Benz's three-wheeler was not a horseless carriage but an entirely new type of vehicle, the marker for a new age of mobility.

Others quickly followed. The Duryea brothers, Charles and Frank, of Springfield, Massachusetts, put America on gas-powered wheels with their motorized carriage in September 1893. Henry Ford's first car, the experimental Quadracycle, sputtered to life in Detroit in June 1896.

By 1901, enough tinkerers had walked in the footsteps of Benz and Daimler that car-building was a full-fledged industry. As for those two German pioneers, they never met face to face, but the rival companies they formed became tightly laced. Daimler proved to be the more successful carmaker. He was quicker to develop his machines, and they entranced a wealthy and colorful Austrian named Emil Jellinek. Jellinek placed large orders for Daimler automobiles, became a member of the company's board, and wielded enough influence to insist that its cars be named for his ten-year-old daughter, Mercedes.

Weathering tough times after World War I, the Daimler and Benz companies formed a syndicate to market their products, and when they merged in 1926, they created a company that combined the names of their autos, which honored the inventor of the car, along with the daughter of Emil Jellinek: Mercedes-Benz.

What Teenager Invented Television?

Responsible for what may have been the most influential invention of the 20th century, Philo T. Farnsworth never received the recognition he was due.

✳ ✳ ✳ ✳

PHILO T. FARNSWORTH's brilliance was obvious from an early age. In 1919, when he was only 12, he amazed his parents and older siblings by fixing a balky electrical generator on their Idaho farm. By age 14, he had built an electrical laboratory in the family attic and was setting his alarm for 4 A.M. so he could get up and read science journals for an hour before doing chores.

Farnsworth hated the drudgery of farming. He often daydreamed solutions to scientific problems as he worked. During the summer of 1921, he was particularly preoccupied with the possibility of transmitting moving pictures through the air.

Around the same time, big corporations like RCA were spending millions of research dollars trying to find a practical way to do just that. As it turned out, most of their work was focused on a theoretical dead-end. Back in 1884, German scientist Paul Nipkow had patented a device called the Nipkow disc. By rotating the disc rapidly while passing light through tiny holes, an illusion of movement could be created. In essence, the Nipkow disc was a primitive way to scan images. Farnsworth doubted that this mechanical method of scanning could ever work fast enough to send images worth watching. He was determined to find a better way.

His "Eureka!" moment came as he cultivated a field with a team of horses. Swinging the horses around to do another row, Farnsworth glanced back at the furrows behind him. Suddenly, he realized that scanning could be done electronically, line-by-line. Light could be converted into streams of electrons and then back again with such rapidity that the eye would be fooled. He immediately set about designing what would one day be called the cathode ray tube. Seven years would pass, however, before he was able to display a working model of his mental breakthrough.

Upon graduating from high school, Farnsworth enrolled at the University of Utah but dropped out after a year because he could no longer afford the tuition. Almost immediately, though, he found financial backers and moved to San Francisco to continue his research. The cathode ray tube he developed there became the basis for all television. In 1930, a researcher from RCA named Vladimir Zworykin visited Farnsworth's California laboratory and copied his invention. When Farnsworth refused to sell his patent to RCA for $100,000, the company sued him. The legal wrangling continued for many years and, though Farnsworth eventually earned royalties from his invention, he never did get wealthy from it.

By the time Farnsworth died in 1971, there were more homes on Earth with televisions than with indoor plumbing. Ironically, the man most responsible for television appeared on the small screen only once. It was a 1957 appearance on the game show *I've Got a Secret*. Farnsworth's secret was that "I invented electric television at the age of 15." When none of the panelists guessed Farnsworth's secret, he left the studio with his winnings—$80 and a carton of Winston cigarettes.

What Was the First Synthetic Fabric?

Did you guess nylon? If so, give yourself half a point. Nylon, invented by DuPont scientist Wallace Carothers in 1935, was the first fabric made from nonorganic sources. Water-resistant, strong, and stretchy, nylon was a big hit. DuPont spent seven years and 27 million dollars tweaking its "new silk," which revolutionized the hosiery industry.

✳   ✳   ✳   ✳

BUT THE FIRST true synthetic fabric was rayon, which was introduced back in 1884. Rayon is made from a naturally occurring polymer. And what exactly does that mean? Well, cellulose—which is plant fiber, the most common organic substance on the planet—is technically a polymer. To chemists, this means cellulose is made of molecules that are arranged in repeated units and are connected by covalent chemical bonds.

Cellulose turns into nitrocellulose when it's exposed to nitric acid. Nitrocellulose can be used in explosives, and we all know how some men like to play with explosives. Around 1855, Swiss chemist Georges Audemars was playing, or "experimenting," with nitrocellulose and discovered that certain solvents made it break down into fibers that looked a lot like silk. He called his new fabric "artificial silk," but as it had a tendency to explode, he didn't sell much of it.

Frenchman Hilaire de Chardonnet, the Count of Chardonnet, took the invention further and patented his "Chardonnay silk" in 1884. He made the material from the pulp of mulberry trees, because silk worms fed on mulberry leaves. Soft and pretty, Chardonnay silk didn't explode, though it did have a nasty habit of bursting into flames. In the days of fireplaces and floor heaters that were fueled by gas, ladies were naturally a little nervous about wearing something so flammable. The fabric, initially popular, was banned in several countries.

In 1892, English scientists Charles Cross, Edward Bevan, and Clayton Beadle figured out how to cheaply and safely make artificial silk that didn't catch fire so easily. Their product was called viscose, and it hit U.S. stores in 1910. A committee of textile manufacturers and the folks at the U.S. Department of Commerce held a contest to rename the fabric in 1924. The winning name? Rayon, which is possibly a combination of "ray" (the fabric's sheen may have reminded folks of a ray of sunshine) and the "on" from "cotton."

What Important Stuff Have Women Invented?

If you think men have the market cornered on inventions, think again. It turns out that the fairer sex is responsible for some of history's most notable breakthroughs.

✳ ✳ ✳ ✳

WOMEN CAME UP with ideas and specifications for such useful items as life rafts (Maria Beasley), circular saws (Tabitha Babbitt), medical syringes (Letitia Geer), and underwater lamps and telescopes (Sarah Mather). Giuliana Tesoro was a prolific inventor in the textile industry; flame-resistant fibers and permanent-press properties are among her many contributions. The Tesoro Corporation holds more than 125 of her textile-related patents.

Some well-known inventions by women are associated with the home. In 1930, for example, dietician Ruth Wakefield and her husband Kenneth were operating a tourist lodge near Boston. While mixing a batch of cookies for guests one day, Ruth discovered she had run out of baker's chocolate. In a rush to come up with something, Wakefield substituted broken pieces of Nestlé semisweet chocolate.  She expected them to melt into the dough to create chocolate cookies; they didn't, and the surprising result was the chocolate chip cookie.

In the late 1950s, Ruth Handler drew inspiration from watching her daughter and her daughter's friends play with paper dolls. After noticing that the girls used the dolls to act out future events rather than those in the present, Handler set out to create a grown-up, three-dimensional doll. She even endowed it with breasts (though their proportions were later criticized for being unrealistic). Handler named her creation after her daughter, and the Barbie doll was introduced in 1959. Handler, incidentally, was one of the founders of the toy giant Mattel.

Of course, not all female inventors have been interested in cookies and dolls. Consider Mary Anderson. While taking a trip from Alabama to New York City just after the turn of the 20th century, she noticed that when it rained, drivers had to open their car windows to see. Anderson invented a swinging-arm device with a rubber blade that the driver operated by using a lever. In 1903, she received a patent for what became known as the windshield wiper; by 1916, it was standard on most vehicles.

Movie actress Hedy Lamarr's invention was a matter of national security. Lamarr, born Hedwig Eva Maria Kiesler in Austria, emigrated to the United States in the 1930s. In addition to leading the glamorous life of a film star, she became a pioneer in the field of wireless communication.

Lamarr and composer George Anthiel developed a secret communications system to help the Allies in World War II—their method of manipulating radio frequencies was used to create unbreakable codes. The invention proved invaluable again two decades later when it was used aboard naval vessels during the Cuban Missile Crisis.

The "spread spectrum" technology that Lamarr helped to pioneer became the key component in the creation of cellular phones, fax machines, and other wireless devices. How's that for inventive?

Who Invented Kitty Litter?

Indoor cats and their owners should give thanks to Ed Lowe, the inventor of Kitty Litter.

✳ ✳ ✳ ✳

Stumbling Upon Paydirt

BORN IN MINNESOTA in 1920, Ed Lowe grew up in Cassopolis, Michigan. After a stint in the U.S. Navy, he returned to Cassopolis to work in his family's business selling industrial-strength absorbent materials, including sawdust, sand, and a powdered clay called fuller's earth. Due to its high concentration of magnesium oxide, fuller's earth has an extraordinary ability to rapidly and completely absorb any liquid.

Back in those days, domestic kitties did their business in litter boxes filled with sand, wood shavings, or ashes. One fateful morning in 1947, a neighbor of Lowe's, Kaye Draper, complained to him about her cat tracking ashes all over the house. She asked if she could have a bag of sand from his warehouse.

Instead, Lowe gave her a sack of fuller's earth. Draper was so pleased with the results that she asked for more. After a while, her cat used only fuller's earth—it was the first Kitty Litter-using critter in the world.

Sensing that he was on to a good thing, Lowe filled ten brown bags with five pounds of fuller's earth each and wrote "Kitty Litter" on them. He never explained exactly how he came up with the name, but it was certainly an inspired choice.

The Idea Catches On in Catdom

Initially, convincing pet shop owners to carry Kitty Litter proved to be a challenge. Lowe's suggested price of 65 cents per bag was a lot of money at that time—the equivalent of about $7.50 today. Why would people pay so much for cat litter, the shop owners asked, when they could get sand for a few pennies? Lowe was so sure Kitty Litter would be a success that he told the merchants they could give it away for free until they built up a demand. Soon, satisfied customers insisted on nothing but Kitty Litter for their feline friends, and they were willing to pay for it.

Lowe piled bags of Kitty Litter into the back of his 1943 Chevy and spent the next few years traveling the country, visiting pet shops and peddling his product at cat shows. "Kitty Litter" became a byword among fastidious cat owners. The *Oxford English Dictionary* cites this advertisement from the February 9, 1949, issue of the Mansfield, Ohio, *Journal News* as the phrase's first appearance in print: "Kitty Litter 10 lbs $1.50. Your kitty will like it. Takes the place of sand or sawdust."

The Kitty Litter Kingdom

By 1990, Lowe's company was raking in almost $200 million annually from the sale of Kitty Litter and related products. He owned more than 20 homes, a stable of racehorses, a yacht, and a private railroad. He even bought up 2,500 acres of land outside of Cassopolis, where he established the Edward Lowe Foundation—a think tank dedicated to assisting small businesses. Lowe sold his business in 1990 and died in 1995. As far as anyone knows, he never owned a cat himself.

If Al Gore Didn't Invent the Internet, Who Did?

When the Internet was conceived in the 1960s, Al Gore was consumed by other matters, such as getting to know his future wife, Tipper, at their senior prom. But Gore wasn't completely full of you-know-what when some years later he claimed to have taken "the initiative in creating the Internet." As a congressman, he helped popularize the term "information superhighway" and sponsored a number of bills that aided in forming the Internet as we know it today.

✳   ✳   ✳   ✳

BUT WE DIGRESS. The best candidate to credit with the invention of the most expansive and influential technology of our time is Robert Taylor. Born in 1932, Taylor was trained as an experimental psychologist and mathematician, and he worked for defense contractor Martin Marietta early in his career. Under J. C. R. Licklider (who is now known as computing's Johnny Appleseed), Taylor went to work in the Department of Defense's information processing office in the 1960s.

Back then, communication between several computers was

akin to communication via telegraph—only one machine could talk to another at a time. At the Department of Defense, Taylor had three computers at his disposal: one connected to the System Development

Corporation in Santa Monica, California; one for Project Genie at the University of California-Berkeley; and one hooked into the Compatible Time-Sharing System at MIT. The problem? To talk to the computer at MIT, Taylor had to be sitting at the Department of Defense's MIT-designated computer. To talk to the System Development Corporation in Santa Monica, he had to be on that designated computer. And so on.

Tired of walking from terminal to terminal, Taylor spared us from having hundreds of laptops in our offices by sensing the need for "interactive computing," or one computer terminal that would connect with all others. He and Licklider coauthored the landmark paper "The Computer as a Communication Device," which was published in *Science and Technology* in April 1968.

By the end of the decade, Taylor had spearheaded the creation of the ARPANET (Advanced Research Projects Agency Network), which featured newly developed packet-switching technology (using a communication line to connect to more than one other computer at a time) and was the precursor to the Internet.

In 1973, Vinton Cerf and Robert Kahn began considering ways of connecting ARPANET with other networks that had emerged. Cerf came up with a new computer communications protocol, a gateway between networks, which eventually became known as transmission-control protocol/Internet protocol (TCP/IP). First tested on ARPANET in 1977, TCP/IP was a way that one network could transfer data packets to another, then another, and another. Cerf's innovation proved invaluable when the Internet eventually consisted of a network of networks. It remains the basis of the modern Internet.

The term "Internet" was adopted in 1983, at about the same time that TCP/IP came into wide use. Today, the entire civilized world has jumped on board and, to borrow Gore's catchphrase, is rolling down the information superhighway.

Chapter 4

Health and the Human Body

Can the Cold Give You a Cold?

No, you won't catch a cold by running around in the frigid air while wearing only underwear or traipsing through town with wet hair. Sorry, Mom—and old wives.

✳   ✳   ✳   ✳

WHILE IT'S TRUE that colds are more prevalent during the nippy months from September to April, the cold temperatures are probably not to blame. These just happen to be the months when viruses are typically spread.

One study did conclude that cold temperatures might indeed give you a cold. Researchers at Cardiff Common Cold Centre in Wales asked 180 volunteers to sit with their feet in bowls of ice-cold water for twenty minutes. Over the next five days, 29 percent of the cold-feet volunteers caught a cold, compared to 9 percent of an empty-bowl control group. It's thought that cold temperatures can constrict the blood vessels of the nose, turning off the warm blood supply to white blood cells (the ones that fight infections).

However, most research continues to show that being physically chilled or wet really has nothing to do with catching a cold. We spend more time indoors during the winter, oftentimes exposed to sniffling coworkers who refuse to take sick days. (Are they still hoping to win a gold star for perfect attendance?) Before you know it, January rolls around and you're drowning in a mound of soft ply tissues and begging someone—anyone—to make you a batch of chicken noodle soup.

Who hasn't been there? That's why it's the "common cold." More than two hundred types of viruses can cause it. There are the rhinovirus (the leading cause of the common cold, made famous in Lysol disinfectant TV commercials), the respiratory syncytial virus, and lots, lots more. These nasty bugs lurk on phones, cutting boards, kitchen sponges, computer mice, doorknobs, elevator buttons, shopping carts, hand towels, and pretty much everywhere hands are meant to go.

So wipe those areas down with disinfecting sprays or wipes and be vigilant about cleansing your hands with antibacterial soap and water or hand sanitizer gel. Dr. Neil Schachter, author of *The Good Doctor's Guide to Colds and Flu*, says that people who wash their hands seven times a day get 40 percent fewer colds than the average person.

You know what else? It really can't hurt to throw on your ski mask and thermal snowsuit when the temperature dips below freezing. At least it will make your mom feel better.

What Did They Use for Contraception in the Old Days?

Ever since humans realized how babies were made, they have either tried to conceive children or avoid them altogether. In earlier days, some techniques were more successful than others.

✳   ✳   ✳   ✳

A N ANCIENT GREEK gynecologist told women not wishing to have a child to jump backward seven times after intercourse. Ancient Roman women tried to avoid pregnancy by tying a pouch containing a cat's liver to their left foot or by spitting into the mouth of a frog.

What Can Women Do?

Barrier methods of contraception have included pebbles (Arabs prevented camels' impregnation this way), half a lemon, and dried elephant or crocodile dung. In 1550 B.C., a suggested concoction of ground dates, acacia tree bark, and honey applied locally was probably fairly effective, since acacia ferments into lactic acid, which disrupts a normal pH balance. In eastern Canada, one aboriginal group believed in the efficacy of women drinking a tea brewed with beaver testicles.

As early as the seventh century B.C., a member of the fennel family called silphium was discovered to be an extremely effective "morning-after pill." But since it only grew in a small area on the Libyan mountainside facing the Mediterranean and attempts to cultivate it elsewhere failed, silphium was extinct by the second century.

Getting the Men Involved

Men have almost always used some sort of sheath, dating back to at least 1000 B.C. The ancient Romans and the 17th-century British employed animal intestine (still available, albeit packaged), while the Egyptians and Italians preferred fabric, sometimes soaked in a spermicidal solution. Vulcanized rubber appeared around 1844.

The main responsibility for contraception still lies with women, many of whom alter their body's hormonal balance with "the pill," introduced in 1960. Meanwhile, due to lack of male interest, research into male contraceptive injections, pills and/or nasal sprays has stalled, and "the sheath" remains men's primary resource.

Do Babies Have More Bones Than Adults?

If this question were a bar bet, it would forever be, um, a bone of contention. Before you can even answer it, you and your rival have to agree on your definition of "bone." And if you're arguing over the meaning of the word "bone" while you're in a bar … well, let's just say the likelihood of absurd distraction is fairly high.

✳   ✳   ✳   ✳

THE COMPARISON IN its simplest form goes like this: The average adult skeleton contains 206 parts, while a baby's skeleton is made up of more than 300 parts. Case closed, bet won, pay up—right? Not quite. Note the weasellike omission of the actual word "bones" from that sentence.

The average adult skeleton does contain 206 parts, and they're all bones. But this is where things start to get tricky. When it comes to babies, just what those "parts" are is subject to debate. An adult's bones are lightweight, rigid structures that are strong and hard enough to support and protect the body's internal organs. Mother Nature, in her infinite wisdom, creates babies with some built-in bounce. Many of the parts in a baby's skeleton contain little or no true bone, but are in fact made of soft, flexible cartilage, which is more likely to bend than break in case of a fall.

So you could argue that babies have fewer bones than adults. As the baby grows into childhood and young adulthood, the soft cartilage ossifies into hard, strong bone. The entire process stops when a person is done growing in height, which can take up to twenty-five years. In some cases, two or more parts fuse together, thus creating one larger bone. In the skull, for example, a number of parts gradually fuse together, which is why babies have a soft spot on their heads that adults don't.

Although if you've spent enough time arguing in bars, no doubt you've occasionally wondered if there aren't a few adults whose skulls never fully developed.

What Makes Joints Crack?

Ever wonder why your joints moan like a rusty gate when you get up from sitting, or why it feels good to crack your knuckles?

❋ ❋ ❋ ❋

THOSE PERCUSSIVE POPS and creaks have a number of causes. When larger joints like your knees or your shoulders raise a ruckus, it's likely that the noise is made by your tendons and ligaments as they snap back into place after a temporary repositioning. Conditions like arthritis can also cause some popping and cracking because of the loss of lubricant in the joints.

A good old-fashioned knuckle-cracking is something else entirely. When you crack your knuckles, you're pulling apart the two bones that meet at the joint. The cartilage that connects these bones is protected by a capsule that produces a fluid that lubricates the joint and absorbs shocks and pressure. As the bones are pulled apart, the capsule is stretched rapidly, which causes gas bubbles to form in the fluid; as the capsule is stretched farther, the pressure drops and the bubbles pop, causing the cracking sound. You can't crack your joints while the gas is redissolving into the fluid, which typically takes between twenty and thirty minutes.

Cracking your knuckles relieves some pressure and temporarily increases the mobility of the joint. So go ahead and crack 'em just before you pound out a piano concerto. And if you sound like a one-man percussion section when you stand up, don't worry—your body is merely reassembling itself for the arduous trek to the kitchen.

Why Do Body Parts Fall Asleep?

It happens to all of us. You get up in the middle of the night because nature is calling, but it's hard to walk because one of your feet is "asleep." As a tingling sensation shoots through your foot, you lumber toward the bathroom like Frankenstein's monster.

✳ ✳ ✳ ✳

WHAT'S HAPPENING? IT begins when a limb has had pressure exerted on it for an extended period of time, maybe from kneeling or from crossing your arms. When this happens, the nerves in the limb obviously have pressure exerted on them, too, and this prevents those nerves from sending messages to the brain and the rest of the body. Blood vessels in the limb are also squeezed, which means oxygen being carried to the nerves is blocked and never makes it. Simply put, in the airport that is your body, too much pressure cancels a lot of incoming and outgoing flights.

The brain isn't sure what's going on—some nerves aren't transmitting any information to it, while others are sending impulses erratically. As a sort of warning signal, the limb starts to tingle. It's your body's way of saying, "Get out of that kneeling position, for crying out loud, before you cause nerve damage."

Once you jostle the affected limb, the nerves begin functioning properly again. Of course, it doesn't happen instantly. The tingling sensation often intensifies and is followed by a somewhat uncomfortable semi-numbness.

Why does this occur? Your nerves comprise bundles of fibers, and each transmits different signals to the brain. The fibers that control touch are among the thickest, and they're the last to "wake up" and resume the proper firing of impulses. That's why the final feeling you have before your limb returns to normal is that odd sensation of semi-numbness, the one that makes you look like you're starring in a B-grade horror flick.

What Is Trepanation?

There aren't many medical procedures more than 7,000 years old that are still practiced today. Trepanation, or the practice of drilling a hole in the skull, is one of the few.

∗ ∗ ∗ ∗

An Ancient Practice

HAS ANYONE EVER angrily accused you of having a hole in your head? Well, it's not necessarily an exaggeration. *Trepanation* (also known as "trephination") is the practice of boring into the skull and removing a piece of bone, thereby leaving a hole. It is derived from the Greek word *trypanon*, meaning "to bore." This practice was performed by the ancient Greeks, Romans, and Egyptians, among others.

Hippocrates, considered the father of medicine, indicated that the Greeks might have used trepanation to treat head injuries. However, evidence of trepanning without accompanying head trauma has been found in less advanced civilizations; speculation abounds as to its exact purpose. Since the head was considered a barometer for a person's behavior, one theory is that trepanation was used as a way to treat headaches, depression, and other conditions that had no outward trauma signs. Think of it like a pressure release valve: The hole gave evil spirits inside the skull a way out of the body. When the spirits were gone, it was hoped, the symptoms would disappear.

How to Trepan

In trepanning, the Greeks used an instrument called a *terebra*, an extremely sharp piece of wood with another piece of wood mounted crossways on it as a handle and attached by a thong. The handle was twisted until the thong was extremely tight. When released, the thong unwound, which spun the sharp piece of wood around and drove it into the skull like a drill. Although it's possible that the terebra was used for a single hole, it is more likely that it was used to make a circular pattern of multiple small holes, thereby making it easier to remove a large piece of bone. Since formal anesthesia had not yet been invented, it is unknown whether any kind of numbing agent was used before trepanation was performed.

The Incas were also adept at trepanation. The procedure was performed using a ceremonial tumi knife made of flint or copper. The surgeon held the patient's head between his knees and rubbed the tumi blade back and forth along the surface of the skull to create four incisions in a crisscross pattern. When the incisions were sufficiently deep, the square-shaped piece of bone in the center was pulled out. Come to think of it, perhaps the procedure hurt more than the symptom.

Trepanation Today

Just when you thought it was safe to assume that the medical field has come so far, hold on—doctors still use this procedure, only now it's called a craniotomy. The underlying methodology is similar: It still involves removing a piece of skull to get to the underlying tissue. The bone is replaced when the procedure is done. If it is not replaced, the operation is called a *craniectomy*. That procedure is used in many different circumstances, such as for treating a tumor or infection.

However, good ol'-fashion trepanation still has its supporters. One in particular is Bart Hughes, who believes that trepanning can elevate one to a higher state of consciousness. According to Hughes, once man started to walk upright, the brain lost blood because the heart had to frantically pump it throughout the body in a struggle against gravity. Thus, the brain had to shut down certain areas that were not critically needed to assure proper blood flow to vital regions.

Increased blood flow to the brain can elevate a person's consciousness, Hughes reasoned, and he advocated ventilating the skull as a means of making it easier for the heart to send blood to the brain. (Standing on one's head also accomplishes this, but that's just a temporary measure.) Some of his followers have actually performed trepanation on themselves. For better or gross, a few have even filmed the process. In 2001, two men from Utah pled guilty to practicing medicine without a license after they had bored holes into a woman's skull to treat her chronic fatigue and depression. There's no word as to whether the procedure actually worked, or if she's just wearing a lot of hats nowadays.

How Long Can You Live Without Sleep?

Dr. Nathaniel Kleitman, the father of modern sleep research, said: "No one ever died of insomnia." Still, what doesn't kill you can have some nasty side effects.

✳ ✳ ✳ ✳

STUDIES HAVE REVEALED that missing just one night of sleep can lead to memory loss and decreased activity in certain parts of the brain. So if you're planning an all-night cram session for the evening before the big midterm, you may be better off closing the book and getting a good night's sleep.

Then again, maybe not. Each person's body and brain handle sleep deprivation differently. Some folks are all but useless after one night without shut-eye, while others function normally. It's largely a matter of physiology.

Take Tony Wright. In May 2007, the 43-year-old British gardener kept himself awake for 226 hours. He said that he was aiming for the world's sleeplessness record and wanted to prove that sleep deprivation does not diminish a person's coherence. Wright admitted to some odd sensory effects during his marathon, but he insisted that his mental faculties were not compromised.

Wright's quest didn't amount to much more than a lot of lost sleep. *Guinness World Records* stopped acknowledging feats of insomnia in 1990 after consulting with experts at the British Association for Counseling and Psychotherapy. The experts believe that sleep deprivation threatens psychological and physical well-being. Muscle spasms, reduced reaction times, loss of motivation, hallucinations, and paranoia can all be triggered by sleep deprivation. That Wright apparently didn't suffer any of these ill effects doesn't mean you won't. Sometimes, it seems, you lose if you don't snooze.

What Was the Black Death?

The Black Death, also called the Great or Black Plague, first swept through Europe in the 1340s, killing nearly 60 percent of the population. It returned periodically, spreading panic and death, and then disappeared into history. Was it bubonic plague, as many people believe, or was something else to blame?

✳   ✳   ✳   ✳

"The Great Mortality"

Brought to italy in 1347 by Genoese trading ships, the Black Death spread through Europe like wildfire. Contemporaries described scenes of fear and decay—the sick were abandoned and the dead were piled in the streets because no one would bury them. Anyone who touched the infected, the dead, or their belongings also caught the disease.

It could take as long as a month before symptoms showed, which was plenty of time for the infection to spread. But once the dreaded blackened spots began to appear on a victim's body, death was quick—usually within three days. At least one autopsy recorded that the person's internal organs had almost liquified and that the blood within the body had congealed.

Transmission

One major problem with the bubonic plague theory is that bubonic plague doesn't transmit from person to person—it can only be transmitted through the bites of fleas that have left an infected rat after its death. The signature symptom—the black swellings, or *buboe*—begin showing within two or three days of contraction. Accounts of the Great Plague often mention people who became infected merely by touching an infected person. Some writings describe the infection as spreading via droplets of body fluid (whether sweat, saliva, or blood), which isn't possible for bubonic plague but is a defining characteristic of hemorrhagic fever.

Incubation and Quarantine

It must be mentioned that it is possible for a bubonic plague infection to spread to the lungs and become pneumonic plague, and this kind of infection is transmittable from person to person. However, pneumonic plague is extremely rare—it occurs in only 5 percent of bubonic plague cases. It also isn't easily transmitted, and it certainly isn't virulent enough to have been responsible for the widespread person-to-person infection rates during the Black Death. Both have a very short incubation period, taking only a few days from infection to death. However, historical records show that the Black Plague took as long as a month to manifest. It was no coincidence that cities started to mandate a strict 40-day quarantine. Officials had observed from multiple cases that that much time was needed to determine whether someone was infected. If it had been pneumonic plague, such a long period of quarantine would not have been needed. Those infected would have been dead within a single week.

Another anomaly that casts doubt on the bubonic plague theory is how the plague spread in Iceland. There were no rats in Iceland and there wouldn't be until 300 years later. However, the Black Plague still ravaged the island, killing nearly 60 percent of its population.

Rapid Spread

The Black Death spread throughout Europe faster than any disease people had ever seen. It made the trip from Italy to the

Arctic Circle in less than three years and is recorded as having traveled 150 miles in England within six weeks. Rats can't travel that quickly, but people can. Frightened citizens fled from cities where the epidemic raged, not knowing that they were infected, and they spread the disease as they went. Many parish records indicate that after strangers arrived in town, the plague emerged there within a few weeks.

In contrast, studies of confirmed bubonic plague outbreaks show that the disease spreads very slowly. One outbreak in India in 1907 took six weeks to travel only 100 yards, and another in South Africa from 1899 to 1925 moved only eight miles per year.

What's on Display at the Mütter Museum?

Located at the College of Physicians of Philadelphia, the Mütter Museum is perhaps the most grotesque and shockingly fascinating museum in the United States. Its collection of freaks of nature will entertain those with even the most morbid curiosities.

✳   ✳   ✳   ✳

"Disturbingly Informative"

IT'S ALSO ONE of the most elegant museums open to the public, with red carpet, brass railings, and redwood-lined display cases. It might even appear a bit highbrow if the curators themselves didn't acknowledge what a uniquely abnormal exhibit they were pushing—a refreshing attitude evident in their motto "Disturbingly Informative."

The museum originated in 1859, when Dr. Thomas Mütter donated several thousand dollars and his personal collection of 1,700 medical specimens to the College of Physicians. Merging it with their own meager collection, the institution used Mütter's money to build new quarters to house it all and opened it to both students and the public.

Dem Bones, Dem Bones

Further acquisitions expanded the museum's collection tremendously, as doctors contributed specimens they'd acquired through their own private practices and studies. A large number of them have been skeletal, such as a woman's rib cage that became cartoonishly compressed by years of wearing tight corsets and the 19th-century Peruvian skulls showing primitive trephinations (holes cut or drilled in the head). There are also the combined skeletons of infants born with a shared skull and the bones of a man suffering a condition in which superfluous bone grows in patches, eventually fusing the skeleton together and immobilizing it and its owner. Most popular, though, is the skeleton of a man measuring 7′6″, the tallest of its kind on display in North America, which stands next to that of a 3′6″ female dwarf.

Other items include heads sliced like loaves of bread, both front to back and side to side, and outdated medical instruments, many of which look torturous. Curators also have in their possession more than 2,000 objects removed from people's throats and airways, a vintage iron lung, and photographs of some of medicine's most bizarre human deformities.

Where's the Gift Shop?

The museum even has its own celebrities of sorts. For example, there's Madame Dimanche, an 82-year-old Parisian whose face and the drooping, ten-inch horn growing from her forehead have been preserved in lifelike wax. There's also the unidentified corpse of a woman known simply as the Soap Lady, whose body was unearthed in 1874. The particular composition of the soil in which she was buried transformed the fatty tissues in her body, essentially preserving her as a human-shape bar of soap. And who can forget Eng and Chang, the conjoined brothers who toured the world with P. T. Barnum and inspired the term "Siamese twins"? The Mütter Museum not only has a plaster cast of their torsos, but also their actual connected livers.

Which Organs Can You Live Without?

Don't ask Dr. Frankenstein's creation. Considering this odd gent is stitched together from scraps his master found around town, he would probably grunt that he needs every last one. But the fact is, he doesn't. Frankenstein's monster can lumber on without a number of his organs.

✳ ✳ ✳ ✳

CERTAIN ORGANS, OR at least some semblance of them, are required to live, including the heart, lungs, pancreas, kidneys, liver, intestines, skin, and bladder. But these can be replaced with real or artificial substitutes (for example, an artificial heart or a kidney dialysis machine). Other options might call for regenerating an organ's tissue with donor help (for example, a section of the liver or pancreas). And luckily, most of us are born with two lungs and two kidneys, and can survive with only one of each in a pinch. However, you have only one brain, and it can't be replaced; if something happens to it, you're out of luck.

On the other hand, there are certain organs you can live without entirely, starting with the eyes. Countless blind individuals navigate their way through life quite successfully. Sex organs can also go. Women routinely have hysterectomies, in which the uterus, and sometimes the cervix, is removed. As for men, there is a long tradition of eunuchs (people whose testicles have been removed) who have gone on to sing high notes and live long and productive lives.

The spleen—which is attached to the stomach, left kidney, and colon, and helps fight bacterial infection—is also disposable. In cases of excessive bleeding, a rupture, or cancer, patients have had their spleens removed. However, follow-up care must include vaccines or antibiotics.

Believe it or not, people can even live without a stomach. Patients who have undergone a total gastrectomy (the removal of the stomach) have survived thanks to their small intestine, which absorbs nutrients. Surgeons are capable of fashioning the small intestine into a surrogate stomach.

The most incredible story of survival without internal organs comes from Miami, Florida. In March 2008, sixty-three-year-old Brooke Zepp had five internal organs completely removed—stomach, pancreas, liver, spleen, and small intestine—so doctors could cut a cancerous tumor out of her abdomen. The organs were chilled during the fifteen-hour surgery and then reinserted. It was a procedure right out of Dr. Frankenstein's notebook.

What Causes Hiccups?

Hic! Hic! Hic-cup! Got the hiccups? Breathe into a paper bag. Swallow a spoonful of sugar. Drink lemon juice. Eat peanut butter. Pinch your ear. Pull your tongue. Stand on your head and count to ten. Yes, the hiccups can be confounding.

✳ ✳ ✳ ✳

EONS AGO, WHEN life was still evolving from the ocean to the land, tadpoles had a problem: They had to take in water via their gills in order to breathe, but they didn't want the water to fill their lungs, which they would need when they grew up to be frogs hopping around on dry land. What to do? Develop a reflex. Whenever a tadpole's gills pushed water into its mouth, its tiny voice box, or glottis, would instantly close to prevent the water from flooding its lungs: a sort of evolutionary "hiccup."

Medical researchers have noticed this same hiccup reflex when monitoring human fetuses in utero. They think that this reflex both prevents amniotic fluid from filling the lungs and helps the muscles of the unborn child learn how to suck.

But you're neither floating in your mother's womb nor paddling around a frog pond. So why do you get hiccups? Hiccups occur when you take in too much air too fast. If you've been chowing down food in a hurry or laughing or crying really hard, inrushing air may trigger a spasm in your diaphragm.

The diaphragm is a dome-shape muscle that separates the lungs from the abdominal cavity and whose main job is to control breathing. When the body takes in too much air too quickly, the brain sends frantic messages to the diaphragm saying, "Push the air out"; at the same moment, it tells the glottis, "Don't let any more air in."

The diaphragm contracts, propelling air out of the lungs. The glottis closes, pushing the air back down. This can cause a "synchronous diaphragmatic flutter"—in other words, hic! hic! Spasms, once they start, can be hard to stop. After all, no one ever has just one hiccup.

When it comes to getting rid of hiccups, some doctors believe that the old paper bag trick actually works. Put a paper bag over your nose and mouth and breathe in and out. You'll inhale the same carbon dioxide that you exhale; carbon dioxide has a depressing effect on the nervous system, which will help to break the cycle of spasms.

Do Identical Twins Have Identical Fingerprints?

Can't tell which identical twin is which? Check their fingerprints. Identical twins may look like carbon copies, but research shows they are not exact duplicates of each other. Some differences are skin deep—but most are much deeper.

✳   ✳   ✳   ✳

IDENTICAL TWINS RESULT when a zygote (a fertilized egg) divides in half, forming two embryos. The embryos develop in tandem and, at birth, are identical twin siblings. In the past it was largely assumed that identical twins were exact replicas of each other. After all, they formed from the exact same genetic material. But scientists have found that there are variations in identical twins' individual gene segments. Researchers believe these disparities occur in the womb, when dividing cells cause small genetic differences in each twin. This explains why one identical twin can develop a genetic disorder while the other twin remains healthy. It also is the reason one twin may be right-handed and the other left-handed.

 In addition to subtle differences in their genetic blueprints, there is another difference in identical twins—their fingerprints. Fingerprints are formed while a fetus is growing and are the result of DNA and environmental influences in the womb. By the second trimester of pregnancy, the ridges and loops in our digits are permanently etched into our skin. Factors such as contact with amniotic fluid and the pressure of bone growth affect the unique patterns. Although no two fingerprints are alike, identical twins often have similar patterns.

The unique fingerprints can also assist confused parents who return home from the hospital with their newborn identical twins, remove the ID bracelets, and then can't figure out who is who. The babies can be identified by refingerprinting them and matching the prints with the originals on file at the hospital.

What Really Causes Ulcers?

For years, spicy foods and stress took the rap for causing ulcers. The real culprit, however, has a Latin name.

✳ ✳ ✳ ✳

Y OU CAN HAVE an ulcer and eat your pepperoni pizza, too. Research has proved that certain foods—including hot chilies, coffee, and curry—do not cause ulcers. Nor does stress, no matter how much you have to endure on the job or on the home front.

Your lifestyle is not to blame for the gnawing pain in your gut, though it can exacerbate your symptoms. Ulcers are most frequently caused by a bacterial infection. The little bug is called *Helicobacter pylori*, a corkscrew-shape bacterium that commonly lives in the mucous membranes that line the stomach and small intestine. Antibiotics are usually successful in eliminating such an infection.

H. Pylori

Ulcers can also be caused by excessive use of nonsteroidal anti-inflammatory drugs (NSAIDs), such as ibuprofen or aspirin. That's because these medications inhibit the production of an enzyme that plays an important role in protecting your sensitive stomach lining.

Drinking alcohol and smoking, once also indicated as ulcer-causing habits, don't have primary responsibility for the development of ulcers, but they can be contributing factors. And they can definitely make an existing ulcer worse. Alcohol is an irritant that increases the amount of stomach acid you produce. The nicotine in cigarettes increases stomach acid, too, and prevents healing.

Don't confuse heartburn symptoms—which include burning, pressure, belching, and a bitter taste after eating—with those of an ulcer. Spicy foods *can* aggravate heartburn and gastroesophageal reflux disease (GERD), which are much more common than ulcers.

If you have ulcers, you do not have to worry about spicy foods. But if you have frequent heartburn, it might be wise to stay away from the chicken curry.

Can People Spontaneously Combust?

Proponents contend that the phenomenon—in which a person suddenly bursts into flames—is very real. Skeptics, however, are quick to explain it away.

❋ ❋ ❋ ❋

The Curious Case of Helen Conway

A PHOTO DOCUMENTS THE gruesome death of Helen Conway. Visible in the black-and-white image—taken in 1964 in Delaware County, Pennsylvania—is an oily smear that was her torso and, behind, an ashen specter of the upholstered bedroom chair she occupied. The picture's most haunting feature might be her legs, thin and ghostly pale, clearly intact and seemingly unscathed by whatever it was that consumed the rest of her.

What consumed her, say proponents of a theory that people can catch fire without an external source of ignition, was spontaneous human combustion. It's a classic case, believers assert: Conway was immolated by an intense, precisely localized source of heat that damaged little else in the room. Adding to the mystery, the investigating fire marshal said that it took just twenty-one minutes for her to burn away and that he could not identify an outside accelerant.

If Conway's body ignited from within and burned so quickly she had no time to rise and seek help, hers wouldn't be the first or last death to fit the pattern of spontaneous human combustion.

The phenomenon was documented as early as 1763 by Frenchman Jonas Dupont in his collection of accounts, published as *De Incendis Corporis Humani Spontaneis*. Charles Dickens's 1852 novel *Bleak House* sensationalized the issue with the spontaneous-combustion death of a character named

Krook. That humans have been reduced to ashes with little damage to their surroundings is not the stuff of fiction, however. Many documented cases exist. The question is, did these people combust spontaneously?

How It Happens

Theories advancing the concept abound. Early hypotheses held that victims, such as Dickens's Krook, were likely alcoholics so besotted that their very flesh became flammable. Later conjecture blamed the influence of geomagnetism. A 1996 book by John Heymer, *The Entrancing Flame*, maintained emotional distress could lead to explosions of defective mitochondria. These outbursts cause cellular releases of hydrogen and oxygen and trigger crematory reactions in the body. That same year, Larry E. Arnold—publicity material calls him a parascientist—published *Ablaze! The Mysterious Fires of Spontaneous Human Combustion*. Arnold claimed sufferers were struck by a subatomic particle he had discovered and named the "pyrotron."

Perhaps somewhat more credible reasoning came out of Brooklyn, New York, where the eponymous founder of Robin Beach Engineers Associated (described as a scientific detective agency) linked the theory of spontaneous human combustion with proven instances of individuals whose biology caused them to retain intense concentrations of static electricity.

A Controversy Is Sparked

Skeptics are legion. They suspect that accounts are often embellished or important facts are ignored. That the unfortunate Helen Conway was overweight and a heavy smoker, for instance, likely played a key role in her demise.

Indeed, Conway's case is considered by some to be evidence of the wick effect, which might be today's most forensically respected explanation for spontaneous human combustion. It holds that an external source, such as a dropped cigarette, ignites bedding, clothing, or furnishings. This material acts like an absorbing wick, while the body's fat takes on the fueling role of candle wax. The burning fat liquefies, saturating the bedding, clothing, or furnishings, and keeps the heat localized.

The result is a long, slow immolation that burns away fatty tissues, organs, and associated bone, leaving leaner areas, such as legs, untouched. Experiments on pig carcasses show it can take five or more hours, with the body's water boiling off ahead of the spreading fire.

Under the wick theory, victims are likely to be unconscious already when the fire starts. They're in closed spaces with little moving air, so the flames are allowed to smolder, doing their work without disrupting the surroundings or alerting passersby.

Nevertheless, even the wick effect theory, like all other explanations of spontaneous human combustion, has scientific weaknesses. The fact remains, according to the mainstream science community, that evidence of spontaneous human combustion is entirely circumstantial, and that not a single proven eyewitness account exists to substantiate anyone's claims of "Poof—the body just went up in flames!"

Why Did Doctors Perform Lobotomies?

There's a reason why lobotomies have taken a place next to leeches in the Health Care Hall of Shame.

✳ ✳ ✳ ✳

Beyond Hollywood

FEW PEOPLE HAVE firsthand experience with lobotomized patients. For many of us, any contact with these convalescents comes via Hollywood—that searing image at the end of *One Flew Over the Cuckoo's Nest* of Jack Nicholson, as Randle Patrick McMurphy, lying comatose. Hopefully, we've all experienced enough to know that Hollywood doesn't always tell it like it is. What would be the point of a medical procedure that turns the patient into a vegetable? Then again, even if Hollywood is prone to exaggeration, the fact is that a lobotomy is a pretty terrible thing.

Dissecting the Lobotomy

What exactly is a lobotomy? Simply put, it's a surgical procedure that severs the paths of communication between the prefrontal lobe and the rest of the brain. This prefrontal lobe—the part of the brain closest to the forehead—is a structure that appears to have great influence on personality and initiative. So the obvious question is: Who the heck thought it would be a good idea to disconnect it?

It started in 1890, when German researcher Friederich Golz removed portions of his dog's brain. He noticed afterward that the dog was slightly more mellow—and the lobotomy was born. The first lobotomies performed on humans took place in Switzerland two years later.

The six patients who were chosen all suffered from schizophrenia, and while some did show post-op improvement, two others died. Apparently this was a time in medicine when an experimental procedure that killed 33 percent of its subjects was considered a success. Despite these grisly results, lobotomies became more commonplace, and one early proponent of the surgery even received a Nobel Prize.

The most notorious practitioner of the lobotomy was American physician Walter Freeman, who performed the procedure on more than three thousand patients—including Rosemary Kennedy, the sister of President John F. Kennedy—from the 1930s to the 1960s.

Freeman pioneered a surgical method in which a metal rod (known colloquially as an "ice pick") was inserted into the eye socket, driven up into the brain, and hammered home. This is known as a transorbital lobotomy.

Freeman and other doctors in the United States lobotomized an estimated 40,000 patients before an ethical outcry over the procedure prevailed in the 1950s. Although the mortality rate had improved since the early trials, it turned out that the ratio of success to failure was not much higher: A third of the patients got better, a third stayed the same, and a third became much worse. The practice had generally ceased in the United States by the early 1970s, and it is now illegal in some states.

Who Got Them?

Lobotomies were performed only on patients with extreme psychological impairments, after no other treatment proved to be successful. The frontal lobe of the brain is involved in reasoning, emotion, and personality, and disconnecting it can have a powerful effect on a person's behavior. Unfortunately, the changes that a lobotomy causes are unpredictable and often negative. Today, there are far more precise and far less destructive manners of affecting the brain through antipsychotic drugs and other pharmaceuticals.

So it's not beyond the realm of possibility that Nicholson's character in *Cuckoo's Nest* could become zombie-like. If the movie gets anything wrong, it's that a person as highly functioning as McMurphy probably wouldn't have been recommended for a lobotomy.

The vindictive Nurse Ratched is the one who makes the call, which raises a fundamental moral question: Who is qualified to decide whether someone should have a lobotomy?

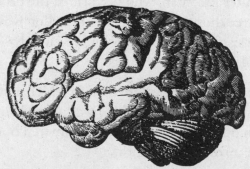

How Did I Get My Birthmark?

In the old days, you would have gone to your mother with some questions. While pregnant with you, did she: Spill wine on herself? Get an X-ray? Suffer a terrible fright? Eat excessive amounts of beets, watermelons, or strawberries? These days, we know those practices don't cause birthmarks. But what does?

✳ ✳ ✳ ✳

THE TRUTH IS, the causes of most birthmarks are unknown. We do, however, know how the two major types of birthmarks—vascular and pigmented—physically form.

Vascular birthmarks—such as macular stains, port-wine stains, and hemangiomas—happen when blood vessels get bunched together, tangled, or just don't grow normally. Pigmented birthmarks—such as café-au-lait spots, Mongolian spots, and congenital moles—form when an overgrowth of cells creates extra pigment on the skin.

Like we said, the experts insist that birthmarks are not caused by what your mother did, craved, ate, or wished for during her pregnancy. Furthermore, they can't be prevented. This earth-shaking news affects a whole lot of people: Up to a third of newborns have some kind of colorful spot, mark, mole, blemish, or blotch. Think of them as nature's tattoos.

Whether brown, red, pink, black, blue, or purple, most birthmarks are harmless. Some will shrink on their own over time. Others can be removed with surgery or the zap of a laser. The rest are permanent fixtures.

If you have a birthmark, don't waste time worrying about it. Instead, you should consider yourself special. Depending on the old wife with whom you consult, it could well be the sign of an angel's kiss or even a battle wound from a previous life. How's that for a mark of honor?

What Is Face-Blindness?

Some people never forget a face; others can't seem to remember one. The latter group might be suffering from a malady called face-blindness.

✳   ✳   ✳   ✳

Faces: They're Everywhere

SOCIOLOGISTS ESTIMATE THAT an adult who lives in a busy urban area encounters more than 1,000 different faces every day. For most of us, picking our friends and loved ones out of a crowd is a snap—homing in on the faces we know is simply an instinct.

But what if you couldn't recognize faces? Not even the ones that belong to the people you know best? If you seem to spend a lot of time apologizing to your nearest and dearest—saying things like, "Sorry, I didn't see you there yesterday. Did you get a new haircut? Were you wearing a different shirt? A pair of Groucho glasses?"—you might be face-blind.

No, you do not need a new pair of contacts. Face-blind people can have 20/20 vision. And chances are, there is nothing wrong with your memory either. You can be a whiz at Trivial Pursuit, an encyclopedia of arcane information, and still not be able to recall the face you see across the breakfast table every morning.

When Faces Blur Together

Many scientists believe facial recognition is a highly specialized neurological task. It takes place in an area of the brain known as the fusiform gyrus, which is located behind your right ear. People who suffer an injury to this part of their brains are likely to have *prosopagnosia*, a fancy medical term for face-blindness. Others seem to be born that way.

Of course, everybody has occasional problems recognizing faces. For the truly face-blind, however, faces may appear only as a blur or a jumble of features that never quite coalesce into the whole that becomes Bill from accounting or Judy from your softball team.

How many people suffer from face-blindness? Statistics are difficult to come by, simply because many people are not even aware that the inability to recognize faces is a bona fide medical syndrome. However, recent research on random samples of college students indicates that prosopagnosia may affect as many as one out of every 50 people, or approximately 2 percent of the population.

The Work-Arounds

What can you do if you think that you are face-blind? Most people with prosopagnosia compensate without even knowing it. They unconsciously learn to distinguish people by the way they walk or talk, or perhaps by distinctive hairdos or articles of dress. Many face-blind people write down the information to remind themselves later. Some people who suffer from this affliction compare it to being tone-deaf or colorblind—an inconvenience but hardly a life-threatening disability.

As with just about anything, a sense of humor helps, too. Ask your friend to warn you before she frosts her hair or he discards that Pearl Jam T-shirt he's proudly worn since you met in 1996. And if you really want to make sure that you see your friends and family in a crowd, tell them to wear something that you'll be sure to remember. Maybe the Groucho glasses. They work like a charm every time.

Why Do Bruises Change Colors While They're Healing?

If you take a lot of beatings, you have no doubt encountered a wondrous rainbow of bruising. Bruises aren't beautiful, but their weird mix of purple, blue, yellow, and even green can be oddly fascinating.

✳   ✳   ✳   ✳

A BRUISE, OR CONTUSION, is an injury in which tiny blood vessels in body tissue are ruptured. As a small amount of blood seeps through the tissue to just below the skin, a deep red or purple bruise forms. The deeper within the tissue the vessels burst, the longer it takes for the blood to reach skin level, and the longer it takes for the bruise to form.

The body is an efficient machine—it's not about to waste the precious iron that's released from the blood when the vessels burst. It dispatches white blood cells to the scene to break down the hemoglobin so the body can salvage the iron.

This chemical breakdown has two notable by-products, each of which has a distinctive color: First, the process produces biliverdin, which is green; then it produces bilirubin, which is yellow. As the deep red hemoglobin, the green biliverdin, and the yellow bilirubin mix, a range of colors results in what we call a bruise. As the body heals, it gradually reabsorbs the by-products, and the skin returns to its normal color.

To minimize bruising, you can apply an ice pack several times a day for a couple of days after you're injured. Or you can invest in some karate classes.

What Are Parasitic Twins?

Ever heard a person say, "There's another person inside of me, just waiting to get out?" For parasitic twins, that's pretty much true.

✳ ✳ ✳ ✳

O Brother, Where Art Thou?

PARASITIC TWINS ARE formed by the same biological defect that causes conjoined twins. Both begin promisingly like any other set of identical twins: A single egg is fertilized and begins dividing into two individual babies. But here the egg hits a snag and doesn't quite finish what it started.

With conjoined twins, both embryos continue to fully develop and both are typically born alive—albeit fused together at the chest or abdomen or, occasionally, the head. But in the case of parasitic twins, only one embryo continues growing normally. The other stops at some point and begins feeding off the blood supply of its twin like a parasite. Though conjoined twins can occasionally share a heart, they usually have their own brains. With parasitic twins, however, the parasitic embryo lacks both heart and brain and so it is never actually alive, although it can go on to grow hair, limbs, and even fully functioning genitalia.

If conjoined twins are rare (1 in 200,000 births), parasitic twins are even rarer (fewer than 1 in 1 million births). In fact, there have been fewer than 200 documented cases of parasitic twins throughout medical history.

Stuck on You

Parasitic twins can be either internal or external—and both are pretty unnerving. In the case of external twins, the parasitic twin appears as an extra set of limbs or a faceless, malformed head growing out of the host twin's abdomen. Usually the limbs just hang there uselessly. But sometimes the nervous systems are attached, so the host twin can actually feel the parasitic twin being touched.

Internal parasites, known as *fetus-in-fetu*, happen when the host embryo envelops the parasitic embryo early in pregnancy. In this case, the parasitic twin continues to grow inside of its host's abdomen. As the parasite grows, the host appears to be pregnant (a weird sight on a man or an infant!). Usually doctors mistake this strange growth for a tumor—and are shocked when they go in to remove it and find they are actually performing a C-section to remove the patient's stillborn twin.

Sideshow Stars

The earliest known case of parasitic twins occurred in Genoa, Italy, in 1617 with the birth of Lazarus and Joannes Baptista Colloredo: Joannes was a fully formed torso growing out of Lazarus's stomach. Lazarus, aka "The Boy with Two-Heads," traveled Europe exhibiting himself, setting a precedent for future generations of parasitic twins to make a living on the carnival circuit.

One of the more fascinating carnival cases is Myrtle Corbin, a Ringling Brothers star in the 1880s known as a *dipygus*, or "double buttocks" parasitic twin. Everything from the waist down was double: two sets of legs, two backsides, and yes, two sets of reproductive organs. Though normally the extra set of limbs is useless, that wasn't so for Myrtle: Her "sister" delivered two of her five children, making Myrtle the only case of dipygus twins to give birth.

Modern Marvels

More recently, an eight-limbed Indian toddler named Lakshmi Tatma made the news in 2007 when her village decided that she was a reincarnation of her namesake, the multilimbed Hindu goddess of wealth. Her parents turned down offers to sell her to the circus, opting instead for surgery to remove her extra arms and legs.

Modern medicine has also made it possible to uncover more cases of fetus-in-fetu. In 2006, the world learned of a 36-year-old Indian farmer who'd been plagued all his life by a very distended belly and a chronic shortness of breath, who went in to have a stomach tumor removed. During surgery, doctors discovered a hand (with fingernails) inside the man, then another, followed by a hair-covered head, teeth, and genitalia.

A similar thing happened to a seven-year-old boy in Kazakhstan in 2003, when the school doctor noticed movement in his swollen stomach. And in 2008, pregnant-looking girls in Greece and China were taken into surgery, where they "delivered" their identical twins.

What Is Heterochromia?

If the eyes are the windows to the soul, the color of a person's irides, (the plural of iris) is the window dressing. The vast majority of human beings have two eyes that are the same color, but some people just can't commit.

✳   ✳   ✳   ✳

What's Up, Doc?

PUT PLAINLY, HETEROCHROMIA is the presence of different-colored eyes in the same person. The condition is a result of the relative excess or lack of pigment within an iris or part of an iris. The causes for having mismatched eyes vary, and some are more worrisome than others.

Heterochromia is largely hereditary; many people are born with eyes that don't quite match and nothing seems to be wrong with them. Females experience it far more than males, and most cases of genetic heterochromia have been found to occur between ages two and nineteen. Some folks who had different-colored eyes as a child report their eyes eventually matching when they reached adulthood.

Diseases such as glaucoma, Waardenberg syndrome, and neurofibromatosis can also cause the condition. Waardenberg syndrome is a rare disorder that affects skin pigmentation and is responsible for varying degrees of hearing loss. Most people with Waardenberg syndrome have two different-colored eyes, making the presence of, say, one green eye and one blue eye, cause for a trip to the doctor.

Another way two eyes might be different colors is due to eye injury. A foreign object in the eye (we're talking about more than an eyelash), ocular inflammation, or other eye injuries can cause trauma to the eye and alter its color.

Now, heterochromia doesn't just mean a person has one brown eye and one green eye; many people with this trait will have one eye that is two colors—part green and part blue, for example. And whatever the color of the iris happens to be, it doesn't have any bearing on the ability of the eye to see. Having heterochromia doesn't mean that a person has poor eyesight.

What (Color) Is It, Lassie?

Animals can also show signs of heterochromia, including cats and horses. However, much more common than heterochromia in humans is heterochromia in dogs. Many breeds, including Siberian huskies, Australian sheep dogs, Great Danes, dalmatians, and Alaskan malamutes exhibit striking cases of the condition—perhaps you've seen a Siberian husky with one ice-blue eye and one dark brown eye. Just as is the case with humans, the dog's vision is completely normal; unlike humans, however, heterochromia in canines is rarely considered a cause for medical concern.

Got Heterochromia? Cool!

If you see multicolored eyes when you look in the mirror, and you have a clean bill of health, then celebrate! Chances are good that you'll never have to think up something interesting to talk about at a cocktail party.

Many people find folks with different-colored eyes fascinating. Some say they find it mysterious (and more than a little sexy) because it's such a rare characteristic. Largely, heterochromia is often seen as really cool, the prevailing notion being that people with mismatched eyes are smarter, more intriguing, possess greater depth, and are generally cooler than everyone else.

If you have heterochromia, you're in good company. Check out this list of famous figures that have boasted dual-tone eye-color:

* actress Mila Kunis
* actor Christopher Walken
* actress Kate Bosworth
* politician Terry McAuliffe
* king and conqueror Alexander the Great
* comedian and actor Dan Aykroyd
* actor Kiefer Sutherland
* singer Carly Simon
* actress Jane Seymour
* pitcher Max Scherzer

Where Did America Send Its Lepers?

Life has never been easy for lepers. Throughout history, they've been stigmatized, feared, and cast out by society. Such reactions—though undeniably heartless—were perhaps understandable because the disease was thought to be rampantly contagious. Anyone suspected of leprosy was forced into quarantine and left to die.

* * * *

LEPROSY HAS AFFECTED humanity since at least 600 B.C. This miserable disease, now known as Hansen's disease, attacks the nervous system primarily in the hands, feet, and face and causes disfiguring skin sores, nerve damage, and progressive debilitation. Medical science had no understanding of leprosy until the late 1800s and no effective treatment for it until the 1940s. Prior to that point, lepers faced a slow, painful, and certain demise.

Misinterpretations of biblical references to leprosy in Leviticus 13:45–46, which labeled lepers as "unclean" and dictated that sufferers must "dwell apart . . . outside the camp," didn't help matters. (The "leprosy" cited in Leviticus referred to several skin conditions, but Hansen's disease was not one of them.) It's really no surprise that society's less-than-compassionate response to the disease was the leper colony.

Cast Out in Misery and Despair

The first leper colonies were isolated spots in the wilderness where the afflicted were driven, forgotten, and left to die.

The practice of exiling lepers continued well into the 20th century. In Crete, for instance, lepers were banished to mountainside caves, where they survived by eating scraps left by wolves. More humane measures were adopted in 1903 when lepers were corralled into the Spinalonga Island leper colony where they were given food and shelter and cared for by priests and nuns. However, once you entered, you never left, and it remained that way until the colony's last resident died in 1957.

Still, joining a leper colony sometimes beat living among the healthy. It wasn't much fun wandering from town to town while wearing signs or ringing bells to warn of one's affliction. And you were always susceptible to violence from townsfolk gripped by irrational fear—as when lepers were blamed for epidemic outbreaks and thrown into bonfires as punishment.

Life in the American Colony

American attitudes toward lepers weren't any more enlightened. One of modern time's most notorious leper colonies was on the Hawaiian island of Molokai, established in 1866.

Hawaiian kings and American officials banished sufferers to this remote peninsula ringed by jagged lava rock and towering sea cliffs. Molokai became one of the world's largest leper colonies—its population peaked in 1890 at 1,174—and more than 8,000 people were forcibly confined there before the practice was finally ended in 1969.

The early days of Molokai were horrible. The banished were abandoned in a lawless place where they received minimal care and had to fight with others for food, water, blankets, and shelter. Public condemnation led to improved conditions on Molokai, but residents later became freaks on display as Hollywood celebrities flocked to the colony on macabre sight-seeing tours.

A Leper Haven in Louisiana

While sufferers of leprosy were being humiliated in Hawaii, they were being helped in Louisiana.

In 1894, the Louisiana Leper House, which billed itself as "a place of treatment and research, not detention," opened in Carville. In 1920, it was transferred to federal authority and renamed the National Leprosarium of the United States. Known today as the National Hansen's Disease (leprosy) Program (NHDP), the facility became a leading research and rehabilitation center, pioneering treatments that form the basis of multidrug therapies currently prescribed by the World Health Organization (WHO) for the treatment of Hansen's disease.

It was here that researchers enlisted a common Louisiana critter—the armadillo—in the fight against the disease. It had always been difficult to study Hansen's disease. Human nerves are seldom biopsied, so direct data on nerve damage from Hansen's was minimal. But in the 1960s, NHDP researchers theorized that armadillos might be susceptible to the germ because of their low body temperature. They began inoculating armadillos with it and discovered that the animals could develop the disease systemically. Now the armadillo is used to develop infected nerves for research worldwide.

A Thing of the Past?

In 1985, leprosy was still considered a public health problem in 122 countries. In fact, the last remaining leper colony, located in Croatia, didn't close until 2002. However, WHO has made great strides toward eradicating the disease; by 2000, the rate of infection had dropped by 90 percent. The multidrug therapies currently prescribed for the treatment of leprosy are available to all patients for free via WHO. In the last two decades, approximately 16 million patients have been cured.

Why Does Helium Make Your Voice Squeaky?

Everyone loves balloons, especially the ones filled with helium. What's great about helium-filled balloons is not just the cheery way they float along, but also the way the gas inside alters your vocal cords. By inhaling small amounts of helium, a person can change his or her voice from its regular timbre to a squeaky, cartoon-like sound. But how does it work?

✳   ✳   ✳   ✳

T HE SIMPLEST EXPLANATION is that since helium is six times less dense than air—the same reason a helium balloon floats—your vocal cords behave slightly differently when they're surrounded by the element. Additionally, the speed of sound is nearly three times faster in helium than in regular air, and this lends quite a bit of squeak to your voice as well.

The opposite reaction can be achieved using a chemical known as sulfur hexafluoride, though it's nowhere near as common as helium and is much more expensive. Whereas helium is readily available in grocery and party stores, sulfur hexafluoride is generally used in electrical power equipment, meaning that one would have to order somewhat large quantities of it from a specially licensed provider. If you do manage to get a hold of some, the results are plenty entertaining: Sulfur hexafluoride drops your voice incredibly low, much like that of a disc jockey or a super villain.

It's important to note, however, that inhaling helium (or other, similar gases) is dangerous. There's a high risk of suffocating, because a person's lungs aren't designed to handle large quantities of helium. What's more, the canisters used to fill balloons contain more than just helium—there are other substances in there that help properly inflate a balloon that can be harmful to your body if they're inhaled. So while a helium-laced voice sounds funny, it actually shouldn't be taken as a joke.

What's Eating You?

There are more than 130 parasites that can inhabit the human body. While it might be a bit creepy to think of all those critters wriggling inside you, just think of it this way: At least you'll never be lonely! Here are some freaky (and intensely gross) facts about human parasites. Warning: Don't eat while reading this list.

✳　✳　✳　✳

✳ Researchers suspect that instances of Crohn's disease, a once-rare inflammatory intestinal disorder, may be on the rise because of the lack of intestinal parasites in much of the first-world population.

✳ Demodex mites are also called "face mites," because they live on human hair follicles, eyelashes, and nose hairs.

✳ As they're only 0.0118 inch long, as many as 25 Demodex mites can live on a single hair follicle.

✳ There are more than 3,000 species of lice in the world.

✳ Head lice are parasites that live on human hair, gripping the shafts with their claws and drinking blood from the scalp.

* Although head lice only live for a month in your hair, each one can lay up to 100 eggs during that time.

* Tapeworms can grow to more than 60 feet long in human intestines.

* The tapeworm's segmented tail contains eggs. This is so that when the segments break off and are expelled from the host's body, the eggs can move on to another animal.

* Instead of a head, the tapeworm has a hooked knob that it uses to cling to the intestinal walls as it sucks nutrients off the surface.

* Tapeworms can only reproduce in humans. When the eggs are eaten by another animal, they reside in the animal's muscle tissue until that flesh is consumed by a human as under-cooked meat.

* Upon attaching to a human host, a chigger (also called red bugs or harvest mites) uses an enzyme to dissolve the flesh at the bite, and then it consumes the liquefied tissue.

* Mosquitoes help transmit botfly eggs to humans, where they hatch and burrow into the skin. To remove them, lay a slice of raw meat on the skin. The maggots will leave the body and enter the meat instead.

* When bathing in the Amazon, men and women always cover their genitals with one hand to prevent the parasitic candiru fish from swimming into their urethra.

* Roundworms grow to 15 inches long and lay as many as 200,000 eggs daily.

* Roundworms are the most common form of intestinal parasite, with an estimated one billion hosts worldwide.

* One out of every three people worldwide is hosting an intestinal parasite.

* Rather than feeding on the material found in human intestines, hookworms attach themselves to feed on the blood and intestinal tissue.

* Occasionally, a whipworm infection is discovered when a worm crawls out of the anus or up through the throat and out through the nose or mouth.

* Whipworms can cause the loss of approximately one teaspoon of blood per day.

* Leeches can suck ten times their body weight in blood.

* After entering the human body in larval form, the two-foot-long adult Guinea worm exits by creating a hole in the flesh of the leg.

* Giardiasis is caused by a one-celled parasite found in dirty water; noticeable symptoms include sulfurous belches and flatulence.

* Mosquitoes that harbor the malarial parasite plasmodia bite more people per night and live longer than uninfected mosquitoes, but they lay fewer eggs.

Why Does the Sun Lighten Hair But Darken Skin?

The key here is a substance called melanin—a bunch of chemicals that combine as a pigment for your skin and hair.

✳   ✳   ✳   ✳

IN ADDITION TO dictating hair and skin colors, melanin protects people from the harmful effects of ultraviolet (UV) light. It does this by converting the energy from UV light to heat, which is relatively harmless. Melanin converts more than 99 percent of this energy, which leaves only a trace amount to mess with your body and cause problems like skin cancer.

When you head out for a day in the sun and don't put on sunscreen, the sun delivers a massive blast of heat and UV light directly to your skin and hair. The skin reacts to this onslaught by ramping up the production of melanin in order to combat that nasty UV radiation. This is where things get a bit tricky. There are two types of melanin: pheomelanin (which is found in greater abundance in people with lighter skin and hair) and eumelanin (which is found in greater abundance in people with darker skin and hair).

If you're unlucky—that is, if your skin has a lot of pheomelanin—the sun can damage the skin cells, causing a splotchy, reddish sunburn and maybe something worse down the road. After the sunburn, the skin peels to rid itself of all these useless, damaged cells. Then you get blisters and oozing pus, and your skin explodes—no, it ain't pretty. People whose skin has an increased production of eumelanin, on the other hand, are saved from these side effects—the sun simply gives their skin a smooth, dark sheen.

And what's the impact on hair? Well, hair is dead—it's just a clump of protein. By the time hair pokes through the scalp, it doesn't contain any melanin-producing cells. So when the sun damages it by destroying whatever melanin is in it, your mane is pretty much toast—no new melanin can be produced. Consequently, your hair loses its pigment until new, darker strands grow.

The moral of the story? Be sensible in the sun—it's a massive flaming ball of gas, and it doesn't care about your health.

Chapter 5

Origins and Traditions

Why Do We Place Flowers on Graves?

Nothing brightens up a grave site quite like a bouquet or two, but how did this tradition get started?

✳   ✳   ✳   ✳

A Path to the Next World

THIS TRADITION CAN be traced to the ancient Greeks, who performed rites over graves that were called *Zoai*. Flowers were placed on the resting places of Greek warriors; it was believed that if the flowers took root and blossomed, the souls of the warriors were declaring that they had found happiness in the next world.

The ancient Romans also used flowers to honor soldiers who died in battle. The Romans held an elaborate eight-day festival during February called *Parentalia* ("Day of the Fathers"), during which roses and violets were placed on the graves of fallen soldiers by friends and family members.

Coming to America

According to acclaimed historian Jay Winik, the tradition began in America at the end of the Civil War, after a train had delivered Abraham Lincoln to his final resting place in Springfield, Illinois. In his Civil War book *April 1865*, Winik writes: "Searching for some way to express their grief, countless

Americans gravitated to bouquets of flowers: lilies, lilacs, roses, and orange blossoms, anything which was in bloom across the land. Thus was born a new American tradition: laying flowers at a funeral."

Following Lincoln's burial, people all over the country began decorating the graves of the more than 600,000 soldiers who had been killed—especially in the South, where women's groups also placed banners on the graves of soldiers. The practice became so widespread that in 1868, General John Alexander Logan—the leader of the Grand Army of the Republic, a Union veterans' group—issued an order designating May 30 as a day for "strewing with flowers or otherwise decorating the graves of comrades who died in defense of their country." The day was originally called Decoration Day, but it later became known as Memorial Day. On May 30, 1868, thousands gathered at Arlington National Cemetery in Virginia to decorate more than twenty thousand graves of Civil War soldiers. In 1873, New York became the first state to declare Decoration Day a legal holiday.

A Boon to the Flower Industry

Today, the tradition is stronger than ever. In addition to being placed on graves, flowers are often displayed in funeral homes and churches for burial services. The most elaborate arrangements are positioned around the casket, perhaps hearkening back to the belief of the ancient Greeks that a flower in bloom signifies happiness in the afterlife.

What's Behind the Tradition of Flying Flags at Half-mast?

As you might have guessed, the custom of flying a flag only midway up its pole has nautical roots. The convention of lowering colors to half-mast to symbolize mourning probably started in the 15th or 16th century, though no one knows precisely when. Nowadays, the gesture is recognized almost everywhere.

❋   ❋   ❋   ❋

THE FIRST HISTORICAL mention of lowering a flag to recognize someone's death comes from the British Board of the Admiralty. In 1612, the British ship *Hearts Ease* searched for the elusive Northwest Passage—a sea route through the Arctic Ocean that connects the Atlantic to the Pacific. During the voyage, Eskimos killed shipmaster James Hall. When the *Hearts Ease* sailed away to rejoin its sister ship, and again when it returned to London, its flag was lowered to trail over the stern as a sign of mourning. That all who saw the *Hearts Ease* understood what the lowered flag meant suggests it was a common practice before then. Starting in 1660, ships of England's Royal Navy lowered their flags to half-mast each January 30, the anniversary of King Charles I's execution in 1649.

In the United States, the flag is to be flown at half-mast (or half-staff) on five designated days: Armed Forces Day (the third Saturday in May), Peace Officers Memorial Day (May 15), until noon on Memorial Day (the last Monday in May), Patriot Day (September 11), and Pearl Harbor Remembrance Day (December 7). In addition, according to the United States Code, the flag goes to half-mast for thirty days following the death of a U.S. president, past or present, and for ten days following the death of the sitting vice president, a current or retired chief justice of the Supreme Court, or the speaker of the House.

But it doesn't stop there. For justices of the Supreme Court other than the chief justice, as well as for governors, former vice presidents, or cabinet secretaries of executive or military departments, the flag is lowered until the person is buried. For a member of Congress, the flag flies at half-mast on the day of and the day after the passing. By presidential order, the flag can also be lowered for the deaths of "principal figures" of the government or foreign dignitaries, such as the pope.

How Did the Days of the Week Get Their Names?

Just like our language itself, the English words for the days of the week embody a hodgepodge of influences. Some of them came from the ancient Babylonians and some came from the Romans. The rest were coined by the Anglo-Saxons, and you have our permission to blame these Germanic settlers of fifth-century Britain for all of the times that you misspelled "Wednesday" when you were a kid.

✳   ✳   ✳   ✳

WHEN THE BABYLONIANS established the seven-day week, they named the first day after the sun and the second day after the moon.

Enter the Romans, who retained the names of those first two days as well as the Babylonians' custom of naming days for heavenly bodies and their representative deities. The Romans named the third day of the week for Mars, which was named after the god of war; the fourth for Mercury, god of merchants and messenger of the gods; the fifth for Jupiter, god of the sky, who brought rain and lightning; the sixth for Venus, goddess of love; and the last day of the week for Saturn, god of seed. The Romans then took along their calendar on a four-hundred-year visit to England. And when the Romans finally skedaddled back to Italy, in barged the Anglo-Saxons.

The Anglo-Saxons were so occupied with pillaging that they found time to rename only four of the seven days—they retained the sun, moon, and Saturn monikers. For the rest, the Anglo-Saxons—like those before them—turned to their gods. Interestingly, the Anglo-Saxons endeavored to identify each of their gods with its Roman predecessor.

So for the third day of the week, the Anglo-Saxons turned to Tiw, their god of war. For the fourth day, they chose Woden, the supreme deity. The fifth day went to Thor, god of thunder. And the sixth was named for their god of love, Frigg. (Yes, we're serious—Frigg.)

Variant spellings exist, but, basically, what the Anglo-Saxons called *sunnan daeg* is now Sunday. *Monan daeg* is now Monday. *Tiwes daeg* evolved into Tuesday. *Wodnes daeg* (which didn't evolve enough) became Wednesday. *Thorsdagr* is Thursday. *Frigedaeg* is Friday. And *Saeterdag* is Saturday. You now have our permission to declare, "Thank Frigg it's Friday!"

When Was Punctuation First Used?

What goes at the end of this sentence, and where would we be without it?

✳ ✳ ✳ ✳

Punctuation is the bane of many an elementary school student, but reading printed text without it would be a terrible chore. Here, give it a try:

forcenturiesmostwrittenlanguagesusedneitherpunctuation-marksnorspacesbetweenwordsreadingwasatediousinterpretive-affairleftlargelytospecialists

The text above isn't very easy to read without punctuation, is it? Here it is again: For centuries, most written languages used neither punctuation marks nor spaces between words. Reading was a tedious, interpretive affair left largely to specialists. And that was just fine, until Latin was adopted as a common language for scholars and clerics throughout Europe in the first century. The practice of reading and writing boomed, as intellectuals from different countries who spoke different languages could now communicate with each other in written text.

Even then, authors and scribes did not use punctuation of any kind, but people who did public readings of texts began marking them up to indicate pauses, bringing rhythm to their presentations and giving themselves a chance to catch their breath. Readers relied on a variety of marks but generally used them to indicate three things—a brief pause, like the modern comma; a middle pause, like the modern semicolon; and a full pause, like the modern period. In the seventh century, Isidore of Seville expanded on this practice by creating a formal punctuation system that not only indicated pauses but also helped clarify meaning. It was only then that authors began to use punctuation as they wrote.

And what about the question mark? Some say ancient Egyptians created it and that they patterned it after the shape a cat's tail made when the feline was perplexed. It's a cute story, but there's absolutely no truth to it. The question mark debuted in Europe in the ninth century; back then, it took the shape of a dot followed by a squiggly line. The modern version—a sickle shape resting atop a dot—was adopted after the invention of the printing press for the convenience of typesetters.

Origins of Standard Symbols

¶—The pilcrow is a typographical character used to indicate a new paragraph. The name may have come from *pylcraft*, a derivation of the word *paragraph*, and the symbol that resembles a backward *P* may have originated as a *C* for "chapter," or to represent a new train of thought.

!—Usually used to indicate strong feeling, the exclamation mark is a pictographic device believed to have originated in the Roman empire. Its resemblance to a pen over a dot was thought to represent a mark a writer might make when surprised or over-joyed at completing a long writing project.

* —The asterisk gets its name from *astrum*, the Latin word for *star*, which the asterisk is also called. It is not an "asterix"—that's the name of the star of a French cartoon. The asterisk was created in feudal times when the printers of family trees needed a symbol to indicate date of birth, which may explain why it's shaped like the branches of a tree.

; —The semicolon was invented by an Italian printer for two main purposes: to bind two sentences that run on in meaning and to act as a "super comma" in a sentence that already contains lots of commas. Excessive use of the semicolon is considered showy by many writers, especially when employed to create long, multisegmented sentences. Author Kurt Vonnegut once said, "Do not use semicolons. All they do is show you've been to college."

? —What is the origin of the question mark? The symbol is generally thought to originate from the Latin *quaestio*, meaning "question," which was abbreviated to *Qo*, with the uppercase *Q* written above the lowercase *o*. The question mark replaces the period at the end of an interrogative sentence. There's a superstition in Hollywood that movies or television shows with a question mark in the title do poorly at the box office. That may explain the mark's absence in the title of the game show *Who Wants to Be a Millionaire*, a program that would not exist without questions!

& —The ampersand, used to replace the word *and*, has been found on ancient Roman sources dating to the first century A.D. It was formed by joining the letters in *et*, which is Latin for *and*. Through the 19th century, the ampersand was actually considered the 27th letter of the English alphabet.

% —The percent sign is the symbol used to indicate a percentage, meaning that the number preceding it is divided by 100. The symbol appeared around 1425 as a representation of the abbreviation of *P cento*, meaning "for a hundred" in Italian.

=—The equal sign is a mathematical symbol used to indicate equality and was invented in 1557 by Welsh mathematician Robert Recorde. In his book *The Whetstone of Witte*, Recorde explains that he invented it "to avoid the tedious repetition of the words 'is equal to.'" Recorde's invention is commemorated with a plaque in St. Mary's Church in his hometown of Tenby, Wales.

Where Did the Swastika Come From?

For thousands of years, it stood as a sacred symbol of fortune and vitality—until Adolph Hitler adopted its eye-catching geometry to lead his rise to power, turning the swastika into the 20th century's ultimate emblem of evil.

✳ ✳ ✳ ✳

ORIGINATING IN INDIA and Central Asia, its name comes from the Sanskrit word *svastika*, meaning well-being and good fortune. The earliest known examples of the swastika date to the Neolithic period of 3000 B.C. A sacred symbol in Hinduism, Buddhism, and Jainism, the symbol was most widely used in India, China, Japan, and elsewhere in Asia, though archaeological examples have also been found in Greco-Roman art and architecture, in Anglo-Saxon graves of the pagan period, in Hopi and Navajo art from the American Southwest, and in Gothic architecture in Europe. Synagogues in North Africa and Palestine feature swastika mosaics, as does the medieval cathedral of Amiens, France.

For thousands of years, the swastika was a symbol of life, the sun, power, and good luck, though in some cultures a counterclockwise mirror image of the swastika, called a *sauvastika*, meant bad luck or misfortune. Pointing to evidence in an ancient Chinese manuscript, astronomer Carl Sagan theorized that a celestial phenomenon occurring thousands of years ago may have given rise to the swastika's use around the world, when gas jets shooting from the body of a passing comet were bent into hooked forms by the comet's rotational forces, creating a similar shape. Other scholars believe that it was so widely known because its geometry was inherent in the art of basket weaving.

The modern revival of the swastika in the Western world began with the excavation of Homer's Troy on the shores of the Dardanelles in the 1870s. German archaeologist Heinrich Schliemann discovered pottery and other artifacts at the site decorated with swastikas. Schliemann and other scholars associated his finds with examples of the symbol uncovered on ancient artifacts in Germany. They theorized that the swastika was a religious symbol linking their German-Aryan ancestors to the ancient Teutons, Homeric Greeks, and Vedic India. German nationalists, including anti-Semitic and militarist groups, began using the symbol at the end of the 19th century. But with its connotations of good fortune, the swastika also caught on in Western popular culture. Swastikas were used to decorate cigarette cases, postcards, coins, and buildings throughout Europe. In the United States, they were used by Coca-Cola, the Boy Scouts, and a railroad company. The U.S. Army's 45th Division used the symbol during WWI; and Charles Lindberg painted one inside the nose cone of the *Spirit of St. Louis* for good luck.

In 1920, Adolf Hitler adopted the symbol for the Nazi Party's insignia and flag—a black swastika inside a white circle on a field of red—claiming he saw in it "the struggle for the victory of the Aryan man." With Hitler's appointment as chancellor, the Nazi flag was raised alongside Germany's national flag on March 14, 1933, and became the nation's sole flag a year later. The symbol was used ubiquitously in Nazi Germany—on badges and arm bands, on propaganda material, and on military hardware. By the end of the war, much of the world identified the symbol only with Hitler and the Nazis. Its public use was constitutionally banned in postwar Germany. Though attempts have been made to rehabilitate its use elsewhere, the swastika is still taboo throughout the Western world.

In Asia, however, the swastika remains a part of several religious cultures and is considered extremely holy and auspicious. In India, it is a symbol of wealth and good fortune, appearing not only in temples and at weddings but on buses, on rickshaws, even on a brand of soap. Hindus in Malaysia, Indonesia, and elsewhere in Southeast Asia also continue its use. In 2005, the government of Tajikistan called for adoption of the swastika as a national symbol.

How Did Friday the 13th Become So Unlucky?

It's perhaps the most pervasive superstition in North America, Western Europe, and Australia. In fact, if you're like lots of other fearful folks, you won't take a flight, get married, sign a contract, or even leave your house on this most doomed of days.

✳ ✳ ✳ ✳

It Started With the Ancients

WHAT EXACTLY MAKES Friday the 13th more luckless than, say, Tuesday the fifth? The answer is deeply rooted in biblical, mythological, and historical events.

Friday and the number 13 have been independently sinister since ancient times—maybe since the dawn of humans. Many biblical scholars say that Eve tempted Adam with the forbidden apple on a Friday. Traditional teachings also tell us that the Great Flood began on a Friday, the Temple of Solomon was destroyed on a Friday, and Abel was slain by Cain on a Friday.

For Christians, Friday and the number 13 are of the utmost significance. Christ was crucified on Friday, and there were

13 people present at the Last Supper. Judas, the disciple who betrayed Jesus, was the 13th member of the party to arrive.

Groups of 13 may be one of the earliest and most concrete taboos associated with the number. It's believed that both the ancient Vikings and Hindus thought it unpropitious to have 13 people gather together in one place. Up until recently, French socialites known as *quatorziens* (fourteeners) made themselves available as fourteenth guests to spare dinner parties from ominous ends.

Some trace the infamy of the number 13 back to ancient Norse culture. According to mythology, twelve gods had arrived to a banquet, when in walked an uninvited 13th guest—Loki, the god of mischief. Loki tricked the blind god Hother into throwing a spear of mistletoe at Balder, the beloved god of light. Balder fell dead, and the whole Earth turned dark.

In modern times, 13 continues to be a number to avoid. About 80 percent of high-rise buildings don't have a 13th floor, many airports skip gate number 13, and you won't find a room thirteen in some hospitals and hotels.

An Infamous Combination

How did Friday and 13 become forever linked as the most disquieting day on the calendar? It just may be that Friday was unlucky and 13 was unlucky, so a combination of the two was simply a double jinx. However, one theory holds that all this superstition came not as a result of convergent taboos, but of a single historical event.

On Friday, October 13, 1307, King Philip IV of France ordered the arrest of the revered Knights Templars. Tortured and forced to confess to false charges of heresy, blasphemy, and wrongdoing, hundreds of knights were burned at the stake. It's said that sympathizers of the Templars then condemned Friday the 13th as the most evil of days.

No one has been able to document if this eerie tale is indeed the origin of this superstition. And really, some scholars are convinced that it's nothing more than a phenomenon created by 20th-century media. So sufferers of paraskevidekatriaphobia (a pathological fear of Friday the 13th), take some comfort—or at least throw some salt over your shoulder.

What Are Redhead Days?

Red hair occurs naturally in approximately 1–2 percent of the world's population. The highest frequency of redheads is found in northern and western Europe. Scotland boasts the highest percentage of natural redheads with 13 percent, followed closely by Ireland with 10 percent.

* * * *

REDHEAD DAYS, A three-day festival celebrating red hair, has been held in the Netherlands since 2005. It all started when Dutch painter Bart Rouwenhorst placed an ad in a local newspaper seeking 15 redheaded female models. To his astonishment, 150 "ginger" women applied. In an attempt to not turn any of the ladies away, Mr. Rouwenhorst held a lottery event to select the women, and thus the first incarnation of the festival was born.

It's important to state, that one need not be a redhead to attend Redhead Days. Friends, family, and redhead admirers are welcome at the free event. Originally referred to by the Dutch name, *Roodharigendag*, the name was officially changed to Redhead Days in 2012 to account for the fest's broader international appeal. Attendance at the festival has reached upwards of 6,000 visitors coming from as many as 80 countries.

Activities at Redhead Days include biking tours, live music, photoshoots, redhead centered question and answer sessions, lectures, wine tastings, portrait drawing, boat trips, baking workshops, and much more. There's also an evening redhead pub crawl and food trucks on site serving diverse cuisines.

The most anticipated event of Redhead Days, the annual group photo, takes place on the final day of the festival. This group photo is the one activity explicitly limited to natural redheads only. Each year the photo shoot gathers more than 1,000 natural redheads. In 2013, a Guinness World Record was set for most redheads in one place at 1,672 people.

After a decade plus run in the town of Breda, 2019 marked the debut of a new location for Redhead Days in the city of Tilburg, Netherlands.

Why Do People Wear Costumes on Halloween?

Why do we deck ourselves out in costumes on Halloween? When you think about it, it's a pretty silly way to celebrate the eve of All Saints' Day. As it turns out, dressing in masks and costumes started along with trick-or-treating about 350 years ago.

✳ ✳ ✳ ✳

THE EARLIEST MENTION of wearing disguises on Halloween comes in the 17th century from Ireland and Scotland. In small villages and rural areas, folks dressed up in costumes and got rowdy. Why? Well, since the first few centuries of the Christian era, Halloween in those Celtic lands had a reputation of being the night when ghosts, witches, demons, and faeries were free to wander. This made it the perfect time to get away with a bit of mischief-making. People also wore masks to avoid being recognized by the wandering ghosts. Men and boys hid behind masks or rubbed charcoal all over their faces, then ran around making noise, throwing trash, and harassing their neighbors (playing tricks, in other words). Sometimes they chased pretty girls or went begging for gifts (the treats). Girls joined in the fun on occasion, always in disguise. But mostly it was a night of male bonding, showing off, and trying to outdo each other.

By the end of the 19th century, more than two million men and women had emigrated from Ireland to live in North American cities. Quite naturally, they tended to live near other Irish families in gentrified neighborhoods, and they celebrated the holidays the way they had in the Old Country. On Halloween, that meant dressing up in disguises and running around, dumping trash in the streets, or begging for gifts. Among more genteel families, it meant costume parties—a practice that quickly became popular with all city folks.

In the United States, it didn't take long for storekeepers to realize they could make profits off this curious custom. By the late 19th century, shops were selling masks for children and adults throughout October. By the 20th century, Halloween was celebrated coast to coast, and families, schools, and churches all hosted costume parties. The first citywide Halloween celebration happened in Anoka, Minnesota, in 1921.

The long-term result? Halloween is big business. More than 175 million Americans celebrated Halloween in 2018. The average consumer spent $86.79 on decorations, candy, costumes, and more—totalling $9 billion.

How Did Piggy Banks Come About?

The piggy bank sprang from a play on words.

✳   ✳   ✳   ✳

THE PIGGY BANK is one of America's favorite ways to save. Kids love to hoard their pennies in them, and adults often use them to hold spare change. But the origin of the venerable piggy bank has nothing to do with pigs. It can be traced to an English play on words that dates back hundreds of years.

According to historians, the concept of the piggy bank most likely started in England around the mid-1500s. Back then, metal was precious and quite expensive, so the average family used dishes, jars, and cookware made from an inexpensive orange clay called *pygg*, which was probably initially pronounced "pug."

It was common for families to keep extra coins in a pygg jar, which eventually came to be known as the "pygg bank." In the 1700s, the name evolved to "piggy bank." Amused British potters started making clay banks in the shape of pigs, and that's how the piggy bank as we now know it was born.

People quickly became enamored with piggy banks, and their popularity soared throughout England. The earliest piggy banks were ceramic and had to be broken to retrieve the money inside. Later versions came with a hole or other retrieval method so that the banks could be used over and over.

Piggy banks eventually spread outside of England to equal popularity. Adults found them a good way to instill a sense of financial responsibility among children, and versions of the piggy bank can now be found throughout the world.

What's the History of the Birthday Cake?

This ubiquitous candlelit confection has been a tradition in Western countries for centuries. Read on for the full scoop!

❋ ❋ ❋ ❋

Whose Cake Is This?

THE ORIGIN OF the birthday cake is up for debate. Some scholars place its creation with the ancient Greeks, who made celebratory round honey cakes to offer up to the goddess Artemis; or with the Romans, who would make small savory cakes with honey, cheese, and olive oil. Other folks claim the birthday cake was born in the Middle Ages. At that time in Germany, sweet dough was formed into a petite cake to represent the baby Jesus wrapped in his swaddling clothes. The cake was eaten on Jesus's birthday (or rather, Christmas Day). Later, it became tradition for the cake to be given to children on their own birthdays.

Cake Customs and Custom Cakes

However the trend began, the birthday cake has been claimed by many birthday-celebrating cultures and cake customs have evolved over time. In England starting in the late 1600s, small charms were baked into birthday cakes; each charm foretold the recipient's future: If you bit into a coin, you'd be rich. Got the thimble? Be prepared to die lonely.

For many years, however, only the rich enjoyed birthday cakes. Before the industrial revolution (when cake mixes and home baking became more commonplace), frosted tiers of sugary cake were luxuries afforded only by the wealthy. These days, a birthday cake can be cheaply made at home or purchased at a bakery or grocery store.

Not everyone loves to celebrate their birthday, and plenty of cultures don't celebrate it at all. Jehovah's Witnesses believe the birthday celebration to be a pagan tradition and refuse to celebrate birthdays—no cake for them. Other people do celebrate the anniversary of their birth, but not with cake. In Korea, seaweed soup is the special birthday dish. In the Netherlands, birthdays are all about fruit tarts served with cream.

Who Started Mother's Day?

Celebrations of mothers date back to antiquity, but Mother's Day proper was the brainchild of Anna Jarvis.

✳ ✳ ✳ ✳

RAISED IN GRAFTON, West Virginia, Jarvis was the daughter of a woman who organized events called Mother's Friendship Days, which reunited West Virginia families that had been separated during the Civil War. After her mother died in 1905, Jarvis paid homage to her with an aggressive letter-writing campaign that began in 1907 and urged elected officials and newspaper editors to promote an official holiday to honor all mothers.

Within six years, most states observed Mother's Day. In 1914, President Woodrow Wilson signed a congressional resolution that designated the second Sunday in May as Mother's Day across the nation. Jarvis had succeeded, but little did she know that, just like Dr. Frankenstein, she had created a monster that would lead to her ruin.

Jarvis suggested that people wear white carnations, her mother's favorite flower, on Mother's Day. But when florists started charging more for carnations, she denounced the practice and chose instead to wear a button to commemorate the day. This was just one of many futile battles that Jarvis waged for the rest of her life against the quick and thorough commercialization of the holiday. Anybody who profited from Mother's Day felt her wrath. She considered Mother's Day cards especially nefarious, opining that giving one was a lazy way to show appreciation for the person who gave you the gift of life.

Jarvis lived off the considerable inheritances that she received after the deaths of her mother and her brother, Claude, who had founded a taxi service in Philadelphia. But while wholeheartedly devoting herself to fighting the exploitation of Mother's Day, Jarvis neglected to tend to her own finances. By 1943, she was living in poverty and her health was in serious decline. Friends raised enough money to allow her to live in a sanatorium in West Chester, Pennsylvania, where she died in 1948, childless.

If Jarvis were alive today, she wouldn't be at all pleased with what has happened to Mother's Day. According to the National Retail Federation, Americans spent $23.1 billion on Mother's Day in 2018 and planned to spend a record $25 billion celebrating mothers in 2019.

Which Came First, the Turkey or Thanksgiving?

Did the Pilgrims start a tradition by eating turkey at the first Thanksgiving—or was that Tiny Tim's doing?

✳ ✳ ✳ ✳

Which came first, the turkey or Thanksgiving? Governor William Bradley's journal from around that time indicates that "besides waterfowl there was great store of wild turkeys, of which they took many." Another record notes that "our governor sent four men on fowling…they four in one day killed as much fowl, as with a little help beside, served the company almost a week."

Of course, "fowl" doesn't necessarily mean turkey, so the best we can say is that the Pilgrims may have eaten it. The only food we know for certain they ate was venison, and that was provided by their guests, the Native Americans. They probably also ate codfish, goose, and lobster, but not a lot of vegetables—you can catch fish and fowl, but it takes time to grow crops. And mashed potatoes? Nope—potatoes hadn't yet been introduced to New England.

So how did the gobbler become the centerpiece of Thanksgiving celebrations? It may have had something to do with the prevalent diet at the time the national holiday was founded in 1863. Beef and chicken were too expensive to serve to a crowd, and even if you had your own farm, you needed the animals' continuous supply of milk and eggs. Venison was an option, but you couldn't always count on bagging a deer in time for the holiday. Turkey was readily available, not too expensive— and very popular, perhaps in part due to the scene at the end of Charles Dickens's *A Christmas Carol* in which Scrooge buys "the prize turkey" for Bob Cratchit's family. The novel, published in 1843, was immensely popular in America and may have secured the humble fowl's center-stage spot on the Thanksgiving table.

How Did the 911 System Originate?

The 911 emergency system was modeled after the United Kingdom's 999.

✳ ✳ ✳ ✳

FOR AMERICANS BORN after 1968, reaching emergency aid—whether police, fire department, or ambulance—has always been as simple as dialing 911. Before then, people in need had to dial the services directly or reach an operator who could place the call for them. The 911 system is a remarkable achievement in public safety and has saved countless lives—but it's not an American invention.

Some historians believe that the first telephone call ever made—by Alexander Graham Bell to his assistant, Thomas A. Watson, on March 10, 1876—was also the first emergency call. Bell and Watson were in separate rooms testing a new transmitter when Bell supposedly spilled battery acid on his clothing. Watson heard Bell say "Mr. Watson, come here. I want you!" over the transmitter and rushed to his aid.

999

Great Britain introduced the first universal emergency number in 1937. Citizens calling 999 reached a central operator who would dispatch the police, fire department, or ambulance, as needed. According to records, the wife of John Stanley Beard of 33 Elsworthy Road, London, made the first 999 call to report a burglar outside her home. The police arrived promptly, and the 24-year-old intruder was arrested. The British system proved so successful that other countries ultimately followed. Today, most industrialized nations now employ some sort of universal emergency number.

911

In the U.S., the idea of a universal emergency number

was introduced in 1967 at the urging of the Presidential Commission on Law Enforcement. Congress quickly established a series of committees to determine how to make the system a reality. The committees had to work out several issues, foremost being the selection of a three-digit number that was not already a United States area code or an international prefix. Another consideration was ease of dialing on a rotary telephone. After much discussion, they finally decided on 911.

On January 12, 1968, AT&T, the nation's primary telephone carrier at the time, announced the designation of 911 as the universal emergency number during a press conference in the office of Indiana Representative Ed Roush, who had championed the cause before Congress. The AT&T plan initially involved only the Bell companies, not the small number of independent telephone companies across the country.

The first 911 call was placed on February 16, 1968, in Haleyville, Alabama. But it wasn't made through AT&T. Instead, the Alabama Telephone Company (a subsidiary of Continental Telephone) holds that honor, primarily because its president, Bob Gallagher, had read about AT&T's plan in *The Wall Street Journal* and decided to beat the telecommunications giant to the punch. Haleyville was determined to be the best place to roll out the program, and the company immediately set to work on the local circuitry system, with a scheduled activation date of February 16. Interestingly, that first call wasn't an emergency. It was a test call placed by Alabama Speaker of the House Rankin Fite from Haleyville City Hall to U.S. Representative Tom Bevill at the town's police station.

The first 911 systems sent callers to a predetermined emergency response agency, where an operator would dispatch the needed services based on what the caller reported. This occasionally proved problematic, especially when the caller was panicked, disoriented, or lacked the necessary information, such as an address.

A more sophisticated system, called "Enhanced 911," eliminated much of the confusion by providing an operator with a caller's location information and telephone number through special computers and display screens. Enhanced 911 also allows for selective routing and selective transfer of 911 calls to multiple emergency response jurisdictions.

Does Easter Have Pagan Roots?

Easter, which celebrates Jesus Christ's resurrection from the dead, is thought by some to be nothing more than a pagan holiday. Despite all the bunnies and bonnets, though, its religious roots hold firm.

✳ ✳ ✳ ✳

SOME PEOPLE THINK Easter has its origins in paganism because it falls roughly at the time of the spring equinox, when the earth comes back to life from the dead of winter.

It *is* a significant Christian holiday. True, but Easter is actually associated with Passover, the Jewish holiday that celebrates the Hebrews' release from bondage in Egypt. Jesus and his disciples were in Jerusalem to celebrate Passover when he was arrested, tried, and crucified. Following his resurrection, the disciples understood Jesus to be the sacrificial lamb that took away the sins of the world, a fulfillment of the Passover lambs that were sacrificed each year. Hence the original name for Easter was *Pasch*, from the Hebrew word for Passover, *Pesach*.

So where does the word *Easter* come from? It derives from Eostre, the Old English name for the month of April. According to the ancient historian Bede (writing in the eighth century), the month of Eostre was named after a goddess of the same name. Much later, Jacob Grimm (of the Brothers Grimm) speculated that Eostre was named for the ancient German goddess Ostara. The reference could also come from the word *east*—the direction of the sunrise—or from the old Germanic word for "dawn," which makes sense, given that dawn comes earlier in the spring.

As for the date of Easter, which varies from year to year, it's calculated based on the lunar calendar and some complex ecclesiastical rules. These calculations include the spring equinox, when the sun is directly above Earth's equator. But whether the equinox and Easter fall close together is purely a matter of chance.

How Did the Easter Bunny Come About?

Everyone knows that rabbits do not lay eggs. So how did a colored-egg-toting bunny become associated with Easter?

✳ ✳ ✳ ✳

IT IS SOMETIMES claimed that rabbits and eggs are fertility symbols associated with springtime, and their connection to Easter is a simple derivation of ancient pagan practices. Not so fast. Rabbits are indeed a symbol of fertility, because they reproduce like—well, rabbits. And it makes sense that ancient pagans associated the advent of spring—the time of rebirth, renewal, and new life—with rabbits and eggs.

Why decorate hard-boiled eggs for Easter? This custom may have originated among Christians in the Middle Ages, when eating eggs was prohibited during Lent, the 40 days leading up to Easter. The faithful broke the Lenten fast with an Easter celebration that included feasting on brightly colored hard-boiled eggs—which were probably plentiful by that time.

Where did the idea of an egg-carrying rabbit come from? One theory points to hares' tendency to overbuild when it comes to home construction. Hares raise their young in hollows in the ground and sometimes separate them into multiple nests for safety's sake. People hunting for eggs may have found them near, or even in, an unused hare's nest—appropriated by some resourceful bird—and came to the mistaken conclusion that the hares had laid eggs.

This confusion may have become the foundation for an old German myth about "Oschter haws" (Easter hare), which laid eggs in gardens for good children to find. German immigrants brought the legend of the Easter hare to America (along with the story about a shadow-sighting groundhog). In the United States, rabbits are more plentiful than hares, and the egg-bearing bunny soon became part of the folklore of Easter.

When Were Forks First Used as Utensils?

Using a fork was not always a demonstration of good manners. In fact, according to an anonymous writer, "It is coarse and ungraceful to throw food into the mouth as you would toss hay into a barn with a pitchfork."

✳ ✳ ✳ ✳

IN THE CASE of the fork, the tool preceded the utensil. The English word *fork* comes from the Latin *furca*, which means "pitchfork." Thousands of years ago, large bronze forks were part of Egyptian sacrificial rituals. By the seventh century A.D., members of Middle Eastern royal courts were using small forks to eat.

Venice and the Fork

Table forks appeared in noble Italian homes in the 11th century, and over the next 500 years, they slowly made their way onto tables throughout Europe. The first forks arrived in Venice at the outset of the 11th century, when a Doge—the head of the government—wed a Byzantine princess. Her forks, however, were despised as an affectation and an example of oriental decadence. According to John Julius Norwich, "Such was the luxury of her habits that she scorned even to wash herself in common water, obliging her servants instead to collect the dew that fell from the heavens for her to bathe in. Nor did she deign to touch her food with her fingers, but would command her eunuchs to cut it up into small pieces, which she would impale on a certain golden instrument with two prongs and thus carry to her mouth." People in the West associated forks with the devil, and it was considered an affront to God to eat with something other than the hands and fingers he had designed for the job. When the princess died young, it was widely regarded as divine retribution.

Exotic Object to Mainstream Convenience

Stories describing forks and their use appear in documents from the 13th century onward. Cookbooks and household inventories, however, suggest that forks remained rare, valuable, and esoteric items. When the Italian aristocrat Catherine de Medici married the future Henry II of France in 1533, her dowry included several dozen table forks wrought by famous goldsmith Benvenuto Cellini. In 1588, forks were removed from *La Girona*, a boat in the Spanish Armada that wrecked off the coast of Ireland. During the 17th century, forks became more common in England, although numerous writers from the period scoffed at the utensil and the class of people who routinely used it.

During the reign of Charles I of England, the fork was relatively common among the upper classes; King Charles himself declared in 1633, "It is decent to use a fork." Soon, sets of forks and knives were sold with a carrying case, as only very wealthy households could provide eating utensils for everyone at the table. Travelers also had to provide their own knives and forks during stopovers at inns. Governor John Winthrop of the Massachusetts Bay Colony owned the first fork—and for some time, the only fork—in colonial America. George Washington was inordinately proud of his set of 12 forks.

Forks, Forms, and Fashion

The first dinner forks had two tines, which were often quite long and sharp. Eventually three- and four-pronged forks were made, with wider, blunted tines arranged in a flattened, curved shape. During the 19th century, forks became commonplace in the United States and were sometimes referred to as "split spoons."

Silver from the Comstock Lode flooded the market after 1859, and the electroplating process made silverware affordable to nearly all people. Middle-class families subsequently claimed social refinement by acquiring complicated table settings featuring a unique utensil for every food. These place settings expanded from a few pieces to hundreds. Finally, in 1926, then Secretary of Commerce Herbert Hoover decreed that there could be no more than 55 pieces in a silver service, reducing, among other things, the number of forks dedicated to a single purpose. Indeed, it was time to put a fork in it.

Who Started Labor Day?

Next time you're enjoying time off for Labor Day, relishing cold beer and grilled bratwurst in the backyard, you can thank Peter J. McGuire of New York. Or maybe Matthew Maguire (no relation).

✳   ✳   ✳   ✳

IN THE 1880s, Peter J. McGuire, one of the cofounders of the American Federation of Labor (AFL), is said to have developed the idea of a holiday for American workers in homage to those "from whom rude nature have delved and carved all the grandeur we behold." On the other hand, Matthew Maguire, a machinist and secretary of the Central Labor Union (CLU), is also credited with that honor.

In any case, the CLU and the Knights of Labor decided to go ahead with the holiday in New York City, and the first Labor Day was observed on September 5, 1882, with a grand parade and festival in Union Square. By 1885, as the labor movement continued to gain ground and organized labor lobbied in state legislatures vigorously, Labor Day was celebrated in cities around the country. The first Monday of September was agreed upon as the official date, roughly halfway between the Fourth of July and Thanksgiving.

Prompted by widespread labor unrest, and perhaps the fact that 1894 was an election year, President Grover Cleveland was eager to appease the labor movement. On June 28, 1894, Congress unanimously named the first Monday in September a legal holiday. That didn't stop labor unrest—the 1894 Pullman strike was still going strong—but it was a step forward.

Today, Labor Day is still marked with speeches and celebrations, though with fewer large parades. But many still regard it, as AFL leader Samuel Gompers did in 1898, as "the day for which the toilers in past centuries looked forward, when their rights and their wrongs would be discussed . . . that the workers of our day may not only lay down their tools of labor for a holiday, but upon which they may touch shoulders in marching phalanx and feel the stronger for it."

Where Did Toilet Paper Originate?

Toilet paper is one invention that has been flushed with success since its 14th-century origins.

✳   ✳   ✳   ✳

LIKE PASTA AND gunpowder, toilet paper was invented in China. Paper—made from pulped bamboo and cotton rags—was also invented by the Chinese, although Egyptians had already been using papyrus plants for thousands of years to make writing surfaces. Still, it wasn't until 1391, almost 1,600 years after the invention of paper, that the Ming Dynasty Emperor first used toilet paper. The government made 2×3 foot sheets, which either says something about the manufacturing limitations of the day or the Emperor's diet!

Toilet paper didn't reach the United States until 1857 when the

Gayetty Firm introduced "Medicated Paper." Prior to the industrial revolution later that century, many amenities were available only to the wealthy. But in 1890, Scott Paper Company brought toilet paper to the masses. The company employed new manufacturing techniques to introduce perforated sheets. In 1942, Britain's St. Andrew's Paper Mill invented two-ply sheets (the civilized world owes a great debt to the Royal Air Force for protecting this London factory during The Blitz!). Two-ply sheets are not just two single-ply sheets stuck together; each ply in a two-ply sheet is thinner than a single-ply sheet. The first "moist" toilet paper—Cottonelle Fresh Rollwipes—appeared in 2001.

What was the rest of the world doing? Some pretty creative stuff! Romans soaked sponges in saltwater and attached them to the end of sticks. There is little information about what happened when the stick poked through the sponge, but the Romans were a hearty, expansionist people and probably conquered another country for spite. Medieval farmers used balls of hay. American pioneers used corncobs. Leaves have always been a popular alternative to toilet paper but are rare in certain climates, so Inuit people favor Tundra moss. Of all people, the Vikings seemed the most sensible, using wool. It's not easy being a sheep.

Chapter 6

Sports and Leisure

What Were the Ancient Olympic Games Like?

Imagine attending a sporting event where blood and broken limbs are the norm. It's hot out but water is scarce; the food is overpriced and lousy. Motels are few, pricey, and crummy. Almost everyone has to camp out. Your bleacher seat feels like freshly heated limestone. Forty thousand drunken, screaming savages surround you.

✳ ✳ ✳ ✳

N<small>O, YOU AREN'T</small> at a modern Division I-A college football game hosted by an eastern Washington agricultural university. You're at the ancient Greek Olympic Games! Millennia later, nations will suspend the Games in wartime; for these Olympics, Greek nations will (for the most part) suspend wartime.

What, When, Where, Why

Olympia was a remote, scenic religious sanctuary in the western Greek boonies. The nearest town was little Elis, 40 miles away.

According to chroniclers, the ancient Olympic Games started in 776 B.C. That's about a century after Elijah and Jezebel's biblical difference of opinion. Rome wasn't yet founded; the Assyrian Empire ruled the Near East. Greece's fractious city-states waged constant political and military struggle. In 776, with disease and strife even worse than usual in Greece, King Iphitos of Elis consulted the Delphic Oracle. She said, roughly translated: "Greece is cursed. Hold athletics at Olympia, like you guys used to do, to lift the curse."

"Done deal," said the king. Greek legend spoke of games of old held at Olympia in honor of Zeus, occurring perhaps every four or five years, so Iphitos cleared some land at Olympia and put on a footrace. The plague soon petered out. "Wish it was always that easy," Iphitos probably said.

Play It Again, Iphitos

It's uncertain why the Eleans decided to repeat the Olympics every four years; that was probably the most prevalent version of the ancient tradition. Likely, they lacked the resources to do it more often. Whatever the reason, the Games became Elis's reason for being. Its people spent the intervening years preparing for the next Olympiad. Given the amount of feasting and drinking that happened at the Games, the first year was likely spent recuperating.

Over the centuries, the event program extended to five days. The Eleans added equestrian and combat events. Any male Greek athlete could try out for the Games. Winners became rock stars, with egos and fringe benefits to match. There were no silver or bronze medals; losers slunk away in shame.

Temples and facilities sprang up at Olympia over the years: a great arena, shrines, and training facilities. In their lengthy heyday, historians believe 40,000-plus people would converge on Olympia to see a sport program ranging from chariot racing to track-and-field events to hand-to-hand combat.

Except for the boxers, wrestlers, charioteers, and *pankratists* (freestyle fighters)—who were frequently maimed or killed— the athletes had it easy compared to the attendees. The climate was hot and sticky, without even a permanent water source for most of the ancient Olympic era (a rich guy finally built an aqueduct). Deaths from sunstroke weren't rare. Sanitation? Most people had no way to bathe, so everyone stank, and disease ran rampant.

Married women couldn't attend, except female racing-chariot owners. The only other exception was a priestess of Demeter, who had her own special seat. Unmarried girls and women, especially prostitutes, were welcome. According to historians and pottery depictions, athletes competed nude, so there was no chance a woman could infiltrate as a competitor.

An Endurance Event for All

For five days every four years, Olympia combined the features of church, carnival, track meet, martial arts, banquet, racing, bachelor party, brothel, and tourist trap into a Woodstock-like scene of organized bedlam. The Olympics weren't merely to be watched or even experienced. They were to be endured and survived.

In A.D. 393, Roman Emperor Theodosius I, a first-rank killjoy, banned all pagan ceremonies. Since the Games' central ritual was a big sacrifice to Zeus, this huge heathen debauch clearly had to go.

The party was over. It wouldn't start again until 1859.

What Are Baseball's Predecessors?

The Abner Doubleday Fan Club isn't going to like this.

✳   ✳   ✳   ✳

IT WAS LONG believed that Abner Doubleday invented baseball in 1839. While we now know this is not true, we still don't know exactly how baseball came about. Games involving sticks and balls go back thousands of years. They've been traced to the Mayans in the Western Hemisphere and to Egypt at the time of the Pharaohs. There are historical references to Greeks, Chinese, and Vikings "playing ball." And a woodcut from 14th-century France shows what seem to be a batter, pitcher, and fielders.

Starting with Stoolball

By the 18th century, references to "baseball" were appearing in British publications. In an 1801 book entitled *The Sports and Pastimes of the People of England,* Joseph Strutt claimed that baseball-like games could be traced back to the 14th century and that baseball was a descendant of a British game called "stoolball." The earliest known reference to stoolball is in a 1330 poem by William Pagula, who recommended to priests that the game be forbidden within churchyards.

In stoolball (which is still played in England, mostly by women), a batter stands before a target, perhaps an upturned stool, while another player pitches a ball to the batter. If the batter hits the ball (with a bat or his/her hand) and it is caught by a fielder, the batter is out. Ditto if the pitched ball hits a stool leg.

The Game Evolves

It seems that stoolball eventually split into two different styles. One became English "base-ball," which turned into "rounders" in England but evolved into "town ball" when it reached the United States. The other side of stoolball turned into cricket. From town ball came the two styles that dominated baseball's development: the Massachusetts Game and the New York Game. The former had no foul or fair territory; runners were put out by being hit with a thrown ball when off the base ("soaking"), and as soon as one out was made, the offense and defense switched sides. The latter established the concept of foul lines, and each team was given three "outs" to an inning. Perhaps more significantly, soaking was eliminated in favor of the more gentlemanly tag. The two versions coexisted in the first three decades of the 19th century, but when the Manhattanites codified their rules in 1845, it became easier for more and more groups to play the New York style.

A book printed in France in 1810 laid out the rules for a bat/ base/running game called "poison ball," in which there were two teams of eight to ten players, four bases (one called "home"), a pitcher, a batter, and flyball outs. Different variations of the game went by different names: "Tip-cat" and "trap ball" were notable for how important the bat had become. It was no longer used merely to avoid hurting one's hand; it had become a real cudgel, to swat the ball a long way.

The Knickerbocker Club

In the early 1840s, Alexander Cartwright, a New York City engineer, was one of a group who met regularly to play baseball, and he may have been the mastermind behind organizing, formalizing, and writing down the rules of the game. The group called themselves The Knickerbocker Club, and their constitution, enacted on September 23, 1845, led the way for the game we know today.

The Myth Begins

Even though the origins of baseball are murky, there's one thing we know for sure: Abner Doubleday had nothing to do with it. The Mills Commission was organized in 1905 by Albert Spalding to search for a definitive American source for baseball. They "found" it in an ambiguous letter spun by a Cooperstown resident (who turned out to be crazy). But Doubleday wasn't

even in Cooperstown when the author of the letter said he had invented the game. Also, "The Boy's Own Book" presented the rules for a baseball-like game ten years before Doubleday's alleged "invention." Chances are, we'll never know for sure how baseball came to be the game it is today.

How Long Was the Longest Game in MLB History?

Here's a look at the longest professional game of all time.

✳   ✳   ✳   ✳

T HE LONGEST GAME in professional baseball history took 33 innings and parts of three days to complete, and while many of the players who suited up for the Class AAA epic between the Pawtucket Red Sox and Rochester Red Wings on April 18, 1981, later saw action in the majors, this is one minor-league contest they would never forget. Both starting third basemen are in the Hall of Fame, as is the scorecard.

The "PawSox"—Boston's top farm club, led by star third baseman Wade Boggs—played host for the game, which began on a cold and windy Rhode Island night before 1,740 fans at McCoy Stadium. They watched the visitors (affiliates of the Baltimore Orioles) take a 1–0 lead in the seventh, but Pawtucket knotted the score in the ninth. And there the seemingly endless string of zeroes on the scoreboard began, altered only with matching "1s" when both teams scored in the 21st.

Conditions grew so frigid after midnight that pitchers broke up benches and lit fires in the bullpen. Umpires could not find a rule about International League curfews, so action continued until league president Harold Cooper was reached by phone and suspended play after 32 innings at 4:07 A.M. on Easter Sunday. At that time only 19 fans remained, and Red Wings third baseman Cal Ripken (like Boggs, destined for Cooperstown) later remembered that it was the only time in his distinguished career that his post game meal consisted of breakfast.

The 2–2 contest made national headlines, both in the days that followed and when it resumed on June 23. By then Major League Baseball players were on strike, so reporters descended

140 strong on Pawtucket. They were joined by a sellout crowd of 5,746, who waited just 18 minutes before Dave Koza singled in Marty Barrett to give Pawtucket a 3–2 victory in the bottom of the 33rd. All told, 41 players saw action over 8 hours, 25 minutes of play, but only one stat mattered to Pawtucket center fielder Dallas Williams: 0-for-13, the worst one-game batting line ever.

Which Hockey Player Has Spent the Most Time in the Penalty Box?

This is the time-out seat of professional sports, where hotheaded hockey players go "to feel shame." It is the penalty box, an off-ice office of purgatory for on-ice transgressors.

❋ ❋ ❋ ❋

For the first 50 years of the National Hockey League's existence, every league arena had only one penalty box, which meant that players who engaged in a lively tussle on the ice served their penance together, with only an obviously nervous league official sitting between them to act as a buffer. Quite often, the combatants would continue their fisted arguments off the ice and inside their temporary, cramped quarters.

On one occasion, this led to the infamous "pickling" of New York Rangers' forward Bob Dill. On December 17, 1944, Dill and Montreal Canadiens fireball Maurice "The Rocket" Richard engaged in a raucous set-to that banished them both to the shower stall of shame. Inside the box, the obviously dazed and confused Dill attacked The Rocket again and received another sound thumping for his lack of common sense.

It wasn't until midway through the 1963–1964 season that the league introduced a rule requiring every rink to have separate penalty benches. A particularly vicious confrontation between Toronto Maple Leaf Bob Pulford and Montreal Canadien Terry Harper on October 30, 1963, precipitated by Harper's questioning of Pulford's sexual preference, spearheaded the NHL's decision to arrive at a sensible solution.

The undisputed king of the sin bin was Dave "Tiger" Williams, who logged nearly 4,000 minutes sitting on his punitive throne during his 15-year career in the NHL. Having spent his formative years with the Toronto Maple Leafs, Williams had a personal affinity for the Maple Leaf Gardens' penalty box, which he described as "a gross place to go. The guys in there are bleeding…and no one's cleaned the place since 1938."

Williams may hold the career mark for sin bin occupancy, but the rap sheet for a single-season sentence belongs to Dave "The Hammer" Schultz. During the 1974–1975 campaign, the Philadelphia Flyers enforcer cooled his carcass in the hotel of humility for 472 minutes, nearly 8 full games. He was so at home in the house, he actually recorded a single titled "The Penalty Box," which became something of a cult hit in and around the City of Brotherly Love.

Philadelphia's post of punition was also the scene of one of hockey's most hilarious highlights. During a game between the Flyers and Maple Leafs in 2001, Toronto tough guy Tie Domi was sent to the box. Upon his arrival in the cage, he was verbally accosted by a leather-lunged Philly fan named Chris Falcone, who wisely used the glass partition to shield himself from Domi. Known as "The Albanian Assassin," Domi responded to the goading by spraying his heckler with water. The broad-shouldered Falcone lunged toward Domi, fell over the glass, and landed in a heap at Domi's feet, which resulted in a comic wrestling match between lug head and lunatic.

Why Is a Football
Shaped That Way?

Would you rather call it a bladder? Because that's what footballs were made of before mass-produced rubber or leather balls became the norm.

✳ ✳ ✳ ✳

THE ORIGINS OF the ball and the game can be traced to the ancient Greeks, who played something called harpaston. As in football, players scored by kicking, passing, or running over the opposition's goal line. The ball in harpaston was often made of a pig's bladder. This is because pigs' bladders were easy to find, roundish in shape, relatively simple to inflate and seal, and fairly durable. (If you think playing ball with an internal organ is gross, consider what the pig's bladder replaced: a human head.)

Harpaston evolved into European rugby, which evolved into American football. By the time the first "official" football game was played at Rutgers University in New Jersey in the fall of 1869, the ball had evolved, too. To make the ball more durable and consistently shaped, it was covered with a protective layer that was usually made of leather.

Still, the extra protection didn't help the pig's bladder stay permanently inflated, and there was a continuous need to reinflate the ball. Whenever play was stopped, the referee unlocked the ball—yes, there was a little lock on it to help keep it inflated—and a player would pump it up.

Footballs back then were meant to be round, but the sphere was imperfect for a couple reasons. First, the bladder lent itself more to an oval shape; even the most perfectly stitched leather covering couldn't force the bladder to remain circular. Second, as a game wore on, players got tired and were less enthused about reinflating the ball. As a result, the ball would flatten out and take on more of an oblong shape. The ball was easier to grip in that shape, and the form slowly gained popularity, particularly after the forward pass was introduced in 1906.

Through a series of rule changes relating to its shape, the football became slimmer and ultimately developed its current look. And although it's been many decades since pigs' bladders were relieved of their duties, the football's nickname—a "pigskin"—lives on.

How Come Nobody Else Calls It Soccer?

Millions of kids across the United States grow up playing a game that their parents hardly know, a game that virtually everyone else in the world calls football. It's soccer to us, of course, and although Americans might be ridiculed for calling it this, the corruption is actually British in origin.

✳ ✳ ✳ ✳

SOCCER—FOOTBALL, AS THE Brits and billions of others insist—has an ancient history. Evidence of games resembling soccer has been found in cultures that date to the third century B.C. The Greeks had a version that they called *episkyro*. The Romans brought their version of the sport along when they colonized what is now England and Ireland. Over the next millennium, the game evolved into a freewheeling, roughneck competition—matches often involved kicking, shoving, and punching.

In England and Ireland, the sport was referred to as football; local and regional rules varied widely. Two different games—football and rugby—slowly emerged from this disorganized mess. The Football Association was formed in 1863 to standardize the rules of football and to separate it from rugby. The term "soccer" most likely is derived from the association's work.

During the late 19th century, the Brits developed the linguistic habit of shortening words and adding "-ers" or "-er." (We suffer this quirk to this day in expressions like "preggers." A red card to the Brits on this one.) One popular theory holds that given the trend, it was natural that those playing "Assoc." football were playing "assoccers" or "soccer." The term died out in England, but was revived in the United States in the early part of the 20th century to separate the imported sport with the round white ball from the American sport with the oblong brown ball.

Soccer has long struggled to catch on as a major spectator sport in the United States. For most Americans, there just isn't enough scoring or action. In fact, many Yanks have their own word for soccer: boring.

Who Was the First Heavyweight Champion to Retire Undefeated?

This heavyweight boxing champ achieved a feat no one else has ever managed.

✳ ✳ ✳ ✳

BORN ON SEPTEMBER 1, 1923, in Brockton, Massachusetts, Rocco Francis Marchegiano was the heavyweight champion of the world from 1952 to 1956. To this day, with 43 knockouts to his credit, he remains the only heavyweight champion in boxing history to retire without a defeat or a draw.

Solid as a Rock

When he was a year old, Rocky Marciano survived a near-fatal bout of pneumonia. This was perhaps the first evidence of the strength and resilience that led him to spend his childhood and young adulthood wrestling and playing baseball and football. He worked out on homemade weight-lifting equipment, including a makeshift heavy bag formed from an old mailbag that hung from a tree in his backyard. He dropped out of high school in tenth grade and worked as a ditchdigger, sold shoes, and found employment at a coal company.

In 1943, Marciano was drafted into the army, where he spent two years ferrying supplies across the English Channel to Normandy. During his stint in the military, Marciano won the 1946 amateur armed forces boxing tournament. He ended his amateur year with an 11–3 record—the last time Marciano ever experienced a loss.

"Timmmberrr!"

In 1947, Marciano tried out for the Chicago Cubs baseball team but was cut three weeks later. Subsequently, he turned professional in the boxing ring. *Sports Illustrated* reported, "He was too short, too light, and had no reach . . . Rough and tough, but no finesse."

Marciano's hometown fans were believers, and they traveled in groups to watch his fights. When Rocky had an opponent ready to go down, they would yell, "Timmmberrr!" as they would for a falling tree, and the audience would go wild.

Rocky catapulted to stardom in 1951, when he was pitted against Joe Louis, his most formidable opponent and also his childhood idol. The match, which was the last of Louis's career, was aired on national television. Marciano KO'd Louis in the eighth round—and later sobbed in Louis's dressing room after the fight.

The KO Kid

Marciano's trainer, Charley Goldman, taught Rocky his trademark technique—a short, overhand right to the jaw. This move served Marciano well when, in the 13th round against the defending heavyweight champion, lagging behind in points and struggling offensively, he suddenly KO'd Jersey Joe Walcott. The year was 1952.

Firmly established as a "marquee" fighter, Marciano went on to defend his title six times, including a first-round knockout

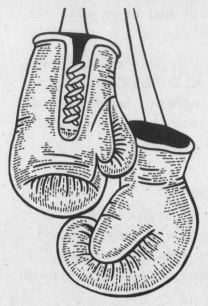

victory in a 1953 rematch with Walcott and another knockout win over Roland La Starza later that year. With a left and a quick right to the jaw, Marciano won a decision against Ezzard Charles in 1954. But fans had a moment of panic when, in a rematch later that year, Marciano nearly lost his title in the sixth round. Charles cut Marciano's nose so badly that his corner trainer couldn't stop the bleeding. When the ring doctor considered stopping the fight, Marciano erupted against Charles and knocked him out in the eighth round. Ding!

A year later, despite organized crime enticements to throw the fight, Rocky KO'd European champion Don Cockell in an exciting nine rounds. Marciano's last fight was in Yankee Stadium on September 21, 1955. He knocked out Archie Moore in the ninth round as more than 400,000 people watched over closed-circuit television.

The Rock

Marciano spent his retirement years working as a boxing show host and commentator and making personal appearances. He died at the age of 46 when a small private plane he was riding in crashed into a tree as it attempted to land in Newton, Iowa.

Inducted into the Boxing Hall of Fame in 1990, Rocky Marciano was honored in 1999 on a commemorative U.S. postage stamp. Marciano lives on through a myriad of books, films, and of course, in the minds and hearts of fans.

And although he may not rank among the top five boxers of all time, one sportswriter summed Marciano up accurately: "If all the heavyweight champions of all time were locked together in a room, Marciano would be the only one to walk out."

What Is Cornhole?

Cornhole, or bags, is the popular backyard game in which teams toss beanbags at a target—a hole in the slanted game board.

✳ ✳ ✳ ✳

To play cornhole, you need two slanted wooden game boards with a hole near one end, two sets of four beanbags (eight beanbags total), and two teams of two players.

Cornhole boards are placed 27 feet apart and facing one another. Two opposing players stand by each board and toss at the farther board. Each player tosses four bags per inning, with the pair of opponents at one end of the court alternately pitching all the bags before the other pair plays. The objective is to land your bag in the hole. A bag in the hole (a "cornhole") is worth 3 points, while a bag landing on the board (a "woody") is worth 1 point. The first team to reach 21 wins the game.

Cornhole can be played at tailgates, outdoor bars, barbecues, campgrounds, beaches, parks, or at home. All you need is a little open space to play this fun, easy to learn, and competitive game. It has wide appeal across all genders and age groups. Plus, it only takes an average of 15 minutes to play a game.

The game of cornhole has reached such a heightened level of popularity that it has multiple associations that claim to be the authority on the sport. There is the American Cornhole Organization (ACO), based in Milford, Ohio, that states it is the governing body for the sport of cornhole. Another, the American Cornhole League (ACL), inked a three-year deal with ESPN to air some of their tournament events. Not too shabby for a backyard sport.

Why Do Most Sports Go Counterclockwise?

For most nonathletes living their quiet day-to-day lives, doing things clockwise seems pretty intuitive. Doorknobs turn clockwise, screws are tightened clockwise, and yes, clocks run clockwise. Board games usually move clockwise, blackjack dealers hand out cards clockwise, and people in restaurants usually take turns ordering in a clockwise direction.

✳ ✳ ✳ ✳

YET IN MANY of our sports, such as baseball and all types of racing, play moves in a counterclockwise direction. This can cause some serious confusion for clockwise-oriented individuals—just ask any T-ball coach trying to shepherd a young hitter down the first-base line.

How did this counterintuitive situation come to be? Part of the answer is rooted in history, of course. In ancient times, when the Roman Empire ruled virtually the entire known Western world, a popular form of entertainment was chariot racing. As Charlton Heston fans know, chariot racing moved in a counterclockwise direction.

Roman horses were invaluable in war and were trained to turn to the left to give right-handed spear-wielding riders an advantage in battle; in the Circus Maximus, it was natural to build the track to suit this. Considering the power of habit in human social development, it seems reasonable to assume that future forms of racing simply adopted the same direction of travel as the mighty Romans.

Some science-minded individuals postulate that foot racing goes counterclockwise due to physical forces. Because most people are right-handed (and right-footed), a counterclockwise motion tends to help those with a dominant right leg speed around turns. This is because of centrifugal force, which we're sure everybody remembers from high school physics. For those who have forgotten (or never knew), centrifugal force is that sense of momentum—called inertia—that tries to keep you going in a straight line when you're trying to turn. A right-legged individual moving counterclockwise, this explanation contends, will have a better chance of counteracting this force.

Some sports move the other way. In England, for example, horse races travel in a clockwise direction. This seems particularly baffling, considering that American horse racing—which was brought over by the British during colonial times—moves counterclockwise. It turns out, though, that counterclockwise horse racing actually developed in the United States in response to the British tradition.

One of the first American horse tracks built after the Revolutionary War was established in 1780 by Kentuckian William Whitley. Flushed with pride at the newly won independence of the colonies, Whitley declared that horse racing in the new country should go in the opposite direction of those stodgy, tyrannical Brits.

Baseball, in which runners move counterclockwise around the bases, also may have descended from a British ancestor. Some baseball historians have postulated that the modern national pastime may be based on a British bat-and-ball game called rounders. Interestingly, rounders players moved in a clockwise direction around the bases; why this was reversed in the rules of baseball is not known.

Possibly, the counterclockwise movement has to do with the orientation of the diamond. It's far easier for righthanders to throw across the diamond to first base if the runner is moving in a counterclockwise direction (which is also why you almost never see lefthanders playing any infield positions except for first base).

Of course, from one perspective, clockwise and counterclockwise are meaningless terms. Some physicists enjoy pointing out (somewhat smugly, we might add) that direction is entirely relative. Which means that those seemingly confused T-ball toddlers might be a lot smarter than we think.

How Are Karate, Kung Fu, and Tae Kwon Do Different?

To the casual observer, karate, kung fu, and tae kwon do can be difficult to tell apart. It's all just a bunch of barefoot dudes kicking each other, right?

* * * *

THE THREE DISCIPLINES do share similarities and have surely influenced each other over the centuries; each evolved in East Asia, after all. For clarity and a bit of simplicity, we can associate each discipline with a country: karate with Japan, kung fu with China, and tae kwon do with Korea. All are mainly unarmed forms of combat (some styles of kung fu involve weapons) that are also practiced as sport or exercise and emphasize self-defense and spiritual development.

Karate stresses timing and coordination to focus as much power as possible on the point of impact. Blows are delivered with the hands, forearms, feet, knees, and elbows. At the height of his or her powers, a karate practitioner can split boards with a swift kick or punch.

Kung fu teaches self-discipline, with all of its moves beginning from one of five basic foot positions, most of which pay tribute to animals. Traditionally, kung fu places less emphasis on levels or rankings than do the other two (indicated, for example, by the different belt colors awarded in karate).

Tae kwon do is partially based on karate and features distinctive standing and jump kicks, but punching and blocking are also integral to it, just as they are to the other two disciplines. As in karate, students of tae kwon do often spar with each other; they try to avoid injury by learning to land their kicks and punches within inches of an opponent's body.

Each discipline requires years of study to master—but, despite what you may have learned from Hollywood, none involves much use of Turtle Wax.

Why Is a Marathon 26.2 Miles?

To most of us, running a marathon is incomprehensible. Equally incomprehensible is the number itself, 26.2. Why isn't a marathon 26.4 miles? Or 25.9?

✳ ✳ ✳ ✳

The Answer Is Rooted in History

To FIND OUT why a marathon is 26.2 miles, we must examine the history of the marathon. Our current marathon is descended from a legend about the most famous runner in ancient Greece, a soldier named Philippides (his name was later corrupted in text to Pheidippides). For much of the fifth century B.C., the Greeks were at odds with the neighboring Persian Empire; in 490 B.C., the mighty Persians, led by Darius I, attacked the Greeks at the city of Marathon. Despite being badly outnumbered, the Greeks managed to fend off the Persian troops (and ended Darius's attempts at conquering Greece).

After the victory, the legend holds, Philippides ran in full armor from Marathon to Athens—about 25 miles—to announce the good news. After several hours of running through the rugged Greek countryside, he arrived at the gates of Athens crying, "Rejoice, we conquer!" as Athenians rejoiced. Philippides then fell over dead. Despite a great deal of debate about the accuracy of this story, the legend still held such sway in the Greek popular mind that when the modern Olympic Games were revived in Athens in 1896, a long-distance running event known as a "marathon" was instituted.

Homing In on 26.2

How did the official marathon distance get to be 26.2 miles if the journey of Philippides was about 25? In the first two Olympic Games, the "Philippides distance" was indeed used. But things changed in 1908, when the Olympic Games were held in London. The British Olympic committee determined that the marathon route would start at Windsor Castle and end in front of the royal box in front of London's newly built Olympic Stadium, a distance that happened to measure 26 miles, 385 yards.

There was no good reason for the whims of British lords to become the standard, but 26.2 somehow got ingrained in the sporting psyche. By the 1924 Olympics in Paris, this arbitrary distance had become the standard for all marathons.

Today, winning a marathon—heck, even completing one—is considered a premier athletic accomplishment. In cities such as Boston, New York, and Chicago, thousands of professionals and amateurs turn out to participate. Of course, wiser people remember what happened to Philippides when he foolishly tried to run such a long distance.

How Did the Biathlon Become an Olympic Event?

It's one thing to ski through the frozen countryside; it's quite another to interrupt that heart-pounding exertion and muster up the calm and concentration needed to hit a target that's a few centimeters wide with a .22-caliber bolt-action rifle.

* * * *

YES, THE BIATHLON is an odd sport. Cross-country skiing combined with rifle marksmanship? Why not curling and long jump? Figure skating and weight lifting? In actuality, however, the two skills that make up the biathlon have a history of going hand in hand, so combining them as an Olympic event makes perfect sense.

It's no surprise that the inspiration for the biathlon came from the frigid expanses of northern Europe, where there's not much to do in the winter besides ski around and drink aquavit. Cross-country skiing provides a quick and efficient way to travel over the snowy ground, so northern cultures mastered the technique early—and it was especially useful when it came time to hunt for winter food. People on skis were killing deer with bows and arrows long before such an activity was considered a sport.

But skiing and shooting (with guns, eventually) evolved from an act of survival into a competition. The earliest biathlon competitions were held in 1767 as informal contests between Swedish and Norwegian border patrols. The sport spread through Scandinavia in the 19th century as sharpshooting skiers formed biathlon clubs. In 1924, it was included as a demonstration sport in the Winter Olympics in Chamonix, France, although it was called military patrol.

In 1948, the Union Internationale de Pentathlon Moderne et Biathlon—the first international governing body for the sport—was formed. The official rules for what would come to be the modern biathlon were determined over the next several years.

During the 1960 Olympics at Squaw Valley Ski Resort in California, a biathlon was contested as an official Olympic event for the first time. The sport has evolved over the decades—it now features smaller-caliber rifles, different distances, various types of relays, and the participation of women. (A women's biathlon was first staged as an Olympic event in 1992 in Albertville, France.)

Today, biathlon clubs and organizations are active all over the world, and there are versions of the sport for summer in which running replaces skiing. Still, the biathlon's popularity remains strongest in its European birthplace.

What Is Esports?

Esports, or competitive video gaming, is becoming big business—and a legitimate sport.

✳ ✳ ✳ ✳

VIDEO GAMING IS now an official high school varsity sport in nine states. Universities across the country are getting into the esports game. Robert Morris University in Illinois became the first college in the U.S. to offer video gaming scholarships in 2014. University of California–Irvine, Boise State University, Western Kentucky University, and the University of Utah are among the growing number of schools now offering esports scholarships.

In the fall of 2019 Marquette University in Milwaukee became the first NCAA Division I power-conference school to place varsity esports within its athletics program. This is a significant step as other universities have housed esports and run their scholarship programs through academic departments. Although there is currently no central governing body for esports, like the NCAA, there *are* collegiate esports conferences and leagues, including the National Association of Collegiate Esports and the Electronic Gaming Federation.

Another development coinciding with the rising profile of esports is users sharing their gaming experience online. Twitch is a live video streaming platform that allows users to broadcast their video gaming, as well as watch others play either live or on demand. The site has spawned streaming celebrities and allows everyday folks the chance to earn money via fan donations, shared ad sales, and sponsorships.

The most popular streamer far and away on Twitch is Tyler "Ninja" Blevins who has over 14 million followers. "Ninja" was reportedly paid $1 million to play the game Apex Legends on the day of its release in 2019. Another streaming gamer, Benjamin Lupo, also known as "Dr. Lupo," has an endorsement deal with State Farm. Part of the deal features a State Farm-branded game replay. The participation of a company like State Farm speaks volumes about the legitimacy of esports as they also advertise with the major sports leagues like the NBA, NFL, MLB, college basketball, and college football.

How Do Bookies Set Odds on Sporting Events?

First, we need to learn a little about the sports book biz. Consider this gambling primer: Bookies take a small percentage of every bet that comes in; this is known as the vig. The ideal situation for any bookie is to have an equal amount of money riding on both sides of a bet; this way, no matter what happens in the game, the bookie will make money. The bookie will pay out money to those who bet on the winner, take in money from those who bet on the loser, and come out ahead because of the vig.

✳ ✳ ✳ ✳

I F EVERYONE BETS on one team and that team wins, the bookie will lose a lot of money. Sports odds are designed to keep an even number of bettors on each side of the bet.

Major sports books in Las Vegas and Europe employ experienced oddsmakers to set the point spread, odds, or money line on a game. Oddsmakers must know a lot about sports and a lot about gamblers: They examine every detail of an upcoming game—including public perceptions about it—to determine which team has the better chance of winning. Several days or weeks prior to the game, the oddsmakers meet, compare information, and reach a consensus on the odds.

Here's a simple example: Team A is thought to be much better than Team B in an upcoming game. If both sides of the bet paid off the same amount of money, almost everyone would bet on Team A. The oddsmakers try to determine what odds will even out the betting. Giving Team B five-to-one odds means anyone who bets on Team B will make five times his bet if Team B wins. Team B may not have much of a chance of winning, but the increased reward makes the risk worthwhile to gamblers.

Or, depending on the sport and the country, the oddsmakers might set a money line, which is usually expressed as a "plus" or "minus" dollar amount. This is effectively the same thing as setting odds—the money line simply reflects the payoff that a bettor can expect from a winning bet.

Another way to balance the betting market is with a point spread. In this case, winning bets always pay off at one-to-one, or even odds, usually with a 10 percent vig on top, which means you would have to bet eleven dollars to win ten dollars. The point spread handicaps the game in favor of one team. In, say, football, Team A might get a spread of minus-seven. This means gamblers aren't just betting on whether Team A will win, but on whether it will do so by more than seven points.

Odds can change leading up to an event. This might indicate something significant happened, such as an injury to a key player, or it might mean that bookies are adjusting the odds because too many bets were coming in on one side. Adjusting the odds reflects their attempt to balance the betting and minimize their potential loss. Remember, a bookie isn't in this for

fun and games—he's in it to make profits. And at the end of the day, he's the one who almost always wins.

When and Where Was NASCAR Founded?

The 1930s and 1940s saw a new breed of driver tearing up the back roads of the American South.

✳ ✳ ✳ ✳

YOUNG, HIGHLY SKILLED, and full of brass, these road rebels spent their nights outwitting and outrunning federal agents as they hauled 60-gallon payloads of illegal moonshine liquor from the mountains to their eager customers in the cities below. In this dangerous game, speed and control made all the difference. The bootleggers spent as much time tinkering under their hoods as they did prowling the roads. A typical bootleg car might be a Ford Coupe with a 454 Cadillac engine, heavy-duty suspension, and any number of other modifications meant to keep the driver and his illicit cargo ahead of John Law.

And They're Off!

With all that testosterone and horsepower bundled together, it was inevitable that these wild hares would compete to see who had the fastest car and the steeliest nerve. A dozen or more of them would get together on weekends in an open field and spend the afternoon testing each other's skills, often passing a hat among the spectators who came to watch. Promoters saw the potential in these events, and before long organized races were being held all across the South. As often as not, though, the promoters lit out with the receipts halfway through the race, and the drivers saw nothing for their efforts.

Seeking to bring both legitimacy and profitability to the sport, driver and race promoter William "Bill" Henry Getty France Sr. organized a meeting of his colleagues at the Ebony Bar in Daytona Beach, Florida, on December 14, 1947. Four days of haggling and backslapping led to the formation of the National Association for Stock Car Auto Racing (NASCAR), with

France named as its first president. The group held its inaugural race in 1948, on the well-known half-sand, half-asphalt track at Daytona. Over the next two decades, the upstart organization built a name for itself on the strength of its daring and charismatic drivers. Junior Johnson, Red Byron, Curtis Turner, Lee Petty, and the Flock Brothers—Bob, Fonty, and Tim—held regular jobs (some still running moonshine) and raced the circuit in their spare time. And these legendary pioneers were some colorful characters: For example, Tim Flock occasionally raced with a pet monkey named Jocko Flocko, who sported a crash helmet and was strapped into the passenger seat.

Dawn of a New Era

During these early years, NASCAR was viewed as a distinctly Southern enterprise. In the early 1970s, however, Bill France Jr. took control of the organization from his father, and things began to change. The younger France negotiated network television deals that brought the racetrack into the living rooms of Middle America. In 1979, CBS presented the first flag-to-flag coverage of a NASCAR event, and it was a doozy. Race leaders Cale Yarborough and Donnie Allison entered a bumping duel on the last lap that ended with both cars crashing on the third turn. As Richard Petty moved up from third to take the checkered flag, a fight broke out between Yarborough and Allison's brother Bobby. America was hooked.

France also expanded the sport's sponsorship beyond automakers and parts manufacturers. Tobacco giant R. J. Reynolds bought its way in, as did countless other purveyors of everyday household items, including Tide, Lowe's Hardware, Kellogg's Cereal, the Cartoon Network, Nextel, and Coca-Cola. Today, NASCAR vehicles and their beloved drivers are virtually moving billboards. Plastered with the logos of their sponsors as they speed around the track, Kurt Busch, Jimmie Johnson, Kyle Busch, Chase Elliott, Kevin Harvick, and their fellow daredevils draw the eyes of some 75 million regular fans and support a multibillion-dollar industry.

How Are Tennis and Handball Related?

Ever watch people playing handball and wonder, "Ow! Isn't that hell on their hands?" Well, it can be. That's why some players decided to take a different approach to handball, and used a racket instead. Here's more on the origins of tennis.

✳   ✳   ✳   ✳

Tennis: Sport of Monks

INTERESTINGLY, NO ONE is quite sure exactly when tennis was invented. Some folks believe it's an ancient sport, but there's no credible evidence that tennis existed before A.D. 1000. Whenever the time period, most people can agree that tennis descends from handball.

The first reliable accounts of tennis come from tales of 11th-century French monks who needed to add a little entertainment to their days spent praying, repenting, and working. They played a game called *jeu de paume* ("palm game," that is, handball) off the walls or over a stretched rope. The main item separating tennis from handball—a racket—evolved withinin these French monasteries. (The first rackets were actually used in ancient Greece, in a game called *sphairistike* and then in *tchigan*, played in Persia.) The monks had the time and means to develop these early forms of the tennis racquet: Initially, webbed gloves were used for hand protection, then paddles, and finally a paddle with webbing. The first balls were made from leather or cloth stuffed with hair, wool, or cork.

Banned by the Pope

Once outside the cloister, the game's popularity spread across the country with the speed of an Amélie Mauresmo backhand. According to some sources, by the 13th century, France had more than 1,800 tennis courts. Most of the enthusiasts were from the upper classes. In fact, the sport became such a craze that some leaders, including kings and the pope, tried to discourage or ban the game as too distracting. Not to be torn from their beloved game, the people played on.

It didn't take long for tennis to reach merry olde England. There the game developed a similar following, counting kings Henry VII and Henry VIII among its fans. Even The Bard, William Shakespeare, refers to the game in his play *Henry V.* At England's Hampton Court Palace, research suggests that the first tennis court was built there between 1526 and 1529. Later, another court was built, The Royal Tennis Court, which was last refurbished in 1628 and is still in use.

15-Love!

Those who believe that tennis originated in ancient Egypt argue that the word "tennis" derives from the Egyptian town of Tinnis. It is also possible that the term comes from the French cry of *"Tenez!"* which in this context could mean, "take this!" or "here it comes!" using the formal address. A similar version would be *"Tiens!"* As with any living language, French pronunciation has evolved, so it's difficult to know precisely whether the word came from French monastery trash-talk—but it's quite plausible.

Ever wonder what's up with tennis's weird scoring system? And what does any of it mean, anyway? Here are a few tennis pointers.

The term "Love," meaning a score of zero, may descend from *"L'Oeuf!"* which means "the egg"—much like "goose egg" means zero in American sports slang.

Evidently, the scoring once went by 15s (0, 15, 30, 45, and Game). But for some reason, it was decided that the numbers should have the same number of syllables. Hence, the "5" got dropped from the French word *quarante-cinq* (45), leaving just *quarante* (40), which is in use today.

The term "Deuce" (when the game ties 40–40 and is reset to 30–30) likely comes from "*À Deux!*" which loosely translates as "two to win!" This is because in tennis, one must win by two.

What Is World Naked Bike Ride?

The World Naked Bike Ride (WNBR) is an annual event generally held in mid-June in the Northern Hemisphere and mid-March in the Southern Hemisphere. And the event is just what it sounds like, a group of adults riding their bikes with a dress code of "as bare as you dare." As such, the rides are clothing optional. Participants can go totally or partially nude, wear underwear, body paint, or fanciful costumes.

✳ ✳ ✳ ✳

So, WHY RIDE bikes naked? The stated objectives are opposition to oil dependency, curbing car culture, real rights for bikes, and celebration of body freedom. Since the first World Naked Bike Ride in 2004, the annual event has steadily grown to include 70 cities in 20 countries. The United States and Great Britain are the countries with the greatest number of cities participating. Exact locations of rides are usually not disclosed in advance to prevent word spreading and leering. In Chicago, the ride is done at night between 8:00 P.M. and midnight, covering a distance of 12 to 22 miles. However, many cities across the globe have daytime rides, so sunscreen is a must!

In addition to traditional two-wheeled bikes, unicycles, tricycles, tandem bikes, skateboards, and any sort of skates are allowed. Gas-powered bikes and scooters run counter to the WNBR's objectives and are excluded. Each city runs their own event as there is no collective managing body that governs the World Naked Bike Ride.

Do participants get arrested? According to the WNBR website, while it is illegal almost everywhere in the world to ride your bike naked, laws on nudity are often vague and difficult to enforce. There is a risk of getting fined for indecent exposure, but organizers advise riders to wear clothes before and after the event to avoid issues with officials. Typically, police are aware when their city is participating in a World Naked Bike Ride; in fact, they may be providing road closures for rider safety.

How Did the Ironman Triathlon Start?

"Faster, higher, stronger" may be the motto for the modern Olympic Games, but it's also an apt description for the athletes who stretched the boundaries of human endurance and initiated the Ironman competition.

✳   ✳   ✳   ✳

THE OLD CLICHÉ "anything you can do, I can do better," along with a spirited discussion over the true meaning of "better," ultimately led to the creation of the Ironman Triathlon. During the awards ceremony for the 1977 Oahu Perimeter Relay, a running race for five-person teams held in Hawaii, the winning participants, among them both runners and swimmers, became engrossed in a debate over which athletes were more fit.

As both sides tossed biting barbs, rousing rhetoric, and snide snippets back and forth, a third party entered the fray. Navy Commander John Collins, who was listening to the spirited spat, mentioned that a recent article in *Sports Illustrated* magazine claimed that bike racers, especially Tour de France winner Eddy Merckx, had the highest recorded "oxygen uptake" of any athlete ever measured, insinuating that cyclists were more fit than anyone. Collins and his wife, Judy, suggested the only way to truly bring the argument to a rightful conclusion was to arrange an extreme endurance competition, combining a swim of considerable length, a bike race of taxing duration, and a marathon foot race. The first Ironman Triathlon was held on February 18, 1978, in Honolulu, Hawaii. Participants were invited to "Swim 2.4 miles! Bike 112 miles! Run 26.2 miles! Brag for the rest of your life." This rousing slogan has since become the registered trademark of the event.

But the Ironman competition was not the first triathlon event. The first competition to combine swimming (500-yard race), bike racing (5-mile course), and running (2.8 miles) was held on September 25, 1974, in San Diego, California.

What Is Punkin Chunkin?

What's punkin chunkin? It's the term used for competitively chucking pumpkins as far as possible using machinery built for this express purpose.

✳   ✳   ✳   ✳

THE FIRST WORLD Championship Punkin Chunkin contest was held in 1986 in Delaware. The annual event moved to Rantoul, Illinois, in 2019. The World Championship Punkin Chunkin Association (WCPCA) governs this engineering and science-based event that tracks the longest launched pumpkin, and also raises money for scholarships and charitable programs. Teams compete in various classes depending on machine type and age group. The team that launches an 8- to 10-pound pumpkin of approved breed and species during the annual event becomes the World Champion Punkin Chunker, regardless of class entered.

Here are the particulars on some punkin chunkin devices used at the competition:

✳ A *pneumatic air cannon* launches a pumpkin by suddenly releasing compressed air from a high pressure tank behind the pumpkin. When the valve is opened, all of the compressed air pushes the pumpkin out of the tube.

* A *trebuchet* hurls a pumpkin by using a change in gravitational potential energy. It uses a short arm, which is weighed down with a heavy object to counterbalance against the long arm, where the pumpkin is placed. When the heavy mass of the short arm falls down, it provides the energy to fling the long arm.

* A *centrifugal* is a machine with an arm that spins at least 360 degrees to launch a pumpkin. The idea is to accelerate a pumpkin by spinning it in a circle, gaining momentum with each rotation until enough energy is built up to propel the pumpkin forward.

* A *catapult* uses stretched springs or rubber bands. When the springs or bands are pulled and released, the stored-up energy is transferred to the arm of the device, which then hurls the pumpkin.

* A *slingshot launcher* has two posts mounted in the ground. As the sling is pulled back and released, the stored elastic energy vaults the pumpkin.

The World Championship Punkin Chunkin has grown from its humble beginnings of three contestants and a handful of spectators to more than 100 teams and upwards of 60,000 fans attending the festivities. The record for longest distance launch at the World Championship Punkin Chunkin stands at 4,694.68 feet.

Where Are the Lumberjack World Championships Held?

Each year the Lumberjack World Championships take place in Hayward, Wisconsin. Sometimes referred to as the "Olympics of the Forest," the three-day event welcomes men and women to compete in 21 timber sporting events.

LUMBERJACKS AND LUMBERJILLS come from across the United States, Canada, Australia, and New Zealand to the small town of Hayward (population 2,300) to vie for world records and over $50,000 in prize money.

Let's take a closer look at some of the events:

* * * *

* *Log rolling*, also known as birling, is a test of balance. This involves rotating a log rapidly with your feet while floating in water. In this event, men and women are essentially running in place trying to knock their opponent off the spinning log. The act of landing your opponent in the water is called wetting. Pro tip: Always keep your eyes on your opponent's feet.

* In *boom running*, competitors run across a series of linked, floating logs (a boom) as fast as possible from one dock to another and back.

* *Chopping* is just what it sounds like. Lumberjacks and lumberjills test their endurance using axes to compete in the standing chop, underhand chop, springboard chop, and standing block chop. The springboard chop is particularly impressive to watch as contestants climb nine feet up a spar pole and chop while standing on a springboard.

* *Throwing* is a test of accuracy. It's a bit like archery except instead of using a bow and arrow, competitors throw a double-bit ax at a target. Points are awarded based on how close to the center of the bull's-eye the ax lands.

* *Sawing* is a battle of both speed and brute strength. Lumberjacks and lumberjills face off using a crosscut saw (or sometimes a chain saw) to see who can slice through a 16- or 20-inch white pine log the fastest.

* *Speed pole climbing* is a fan favorite. Competitors scale either a 60- or 90-foot cedar spar pole and then return to the ground in a timed head-to-head event. The descent, or free-fall back down, can be done in a shocking 15 or 16 seconds.

What Is Parkour?

Parkour is the act of moving from point A to point B using the obstacles in one's path to increase your efficiency. Parkour uses the acts of running, vaulting, jumping, climbing, rolling, and other improvisational skills to make traversing the world a more interesting experience.

✳ ✳ ✳ ✳

THE NAME PARKOUR comes from the French term "*Parcours du combattant*" or "The Path of the Warrior." The term warrior is no understatement. At its most dramatic, parkour can involve jumping from rooftop to rooftop or leaping across a 10-foot gap, often from extreme heights.

Practitioners of parkour are referred to as "traceurs." David Belle, a man from suburban Paris, is considered the founder of parkour. Belle founded the discipline in the late 1980s learning techniques directly from his father, Raymond, who was an extremely adept and acrobatic fireman.

Parkour moves revolve around a set of core maneuvers: leaps, jumps, rolls, drops, and vaults. The moves employed by traceurs bear a striking resemblance to gymnastics and martial arts moves. A tic-tac is a combination of a wall-climb and a jump, in which a traceur takes at least one step along a wall and launches herself or himself from it. Popular vaults go by names like lazy vault, reverse vault, speed vault, dash vault, and kong vault, which involves running straight at a wall or railing, planting one's hands on top, and bringing the feet through the hands.

Parkour has found its way into pop culture, most notably in the opening scene of the James Bond film *Casino Royale*. The *Casino Royale* scene features the parkour heroics of David Belle's childhood friend Sébastien Foucan being chased through a construction site. Foucan is the founder of parkour's parallel discipline, called freerunning.

Parkour is a communal activity and is often performed in groups. Many big cities have parkour meet-ups, or "parkour jams." In addition, there is a healthy online community sharing parkour videos on YouTube and other social media platforms.

Who Started Lacrosse?

Lacrosse is Canada's national summer sport and is the fastest growing high school and college sport in the United States. Along with basketball, it is arguably the most North American game there is—First Peoples/Native Americans invented it.

✳   ✳   ✳   ✳

First Nations Origins

ALGONQUINS CALLED LACROSSE baggataway and the Iroquois called it teewaarathon. Natives played the game to honor the Great Spirit or revered elders, or to celebrate. Lacrosse also served a diplomatic role. Suppose you were a Mohawk elder and you learned that the Oneidas were fishing on your side of the lake (violating your long-standing agreement). Rather than sending your warriors to fight the Oneida, you'd send an emissary to challenge them to settle the dispute with a teewaarathon match. These early games, which were quite violent, took place on fields that were miles long and involved as many as 1,000 participants. We can thank French Canadians for its name: La crosse means "the bishop's staff," because that's what the stick looked like.

Settlers' Adoption

Europeans' first record of a lacrosse match dates to the 1630s in southern Ontario, when missionary Jean de Brébeuf watched the Hurons play. By the 1800s, the game was popular with French Canadian settlers. In 1867, the same year Canada became a dominion, Canadian dentist W. George Beers standardized the rules of lacrosse. By 1900, the Canadian game had spread well across its native land and into the United States, with men's and women's versions.

The Game Today

There are two primary forms of lacrosse today: box (indoor) and field (outdoor). Box lacrosse is largely a Canadian sport, but Canadians also compete well in men's and women's field lacrosse. The game values speed and agility above brawn. The crosse (stick) takes skill to manipulate as players move the ball around. Play flow is similar to hockey or soccer; a team tries to control the ball and send it past a goaltender into the net. Fouls are similar to those in hockey, as is the penalty box. Lacrosse is a physical, speedy, demanding game that requires the toughness of rugby and the stamina of soccer.

First Nations in the Game

Only one First Nations team is sanctioned for international sport competition: the Iroquois Nationals, in field lacrosse. They're even sponsored by Nike!

Positions in Men's Lacrosse

Attack: There are three attackers on the field at one time. The attackers use "short-sticks" and must demonstrate good stick-handling with both hands; they must know where their teammates are at all times and be able to handle the pressure of opposing defense. Attackers score most of the goals.

Defense: Three defensive players with "long-poles" and one long-stick midfielder are allowed on the field at a time, using their sticks to throw checks and trying to dislodge the ball. One of the "long-poles" may also play midfield as a strategic defender, aka a long-stick middie. Teams usually use this to anticipate losing the face-off and to be stronger on defense.

Midfield: Three "middies" are allowed on the field at once. There are two types of midfielders, defensive and offensive. The two can rotate by running off the sidelines. Midfielders are allowed to use short-sticks and up to one long-pole. While on offense, three short-sticks are generally used for their superior stick-handling. While on defense, two short-sticks are used with one long-pole. Some teams have a designated face-off middie who takes the majority of face-offs and is usually quickly substituted after the face-off is complete.

Goalkeeper: Goalies try to prevent the ball from getting into the goal, and they also direct the team defense. A goalkeeper needs to be tough both physically and mentally, and he has to be loud enough to call the position of the ball at all times so the defense can concentrate on where the players are.

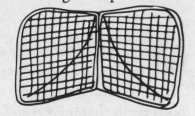

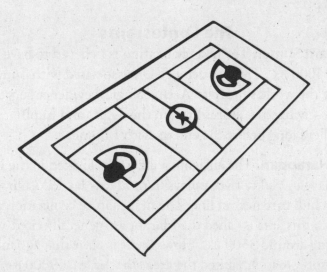

Chapter 7

History

What Was the World's First Civilization?

The fame of the ancient Egyptians—pyramids, pharaohs, eye makeup!—has led to the common misconception that ancient Egypt was the world's first civilization.

✳   ✳   ✳   ✳

MOST WESTERN SCHOLARS agree that the Sumerian civilization in Mesopotamia, located between the Tigris and Euphrates rivers in modern-day Iraq, was the first. Yet a deeper look reveals that there is a whole pageant of contenders for that coveted prize.

The Contestants

1. Ancient Sumer. The first civilization is believed to have begun around 4000 B.C. The great city of Ur, associated with Sumer, is possibly the world's first city. Archaeological evidence suggests that "pre-civilized" cultures lived in the Tigris and Euphrates river valleys long before the emergence of Sumer.

2. The Harappan. The ancient civilizations located in the Indus and Ghaggar-Hakra river valleys in modern-day Pakistan and western India are next in line. The first mature civilization associated with this area is called the Harappan, generally cited as beginning around 3500 B.C. However, it is clear that agricultural communities had inhabited the area since at least 9000 B.C.

3. Ancient Egypt. Located in Africa's Nile Valley, it is generally cited as beginning in 3200 B.C. But as with the Indus Valley civilization, it is difficult to establish a firm beginning date because agricultural societies had settled in the Nile River Valley since the tenth millennium B.C.

4. and 5. Ancient China and Elam. The final two, and least known, contestants (from the Western perspective) are the ancient Chinese civilizations and the Elam civilization of modern-day Iran. The Elamite kingdom began around 2700 B.C., though recent evidence suggests that a city existed in this area at a far earlier date—perhaps early enough to rival Sumer. Meanwhile, the ancient Chinese civilizations, located in the Yangtze and Yellow river valleys, are said to have begun around 2200 B.C.

The Criteria

The most salient feature of a civilization is a city, which, unlike a village, should have large religious and government buildings, evidence of social stratification (mansions for the rich and shacks for the poor), and complex infrastructure such as roads and irrigation. Civilizations are also defined by elaborate social systems, organized trade relations with outside groups, and the development of writing.

Marking a "civilization" is difficult because in all five possible cradles of civilization described above, complex societies lived in the same areas long before true civilization emerged. In fact, this is surely why civilizations first developed in these regions—human groups lived in the areas before the development of agriculture. Human populations have roamed the sprawling Eurasian continent for at least 100,000 years.

The emergence of civilization can be seen as the result of culture after culture living in one geographic area for countless generations until something happened that set these seminomadic groups on the path to civilization.

That Certain Something

Historians agree that the development of agriculture around 10,000 B.C. was the "something" that led to civilization. There is a strong correlation between agriculture, population size and density, and social complexity. Once agriculture began, human populations were increasingly tied to the land. They could no longer be nomadic, moving around at different times of the year and setting up temporary villages. As people continued to stay in one place and social relationships became more hierarchical, permanent villages developed into cities.

Who Has the World's Oldest Parliament?

Contrary to popular belief, the world's oldest parliament is not in Britain. It's not in the United States, either.

✳   ✳   ✳   ✳

First, a Definition

A PARLIAMENT IS A representative assembly with the power to pass legislation and most commonly consists of two chambers, or houses, in which a majority is required to create and amend laws. Congress became the supreme legislative body of the United States in 1789. The roots of the British Parliament date back to the 12th century, but it wasn't until 1689 that the Bill of Rights established Parliament's authority over the British monarch and gave it the responsibility of creating, amending, and repealing laws.

The title of Oldest Functioning Legislature in the World belongs to the Parliament of Iceland, known as Althing, which is Icelandic for "general assembly." Althing was established in A.D. 930 during the Viking age. The legislative assembly met at Thingvellir (about 30 miles outside of what is now the country's capital, Reykjavík) and heralded the start of the Icelandic Commonwealth, which lasted until 1262. Althing convened annually and served as both a court and a legislature. One of Althing's earliest pieces of legislation was to ban the Viking explorer Erik the Red from Iceland in 980 after he was found guilty of murder.

Even after Iceland lost its independence to Norway in 1262, Althing continued to hold sessions, albeit with reduced powers, until it was dissolved in 1799. In 1844, Althing was restored as an advisory body, and in 1874 it became a legislative body again, a function it maintains to this day. The parliament is now located in Reykjavík.

Why Didn't the Vikings Stay in North America?

According to ancient Norse sagas that were written in the 13th century, Leif Eriksson was the first Viking to set foot in North America. After wintering at the place we now call Newfoundland in the year 1000, Leif went home. In 1004, his brother Thorvald led the next expedition, composed of thirty men, and met the natives for the first time. The Vikings attacked and killed eight of the nine native men they encountered. A greater force retaliated, and Thorvald was killed. His men then returned home.

✳ ✳ ✳ ✳

SIX YEARS LATER, a larger expedition of Viking men, women, and livestock set up shop in North America. They lasted two years, according to the sagas. The Vikings traded with the locals initially, but they soon started fighting with them and were driven off. There may have been one further attempt at a Newfoundland settlement by Leif and Thorvald's sister, Freydis.

In 1960, Norse ruins of the appropriate age were found in L'Anse aux Meadows, Newfoundland, by Norwegian couple Helge and Anne Stine Ingstad. The Vikings had been there, all right. Excavations over the next seven years uncovered large houses and ironworks where nails and rivets were made, as well as woodworking areas. Also found were spindlewhorls, weights that were used when spinning thread; this implies that women were present, which suggests the settlement was more than a vacation camp.

The ruins don't reveal why the Vikings left. However, they do confirm what the old sagas claimed: The Vikings were in North America.

The sagas say that the settlers fought with the local *Skraelings*, a Norse word meaning "natives," until the *Skraelings* came at them in large enough numbers to force the Vikings out.

This sounds plausible, given the reputation of the Vikings—they'd been raiding Europe for centuries—and the Eriksson family's history of violence. Erik the Red, the father of Leif, founded a Greenland colony because he'd been thrown out of Iceland for murder, and Erik's father had been expelled from Norway for the same reason. Who'd want neighbors like them?

How Did the First Crusade Start?

Pope Urban II's call to arms in 1095 set off a war for the Holy Land that would change the course of human history for the next thousand years.

❊　❊　❊　❊

THE FIRST CRUSADE (1096–1099) was born of a pope's desire to safeguard the holy sites of Palestine for Christian pilgrims and to assert papal influence over the kingdoms of Western Europe. One sermon, given in late 1095, did more to change the course of the second millennium than any other speech in history.

Birth of the Crusades
The Crusades were born of a desire to roll back a loose Islamic empire that stretched from Afghanistan to northern Spain. In

the seventh and eighth centuries, while many European nobles spent their time fighting one another, a wave of Arab-led, Islam-inspired armies thundered across North Africa, Central Asia, the southern Mediterranean, and the Iberian Peninsula, gobbling up huge chunks of territory—many of which were torn out of the predominantly Orthodox Christian Byzantine Empire.

It did not take a political genius to figure out that Western Europe could set aside brewing political and social differences by uniting against a dangerous enemy espousing a different religion. In 1074, Pope Gregory VII issued a call for Christian soldiers to rush to the aid of the Byzantine Empire; they may have been Orthodox Christians, but they were Christians nonetheless, and they were being threatened by the great imperial powers of the age, the Islamic Caliphates.

Gregory's call went nowhere, but the publicity surrounding the pope's pleas attracted the attention of Christian pilgrims, who began visiting the Holy Land in record numbers. When priests with names like Walter the Penniless and Peter the Hermit began spreading tales of Muslims robbing Christian pilgrims on their way to Jerusalem, Europe was ripe for a battle over Palestine.

Urban's Call to Arms

Enter Pope Urban II. Elected in 1088, this savvy French priest carried out his diplomatic duties with finesse, and when Emperor Alexius I of Byzantine called for help against the Muslim hordes, Urban was happy to oblige. He summoned bishops from all over Europe to Clermont, France, and when some 300 bishops had assembled in an open-air forum, Urban gave them a barn-burner of a sermon. He exhorted the Christians of Europe to take up arms, to drive back the Seljuk Turks and the other Muslim armies occupying the Holy Land.

Knowing his real audience was the kings, princes, and nobles who would be asked to send soldiers into battle, the cagy Urban was quick to point out the material benefits of a conquest of eastern lands. He proclaimed:

"This land which you inhabit, shut in on all sides by the seas and surrounded by the mountain peaks, is too narrow for your large population; nor does it abound in wealth; and it furnishes scarcely food enough for its cultivators . . . Enter upon the road to the Holy Sepulcher; wrest that land from the wicked race, and subject it to yourselves."

The kicker, of course, was that the crusaders would have a spiritual carte blanche to kill and conquer, all with divine sanction. "God has conferred upon you above all nations great glory in arms. Accordingly undertake this journey for the remission of your sins, with the assurance of the imperishable glory of the kingdom of heaven," Pope Urban II said.

Urban's sermon wowed the bishops and nobles in attendance, who left the council chanting, *Deus vult!* ("God wills it!"). Peasants, knights, and nobles from France, Italy, and Germany answered Urban's call, and over the next year, a hodgepodge of crusaders (generally grouped into the unsuccessful "People's Crusade" and the more successful "Princes' Crusade") took up the Cross, looking for heavenly rewards, material treasure, and great victory.

Conquest of the Holy Land

The Crusades didn't get off to much of a start. The thousands of hungry, ill-supplied peasants who had joined the People's Crusade were neither trained nor organized, and they were quickly massacred once they set foot into Seljuk Turk territory. But the roughly 7,000 knights of the Princes' Crusade managed to capture Antioch, north of Jerusalem, in 1098. The following year, the crusading army—about 1,500 knights, supported by some 12,000 men-at-arms—reached Jerusalem, which it captured after a brief siege. The crusaders capped their victory by massacring men, women, and children of all faiths in all sections of the holy city. They set up the Kingdom of Jerusalem, which they ran as a Christian fiefdom until it fell to Saladin and his Arabian armies in 1187.

Echoes Through the Ages

The First Crusade set in motion a seesaw battle between the Christian west and the Islamic east that lasted another two centuries. As chunks of the Holy Land fell to one army or another, Urban's successor popes used the Crusades as a way to unite Europe. But the Crusades, and the orgies of blood they incited, left a bitter legacy. The rancor that the Crusades caused among both Christians and Muslims has persisted to this day, and even now the word "crusader" evokes very different feelings among Westerners and Middle Easterners.

How Long Was the Hundred Years' War?

Although a monumental medieval-era struggle between England and France lasted more than 100 years, the actual fighting took only a fraction of that period. So how long did the war really last? It depends how you do the math.

✳ ✳ ✳ ✳

King of England, King of France

THE HUNDRED YEARS' War started in 1337 when a legal dispute over the French crown turned violent. English nobles believed that their king, Edward III, was next in line to rule France because his mother was sister to French King Charles IV, who had no direct male heir. French nobles, uneasy at the idea of an English king of France, disagreed. Their choice was nobleman Philip of Valois, who claimed that his own lineage from a 13th-century French king—through his father—gave him the more legitimate claim to the throne.

Valois's ships raided English ports, and Edward invaded French territory. The hostility was rooted in the time after Charles IV died in early 1328, when Valois was crowned Philip VI. Philip attacked Edward's forces in Aquitaine, a region in France long ruled by England. Many English invasions of France followed, with the English—whose claims to French lands dated to 1066—repeatedly gaining ground and the French repeatedly striking back.

Peace Breaks Out

Although successive English kings steadfastly claimed the right to rule France, England lacked the resources for non-stop fighting over many decades. It had other conflicts to deal with—military campaigns in Ireland, for example—and domestic strife such as the 1399 coup when Henry Bolingbroke stole the English crown from his cousin Richard II and became Henry IV.

France, meanwhile, fought other battles, too—including rebellious outbreaks by French nobles against the crown. Out of necessity, both sides agreed to long truces with one another. For example, peace erupted in 1360 and lasted nine placid years.

Sometimes the warring royal families cemented a truce with intermarriage. In 1396, England's Richard II married the child princess Isabelle, a daughter of French king Charles VI. Twenty-four years later, England's Henry V married Isabelle's little sister Catherine as part of a treaty he imposed on the French after his crushing victory at the battle of Agincourt in 1415 and after another successful campaign in 1417–1419.

The Culmination

Although English invaders won major territorial concessions from the French over most of the war's duration, the tide turned in France's favor in 1429. That was when the peasant girl Joan of Arc rallied French forces and freed the city of Orléans from an English siege. The next 23 years saw the most intense fighting of the Hundred Years' War, culminating with a French victory at the Battle of Castillon in 1453. England lost all of its lands on the European continent except for the port city of Calais.

The English didn't give up their claim to France for centuries—but with a civil conflict called the Wars of the Roses breaking out at home, they stopped attacking their continental neighbor. The Hundred Years' War was over, after 116 years. It's correct to say that the war lasted well over a century. However, it's just about impossible to subtract all the lulls and truces with accuracy. If you could, you would come out with fewer than 100 years of war.

What Were the Wars of the Roses?

Power—not flowers—was at stake in the Wars of the Roses, a series of battles and skirmishes between two branches of England's royal family. The Lancaster clan had the throne, and the York clan wanted it. Then the tables turned and turned again.

✳ ✳ ✳ ✳

A Family Feud

ONE DRAWBACK OF monarchies is that they often lead to quarrels over whose turn it is to sit on the throne. Brother turns against brother, son against father, and so on. More than 500 years ago, such a disagreement between noble cousins grew into a squabble that split England's ruling class into armed camps and repeatedly tore up the countryside.

The House of Lancaster and the House of York were branches of the royal Plantagenet family, descendants of King Edward III, who ruled from 1327 to 1377. The Wars of the Roses began in 1399, when Henry of Bolingbroke, a grandson of Edward III, ended the disastrous reign of his cousin, Richard II, and took the throne himself. Also known as the Duke of Lancaster, the new king, now Henry IV, founded the Lancastrian Dynasty. He passed his scepter down to son Henry V, who in turn passed it to his then nine-month-old son, Henry VI in 1422.

The Yorkist Claim

Lancastrian heirs might have continued this streak indefinitely, but pious Henry VI preferred the spiritual realm of prayer to his worldly kingdom, which sorely needed leadership. Worse, the king developed a mental disorder resulting in periodic breakdowns.

After Henry VI lapsed into temporary insanity in 1453, the powerful Earl of Warwick appointed the Duke of York to fill in as the protector of the realm. York, an able leader, was also a descendent of Edward III and boasted a family tree that arguably made him a better claimant to the crown than the sitting king.

York earned the fierce enmity of the queen, Margaret of Anjou, who wielded more actual power than her husband did and who feared York would steal the throne. Battles ensued, beginning in 1455, with York defeating the royal forces more than once. In 1460, Lancastrian forces killed York in a sneak attack. The Yorkist cause passed to his 18-year-old son, Edward, who won a decisive battle, ran King Henry and Queen Margaret out of the country, and had himself crowned Edward IV in 1461.

The wars went on, however, as the new king clashed with his father's old supporter, the Earl of Warwick. For a time, Warwick got the upper hand and put addled King Henry back on the throne. Edward prevailed in 1471, however, and maintained order until his death in 1483.

The Fight Resumes and Ends

Edward IV's young son briefly succeeded him as Edward V, but the boy's uncle, brother of the late king, appears to have pulled a fast one. The uncle pushed little Eddie aside and became Richard III, one of England's most notorious monarchs. His notoriety is based on the widespread belief that Richard III murdered his two defenseless young nephews—Edward V and a younger brother.

For that reason and others, Richard lost the backing of many nobles, who flocked to support another royal claimant, Henry Tudor, the Earl of Richmond. A Welshman, this new contender also descended from Edward III on the Lancaster side.

Tudor famously killed Richard III in battle and became Henry VII, founder of England's Tudor Dynasty. He married the Yorkist heiress, the late Edward IV's daughter Elizabeth, in 1485, consolidating the family claim and ending, finally, the Wars of the Roses.

How Did Europe Divvy Up the New World?

Initially, it was quite simple: The pope decided who got what. In 1493—one year after Christopher Columbus's first voyage—the largely Catholic kingdoms of Spain and Portugal were the only European players in the New World. Other countries were decades away from investigating the strange land; the Pilgrims wouldn't arrive at Plymouth Rock for more than a century.

※　※　※　※

FERDINAND AND ISABELLA of Spain had financed Columbus's voyage and figured that they had an obvious claim to the lands he had discovered. But Portugal's King John II disagreed. He cited the 14-year-old Treaty of Alcaçovas, drafted when Portugal was exploring the coast of Africa. The treaty, which Spain had signed, gave Portugal all lands south of the Canary Islands. The New World was south of the Canaries, so it belonged to Portugal. Columbus, according to John, was trespassing on his land.

Isabella and Ferdinand of Spain were indignant. They brought up a law that dated back to the Crusades that said Christian rulers could seize control of any heathen land in order to spread the Catholic faith. So there. Rather than go to war, they asked the pope to resolve the issue because, frankly, Portugal had a big, powerful navy and Spain did not. (No one bothered to ask the native people in the New World what they had to say about this, in case you're wondering.)

Pope Alexander VI, of the infamous Borgia family, drew a line from the North Pole to the South Pole, one hundred leagues west of the Cape Verde Islands, which was the site of a Portuguese colony. Portugal received every heathen land east of that line: the Azores, the Canary Islands, Africa (including Madagascar), and Saudi Arabia. Years later, explorers found that the north-south line went right through South America; this gave Portugal a chunk of that continent as well. That's why most Brazilians speak Portuguese to this day.

Spain got everything to the west of the pope's line. In 1494, when the treaty was signed at Tordesillas, no one realized that the majority of two huge continents sat in Spain's portion. Isabella and Ferdinand thought that they were getting only the puny Caribbean islands that Columbus had spotted. In fact, they were upset and felt cheated, but the pope's decision was final.

At least for a while. A later treaty changed the line, and then the British, French, Russians, and Dutch got in on the action and began claiming parts of the New World for themselves. The Treaty of Tordesillas was forgotten.

What Really Happened at the First Thanksgiving?

Most people were taught that Thanksgiving originated with the Pilgrims when they invited local Native Americans to celebrate the first successful harvest. Here's what really happened.

✳ ✳ ✳ ✳

THERE ARE ONLY two original accounts of the event we think of as the first Thanksgiving, both very brief. In the fall of 1621, the Pilgrims, having barely survived their first arduous year, managed to bring in a modest harvest. They celebrated with a traditional English harvest feast that included food, dancing, and games. The local Wampanoag Indians were there, and both groups demonstrated their skill at musketry and archery.

So that was the first Thanksgiving, right? Not exactly. To the Pilgrims, a thanksgiving day was a special religious holiday that consisted of prayer, fasting, and praise—not at all like the party atmosphere that accompanied a harvest feast.

Our modern Thanksgiving, which combines the concepts of harvest feast and a day of thanksgiving, is actually a 19th-century development. In the decades after the Pilgrims, national days of thanksgiving were decreed on various occasions, and some states celebrated a Thanksgiving holiday annually. But there was no recurring national holiday until 1863, when a woman named Sarah Josepha Hale launched a campaign for an annual celebration that would "greatly aid and strengthen public harmony of feeling."

Such sentiments were sorely needed in a nation torn apart by the Civil War. So, in the aftermath of the bloody Battle of Gettysburg, President Lincoln decreed a national day of thanksgiving that would fall on the last Thursday in November, probably to coincide with the anniversary of the Pilgrims' landing at Plymouth. The date was later shifted to the fourth Thursday in November, simply to give retailers a longer Christmas shopping season.

What Was the Boston Tea Party All About?

We've all learned that our colonial forebears helped touch off the American Revolution by turning Boston Harbor into a big tea caddy to protest "taxation without representation." In fact, wealthy smugglers set the whole thing up.

✳   ✳   ✳   ✳

IS THE ORIGINAL not a great tale of democracy? Angry patriots, righteously fed up with burdensome taxes and British oppression, seize a British ship and spoil the cargo. In reality, there's much more to the story.

The Backdrop

This tale begins with the 1765 Stamp Act, eight years before the start of the Revolution. Because it cost Britain money to defend the colonies, the king wanted help paying the bill. This would happen through tax stamps, similar to modern postage stamps, required on various documents, printed materials, goods, etc. For the same reason that proclaiming "I will raise taxes" is the same as saying "Don't elect me" twelve generations later, this caused an outcry. Then, as now, most Americans would rather part with their lifeblood than pay an extra dime in taxes.

The colonists resorted to various forms of terrorism. Mobs tarred and feathered government officials, burned them in effigy, and torched their homes and possessions. Within months, the horrified British gave up on the Stamp Act fiasco.

What's the Price of Tea?

Next the British tried the Townshend Act (1767), imposing customs duties and hoping the average citizen wouldn't notice. Tea, much loved in the colonies, was among the taxed imports. Of course, Britain lacked the resources to patrol the entire colonial coastline against enterprising Dutch smugglers, who snuck shiploads of tea past customs officials. Seeing opportunity, clever colonial businessmen bought and distributed smuggled tea; like teen-clothing branders two centuries later, they marketed their product by associating it with defiant rebellion. It worked: Colonials boycotted legally imported tea, often refusing to let it be unloaded from ships.

The Boston Massacre of 1770 (a shooting incident that escalated from heckling and a snowball fight) didn't help. The British realized that the Townshend Act wasn't working, but they maintained the tea tax as a symbol of authority. The British East India Company (aka John Company), which monopolized the importation of Indian tea to America, was losing a lot of money. In response, Parliament passed the 1773 Tea Act, which relaxed customs duties and allowed John Company to bypass costly London middlemen. It was a brilliant idea: John Company could unload ruinously vast inventories of tea while pacifying the tax-hating, bargain-hunting colonials.

Tea and Cakes in the Harbor

In November 1773, three British merchant ships anchored in Boston Harbor with the first loads of tea. Amid much social brouhaha, the smugglers roused mobs that prevented the tea from being unloaded. But by December 16, it was clear that the ships would land their tea the next day.

One group of protesters fortified itself with lots of liquor, dressed up in "Indian" costumes, and staggered toward the wharf in an outrage. Those who didn't fall into the water along the way boarded the British ships and began dragging the cargo up from the holds, cracking open designated cases, and heaving tea leaves into the water. By the end of the night, approximately 45 tons of tea had been dumped overboard, and tea leaves washed up on Boston shores for weeks.

Afterward, the Sons of Liberty wandered home, proud of their patriotic accomplishment. Similar tea "parties" occurred in other colonial ports. The colonies had successfully impugned King George III and maintained a healthy business climate for smugglers.

Who Cracked the Liberty Bell?

The Liberty Bell is one of the most enduring symbols of America. It draws millions of tourists to its home in Philadelphia each year. Yet for all of its historical resonance, anybody who has seen it will attest that it looks kind of cruddy, due mostly to the enormous crack that runs down its side. Whom can we blame for the destruction of this national treasure?

✳ ✳ ✳ ✳

A QUICK SURVEY OF the Liberty Bell's rich history shows that it has been fraught with problems since it was struck. The original bell, which was constructed by British bell-founder Lester & Pack, arrived in Philadelphia in 1752. Unfortunately, it cracked upon its very first tolling—an inauspicious beginning for a future national monument. Disgruntled Philadelphians called upon two local foundry workers, John Pass and John Stow, to recast the bell, with firm instructions to make it less brittle. The artisans did as they were told, but the new bell was so thick and heavy that the sound of it tolling resembled that of an ax hitting a tree. Pass and Stow were told to try again, and finally, in June 1753, the bell that we see today was hung in the Pennsylvania State House (later called Independence Hall).

Of course, in those days, it wasn't known as the Liberty Bell. It got that nickname about seventy-five years later, when abolitionists adopted its inscription—PROCLAIM LIBERTY THROUGHOUT ALL THE LAND UNTO ALL THE INHABITANTS THEREOF—as a rallying cry for the antislavery movement. By that time, the bell was already an important part of the American mythos, having been rung in alarm to announce the onset of the Revolutionary War after the skirmishes at Lexington and Concord, and in celebration when independence was proclaimed in 1776.

Exactly when the crack happened is a matter of debate amongst historians, though experts have been able to narrow it down to between 1817 and 1846. There are several possible dates that are offered by the National Park Service, which is charged with caring for the bell (though it obviously wasn't charged with this task soon enough). The bell may have been cracked:

* in 1824, when it tolled to celebrate French Revolutionary War hero Marquis de Lafayette's visit to Philadelphia,

* in 1828, while ringing to honor the passage of the Catholic Emancipation Act in England, or

* in 1835, while ringing during the funeral procession of statesman and justice John Marshall.

All of these theories, however, are discounted by numerous contemporary documents—such as newspaper reports and town-hall meeting minutes—that discuss the bell without mentioning the crack. In fact, the first actual reference to the Liberty Bell being cracked occurred in 1846, when the Philadelphia newspaper *Public Ledger* noted that in order for the bell to be rung in honor of George Washington's birthday that year, a crack had to first be repaired. The newspaper states that the bell had cracked "long before," though in an article published several years later, "long before" is specified as having been during the autumn of 1845, a matter of a few months.

Unfortunately, the paper gives no explanation as to how the bell cracked or who did it. Nor does it explain something that, when confronted by the crack in the bell, many viewers ignore: Not only were the bell-makers fairly shoddy craftsmen, they were also terrible spellers. In the inscription, the name of the state in which the bell resides is spelled "Pensylvania."

What Was America's First Foreign War?

Ever wonder why the U.S. Marines will fight their country's battles "to the shores of Tripoli"? Here's the answer.

❋ ❋ ❋ ❋

ON NOVEMBER 26, 1804, William Eaton, acting as an agent for the U.S. government, disembarked from the brig *USS Argus* at Rosetta, Egypt, to find Hamet Karamanli, the former ruler of Tripoli and leader of the Barbary pirates. A few years earlier, Hamet had been deposed in a coup and ultimately replaced by his brother Yusuf Karamanli. Eaton wanted Hamet to become the ostensible leader of an expedition to overthrow Yusuf, whose pirates had captured the frigate *USS Philadelphia* and its crew. The small U.S. Mediterranean Squadron was spread too thin, and the ships could never fight their way past the hundreds of guns guarding the port of Tripoli, so the town had to be taken by land. And Eaton needed to produce an army to do that.

Unsafe at Sea

For hundreds of years Britain, France, and Spain had been paying protection money to the Barbary pirates to leave their ships alone. The United States, now independent from Britain and no longer under its system of payments, became fair game. In 1785, after the merchant ships *Maria* and *Dauphin* were captured by swift pirate raiders, America suddenly became aware that there was a problem. American preachers and journalists thundered about "dark-skinned monsters holding Americans as slaves" (conveniently ignoring the fact that Americans held many thousand slaves of their own). Captured sailors of all nations wound up in the dungeons of Tripoli, Tunis, and Algiers, including Miguel de Cervantes, author of *Don Quixote*, who spent five years as a Barbary captive in the late 16th century.

Secretary of State Thomas Jefferson thought the United States had but three choices: Pay tribute to the pirates like the European countries (which he didn't favor); forbid American vessels to sail in the Mediterranean (which he couldn't enforce); or go to war (which he preferred). But in this case, Jefferson's preferences weren't taken into account. Instead, Congress allocated $40,000 to ransom the captives and $100,000 a year in payment. Apparently the pirates thought they could do better raiding, because they refused the offer.

Representative Robert Goodloe Harper made a stirring promise to spend "millions for defense, but not one cent for tribute," and Congress authorized $688,888.82 for the construction of six frigates, but an agreement on tribute was reached nonetheless. America would pay the pirates a large ransom (more than a million dollars) and yearly tribute. It was expensive and embarrassing, but cheaper than a full-scale war. America had a rich merchant fleet to protect.

This Means War

By 1797, John Adams had become president and all of the American captives had either died in prison or been released. For four years there was relative peace. Then, near the end of Adams's term, Yusuf Karamanli decided that the Americans weren't paying enough and declared war on the United States. That was fine with most Americans, who were fed up with paying tribute. Jefferson became president in 1801, and he saw America's fight with the Barbary pirates as a test of the young nation's mettle. He sent a six-ship squadron to the Mediterranean under Commodore Edward Preble.

Those six ships had to patrol more than 1,200 miles of coastline, a nearly impossible task. This was made more difficult when the frigate *Philadelphia* ran aground off Tripoli and was captured in October 1803. Something had to be done—such a warship could not be left in the hands of pirates.

On the night of February 16, 1804, Lieutenant Stephen Decatur led a raiding party, armed with cutlasses and tomahawks, into Tripoli harbor in small boats. He and his crew annihilated the Tripolitan prize crew and burned the *Philadelphia*—a feat that Britain's Admiral Nelson called "the most daring act of the age." But the biggest problem remained—the crew of the *Philadelphia* and Americans from other ships were still in the dungeons of Tripoli.

The American captives couldn't just wait out the war. While those with exploitable talents were treated well, most were tortured and forced to do hard labor. A favorite method of torture was the bastinado, where a captive was beaten on the soles of his feet, a tremendously painful punishment. Men were dying, committing suicide, or converting to Islam and fighting for Yusuf.

Rescue Party

Back in Egypt, Eaton managed to scrape together 90 of Hamet's followers, joined by 50 Greek mercenary soldiers, 20 Italian gunners, and a fire-eating Englishman named Farquhar. About 300 Bedouin Arab cavalry completed the local contingent.

Eaton wanted to include 100 U.S. Marines from the fleet, now commanded by Captain Samuel Barron, but Barron refused. In the end, the only Americans who took part were Eaton, Lieutenant Presley O'Bannon of the marines with a sergeant and a few enlisted soldiers, and Midshipman Pascal Paoli Peck, U.S. Navy. So the sum total of marines going to "the shores of Tripoli" was ten.

On March 5, 1805, the expedition set off across the desert. Lacking most necessary equipment (such as water bottles), they stumbled into Bomba on April 15. They had been 25 days without meat and 15 days without bread. For two days, they'd eaten nothing at all. Smoke signals brought the USS *Argus*, which had ample provisions and one of two promised cannons.

The Battle of Derna

They set off for Derna, arriving on April 26. When an attempt to negotiate with the governor of the town brought the response "your head or mine," Eaton attacked.

After some hours, during which his force took casualties and had its one cannon put out of action, Eaton decided on an all-out assault. Brandishing a sword and leading his force, Eaton swept through the barricades and took the town. Resistance collapsed, and the governor took refuge within his harem. It wasn't Tripoli, but it was close enough. Yusuf agreed to release American captives and leave American ships alone. The war was finally over.

In addition to the "Shores of Tripoli," there is one other lasting legacy of the Tripolitan War. To this day, when a marine officer is commissioned, he proudly receives a Mameluke saber like the one presented to the valiant Lieutenant O'Bannon by Hamet Karamanli.

Why Are We Supposed to Remember the Alamo?

The average three-year-old in Texas can probably tell you about the Alamo, complete with names, dates, and cool sound effects. But it's understandable if the details are a little hazy for the rest of us. We have our own state histories to worry about.

✳ ✳ ✳ ✳

THE ALAMO BEGAN as a Roman Catholic mission called Misión San Antonio de Valero, which was established by the Spanish in the early 18th century to convert Native Americans to Christianity. The missionaries moved out in 1793, and nine years later, a Spanish cavalry company moved in, turning it into a fort that it called the Alamo (after Alamo de Parras, the city in Mexico that had been the company's home base). When the Mexican War of Independence ended in 1821, Mexican soldiers had control of all of San Antonio, including the Alamo, and they built up the fort's defenses.

But no one cares if you remember any of this stuff. You're supposed to remember the Alamo because of what happened there during the Texas Revolution. This was a conflict between the Mexican government and the Texians—people who had moved to Mexican territory from the United States. The Texians chafed under the government of Mexican president General Antonio López de Santa Anna Pérez de Lebrón (or Santa Anna to his friends), who was trying to assert more central control over the region. The Texians rebelled against this crackdown and took control of San Antonio and the Alamo, among other places.

A Desperate Situation

On February 23, 1836, General Santa Anna and thousands of soldiers showed up to reclaim the Alamo. William Travis, the commander of the Texian insurgents who held the Alamo, sent messengers out to request help from surrounding communities. He got only 32 more volunteers, bringing his fighting force up to about 200 men. Though they were clearly outnumbered, Travis and his men decided that they would rather die than surrender the fort. They held out for 13 days, but in a final assault on March 6, Santa Anna's soldiers took control of the fort and killed Travis and all of his men.

Remember the Alamo!

The defeat infuriated the Texian revolutionaries and strengthened their resolve. Two months later at the Battle of San Jacinto, Texian soldiers led by General Sam Houston shouted, "Remember the Alamo!" as they charged into the fray. The rebels defeated the Mexican army, captured Santa Anna, and won Texas its independence. "Remember the Alamo!" became a rallying cry, and the battle went down in history as a tale of brave men standing their ground against terrible odds.

The resulting Republic of Texas was short-lived and unstable, thanks in part to continued skirmishes with the Mexican army. On December 29, 1845, Texas became a U.S. state, and it wasn't long before Mexico and the United States were embroiled in the Mexican-American War. But that's another story for another book.

Why Didn't the Irish Eat Stuff Other Than Potatoes During the Great Famine?

More than a million people starved to death in Ireland from 1845 to 1851, but only one crop failed: the potato. How could this have killed so many? Why didn't the Irish just eat other stuff?

✳   ✳   ✳   ✳

As Usual, the Poor Get the Shaft

THE REASON THE Great Famine, as it is dubbed, took such a toll is simple: Those who starved were poor. For generations, the impoverished in Ireland had survived by planting potatoes to feed their families. They had nothing else. Ireland's wealthy landowners grew a wide variety of crops, but these were shipped away and sold for profit. Most of the rich folks didn't care that the poor starved.

How did things get so bad? Irish History 101: The Catholics and the Protestants didn't like each other, and neither did the English and the Irish. Back then, the wealthy landowners were mostly Protestants from England, while the poor were Catholic peasants. The Irish peasants grew their food on small parcels of land that were rented from the hated English.

In the 16th century, a hitherto unknown item crossed the Atlantic from Peru, originally arriving in England and finally getting to Ireland in 1590: the potato. Spuds grew well in Ireland, even on the rocky, uneven plots that were often rented by peasants, and they quickly became the peasants' main food source. Potatoes required little labor to grow, and an acre could yield twelve tons of them—enough to feed a family of six for the entire year, with leftovers for the animals.

We think of potatoes as a fattening food, but they're loaded with vitamins, carbohydrates, and even some protein. Add a little fish and buttermilk to the diet, and a family could live quite happily on potatoes. Potatoes for breakfast, lunch, and dinner might sound monotonous, but it fueled a population boom in Ireland. By the 19th century, three million people were living on the potato diet.

Nature's Wrath

In 1845, though, the fungus *Phytophthora infestans*, or "late blight," turned Ireland's potatoes into black, smelly, inedible lumps. Impoverished families had no options, no Plan B. Their pitiful savings were wiped out, and they fled to the work houses—the only places where they could get food and shelter in return for their labor.

When the potato crop failed again the next year, and every year through 1849, people began dying in earnest—not just from starvation, but from scurvy and gangrene (caused by a lack of vitamin C), typhus, dysentery, typhoid fever, and heart failure. Overwhelmed and underfunded, the work houses closed their doors. Many people who were weakened by hunger died of exposure after being evicted from their homes. To top the disaster off, a cholera epidemic spread during the last year of the blight, killing thousands more.

The exact number of those who perished is unknown, but it's believed to be between one and two million. In addition, at least a million people left the country, and many of these wayward souls died at sea. All during that terrible time, plenty of food existed in Ireland, but it was consumed by the wealthy. The poor, meanwhile, had nothing. They were left to starve.

What Did Custer Stand For in His Last Stand?

Gold and his own ego, mostly. Custer's Last Stand (aka the Battle of Little Bighorn) was the culmination of years of hostility between the United States government and the Sioux tribe.

✳ ✳ ✳ ✳

The Wild, Wild West

CUSTER'S LAST STAND, the legendary designation for the Battle of Little Bighorn, occurred during the climax of the Indian Wars of the 1860s and '70s, when the U.S. government corralled the western Native American tribes onto small reservations. In the 1860s, the U.S. Army battled the Sioux and other tribes in the Dakota and Wyoming territories for control of the Bozeman Trail, a path that passed through Sioux buffalo-hunting grounds to gold mines in Montana. The government abandoned the effort in 1868 and negotiated the Fort Laramie Treaty, which gave the Sioux, Cheyenne, and Arapaho tribes ownership of much of what is now South Dakota.

Then in 1874, Lieutenant Colonel George Armstrong Custer led an expedition to the area to find a suitable location for an army post and to investigate rumors of gold. He verified that there was gold in the Black Hills, on Native American land. The government tried to buy back the land, but renegade Sioux who refused to abide by U.S. regulations blocked the sale. The government issued an ultimatum that all Sioux warriors and hunters report to reservation agency outposts by a certain date;

failure to comply would be viewed as an act of hostility.

When the renegade Sioux warriors ignored the order, the army mounted a campaign to round them up and force them into designated areas on the reservation. Brigadier General Alfred Terry led the campaign, and Custer commanded one of the regiments, the Seventh Cavalry. At the time, Custer was already a Civil War hero known for his reckless yet successful military campaigns. Terry ordered Custer to lead his regiment to the south of the presumed Sioux location and wait until Terry positioned the rest of the soldiers to the north; this way, they could advance simultaneously from both sides.

But on June 25, 1876, Custer came across a Sioux village in the Valley of Little Bighorn and decided to attack it by himself. Against the advice of his officers, he divided his regiment into three groups: one to scout the bluffs overlooking the valley; one to start the attack on the upper end of the village; and one—made up of 210 men, including Custer—to attack from the lower end of the village.

Bad plan. As many as three thousand Sioux and Cheyenne men (many more than Custer had expected) forced the first group of soldiers into retreat, and then they turned their full attention to Custer and his men, killing every last one in less than an hour. News reports right after the incident said that Custer's actions were the result of foolish pride. But before long, he had morphed into a heroic figure, one who fueled outrage against the Native Americans in the West.

Drawings and paintings depicting the battle, usually titled "Custer's Last Fight" or "Custer's Last Stand," kept the battle fresh in people's minds for decades to follow. "Stand," in the military terminology of the day, meant simply the act of opposing an enemy rather than retreating or yielding. Custer definitely stood for that, if nothing else.

How Were the World's Great Canals Built?

The construction of great canals such as Suez and Panama cost vast amounts of money and required incredible feats of engineering to link seas and oceans with only a few miles of artificial waterway. But it sure beat sailing thousands of miles around entire continents.

✳ ✳ ✳ ✳

IN SEPTEMBER 1513, Vasco Núñez de Balboa left the Spanish colony of Darién on the Caribbean coast of the narrow Panamanian isthmus to climb the highest mountain in the area—literally, to see what he could see. Upon reaching the summit, he gazed westward and became the first European to see the eastern shores of the vast Pacific Ocean.

From there, he led a party of conquistadors toward his discovery. They labored up and down rugged ridges and hacked their way through relentless, impenetrable jungle, sweating bullets under their metal breastplates the entire way. It took four days for Balboa and his men to complete the 40-mile trek to the beach.

Of course, Balboa's journey would have been much easier if someone had built the Panama Canal beforehand.

For 2,500 years, civilizations have carved canals through bodies of land to make water transportation easier, faster, and cheaper. History's first great navigational canal was built in Egypt by the Persian emperor Darius I between 510 and 520 B.C., linking the Nile and the Red Sea. A generation later, the Chinese began their reign as the world's greatest canal builders, a distinction they would hold for 1,000 years—until the Europeans began building canals using technology developed centuries earlier during the construction of the world's longest artificial waterway: the 1,100-mile Grand Canal of China.

Here's a brief look at three great canals.

The Erie Canal—Clinton's Big Ditch

At the turn of the 19th century, the United States was bursting at its seams, and Americans were eyeing new areas of settlement west of the Appalachians. However, westward overland routes were slow and the cost of moving goods along them was exorbitant.

The idea of building a canal linking the Great Lakes with the eastern seaboard as a way of opening the West had been floated since the mid-1700s. It finally became more than wishful thinking in 1817, when construction of the Erie Canal began.

Citing its folly and $7-million price tag, detractors labeled the canal "Clinton's Big Ditch" in derisive reference to its biggest proponent, New York governor Dewitt Clinton. When completed in 1825, however, the Erie Canal was hailed as the "Eighth Wonder of the World," cutting 363 miles through thick forest and swamp to link Lake Erie at Buffalo with the Hudson River at Albany. Sadly though, more than 1,000 workers died during its construction, primarily from swamp-borne diseases.

The Erie Canal fulfilled its promise, becoming a favored pathway for the great migration westward, slashing transportation costs a whopping 95 percent, and bringing unprecedented prosperity to the towns along its route.

The Suez Canal—Grand Triumph

The centuries-old dream of a canal linking the Mediterranean and the Red Sea became reality in 1859 when French diplomat Ferdinand de Lesseps stuck the first shovel in the ground to commence building of the Suez Canal.

Over the next ten years, 2.4 million laborers would toil—and 125,000 would die—to move 97 million cubic yards of earth and build a 100-mile Sinai shortcut that made the 10,000-mile sea journey from Europe around Africa to India redundant.

De Lesseps convinced an old friend, Egypt's King Said, to grant him a concession to build and operate the canal for 99 years. French investors eagerly bankrolled three-quarters of the 200 million francs ($50 million) needed for the project. Said had to kick in the rest to keep the project afloat because others, particularly the British, rejected it as financial lunacy—seemingly justified when the canal's final cost rang in at double the original estimate.

The Suez dramatically expanded world trade by significantly reducing sailing time and cost between east and west. De Lesseps had been proven right and was proclaimed the world's greatest canal digger. The British, leery of France's new back-door to their Indian empire, spent the next 20 years trying to wrest control of the Suez from their imperial rival.

The Panama Canal—Spectacular Failure

When it came time to build the next great canal half a world away in Panama, everyone turned to de Lesseps to dig it.

But here de Lesseps was in over his head. Suez was a walk in the park compared to Panama. In the Suez, flat land at sea level had allowed de Lesseps to build a lockless channel. A canal in Panama, however, would have to slice through the multiple elevations of the Continental Divide.

Beginning in 1880, de Lesseps, ignoring all advice, began a nine-year effort to dig a sea-level canal through the mountains. This futile strategy, combined with financial mismanagement and the death of some 22,000 workers from disease and land-slides, killed de Lesseps's scheme. Panama had crushed the hero of Suez.

The Panama Canal—Success!

The idea of a Panama canal, however, persevered. In 1903, the United States, under the expansionist, big-stick leadership of Theodore Roosevelt, bought out the French and assumed control of the project. Using raised-lock engineering and disease-control methods that included spraying oil on mosquito breeding grounds to eliminate malaria and yellow fever, the Americans completed the canal in 1914.

The Panama Canal made sailing from New York to San Francisco a breeze. A trip that once covered 14,000 miles while circumnavigating South America was now a mere 6,000-mile pleasure cruise.

What Happened to Russia's Imperial Family?

The fate of Russia's imperial family remained shrouded in mystery for nearly a century.

✳ ✳ ✳ ✳

The End of a Dynasty

IN THE WAKE of Russia's 1917 uprisings, Tsar Nicholas II abdicated his shaky throne. He was succeeded by a provisional government, which included Nicholas and his family—his wife, Tsarina Alexandra; his four daughters, Grand Duchesses Olga, Tatiana, Maria, and Anastasia; and his 13-year-old son, Tsarevich Alexei—under house arrest.

When the radical Bolshevik party took power in October 1917, its soldiers seized the royal family and eventually moved them to the Ural Mountain town of Yekaterinburg, where they were held prisoner in the home of a wealthy metallurgist. As civil war waged between the "White" and "Red" factions in Russia, the Bolsheviks worried that the White Army might try to free the royal family and use its members as a rallying point. When White troops neared Yekaterinburg in July 1918, the local executive committee decided to kill Nicholas II and his family.

The bedraggled imperial family was rudely awakened by their captors in the middle of the night. Sounds of battle echoed not far from the spacious home that had become their makeshift prison, and the prisoners were ordered to take shelter in the basement. Outside the basement, a waiting truck revved its engine.

After a long wait, the head jailer reappeared, brandishing a pistol and backed by ten men armed with rifles and pistols. He declared, "Because your relatives in Europe carry on their war against Soviet Russia, the Executive Committee of the Ural has decided to execute you." Raising his revolver, he fired into Tsar Nicholas II's chest as his family watched in horror.

With that shot, the militia opened fire. Bullets ricocheted around the room as family members dove for cover, trying to escape the deadly fusillade. None made it. The wounded children who clung to life after the firing stopped were dragged into the open and set upon with rifle butts and bayonets until all lay quiet. Tsar Nicholas II, the last of the Romanov emperors, died alongside his beloved family.

A Bungled Disposal of Bodies

After the murders, the bodies were taken into the nearby woods, stripped, and thrown into an abandoned mine pit. The corpses were visible above the pit's shallow waterline. Fearing the bodies would be discovered, the communist officials tried to burn them the following day. When that didn't work, they decided to move the bodies to a deeper mine pit farther down the road. The truck got stuck in deep mud on the way to the mines, so the men dug a shallow grave in the mud, buried the bodies, and covered them with acid, lime, and wooden planks, where they remained untouched until their discovery in 1979.

In his official report, the lead executioner, Yakov Yurovsky, stated that two of the bodies were buried and burned separately, giving rise to speculation that one or two of the Romanov children escaped the massacre. Several pretenders came forth claiming to be Tsarevich Alexei, heir to the Russian throne, and his sister Grand Duchess Maria. But the most famous of the "undead Romanovs" was young Anastasia.

Did Anastasia Survive?

Anastasia, the fourth daughter of Nicholas and Alexandra, was 17 at the time of the executions. At least ten women have stepped forward claiming to be the lost grand duchess. The most famous of these was the strange case of Anna Tchaikovsky.

Two years after the murders, Ms. Tchaikovsky—who was hospitalized in Berlin after an attempted suicide—claimed to be Anastasia. She explained that she had been wounded but survived the slaughter with the help of a compassionate Red Army soldier, who smuggled her out of Russia through Romania.

Anna bore a striking physical resemblance to the missing Anastasia, enough to convince several surviving relatives that she was indeed the last of the imperial family. She also revealed details that would be hard for an impostor to know—for instance, she knew of a secret meeting between Anastasia's uncle, the grand duke of Hesse, and Nicholas II in 1916, when the two men's countries were at war.

Other relatives, however, rejected Anna's claim, noting, among other things, that Anna Tchaikovsky refused to speak Russian (although she understood the language and would respond to Russian questions in other languages). A drawn-out German court case ended in 1970 with no firm conclusions.

Anna, later named Anna Anderson, died in 1984. It was not until DNA evidence became available in the 1990s that her claim to imperial lineage could finally be disproved.

The Romanov Ghosts

But what of the hidden remains?

After the location of the royal resting place was made public in 1979, nine skeletons were exhumed from the muddy pit. The bodies of the royal couple and three of their children—Olga, Tatiana, and Anastasia—were identified by DNA tests as Romanov family members. Their remains, as well as those of four servants who died with them, were interred in 1998 near Nicholas's imperial predecessors in St. Petersburg.

By all accounts, 11 people met their deaths that terrible night in July 1918. In late August 2007, two more sets of remains were found in a separate grave near Yekaterinburg. Based on results of DNA analysis that was completed in 2009, experts agree that the sets of remains were those of Tsarevich Alexei and Maria.

How Did American Women Get the Vote?

Between 1818 and 1820, Fanny Wright, a feminist from Scotland, lectured throughout the United States on such topics as voting rights for women, birth control, and equality between the sexes in education and marriage laws. Little did she know that it would take another 100 years for American women to achieve the right to vote on these issues.

❋ ❋ ❋ ❋

The Beginning

To be technical, Margaret Brent, a landowner in Maryland, was the very first woman in the United States to call for voting rights. In 1647, Brent insisted on two votes in the colonial assembly—one for herself and one for the man for whom she held power of attorney. The governor rejected her request.

Then there was Abigail Adams. In 1776, she wrote to her husband John, asking him to remember the ladies in the new code of laws he was drafting. She was summarily dismissed.

Almost half a century later, Fanny Wright showed up from Scotland. Although she recognized the gender inequities in the United States, she still fell in love with the country and became a naturalized citizen in 1825.

It wasn't until the 1840s, however, that the feminist ball really got rolling. Because progress was achieved in fits and spurts, women's suffrage eventually took the good part of a century after that to come to fruition.

The Middle

Before the Civil War, the women's suffrage movement and abolition organizations focused on many of the same issues. The two movements were closely linked in action and deed, specifically at the World Anti-Slavery Convention in London in 1840. However, female delegates to the convention, among them Lucretia Mott and Elizabeth Cady Stanton, were not allowed to participate in the activities because of their gender. London is a long way to travel to sit in the back of a room and be silent. Stanton and Mott resolved to organize a convention to discuss the rights of women.

The convention was finally held in 1848 in Seneca Falls, New York. Stanton presented her *Declaration of Sentiments*, the first formal action by women in the United States to advocate civil rights and suffrage.

Two groups formed at the end of the 1860s: the National Woman Suffrage Association (NWSA) and the American Woman Suffrage Association (AWSA). The NWSA, led by Susan B. Anthony and Stanton, worked to change voting laws on the federal level by way of an amendment to the U.S. Constitution. The AWSA, led by Lucy Stone and Julia Ward Howe, worked to change the laws on the state level. The two groups were united in 1890 and renamed the National American Woman Suffrage Association.

The End

In 1916, Alice Paul formed the National Woman's Party (NWP). Based on the idea that action, not words, would achieve the suffragists' mission, the NWP staged Silent Sentinels outside the White House during which NWP members held banners and signs that goaded the president. When

World War I came along, many assumed the Silent Sentinels would end. Instead, the protesters incorporated the current events into their messages and were ultimately arrested. Once the public got wind of the horrendous treatment the women were subjected to in jail, the public tide turned in their favor. In 1917, President Woodrow Wilson announced his support for a suffrage amendment. In the summer of 1920, Tennessee ratified the 19th Amendment—the 36th state to do so—and in August of that year, women gained the right to vote. It had certainly been a long time coming.

What Was World War I Called Before World War II?

We certainly don't name wars like we used to. Once, we had poetry in our conflicts. We had the Pastry War, the Wars of the Roses, and the War of the Oranges. We had the War of the Three Sanchos, the War of the Three Henries, and the War of the Eight Saints. We even had something called the War of Jenkins' Ear.

✳ ✳ ✳ ✳

As the 20th century dawned, this convention of applying sweet nicknames to wars—and everything else—was still going strong. Ty Cobb was given the moniker "The Georgia Peach." The 1904 World's Fair was not-so-humbly called "The Greatest of Expositions." It was an optimistic time. Advances in medicine were helping people live longer and Henry Ford's mass production of the automobile made the world seem smaller than ever.

This combination of optimism and the tradition of poetic nicknames led to some understandable debate in 1914, when an assassin's bullet felled Archduke Franz Ferdinand and launched Europe—and much of the world—into all-out war. For the next few years, Germans rampaged through the continent, looking rather silly in spiked hats; mustard gas (which is not nearly as delicious as it sounds) crippled and killed countless men and women; and all across Europe, an entire generation was slowly wiped out.

What to name this gruesome conflict? The journalists and historians went to work. A number of possibilities were discarded, including "The German War" and "The War of the Nations," before two names were settled upon, which are still used today in conjunction with World War I: "The Great War," which retains a simplistic elegance, and, more popularly, "The War to End All Wars."

Melodramatic? Yes. Full of hubris? Definitely. Remember, though, these were the same people who famously labeled the *Titanic* "unsinkable."

No, we don't name wars like we used to. But even if the stylistic flourishes of yore have mostly disappeared, it is comforting to know that we're still not above a little hubris and melodrama. Anyone remember "Mission Accomplished"?

Who Betrayed Anne Frank?

Anne Frank and her family thwarted Nazis for two years, hiding in Amsterdam. They might have remained hidden and waited out the war, but someone blew their cover.

✳ ✳ ✳ ✳

ANNELIES MARIE FRANK was born in Frankfurt am Main, Germany, on June 12, 1929. Perhaps the most well-known victim of the Holocaust, she was one of approximately 1.5 million Jewish children killed by the Nazis. Her diary chronicling her experience in Amsterdam was discovered in the Franks' secret hiding place by friends of the family and first published in 1947. Translated into more than 60 languages, *Anne Frank: The Diary of a Young Girl* has sold 30 million copies and is one of the most read books in the world.

The diary was given to Anne on her 13th birthday, just weeks before she went into hiding. Her father, Otto Frank, moved his family and four friends into a secret annex of rooms above his office at 263 Prinsengracht on July 6, 1942. They relied on trustworthy business associates, employees, and friends, who risked their own lives to help them. Anne poignantly wrote her thoughts, yearnings, and descriptions of life in the secret annex in her diary, revealing a vibrant, intelligent young woman struggling to retain her ideals in the direst of circumstances.

On August 4, 1944, four or five Dutch Nazi collaborators under the command of an Austrian Nazi police investigator entered the building and arrested the Franks and their friends. The family was deported to Auschwitz, where they were separated and sent to different camps. Anne and her sister, Margot, were sent to Bergen–Belsen, where they both died of typhus in 1945, a few weeks before liberation. Anne was 15 years old. Otto Frank was the only member of the group to survive the war.

Dutch police, Nazi hunters, and historians have attempted to identify who betrayed the Franks. Searching for clues, the Netherlands Institute for War Documentation (NIWD) has examined records on Dutch collaboration with the Nazis, the letters of Otto Frank, and police transcripts dating from the 1940s. The arresting Nazi officer was also questioned after the war by Nazi hunter Simon Wiesenthal, but he could not identify who informed on the Franks. For decades suspicion centered on Willem Van Maaren, who worked in the warehouse attached to the Franks' hiding place, but two police investigations found no evidence against him.

British author Carol Anne Lee believes it was Anton Ahlers, a business associate of Otto's who was a petty thief and a member of the Dutch Nazi movement. Lee argues that Ahlers informed the Nazis to collect the bounty paid to Dutch civilians who exposed Jews. She suggests he may have split the reward with Maarten Kuiper, a friend of Ahlers who was one of the Dutch Nazi collaborators who raided the secret annex. Ahlers was jailed for collaboration with the Nazis after the war, and members of his own family, including his son, have said they believe he was guilty of informing on the Franks.

Austrian writer Melissa Müller believes that a cleaning lady, Lena Hartog, who also worked in the warehouse, reported the Franks because she feared that if they were discovered, her husband, an employee of Otto Frank, would be deported for aiding Jews.

The NIWD has studied the arguments of both writers and examined the evidence supporting their theories. Noting that all the principals involved in the case are no longer living, it concluded that neither theory could be proved.

In 2016, the Anne Frank House museum published its own research suggesting that the Franks may have been uncovered by chance instead of being betrayed. Nazi officers investigating illegal work and/or ration fraud at the warehouse may have accidentally stumbled upon the Franks hiding in the annex.

Why Did the Nazis Keep a Record of the Holocaust?

The events of World War II were recorded to an extent far beyond that of preceding conflicts. Events were captured in print, photographs, and moving pictures. The most chilling of all was the exhaustive documentation of the Holocaust, much of it created by the very people who committed the crimes.

✳   ✳   ✳   ✳

KNOWLEDGE OF THE Holocaust stems from many sources, the most compelling of which are the eyewitness testimonies of victims. But there is another source that helps confirm the extermination's unthinkable scale, as well as the fates of individuals. That source is the accounts kept by the Nazis themselves.

Seized by the liberating armies in the last days of the war, the documentation exists in various collections, but the bulk of the records have been under the care of the Red Cross. The files are extensive: millions upon millions of papers covering 16 miles of shelves. So why would a group of people intent on murder risk putting their activities in writing?

The answer may be surprisingly prosaic. In the opinion of Paul Shapiro, director of Holocaust studies at the United States Holocaust Memorial Museum, "They wanted to show they were getting the job done." Many accounts suggest that he may be correct.

Just a Job: The Bureaucracy of the Devil

A stereotypical but not entirely inaccurate image of the prewar German government is one of bureaucracy. Everything was documented, and paper authorizations were generated by the handful for the most mundane of tasks. This attitude extended into the war. The task of running an empire, even a despicable one, is complex, requiring extensive procedures and paper trails. Like many governments, Nazi Germany employed an array of middle managers who wanted to prove their efficiency. The only way an official could show he was performing up to par was to keep records.

Prisoners who were immediately executed had the least documentation, sometimes being reduced to a mere entry in the number of arrivals for the day. Individuals who stayed in the camps longer typically had more comprehensive records. Because of the sheer number of people involved—some 17 million in all—some startling documents survived, such as the original list of Jews transferred to safety in the factories of Oskar Schindler. Another file contains the records of Anne Frank.

Why Worry?

For most of the war, the Nazis showed little compunction about documenting their activities. In their minds, why should they? To whom would they be accountable? After all, many thought the Third Reich would last a thousand years. In the closing months of the war, there was a slight reversal of this policy, and the commandants of some camps sought to destroy records and eliminate the remaining witnesses as the Allied forces closed in. Fortunately, they were not able to erase the record of their own atrocities.

Private memoirs of the Holocaust also exist. Participants at all levels wrote letters about their experiences, and some SS guards took photographs of the camps and inmates with their personal cameras. Some of the Nazi leadership was also prone to recording daily activities; Joseph Goebbels kept a journal throughout the war, viewing it as a "substitute for the confessional."

Much like Goebbels's diary, the official records of the Holocaust have become the unintentional confession of a Nazi machine that had uncountable crimes for which to answer. The archive exists in Bad Arolsen, Germany, and was opened to the online public in late 2006. Survivors of the camps hope that its presence serves as a counterargument to those who inexplicably deny that the Holocaust ever happened, and as a reminder that humankind must never allow it to happen again.

How Did the United Nations Start?

Countries from around the world come together to try to work out their differences at the United Nations in New York. How did this organization start? What was the impulse that made the world strive for international cooperation?

* * * *

THE UNITED NATIONS was officially born October 24, 1945, but it wasn't a new idea. Actually, an international peace-keeping organization was established after World War I. The 1919 Treaty of Versailles that ended that conflict created the League of Nations. American President Woodrow Wilson was one of the main backers of the League, but he couldn't win support for it from Congress, so the United States never joined its membership. When the League was unable to prevent World War II, it fell apart.

In January 1942, midway through the war, representatives from 26 nations fighting the Axis powers pledged to hold together until victory was achieved. President Franklin Roosevelt first coined the phrase *United Nations* to describe the group. The name became official when it was used in the title of *The Declaration by the United Nations*. Months earlier, Roosevelt and British Prime Minister Winston Churchill had secretly negotiated the Atlantic Charter, which set up principles for a postwar world. In the declaration, the Allies committed to follow those ideas. It also officially referred to the alliance as the United Nations Fighting Force, a rather inauspicious name for a group meant to abolish war and promote peace.

Organizing the War's Aftermath

Various configurations of Allies met in Tehran, Moscow, and Cairo throughout the war. In summer and fall 1944, representatives of four key Allied nations—the United States, the Republic of China, Great Britain, and the Soviet Union—gathered at the ten-acre Dumbarton Oaks estate in

Washington, D.C., to discuss and formulate the ground rules for an organization that would strive to maintain international peace and security. On April 25, 1945, San Francisco hosted representatives from 50 nations to draft a charter to that effect. On October 24, the charter was ratified by the five permanent Security Council members—those nations represented at the Dumbarton Oaks conference, with the addition of France—and endorsed by most of the additional signatories. Poland, which was invited but did not attend the conference, later signed the charter and brought the initial membership to 51 nations.

Continuing to Work Together

As of this writing, 193 member states represent virtually all recognized independent nations. The first session of the general assembly convened January 10, 1946, in the Westminster Central Hall in London under the auspices of acting Secretary-General Gladwyn Jebb, a prominent British diplomat. On February 1, Norway's Trygve Lie was chosen to be the United Nations' first secretary-general. The secretary-general is appointed for a renewable five-year term; to date no secretary-general has served more than two terms.

Today the United Nations is headquartered at an 18-acre site on New York's Manhattan Island. The land was purchased in 1946 through a donation from John D. Rockefeller Jr.; even though it's physically located in New York City, it is considered international territory. It recognizes six official languages—English, Arabic, Chinese, French, Russian, and Spanish—and is comprised of six principal operating organs: the General Assembly, the Security Council, the Economic and Social Council, the Secretariat, the International Court of Justice, and the Trusteeship Council. The General Assembly operates on a one-state-one-vote system, and a two-thirds majority is required to pass many resolutions. The organization, its specialized agencies, and staff have been honored with the Nobel Peace Prize many times.

What Was Project MKULTRA?

From the mid-1950s through at least the early 1970s, thousands of unwitting Americans and Canadians became part of a bizarre CIA research project codenamed MKULTRA. Participants were secretly "brainwashed"—drugged with LSD and other hallucinogens, subjected to electroconvulsive shock therapy, and manipulated with abusive mind-control techniques.

✳   ✳   ✳   ✳

MKULTRA BEGAN IN 1953 under the orders of CIA director Allen Dulles. The program was developed in response to reports that U.S. prisoners of war in Korea were being subjected to mind-control techniques.

CIA researchers hoped to find a "truth drug" that could be used on Soviet agents, as well as drugs that could be used against foreign leaders (one documented scheme involved an attempt in 1960 to dose Fidel Castro with LSD). They also aimed to develop means of mind control that would benefit U.S. intelligence, perhaps including the creation of mind-controlled people to carry out assassinations. The CIA investigated parapsychology and such phenomena as hypnosis, telepathy, precognition, photokinesis, and "remote viewing."

MKULTRA was headed by Dr. Sidney Gottlieb, a military psychiatrist and chemist who specialized in concocting deadly poisons. More than 30 universities and scientific institutes took part in MKULTRA. LSD and other mind-altering drugs including heroin, mescaline, psilocybin, scopolamine, marijuana, and sodium pentothal were given to CIA employees, military personnel, and other government workers, often without the subjects' knowledge or prior consent.

To broaden their subject pool, researchers targeted unsuspecting civilians, often those in vulnerable or socially compromising situations. Prison inmates, prostitutes, and mentally ill hospital patients were often used. In a project codenamed Operation Midnight Climax, the CIA set up brothels in several U.S. cities to lure men as unwitting test subjects. Rooms were equipped with cameras that filmed the experiments behind one-way mirrors. Some civilian subjects who consented to participation were used for more extreme experimentation. One group of volunteers in Kentucky was given LSD for more than 70 straight days.

Clandestine Research

In the 1960s, Dr. Gottlieb conducted mind-control experiments on prisoners of war being held by U.S. forces in Vietnam. During the same time period, an unknown number of Soviet agents died in U.S. custody in Europe after being given dual intravenous injections of barbiturates and amphetamine in the CIA's search for a truth serum.

MKULTRA experiments were also carried out in Montreal, Canada, between 1957 and 1964 by Dr. Donald Ewen Cameron, a researcher in Albany, New York, who also served as president of the World Psychiatric Association and the American and Canadian psychiatric associations. The CIA appears to have given him potentially deadly experiments to carry out at Canadian mental health institutes so U.S. citizens would not be involved.

Cameron also experimented with paralytic drugs—in some cases inducing a coma in subjects for up to three months—as well as using electroconvulsive therapy at 30 times the normal voltage. The subjects were often women being treated for anxiety disorders and postpartum depression. Many suffered permanent damage. A lawsuit by victims later uncovered that the Canadian government had also funded the project.

There was at least one American subject who died in the experiments. Frank Olson, a biological weapons researcher, was secretly given LSD in 1953. A week later, he was found dead on a New York City sidewalk. A CIA doctor assigned to monitor

Olson claimed he jumped from the window of his 10th-floor hotel room, but an autopsy performed on Olson's exhumed remains in 1994 found that he had been knocked unconscious before the fall.

The U.S. army also conducted experiments with psychoactive drugs. A later investigation determined that nearly all army experiments involved soldiers and civilians who had given their informed consent, and that army researchers had largely followed scientific and safety protocols. Ken Kesey, who would later write *One Flew Over the Cuckoo's Nest* and become one of the originators of the hippie movement, volunteered for LSD studies at an army research center in San Francisco in 1960.

The army's high ethical standards seem to have been absent in at least one case. Harold Blauer, a professional tennis player in New York City who was hospitalized for depression following his divorce, died from apparent cardiac arrest during an army experiment in 1952. Blauer had been secretly injected with massive doses of mescaline.

CIA researchers eventually concluded that the effects of LSD were too unpredictable to be useful, and the agency later acknowledged that their experiments made little scientific sense. Records on 150 MKULTRA research projects were destroyed in 1973 by order of CIA Director Richard Helms. A year later, the *New York Times* first reported about CIA experiments on U.S. citizens. In 1975, congressional hearings and a report by the Rockefeller Commission revealed details of the program. In 1976, President Gerald Ford issued an executive order prohibiting experimentation with drugs on human subjects without their informed consent. Ford and CIA Director William Colby also publicly apologized to Frank Olson's family, who received $750,000 by a special act of Congress.

What Were History's Shortest Wars?

As wars grow costlier and transportation gets faster, battles compress the same level of tragedy into shorter durations. Most consider World War II to have been one big conflict, but for many smaller nations the main conflict amounted to a solo war between themselves and Nazi Germany. Here are some of the shortest conflicts in history.

✳   ✳   ✳   ✳

Anglo-Zanzibar War (9:02–9:40 A.M., August 27, 1896; Great Britain versus Zanzibar): The British liked it when the Sultan of Zanzibar (an island off modern Tanzania) engaged in battles. When a new sultan named Khalid bin Barghash refused to, the Royal Navy gave Zanzibar a taste of British anger. Bin Barghash tapped out after just 38 minutes of shelling in what is the shortest recorded war.

Spanish-American War (April 25–August 12, 1898; United States versus Spain): Spain once had an empire, some of which was very near Florida. After months of tension, the battleship *USS Maine* blew up in Havana harbor. Though no one knew why it exploded, the United States declared war anyway. A few months later, Spain had lost Cuba, Guam, the Philippines, and Puerto Rico.

Nazi-Polish War (September 1–October 6, 1939; Nazi Germany and Soviet Union versus Poland): After Russian and German negotiators signed a secret agreement in August for the division of Poland, the Nazis invaded in vicious armored thrusts with heavy air attacks. Polish forces fought with uncommon valor, but their strategic position was impossible. Russian troops entered from the east on September 17, and Poland became the first European nation conquered in World War II.

Nazi-Danish War (4:15–9:20 A.M., April 9, 1940; Nazi Germany versus Denmark): Arguably the biggest mismatch of World War II (unless one counts Germany's invasion of Luxembourg). Sixteen Danish soldiers died before the Danish government ordered the resistance to cease.

Suez/Sinai War (October 29–November 6, 1956; Israel, Britain, and France versus Egypt): The Egyptians decided to nationalize the Suez Canal, which seems logical today given that the Suez is entirely in Egypt. British and French companies operating the canal didn't agree. The Israelis invaded by land, the British and French by air and sea. The invaders won a complete military victory, but the rest of world got so mad at them that they withdrew under international pressure.

Six-Day War (June 5–10, 1967; Israel versus Egypt, Syria, and Jordan): Israelis launched a sneak attack on the Egyptians, destroying the Egyptian air force on its airfields and sending the Egyptians reeling back toward the Suez Canal. Jordanians attacked the Israelis and immediately regretted it. The Israelis attacked Syria and seized Golan Heights.

Yom Kippur War (October 6–25, 1973; Egypt and Syria versus Israel): Egyptians and Syrians, still annoyed and embarrassed over the Six-Day War, attacked Israelis on a national religious holiday. Israeli forces were caught napping at first but soon regained the upper hand—they struck within artillery range of Damascus and crossed the Suez Canal. The United Nations' ceasefire came as a major relief to all involved, even the Israelis, who had no desire to administer Cairo and Damascus.

Soccer War (July 15–19, 1969; El Salvador versus Honduras): Immigration was the core issue, specifically the forced expulsion of some 60,000 Salvadorean illegal immigrants from Honduras. When a soccer series between the two Central American nations fueled tensions, each managed to insult the other enough to start a bloody yet inconclusive war.

Falklands War (March 19–June 14, 1982; Argentina versus United Kingdom): Argentina has long claimed the Falkland Islands as Las Islas Malvinas. In 1982, Argentina decided to enforce this claim by invading the Falklands and South Georgia. Although the Argentines had a surprise for the Royal Navy in the form of air-launched antiship missiles, the battle for the islands went heavily against Argentina. Its survivors, including most of its marines, were shipped back home minus their weaponry.

Invasion of Grenada (October 25 to mid-December, 1983; United States versus Grenada and Cuba): Concerned about a recent Marxist takeover on the Caribbean island of Grenada, elite U.S. forces invaded by air and sea. The public learned that about 1,000 Americans (including 600 medical students) were in danger in Grenada; after the relatively recent Iran hostage crisis, the lives of U.S. citizens overseas were a powerful talking point in domestic politics.

First Gulf War (January 16–March 3, 1991; Allies versus Iraq): Saddam Hussein misjudged the world's tolerance for military adventurism (at least involving oil-rich Western-friendly Arab emirates) by sending his oversized military into Kuwait. President George W. Bush led a diverse world coalition that deployed into Saudi Arabia and started bombing the Iraqi military. Most remarkable: The primary land conflict of the war lasted just 100 hours, February 23–27.

Chapter 8

Culture

Were the Ancient Egyptians the First to Practice Mummification?

Turns out that the Egyptians—history's most famous embalmers—weren't the first. By the time Egyptians were fumbling with the art, Saharans and Andeans were veterans at mortuary science.

❋ ❋ ❋ ❋

Andes

IN NORTHERN CHILE and southern Peru, modern researchers have found hundreds of pre-Inca mummies (roughly 5000–2000 B.C.) from the Chinchorro culture. Evidently, the Chinchorros mummified all walks of life: rich, poor, elderly, didn't matter. We still don't know exactly why, but a simple, plausible explanation is that they wanted to honor and respect their dead.

The work shows the evolution of increasingly sophisticated, artistic techniques that weren't very different from later African methods: Take out the wet

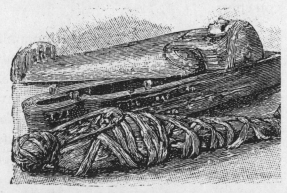

stuff before it gets too gross, pack the body carefully, dry it out. The process occurred near the open-air baking oven we call the Atacama Desert, which may hold a clue in itself.

Uan Muhuggiag

The oldest known instance of deliberate mummification in Africa comes from ancient Saharan cattle ranchers. In southern Libya, at a rock shelter now called Uan Muhuggiag, archaeologists found evidence of basic seminomadic civilization, including animal domestication, pottery, and ceremonial burial.

We don't know why the people of Uan Muhuggiag mummified a young boy, but they did a good job. Dispute exists about dating here: Some date the remains back to the 7400s B.C., others to only 3400s B.C. Even at the latest reasonable dating, this predates large-scale Egyptian practices. The remains demonstrate refinement and specialized knowledge that likely took centuries to develop. Quite possibly some of this knowledge filtered into Egyptian understanding given that some of the other cultural finds at Uan Muhuggiag look pre-Egyptian as well.

Egypt

Some 7,000 to 12,000 years ago, Egyptians buried their dead in hot sand without wrapping. Given Egypt's naturally arid climate, the corpse sometimes dehydrated so quickly that decay was minimal. Sands shift, of course, which would sometimes lead to passersby finding an exposed body in surprisingly good shape. Perhaps this is what inspired early Egyptian mummification efforts.

As Egyptian civilization advanced, mummification interwove with their view of the afterlife. Professionals formalized and refined the process. A whole industry arose, offering funerary options from deluxe (special spices, carved wood case) to budget (dry 'em out and hand 'em back). *Natron*, a mixture of sodium salts abundant along the Nile, made a big difference. If you extracted the guts and brains from a corpse, then dried it out it in natron for a couple of months, the remains would keep for a long time. The earliest known Egyptian mummy dates to around 3300 B.C.

Desert Origins

It's hard to ignore a common factor among these cultures: proximity to deserts. It seems likely that ancient civilizations got the idea from seeing natural mummies.

Ice and bogs can also preserve a body by accident, of course, but they don't necessarily mummify it. Once exposed, the preservation of the remains depends on swift discovery and professional handling. If ancient Africans and South Americans developed mummification based on desert-dried bodies, it would explain why bogs and glaciers didn't lead to similar mortuary science. The ancients had no convenient way to deliberately keep a body frozen year-round without losing track of it, nor could they create a controlled mini-bog environment. But people could and did replicate the desert's action on human remains.

Today

We make mummies today, believe it or not. An embalmed corpse is a mummy—it's just a question of how far the embalmers went in their preservation efforts. To put it indelicately: If you've attended an open-casket funeral or wake, you've seen a mummy.

Why Did Ancient Egyptians Shave Their Eyebrows?

Shaving away all body hair—most notably the eyebrows—was part of an elaborate daily purification ritual that was practiced by Pharaoh and his priests.

✳ ✳ ✳ ✳

THE ANCIENT EGYPTIANS believed that everything in their lives—health, good crops, victory, prosperity—depended on keeping their gods happy, so one of the Pharaoh's duties was to enter a shrine and approach a special statue of a god three times a day, every day. Each time he visited the shrine, the Pharaoh washed the statue, anointed it with oil, and dressed it in fresh linen.

Because the Pharaoh was a busy guy, high-ranking priests often performed this duty for him. But whether it was the Pharaoh or a priest doing it, the person had to bathe himself and shave his eyebrows beforehand.

Shaving the eyebrows was also a sign of mourning, even among commoners. The Greek historian Herodotus, who traveled and wrote in the fifth century B.C., said that everyone in an ancient Egyptian household would shave his or her eyebrows following the natural death of a pet cat. For dogs, he reported, the household members would shave their heads and all of their body hair as well.

Herodotus was known to repeat some wild stories in his books. For instance, he reported that serpents with bat-like wings flew from Arabia into Egypt and were killed in large numbers by ibises. Herodotus claimed he actually saw heaps of these serpent skeletons. So you might want to take his eyebrow-shaving claim with a grain of salt . . . and a pinch of catnip.

If the Maya Were So Brilliant, Why Aren't They Still Around?

They are! Six million people who are living in Mexico, Honduras, Guatemala, and Belize speak Mayan or identify themselves as Maya. The Nobel Peace Prize winner in 1992, Rigoberta Menchú, was Maya.

✳   ✳   ✳   ✳

BUT YOU'RE THINKING of the ancient Maya, right? The temple-building, bloodthirsty warriors seen in the movie *Apocolypto*? The great astronomers and priest-kings who ruled over the sculpted plazas deep in the jungle? Those Maya? Well, today's Maya are the descendents of those Maya—the Mayan people who flourished in southern Mexico and the Yucatan Peninsula for millennia.

Mayan civilization was established well before 1500 B.C. For centuries, the Maya cut and burned jungle land to plant crops, and after 400 B.C., they began building cities, temples, astronomical observatories, and pyramids. Samples of their complex writing date back to before the time of Christ. Their accomplishments peaked between A.D. 300 and A.D. 800, when the Maya engineered reservoirs, canals, and irrigation systems to maximize the food supply that supported their growing network of city-states. It was a remarkable civilization.

Then, abruptly, the Mayan people abandoned their cities, and the great buildings and plazas fell into ruin. Signs of violence and fire mark some (though only some) sites. The population in A.D. 900 was merely a third of what it had been one hundred years earlier. Why? Invasion? Disease? Political upheaval? Recent scientific studies show that a series of multiyear droughts began in A.D. 750 and lasted for nearly three hundred years. No one knows for sure, but the drought could have caused famine, epidemics, invasions, wars, riots, and rebellion. Many Maya died, and others left their cities and took to the jungle, where they tried to survive.

Thanks to GPS and satellite imaging, more Mayan sites and ruins have been spotted in recent years. Digs and explorations are constantly evolving. Mayan writing remained a mystery until the 1980s, when it was finally deciphered. So the answer to the riddle of what drove the Maya from their cities could still be found.

Who Are the Aborigines?

The term Aborigine conjures images of loincloth-clad spear-throwers running across a sweltering savanna. Yet some people are unsure what an Aborigine actually is, and most Aborigines prefer to be called by a different name.

✷ ✷ ✷ ✷

Semantic Antics

ASK SOMEBODY IN the United States what *aboriginal* means, and it is likely that flustered confusion will ensue. In common usage, *aboriginal* (or *aborigine*) refers to the indigenous population of Australia, but aboriginal is also sometimes used to refer to the indigenous populations of other countries. When the word begins with a lowercase a, it can refer to a wide variety of people, places, and things. When it begins with a capital A, it refers only to the indigenous population of Australia. The solution to this semantic puzzle lies in the nuanced differences between the words *indigenous* and *aboriginal*.

The word aboriginal means "the first or earliest known of its kind in a region." The word derives from the Latin for "from" combined with the Latin for "the beginning." The word *indigenous* means "having originated in and being produced, growing, or living in a particular region or environment," and it derives from the Latin for "in" combined with the Latin for "born."

Aboriginal, therefore, is a less-inclusive term than *indigenous*. Technically, anyone born in a particular area is indigenous to that area, though in practical usage, indigenous groups are descendants of those that resided in a region before Eurasian colonization and the worldwide creation of nation-states.

Many indigenous groups besides Australian Aborigines can be said to be the first inhabitants of a given region. Native Americans, for example, are descendants of the first human groups to live in the Americas and thus could be said to have been there "from the beginning." Why is it, then, that indigenous Australians have a monopoly on the term *aborigine*?

There from the Earlier Beginning

Human populations first existed in Africa and from there walked north to the sprawling Eurasian continent. Indigenous Australians separated from these populations far earlier than did Native Americans. Evidence suggests that humans arrived in Australia some 50,000 years ago, probably by boat from southern Asia.

From that time onward until colonization, the population of Australia was completely isolated from the rest of the world. The same can probably be said for Native Americans, but the difference is that the first humans arrived in the Americas at a much later date, approximately 11,500 to 12,000 years ago. When Europeans first met the indigenous Australians in the 17th century, they had stumbled upon a population that had existed in its own geographic bubble for 50,000 years. The colonizers immediately used the term aborigine, "there from the beginning," to describe the indigenous Australians.

Why Did the Romans Sell Urine?

Because there was a demand for it. Why the demand? Because Romans used the stuff by the bucketful to clean and dye clothing. Why urine? Because it worked, it was plentiful, and it was cheap. Why on Earth did it work? Because the nitrogenous urea in urine generates ammonia when the urine is left standing around, and this ammonia is a disinfecting and bleaching agent.

✳   ✳   ✳   ✳

SOME ROMANS, LIKE many other people of the time, used urine to wash their teeth, too. But before you go dissing the Romans, realize that for more than fifteen hundred years after the Roman Empire peaked, Europeans were still using urine to clean clothes. And the Romans were not slovenly people, relatively speaking. They were quite the scientists. For example, it's been argued that after the fall of Rome, battlefield medicine didn't return to Roman levels until World War I, and that's partly a function of hygiene. Besides, lots of people today drink urine in the name of alternative medicine.

The Romans made extensive use of public baths—a bit of a turn-off to many of us today, but actually a sign of their culture's advancement. (The Romans were great innovators in matters hydraulic, as evidenced by their clever work with aqueducts and plumbing.) In the first century A.D., the emperor Vespasian enacted a "urine tax," and with it coined the proverb pecunia non olet ("money does not smell"). But pee does. Imagine the troughs at the more than one hundred public baths where urine vendors would collect their wares, which they sold to the multitude of establishments around Rome and elsewhere that cleaned and bleached and performed a kind of dry-cleaning on woolens. A significant number of Romans were employed in the cleaning industry, experts say.

All in all, we modern folk would be astonished to learn how "green" the ancients were. They didn't pump crude oil from the earth and make gasoline of it, and they didn't make plastics of whatever it is we use to make plastics. No, they used what was at hand in remarkable ways.

Who Were the Druids and the Picts?

What do you know about the druids? How about the Picts? Chances are, what you know (or think you know) is wrong.

✳ ✳ ✳ ✳

MOST CONTEMPORARY PERCEPTIONS of the druids and Picts tend to be derived from legend and lore. As such, our conceptions of these peoples range from erroneous and unlikely to just plain foolish.

The Druids—The Priestly Class

As the priestly class of Celtic society, the druids served as the Celts' spiritual leaders—repositories of knowledge about the world and the universe, as well as authorities on Celtic history, law, religion, and culture. In short, they were the preservers of the Celtic way of life.

The druids provided the Celts with a connection to their gods, the universe, and the natural order. They preached of the power and authority of the deities and taught the immortality of the soul and reincarnation. They were experts in astronomy and the natural world. They also had an innate connection to all things living: They preferred holding great rituals among natural shrines provided by the forests, springs, and groves.

To become a druid, one had to survive extensive training. Druid wannabes and druid-trained minstrels and bards had to endure as many as 20 years of oral education and memorization.

More Powerful than Celtic Chieftains

In terms of power, the druids took a backseat to no one. Even the Celtic chieftains, well-versed in power politics, recognized the overarching authority of the druids. Celtic society had well-defined power and social structures, territories, and property rights. The druids were deemed the ultimate arbiters in all matters relating to such. If there was a legal or financial dispute, it was unequivocally settled in special druid-presided courts. Armed conflicts were immediately ended with druid rulings.

Their word was final.

In the end, however, there were two forces to which even the druids had to succumb—the Romans and Christianity. With the Roman invasion of Britain in A.D. 43, Emperor Claudius decreed that druidism throughout the Roman Empire was outlawed. The Romans destroyed the last vestiges of official druidism in Britain with the annihilation of the druid stronghold of Anglesey in A.D. 61. Surviving druids fled to unconquered Ireland and Scotland, only to become completely marginalized by the influence of Christianity within a few centuries.

Stripped of power and status, the druids of ancient Celtic society disappeared. They morphed into wandering poets and storytellers with no connection to their once illustrious past.

The Picts—The Painted People

The Picts were, in simplest terms, the people who inhabited ancient Scotland before the Scots. Their origins are unknown, but some scholars believe that the Picts were descendents of the Caledonians or other Iron Age tribes who invaded Britain.

No one knows what the Picts called themselves; the origin of their name comes from other sources and probably derives from the Pictish custom of tattooing or painting their bodies. The Irish called them *Cruithni*, meaning "the people of the designs." The Romans called them *Picti*, which is Latin for "painted people"; however, the Romans probably used the term as a general moniker for all the untamed peoples living north of Hadrian's Wall.

A Second-Hand History

The Picts themselves left no written records. All descriptions of their history and culture come from second-hand accounts. The earliest of these is a Roman account from A.D. 297 stating that the Picti and the Hiberni (Irish) were already well-established enemies of the Britons to the south.

The Picts were also well-established enemies of each other.

Before the arrival of the Romans, the Picts spent most of their time fighting amongst themselves. The threat posed by the Roman conquest of Britain forced the squabbling Pict kingdoms to come together and eventually evolve into the nation-state of Pictland. The united Picts were strong enough not only to resist conquest by the Romans, but also to launch periodic raids on Roman-occupied Britain.

Having defied the Romans, the Picts later succumbed to an invasion launched by Irish Christian missionaries. Arriving in Pictland in the late sixth century, they succeeded in converting the polytheistic Pict elite within two decades. Much of the written history of the Picts comes from the Irish Christian annals. If not for the writings of the Romans and the Irish missionaries, we might not have knowledge of the Picts today.

Despite the existence of an established Pict state, Pictland disappeared with the changing of its name to the Kingdom of Alba in A.D. 843, a move signifying the rise of the Gaels as the dominant people in Scotland. By the 11th century, virtually all vestiges of them had vanished.

Were There Female Druids?

The ancient Celts—the culture that produced druids—were far less gender-biased than their Greek and Roman neighbors. Women could buy or inherit property, assume leadership, wage war, divorce men, and, yes, become druids.

✳ ✳ ✳ ✳

DRUIDS WERE THE leaders—spiritually, intellectually, and sometimes politically—of Celtic societies. Because they did not use writing, we don't know exactly what druids (or their followers) believed or what they taught. From ancient stories, we've learned that they were well-educated and served as judges, scientists, teachers, priests, and doctors. Some even led their tribes.

At one time, Celtic tribes covered most of Europe, and their druids embodied wisdom and authority. In the ensuing centuries, however, druids have gotten a bad rap, due to lurid tales of human sacrifice that may or may not be true. Most of the bad-mouthing came from enemies of the Celts, so take what they said with the proverbial grain of salt.

Femme druids were described as priestesses, prophets, and oracles by Greek writers like Plutarch and Romans such as Tacitus. Several ancient authors mention holy women living on island sanctuaries, either alone or alongside male druids.

Irish tales are full of druids, some of them women. They helped win battles by transforming trees into warriors, they conjured up storms and diseases, and sometimes they hid children from murderous fathers. In the Irish epic *Cattle Raid of Cooley*, a beautiful young druid named Fidelma foretells victory for the hero Cúchulainn. Saint Patrick met female druids, and Saint Bridget, by some accounts the daughter of a druid, may have been a druid herself before converting to Christianity.

The ancient Celts knew what the rest of the world has slowly come to realize: Women can wield power as wisely—or as cruelly—as men.

What Happened to the Anasazi?

There is a prevalent belief that the prehistoric Native American culture referred to as the Anasazi mysteriously disappeared from the southwestern United States. Here are the facts.

✳ ✳ ✳ ✳

Who Were the Anasazi?

ACROSS THE DESERTS and mesas of the region known as the Four Corners, where Arizona, New Mexico, Colorado, and Utah meet, backcountry hikers and motoring tourists can easily spot reminders of an ancient people. From the towering stone structures at Chaco Culture National Historical Park to cliff dwellings at Mesa Verde National Park to the ubiquitous scatters of broken pottery and stone tools, these remains tell the story of a culture that spread out across the arid Southwest during ancient times. The Anasazi are believed to have lived in the region from about A.D. 1 through A.D. 1300 (though the exact beginning of the culture is difficult to determine because there is no particular defining event). In their everyday lives, they created black-on-white pottery styles that distinguish subregions within the culture, traded with neighboring cultures (including those to the south in Central America), and built ceremonial structures called kivas, which were used for religious or communal purposes.

The Exodus Explained

Spanish conquistadors exploring the Southwest noted the abandoned cliff dwellings and ruined plazas, and archaeologists today still try to understand what might have caused the Anasazi to move from their homes and villages throughout the region. Over time, researchers have posed a number of theories, including the idea that the Anasazi were driven from their villages by hostile nomads, such as those from the Apache or Ute tribes. Others believe that the Anasazi fought among themselves, causing a drastic reduction in their populations, and a few extraterrestrial-minded theorists have suggested that the Anasazi civilization was destroyed by aliens. Today, the prevalent hypothesis among scientists is that a long-term drought affected the area, destroying agricultural fields and forcing people to abandon their largest villages. Scientists and archaeologists have worked together to reconstruct the region's climate data and compare it with material that has been excavated. Based on their findings, many agree that some combination of environmental and cultural factors caused the dispersal of the Anasazi from the large-scale ruins seen throughout the landscape today.

Their Journey

Although many writers—of fiction and nonfiction alike—

romanticize the Anasazi as a people who mysteriously disappeared from the region, they did not actually disappear. Those living in large ancient villages and cultural centers did indeed disperse, but the people themselves did not simply disappear. Today, descendents of the Anasazi can be found living throughout New Mexico and Arizona. The Hopi tribe in northern Arizona, as well as those living in approximately 20 pueblos in New Mexico, are the modern-day descendants of the Anasazi. The Pueblos in New Mexico whose modern inhabitants consider the Anasazi their ancestors include: Acoma, Cochiti, Isleta, Jemez, Laguna, Nambe, Picuris, Pojoaque, San Felipe, San Ildefonso, Ohkay Owingeh (formerly referred to as San Juan), Sandia, Santa Ana, Santa Clara, Santo Domingo, Taos, Tesuque, Zia, and Zuni.

Who Were the Goths?

We don't mean today's darkly clothed wannabe vampires or the 19th-century purveyors of ghost stories and mysteries. No, the original Goths lived in the days of the Roman Empire.

✳ ✳ ✳ ✳

ROMAN HISTORIANS CLAIMED that the Goths emerged from Scandinavia, but the earliest archaeological evidence of their existence was discovered in Poland and dates back to the first century A.D.—when the Roman Empire was on the rise. Over time, the Goths, a Germanic tribe, moved south; the Roman Empire, meanwhile, pushed north. The two groups met somewhere in between and fought. The Goths sacked Roman frontier cities and annihilated a Roman army, killing Emperor Decius and his son. The Romans eventually drove the Goths back, but the Goths gained a frightening reputation as barbarian bogeymen.

By the fourth century, the Goths had increased their power and had divided into several kingdoms north of the Roman Empire. The Romans saw them as Visigoths (western Goths) and Ostrogoths (eastern Goths), but there may have been more groups that were known by different names.

During the 370s, the Huns—you've heard of Attila? Yup, same guys—attacked the Goths from the east, forcing the Goths to push into the Roman Empire again. This time, having become a bit more civilized, the Goths asked permission of the Romans before crossing the Danube. Predictably, however, things turned ugly. The Romans and the Goths went to war, and another Roman Emperor—Valens—bit the dust at the Battle of Adrianople.

That war lasted six years and marked the twilight of the Roman Empire. After Rome was forced to negotiate a settlement, surrounding tribes saw that the Empire was weak. Fewer than twenty years later, the Visigoths sacked the city of Rome. They then moved west to establish a kingdom in what is today southern France and Spain; this kingdom lasted for almost three centuries.

The Ostrogoths, after years of fighting the Huns in the Balkans, more or less took over the Roman Empire after it fell. Here's how it happened: In A.D. 476, a barbarian named Odoacer deposed the last Roman Emperor in the west. Gothic King Theodoric the Great fought Odoacer several times and laid siege to the city of Ravenna for three years until Odoacer surrendered. At a banquet celebrating the end of the siege, Theodoric raised a toast—then killed Odoacer with his own hands and took over the Italian peninsula.

Theodoric's empire extended from Spain to the Balkans, but after his death, it fell apart. The Eastern Roman Empire attacked, and the Ostrogoths pretty much disappeared. Their former lands were conquered by other rulers.

Think about all of this the next time you're walking down the street and you pass a pale, sullen-looking person who's dressed entirely in black and has piercings galore.

Were the Viking Berserkers Really Berserk?

Depending on whom you ask, the Viking berserkers were either bloodthirsty thugs intent on pillaging everything in their path or an elite corps of buff warriors who had a hard time keeping their shirts on in the heat of battle.

✳ ✳ ✳ ✳

THE WORD "BERSERK" comes from Old Norse. It has been translated as "bare of shirt," meaning that the berserkers entered battle without armor and possibly bare-chested, or more literally as "bear-shirt," for the Vikings also liked to don the skins of their totem animals (bears and wolves). Sometimes they would even wear animals' heads as helmets or masks, the better to frighten their enemies. Such behavior jibes with the English definition of the word: "extremely aggressive or angry."

Vikings first sailed into European history in A.D. 793, when a group of longboats pulled up on the northeast coast of England right outside the abbey of Lindisfarne. Locals thought the boats—with their high, carved prows—were literally sea dragons and that the men who disembarked from them were equally possessed of supernatural powers.

After sacking Lindisfarne, the Vikings terrorized Europeans for the better part of the next two centuries, looting cities and villages, killing men, and seizing women and children and carting them off as slaves. The most fearsome of these raiders called themselves the sons of Odin. According to Norway's epic poet Snorri Sturluson, those who belonged to the cult of Odin "went to battle without armor and acted like mad dogs or wolves. They bit into their shields and were as strong as bears or bulls. They killed men, but neither fire nor iron harmed them. This madness is called berserker-fury."

How did they reach this state of madness or berserkergang, as the Scandinavians say? In 1956, psychiatrist Howard Fabing introduced the theory that the berserkers psyched themselves for battle with bites of *Amanita muscaria*, a potent hallucinogenic mushroom that is native to northern Europe. The notion that the Vikings owed their victories to psychedelic highs is intriguing, but it's unconvincing to many historians. Although the old Norsemen often went heavy on the mead (a fermented beverage made from honey), there's no archaeological evidence that they added mushrooms to their pre-battle menu.

Some scholars think that the berserkers may have been genetically predisposed to bipolar disorder (also called manic-depressive illness). Contemporary accounts depict them as swinging from states of wild rage to utter lassitude, a pattern in keeping with what we know of bipolar disorder. People in manic episodes can experience huge releases of endorphins, which may explain why the berserkers seemed impervious to pain.

Or it is possible that the berserkers simply worked themselves into frenzied states through dancing, drumming, chanting, and other high-energy rituals. Whatever they did, it was certainly effective: The image of the Viking warrior has hardly dimmed through the ages, though their press has gotten slightly better. Today filmmakers are more apt to depict the berserker as a brave hero rather than a rapacious villain. And, of course, there are those fanatics in Minnesota who paint their faces purple just to watch football games. Now that's really berserk.

What Happened to the Knights Templar?

The Crusades, Christendom's quest to recover and hold the Holy Land, saw the rise of several influential military orders. Of these, the Knights Templar had perhaps the greatest lasting influence—and took the hardest fall.

✳   ✳   ✳   ✳

JULY 15, 1099: On that day, the First Crusade stormed Jerusalem and slaughtered everyone in sight—Jews, Muslims, and Christians. This unleashed a wave of pilgrimage, as European Christians flocked to now-accessible Palestine and its holy sites. Though Jerusalem's loss was a blow to Islam, it was a bonanza for the region's thieves, from Saracens to lapsed Crusaders: a steady stream of naive pilgrims to rob.

Defending the Faithful

French knight Hugues de Payen, with eight chivalrous comrades, swore to guard the travelers. In 1119, they gathered at the Church of the Holy Sepulchre and pledged their lives to poverty, chastity, and obedience before King Baldwin II of Jerusalem. The Order of Poor Knights of the Temple of Solomon took up headquarters in said Temple.

Going Mainstream

The Templars did their work well, and in 1127 Baldwin sent a Templar embassy to Europe to secure a marriage that would ensure the royal succession in Jerusalem. Not only did they succeed, they became rock stars of sorts. Influential nobles showered the Order with money and real estate, the foundation of its future wealth. With this growth came a formal code of rules. Some highlights include:

✳ Templars could not desert the battlefield or leave a castle by stealth.

* They had to wear white habits, except for sergeants and squires, who could wear black.

* They had to tonsure (shave) their crowns and wear beards.

* They had to dine in communal silence, broken only by scriptural readings.

* They had to be chaste, except for married men joining with their wives' consent.

A Law unto Themselves

Now with offices in Europe to manage the Order's growing assets, the Templars returned to Palestine to join in the Kingdom's ongoing defense. In 1139, Pope Innocent II decreed the Order answerable only to the Holy See. Now exempt from the tithe, the Order was entitled to accept tithes! The Knights Templar had come far.

By the mid-1100s, the Templars had become a church within a church, a nation within a nation, and a major banking concern. Templar keeps were well-defended depositories, and the Order became financiers to the crowned heads of Europe— even to the Papacy. Their reputation for meticulous bookkeeping and secure transactions underpinned Europe's financial markets, even as their soldiers kept fighting for the faith in the Holy Land.

Downfall

Templar prowess notwithstanding, the Crusaders couldn't hold the Holy Land. In 1187, Saladin the Kurd retook Jerusalem, martyring 230 captured Templars. Factional fighting between Christians sped the collapse as the 1200s wore on. In 1291, the last Crusader outpost at Acre fell to the Mamelukes of Egypt. Though the Templars had taken a hosing along with the other Christian forces, their troubles had just begun.

King Philip IV of France owed the Order a lot of money, and they made him more nervous at home than they did fighting in

Palestine. In 1307, Philip ordered the arrest of all Templars in France. They stood accused of apostasy, devil worship, sodomy, desecration, and greed. Hideous torture produced piles of confessions, much like those of the later Inquisition. The Order was looted, shattered, and officially dissolved. In March 1314, Jacques de Molay, the last Grand Master of the Knights Templar, was burned at the stake.

Whither the Templars?

Many Templar assets passed to the Knights Hospitallers. The Order survived in Portugal as the Order of Christ, where it exists to this day in form similar to British knightly orders. A Templar fleet escaped from La Rochelle and vanished; it may have reached Scotland. Swiss folktales suggest that some Templars took their loot and expertise to Switzerland, possibly laying the groundwork for what would one day become the Swiss banking industry.

Who Were the Incas?

The Inca civilization in South America started out as a highland tribe in present-day Peru. The term "Inka" means ruler or lord in Quechua, the language of the Incas.

✳ ✳ ✳ ✳

IN THE 12TH century, Cusco (also spelled Cuzco) was established as a city-state and later the capital of the Inca Empire. The founder and first Inca emperor was named Manco Cápac. The civilization remained a relatively small tribe until the Inca began their conquests in the early 15th century under Emperor Pachacuti (also called Pachacutec). Within one hundred years, the Inca Empire had expanded from modern-day Peru into parts of what are now Ecuador, Bolivia, Argentina, and Chile. At its height, the Inca Empire included an Andean population of about 12 million people.

The Incas were master stonemasons who created large buildings and walls so precisely engineered that no mortar was needed. They were also adept at road building. In order to connect the vast Inca Empire, an elaborate road system spanning 25,000 miles was constructed. Some of the greatest achievements of the Incas are still in use today. They invented the technique of freeze drying, as well as the rope suspension bridge.

The collapse of the Inca Empire came in 1532, when Spanish explorer Francisco Pizarro and his conquistadors claimed Peru for Spain. The most notable victim of their conquest was the Incan Emperor Atahualpa. Though he first presented himself in friendship, Pizarro soon kidnapped the Incan ruler and murdered him after receiving a ransom. Atahualpa was the 13th and last Inca emperor.

Today, Machu Picchu exists as one of the great legacies of the Incas. The ancient stone town in the Andes is located near Cuzco, Peru. It is believed Machu Picchu was built around A.D. 1460 by Pachacuti as an estate or retreat for himself and his family. The name Machu Picchu means "old mountain" and refers to the lower of the two peaks that stand on each side of the city. It was discovered in 1911 by American explorer Hiram Bingham. Amazingly, the ruins of Machu Picchu stayed intact and the exquisite temples, terraces, and water channels are among the most visited tourist attractions in South America.

What Are Some Notable Fraternal Organizations?

Fraternal organizations have been in operation, often under varying degrees of secrecy, for hundreds of years. Ancient bylaws and traditions mostly forbid women from becoming members, although many have now established sister organizations.

✳ ✳ ✳ ✳

Freemasons

WHILE THE FREEMASONS' symbols of the square and the compass may be derived from the building of King Solomon's Temple in the tenth century B.C., the origins of the society itself are somewhat more modern. The organization developed among the guilds of stonemasons created during the construction of the great cathedrals of Europe in the Middle Ages. From these original professional associations came today's Masons, committed to philanthropy and ethics. Although Freemasonry includes reverence of the "Great Architect of the Universe," it is not a religion. Most lodges serve the communities in which they reside, and many are heavily involved in charity. While they don't consider themselves a secret society, Freemasons argue that they are an esoteric society with certain signs, tokens, and words that are private.

Order of DeMolay

A civic organization dedicated to helping young men grow into the responsible leaders of tomorrow, the Order of DeMolay was started by Frank Land in Kansas City, Missouri, in 1919. Membership is open to young men ages 12–21, and through mentoring relationships with adults, the young men of the society focus on character and leadership skills. While it is not officially affiliated with the Freemasons, the Order developed much of its philosophy and many of its rituals from the Masonic tradition. The name of the group was chosen to honor Jacques de Molay, the last Grand Master of the Knights Templar. Today, the Order of DeMolay has more than 1,000 chapters located around the world.

Rosicrucians

The Rosicrucians are an order that attempts to understand the connection between the soul, the body, and the higher consciousness. Many legends, both oral and written, explain aspects of Rosicrucian thought. The group seems to have roots in the mysticism of ancient Egypt and can trace its evolution through the development of Western philosophy until the group's eventual incorporation in 1915. Alchemy, specifically as applied to the transmutation of people rather than matter, has played a key role in Rosicrucian thought. Today, Rosicrucians focus on history, spirituality, and the humanities as tools for understanding the challenges confronting the people of the modern world.

Knights of Columbus

The Knights of Columbus was established in Connecticut in 1882 by Father Michael McGivney; he brought together the men of his parish to create a brotherhood of the faithful to mutually support each other and fellow Catholics. The group selected its name to honor Christopher Columbus, who had brought Christianity to the Americas. Originally envisioned as a network of social assistance in prewelfare days, the K of C, as it is known, sought to provide for widows and orphans. Since that time, the organization's ideals of charity, civic duty, and evangelism have expanded into a much broader mission. Regardless, providing insurance to the families of members still remains one of its objectives today.

P.E.O. Sisterhood

The P.E.O. (or Philanthropic Educational Organization) started as an on-campus group at Iowa Wesleyan College in 1869. The original seven members founded their association on the ideals of friendship and philanthropy. Since that time, the group has evolved into an all-female society dedicated to furthering educational opportunities for women. The organization has several scholarship and loan funds designed to advance that purpose.

Are There Cultures in Which Women Have Multiple Husbands?

Anthropologists use the term "polygamy" to refer to any marriage system that involves more than two people. The "one husband, many wives" form is called "polygyny." The "one wife, multiple husbands" version is called "polyandry." And if anthropologists have a special word for it, it must exist somewhere.

✳　✳　✳　✳

POLYANDRY IS, HOWEVER, exceedingly rare. Only a few cultures continue to practice it today, and polyandry is gradually being eroded by more modern ideas of love and marriage. The strongholds of polyandry are Nepal and certain parts of India. It is also practiced in Sri Lanka. Other cultures were polyandrous in the past, though it was never widespread.

In many cases, this marriage practice takes the form of fraternal polyandry, in which one woman is married to several brothers. There may be a primary husband, the eldest brother or the first one she married. If additional brothers are born after the marriage, they usually become the woman's husbands as well.

The reasons for polyandry are typically more economic than religious. In the areas where it is practiced, life is difficult and poverty is rampant. If a family divided its property among all the brothers, no one would have enough land to survive on through farming and herding. Keeping all the brothers as part of one family keeps the familial plot in one piece. The herding lifestyle also means one or more brothers are often away tending the livestock for extended periods, so the other husbands can stay at home, protect the family, and tend the farm. Where resources are so limited, polyandry also serves as a form of birth control, since the wife can only get pregnant once every nine months no matter how many husbands she has. No one is ever sure which father sired which child, so each tends to treat all of the kids as if they are his own.

How Are Weddings Celebrated Around the World?

Around the world, different cultures celebrate the bride and groom in some pretty unusual ways.

✳ ✳ ✳ ✳

Tying

HANDFASTING IS A tying ritual practiced in one way or another throughout the world. In some African tribes, it involves tying together the wrists of the bride and groom with cloth or braided grass during the wedding ceremony. For Hindus, a string is used, and for the ancient Celts, handfasting *was* the complete wedding ceremony: A year and a day after the tying ritual, the couple was legally married.

Among the *fellahin* in northern Egypt, the priest conducts the handfasting ceremony by tying silk cord over the groom's right shoulder and under his left arm; then he says a prayer and unties him. Next, the priest ties the wedding rings together with the same cord, and after questioning the bride and groom about their intentions, he unties the rings and places them on the couple's fingers.

Though they don't call it "handfasting," Thai couples link their hands together for the wedding ceremony with a chain of flowers, while Laotians use a simple white cotton string. But why just tie the couple's hands together when you can tie up their whole bodies? Guatemalan couples are "lassoed" together with a silver rope; Mexican couples with a white rope or rosary. In a traditional Scottish wedding, the bride and groom tie strips of their wedding tartans together to symbolize the union of their two clans.

Breaking

Shattering crockery for good luck is a "smash hit" in a number of cultures. Russians throw their champagne glasses on the ground, as do the Greeks (along with their plates). Jewish weddings end with the breaking of a wine glass to symbolize one of three things: the destruction of the ancient Temple of Jerusalem, the end of the bride and groom's past lives, or that the couple will share as many years as there are shards of glass.

Italian couples also count the shards from a broken glass or vase to see how many years they'll be happily married. Ukrainians follow a tradition called *Vatana*, breaking dishes with silver dollars to symbolize future prosperity, while the German custom is to host a pre-wedding dish-smashing party, called the *Polterabend*, during which family and friends shatter china (because glass is considered bad luck) for the engaged couple to clean up—the first of many messes they'll have to deal with as husband and wife. Bulgarian brides raise the stakes by filling the dish with food—wheat, corns, and raw egg—before tossing it over their heads; an English bride might drop a plate of wedding cake from her roof.

Other cultures skip the dish and just break the food. Hungarian brides smash eggs to ensure the health of their future children, and Sudanese ceremonies are marked by the breaking of an egg outside the couple's new home to symbolize the groom's role as master of the house. Many Middle Eastern cultures observe a pre-wedding "grinding" ritual in which the unmarried girls drape a cloth over the heads of the bride and groom and one of the girls—the "grinding girl"—grinds two lumps of sugar over them to repel evil spirits. The Iranian twist on this ceremony involves shaving crumbs from two decorated sugar cones over the heads of the newlyweds for luck.

Circling

This custom may seem a little "loopy," but it's practiced the world over. Hindu couples finalize their union by taking seven steps around a ceremonial fire. Seven is also the magic number for Jewish couples. Traditionally, after stepping under the *chuppah*, or wedding canopy, the bride circles the groom seven times to represent the seven wedding blessings and seven days of Creation—and also to demonstrate her subservience to the groom. (In modern ceremonies, the bride and groom will often circle each other to show equality.)

For other cultures, three is the lucky number for circles. In the Eastern Orthodox tradition, a priest leads the couple in their first steps as husband and wife three times around the altar—to signify the dance around the Ark of the Covenant—while the choir sings three ceremonial hymns. Croatian wedding guests circle a well three times in honor of the holy Trinity. Moroccan brides circle their new home three times before entering it and officially assuming the role of wife.

Kidnapping

Likely a holdover from days of yore when women were stolen by rival tribesmen and forced into marriage, kidnapping is today a lighthearted custom practiced around the world. In a number of small German villages, the couple's friends kidnap the bride days before the wedding and hide her somewhere for the groom to find. The groom typically begins his search in a local pub, where he buys drinks for his friends to persuade them to help. In Latvia, the bride is often kidnapped by the groomsmen during the wedding reception, and the groom must pay a ransom (like buying drinks or singing a song) to get her back.

In some cultures, the bride and groom voluntarily leave. Danish grooms disappear during part of the reception so single men can kiss the bride; then the bride leaves so single girls can have a go at the groom. In the African nation of Burkina Faso,

Fulani brides and grooms take turns hiding from each other—the bride before the wedding, the groom after. In both cases, it's up to the groom's friends to lead the search.

In Scotland, the groom isn't so much kidnapped by his friends as he is embarrassed. On "stag night," his buddies dress him up in drag, parade him to local pubs, and occasionally at the end of the night, strip him of his clothes and tie him to a tree in front of his house.

Do Dutch Couples Always Split the Bill?

Conventional wisdom holds that dating is considerably cheaper for men in Holland—at least if the phrases "going Dutch" and "Dutch treat" have any validity.

❋　❋　❋　❋

ALTHOUGH SOME AMERICANS today might think of the Netherlands (the official name for Holland) as a country of tulips and debauchery, this wasn't always the case. For a brief period in the 17th century, Holland was one of the world's most powerful empires, largely due to its early exploitation of spice-producing lands in Asia and the Pacific. Along with its financial and military might, Holland saw a cultural flowering during this period, with painters like Rembrandt and Vermeer churning out masterpieces and scientists like Christiaan Huygens laying the foundation for the theory of light. (We're told this was important.)

Of course, Holland wasn't the only imperial nation in the 17th century. Most of the other European countries were also getting busy plundering and looting the rest of the world. England, one of the biggest offenders, didn't like the fact that Holland was horning in on its territory. The British expressed their displeasure by waging not one, not two, but three wars against the Netherlands during the 17th century. Unfortunately for the British, they were forced to an unsatisfying draw in the first and were soundly whipped in the next two.

Unable to defeat the Dutch in battle, they did the next best thing: They made fun of them. During the 17th century, a series of phrases deriding the Dutch worked their way into the English language, such as "Dutch concert" (pandemonium), "Dutch courage" (alcohol), "Dutch comfort" (no comfort at all), and "Dutch feast" (when the host of a dinner gets hammered before the guests even arrive). Most of these phrases have gone the way of the Dutch flotilla, but one has made its way through the centuries to our modern lexicon: "going Dutch" or "Dutch treat," meaning that everyone pays his or her own way.

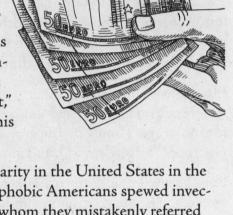

"Dutch treat" regained popularity in the United States in the late 19th century, when xenophobic Americans spewed invectives at German immigrants whom they mistakenly referred to as Dutch (a mispronunciation of the German word *deutsch*, which translates to "German"). Back then, it was considered cheap and rude to make somebody pay his or her own share for an outing that you suggested. Today, however, "going Dutch" is standard in most situations, and it's becoming increasingly so in dating etiquette.

Besides, there isn't any real reason to make fun of the Dutch anymore. By the 18th century, Holland's military power had waned and the country slowly receded from the world stage. Holland remains notable, however, for its progressive social policies on recreational drugs, prostitution, same-sex marriage, and socialized health care.

Do Eskimos Really Have a Thousand Words for Snow?

It stands to reason that the Eskimos would have a lot of words for snow. Their lives revolve around the stuff, after all. But it seems that reports of the exact number of words have, well, snowballed.

✳ ✳ ✳ ✳

THERE ARE FIVE major Eskimo languages. The most widely used is Inuit, which is spoken by people living in northern Alaska, Canada, and Greenland. The notion that Eskimos have lots of words for snow started with anthropologist Frank Boas, who spent much of the late 19th century living with Eskimos in British Columbia and on Baffin Island of Upper Canada.

He wrote in the introduction to his 1911 *Handbook of North American Indians* that the Inuit language alone had four words for snow: *aput* ("snow on the ground"), *qana* ("falling snow"), *piqsirpoq* ("drifting snow"), and *qimuqsoq* ("a snowdrift").

Boas believed that differences in cultures were reflected in differences in language structure and usage. This wasn't to say that Inuits saw snow differently, according to Boas, but that they organized their thinking and their vocabulary about snow in a more complex manner because snow was such a big part of their daily lives.

In 1940, anthropologist Benjamin Whorf claimed that the Eskimo/Inuit language contained seven words for snow. In 1984, Steven Jacobson published the *Yup'ik Eskimo Dictionary*, which placed the figure for the Yup'ik Eskimos at well into the hundreds. Exaggeration piles upon exaggeration, and pretty soon a thousand words for snow sounds quite reasonable.

In a July 1991 article critiquing Jacobson's dictionary, University of Texas linguist Anthony Woodbury claimed the problem is lexemes. Lexemes are individual units of meaning: For example, the word "speak" can be transformed into the words spoken, speech, speaking, spoke, and so on. Woodbury noted that noun lexemes in at least one of the Eskimo languages can be arranged into more than 250 different individual words or phrases, and verbs allow for even more differentiations. He claimed that there were only fifteen individual lexemes for snow shared among the five Eskimo languages. That's not all that different from the English language.

What's the Difference Between Cajun and Creole?

This is a question to ponder the next time you're stumbling down Bourbon Street after a long night of Mardi Gras revelry.

✳ ✳ ✳ ✳

ONCE, ON A visit to a Louisiana bayou, an old Cajun said to us: "I got an ahnvee for some chee wee." We have no idea what that means, but such phrases are part of what makes Cajun culture—its language, its accordion-heavy music, and its crawfish étouffée—an integral part of the romance of New Orleans. The history of Louisiana Cajuns goes back to the French and Indian War of the mid-18th century, when England and France battled over large swaths of colonial land, including what was then known as Acadia (now part of Nova Scotia, Canada).

Though Acadia was at that time part of a British colony, it was populated mostly by French settlers. Wary of having a colony full of French people during an impending war with France, the Brits kicked out everyone of French descent. These displaced settlers scattered all over North America, but a large percentage of them headed down to another French colony, Louisiana.

Though New Orleans was at that time a thriving port community, Acadians instead settled in the surrounding swampy, alligator-infested bayou regions. Through the years, the Acadians, or Cajuns, as they came to be known, developed a close-knit, if isolated, community with its own dialect, music, and folk wisdom. Technically, only people who are descended from the communities settled by those original displaced Acadians are considered Cajun.

Creole, on the other hand, can refer to any number of things. Originally the term, which dates back to the Spanish conquest of Latin America, meant any person descended from colonial settlers; eventually, any people of mixed race who were native to the colonies became known as Creoles. To add further confusion to the definition, there is something called a Creole language, which is most often born of the contact between a colonial language and a native one.

In Louisiana, Creole refers to people of any race born in Louisiana who descended from the original French settlers of the colony. These folks differ from Cajuns in that they came from places other than Acadia. Louisianan Creoles, too, have their own language—which differs from Cajun—that blends French, West African, and Native American languages; music (such as zydeco); and cuisine.

So there you have it—the difference between Cajun and Creole. Now you can think about something else the next time you're staggering down Bourbon Street—like what to do with all the beads you've collected.

What Was the Iroquois League?

Long before English settlers swarmed over the eastern coast of the "New World," Native Americans—the real original settlers—occupied the land around Lake Ontario now known as New York, as well as parts of New England, and parts of Canada. Sometime between the 14th and 16th centuries, the area became home to thousands of Indians in dozens of tribes.

✳ ✳ ✳ ✳

The High Five

FIVE OF THESE tribes experienced much intertribal fighting. According to legend, a wise sachem (chief) named Deganiwidah sought to make peace and foster goodwill among the nations through the efforts of another sachem named Hiawatha (no, not the Hiawatha). These five tribes—Seneca, Cayuga, Onondaga, Oneida, and Mohawk—sent 50 chiefs as a council and formed an alliance between 1500 and 1650 that came to be known as the "Five Nations of the Iroquois League." (A sixth nation, Tuscarora, joined in 1722.) Other names for this tribal organization were "the Woodland Democracy" and "the Iroquois Confederation."

Each tribe in the League had its own unique traits and qualities. The Seneca tribe—"People of the Great Hills"—was the largest, while the Cayuga, called "the Pipe People," was the smallest. The Onondaga were relatively peaceful and known as the "People of the Mountain." The Oneida—"People of the Standing Stone"—were pretty violent. The Mohawk, known as the "People of the Flint," were the fiercest of them all. Yet, the League had four moral principles to which they all agreed: a love of peace, respect for their laws, a sense of brotherhood, and a reverence for their ancestors.

A Longhouse Is a Home

Life in an Iroquois village was based on farming, even though the tribes did not have animals to help cultivate their fields.

As such, many settlements were situated along rivers, where a spiral wooden fence surrounded the main buildings. These structures, known as "longhouses," could be anywhere from 30 to 350 feet long and were home for many, many families in individual living quarters under one roof (a somewhat primitive form of tenement housing). Several longhouses in an Iroquois village could house as few as 100 to as many as 3,000 people. A number of fires were kept burning in the middle of the longhouse, to provide heat in the winter months and allow cooking and baking year-round.

So strong was the concept of the longhouse in the Iroquois League, the tribes actually regarded their occupied land as one enormous longhouse. The Seneca considered themselves the "Keepers of the Western Door," and the Mohawk were the "Keepers of the Eastern Door" on the other end at the Atlantic Ocean. In between, the Onondaga were the "Keepers of the Fire," the Cayuga were the "Younger Brothers of Seneca," and the Oneida were the "Younger Brothers of Mohawk."

The social order of the League was matrilineal—women owned the longhouse, as well as garden plots and farming tools. They also set and maintained rules in the village and could appoint religious leaders. Women in the village were wholly responsible for daily life, as the men were seldom in camp. Their jobs—warfare, trading, trapping, and hunting—kept them away from the longhouse for months at a time.

Make War, Not Peace

Though the League claimed to have a "love of peace," they still engaged in many warlike activities. The Huron and Algonquin tribes were natural enemies of the League, and tribal warfare was an important component of Iroquois society. The Mohawk were known for swift "hit-and-run" techniques of attack, wielding heavy tomahawk axes to kill their enemies and pillage their goods. But the League avoided large-scale war, remaining satisfied with small skirmishes of 20 to 30 warriors. The League, as sophisticated as it may seem, lacked the social economics and organization to maintain standing armies and stage full-blown war with their enemies. Europeans joined the list of foes in the mid-1600s, as they landed in America and hunted beaver and other animals for pelts. As a result, the Iroquois were forced to move out into other territories for their prey, which increased their aggressive attacks.

Still, the Iroquois were masters of psychological warfare. They understood and exploited intimidation through kidnapping and torture, which instilled fear in others. Many captives were tortured, then assigned by the longhouse women as slaves to their families. Hideous instances of cannibalism were also common among the Iroquois. Jesuit priests like Jean de Brebeuf suffered such atrocities while attempting to minister their faith among the League nations.

The Doctor Is In

The Iroquois League held many religious beliefs, including the power of medicine men. One group, known as the "False Face Society," donned fearsome carved wooden masks. They danced, shook turtle shells, and sprinkled ashes to bring about a cure for illness. A similar curing group, called the "Huskface Society," wore cornhusks as masks.

Working with the White Man

These seemingly savage people had much to offer in the way of operating a complex government body. The council of 50 sachems required that all decisions of the village had to be unanimous. If a sachem caused problems in the council, he was given three warnings. After that, he was ousted. Some historians believe that portions of the U.S. Constitution were based on the council of the Iroquois Confederacy. A curious visitor to many of the council meetings in the 1700s was a man named Benjamin Franklin. The Presidential Seal of America features an eagle holding 13 arrows—one for each original colony. Similarly, the Iroquois seal showed an eagle with five arrows in its talon—one for each nation. The Iroquois nations established peace and harmony with the United States, signing a treaty in 1794. Terms of the agreement endure to this day as, according to the 225-plus-year-old document, some nation members receive calico cloth as annual payment, while other tribes receive the handsome amount of $1,800 a year.

Are Good Manners the Same Around the World?

Sit up straight. Say please and thank you. Don't put your elbows on the table. Most of us were drilled from an early age in proper manners and etiquette. But once you leave your home country, things get a bit complicated. Here are some examples of how other cultures do things differently.

✳   ✳   ✳   ✳

1. In China and the Far East, belching is considered a compliment to the chef and a sign that you have eaten well and enjoyed your meal.

2. In most of the Middle and Far East, it is considered an insult to point your feet (particularly the soles) at another person, or to display them in any way, for example, by resting with your feet up.

3. In most Asian countries, a business card is seen as an extension of the person it represents; therefore, to disrespect a card—by folding it, writing on it, or just shoving it into your pocket without looking at it—is to disrespect the person who gave it to you.

4. Nowadays, a bone-crushing handshake is seen as admirable in the United States and UK, but in much of the East, particularly the Philippines, it is seen as a sign of aggression—just as if you gave any other part of a person's body a hard squeeze!

5. Orthodox Jews will not shake hands with someone of the opposite sex, while a strict Muslim woman will not shake hands with a man, although, to confuse matters, a Muslim man will shake hands with a non-Muslim woman. People in these cultures generally avoid touching people of the opposite sex who are not family members.

6. When dining in China, never force yourself to clear your plate out of politeness—it would be very bad manners for your host not to keep refilling it. Instead, you should leave some food on your plate at each course as an acknowledgment of your host's generosity.

7. In Japan and Korea, a tip is considered an insult, rather than a compliment, and, for them, accepting tips is akin to begging. However, this tradition is beginning to change as more Westerners bring their customs with them to these countries.

8. The "okay" sign (thumb and forefinger touching to make a circle) is very far from okay in much of the world. In Germany and most of South America, it is an insult, similar to giving someone the finger in the United States, while in Turkey it is a derogatory gesture used to imply that someone is homosexual.

9. In the UK, when the two-fingered "V for victory" or "peace" salute is given with the hand turned so that the palm faces inward, it is considered extremely rude, having a meaning similar to raising the middle finger to someone in the United States.

10. In Greece, any signal that involves showing your open palm is extremely offensive. Such gestures include waving, as well as making a "stop" sign. If you do wish to wave goodbye to someone in Greece, you need to do so with your palm facing in, like a beauty pageant contestant or a member of the royal family.

11. In many countries, particularly in Asia and South America, it is essential to remove your shoes when entering someone's home, while in most of Europe it is polite to ask your host whether they would prefer you to do so. The reason, as anyone who's ever owned white carpet will attest, is simple hygiene and cleanliness.

12. Chewing gum might be good for dental hygiene, but in many parts of the world, particularly Luxembourg, Switzerland, and France, public gum-chewing is considered vulgar, while in Singapore most types of gum have been illegal since 1992 when residents grew tired of scraping the sticky stuff off their sidewalks.

13. In most Arab countries, the left hand is considered unclean, and it is extremely rude to offer it for a handshake or to wave a greeting. Similarly, it is impolite to pass food or eat with the left hand. If you must know why, let's just say that, historically, people living in deserts didn't have access to toilet paper, so the left hand was used for "hygienic functions," then cleaned by rubbing it in the sand.

Chapter 9

Disasters and Survival

What Are the All-Time Deadliest Disasters?

✳ ✳ ✳ ✳

Dino-B-Gone

THE DEADLIEST DISASTER in Earth's history may have struck long before humans even existed. According to leading scientific theory, the dinosaurs (and many others) checked out when a massive asteroid slammed into Earth about 65 million years ago. The resulting destruction dwarfs anything that's happened since:

✳ Scientists estimate the asteroid was about six miles wide—bigger than Mount Everest.

✳ The energy of the impact was likely equal to hundreds of millions of megatons. That's about a million times more powerful than the explosion you would get if you detonated all the nuclear bombs in the world at once.

✳ The asteroid hit in what is now the Gulf of Mexico, blasting massive amounts of scorching steam and molten rock into the sky and creating tsunamis that were hundreds of yards high and that moved 600 miles per hour.

✳ The resulting shock wave rocked the entire planet and killed everything for hundreds of miles around.

* Molten rock fell back to Earth for thousands of miles around the impact, setting much of the planet on fire.

* The kicked-up material darkened the atmosphere everywhere and generated nitric acid rain.

* All told, the asteroid wiped out as much as 75 percent of all life on the planet.

King of Plagues

The worst disaster on record in terms of human death toll was the Black Death—a pandemic thought to be bubonic plague, pneumonic plague, and septicemic plague, all caused by bacteria carried by fleas:

* The plague infected the lymphatic system, resulting in high fever, vomiting, enlarged glands, and—in the case of pneumonic plague—coughing up bloody phlegm.

* Bubonic plague was fatal in 30–75 percent of cases; pneumonic plague was fatal in 75 percent of cases; and septicemic plague was always fatal.

* Between 1347 and 1350, the plague spread across Europe and killed approximately 75 million people—nearly half the European population.

* Improvements in sanitation helped bring the Black Death to an end, but the plague still pops up now and then in isolated outbreaks.

An Extra Large Shake

The deadliest earthquake and string of aftershocks in recorded history rocked Egypt, Syria, and surrounding areas in 1201:

* Of course, nobody was measuring such things back then, but experts believe the initial quake ranked as a magnitude 9.

* Egypt was already experiencing a major drought, and damage from the quake exacerbated the problem, leading to mass starvation (and a bit of cannibalism to boot).

* Historians put the total death toll at about 1.1 million.

The Storm of Several Centuries

The deadliest storm on record was the Bhola Cyclone, which hit East Pakistan (now Bangladesh) on November 13, 1970:

* The storm's winds were in excess of 120 miles per hour when it finally hit land.

* It generated an astonishing storm surge of 12 to 20 feet, which flooded densely populated coastal areas.

* Parts of the Ganges River actually turned red with blood.

* According to official records, 500,000 people died (mainly due to drowning). Some sources put the total at closer to one million.

Can You Outrun Lava?

You never know when you're going to get stuck in the middle of a volcanic eruption, so it's only appropriate to ask this all-important question: Can a person outrun lava? It would depend on how fast the human could run and how fast the lava flowed.

* * * *

Number-Crunching

THE ABSOLUTE FASTEST humans in the world can run a little better than ten meters per second, but only for 100 meters. For a 5,000-meter Olympic race, peak human performance is just more than six meters per second. Assuming you'll have a major adrenaline boost due to the dire circumstances, we'll say that you can maintain a speed of three to five meters per second. This speed could vary greatly, however, depending on your physical condition and the distance you need to run, which might be several kilometers.

The speed of lava is affected by its temperature and viscosity (which are related), the angle of the slope it is flowing, and the expulsion rate of the volcano. There are different types of volcanoes and varieties of lava. Some, you could probably outwalk; other types of lava would swallow and incinerate an Olympic-class runner before he or she took a single step.

A Pyroclastic Flow: You're Toast

A pyroclastic flow isn't actually made of lava—it's a column of hot ash and gas that collapses under its own weight and roars down the side of the volcano like an avalanche. These flows can reach speeds of 40 meters per second—you have no chance of outrunning them.

A Basaltic Flow: You've Got a Chance

Basaltic lava has a high temperature and low viscosity, which means that it can move quickly, approaching speeds of 30 meters per second. However, many basaltic flows are much slower—two meters per second or less. You could outpace it for a while, but basaltic lava is relentless and often flows ten or more kilometers from the volcano before cooling and coming to a stop. You might outrun the slower flows, but it would be a challenge.

Mount Kilauea in Hawaii has been continuously issuing basaltic lava flows since 1983. Occasionally, the flows extend to nearby towns, most of which have been abandoned. When there are Hawaiians in the path of the lava, however, they are able to run away from the generally slow flows.

A Rhyolitic Flow: You'll Leave It in the Dust

Rhyolitic lava moves very slowly because it has a relatively low temperature and high viscosity. It may move only a few meters in an hour. It is still dangerously hot, however, so while you can easily outpace it with a brisk walk, you shouldn't dilly-dally.

How Do You Survive a Sinking Car?

Thousands of drivers accidentally steer themselves into lakes or rivers every year. Most cars take only a few minutes to submerge. Would you know how to get out alive? If you know how to handle the situation, the disaster doesn't have to turn deadly.

✳ ✳ ✳ ✳

Stay Calm and Unbuckle

THE FIRST RULE of thumb is never panic. Remain calm, unfasten your seatbelt, and get ready to exit the vehicle.

Roll Down the Window

Don't wait: Roll down your driver-side window as quickly as you can. Even electric windows will open if you try soon enough. If it doesn't work, you'll have to smash the glass. A heavy object is your best bet, but you can try to kick out the window with your feet, too. (Take an easy precaution and leave a screwdriver or hammer inside your glove box, just in case.) Aim for the bottom or corner edge of the window. Whatever you do, don't try to open the door—there's too much pressure from the water outside.

Work Your Way Out

Take a deep breath and force yourself out through the open space. Then start swimming upward.

If the Window Won't Open

If you can't get the window open or broken, your only option is to wait until your car has almost been overtaken with water. Climb into the back seat, as it'll be the last to fill up. Unlock the door right away so you don't forget. Then, once the water is as high as your neck, push the door open—once the water is inside the car, there should be enough pressure for the door to give without much trouble. As soon as it opens, swim as fast as you can out of the vehicle and toward the surface.

How Far Do You Have to Dive Underwater to Escape Gunfire?

Unlike outrunning an explosion, this action-hero plan actually works. If someone happens to be shooting at you, you can avert the gunfire by diving underwater.

✳ ✳ ✳ ✳

A Shield of Water

A 2005 EPISODE OF THE Discovery Channel's *MythBusters* proved that bullets fired into the water at an angle will slow to a safe speed at fewer than four feet below the surface. In fact, bullets from some high-powered guns in this test basically disintegrated on the water's surface.

It might seem counterintuitive that speeding bullets don't penetrate water as easily as something slow, like a diving human or a falling anchor. But it makes sense. Water has considerable mass, so when anything hits it, it pushes back. The force of the impact is equal to the change in momentum (momentum is velocity times mass) divided by the time taken to change the momentum.

In other words, the faster the object is going, the more its momentum will change when it hits, and the greater the force of impact will be. For the same reason that a car suffers more damage in a head-on collision with a wall at 50 miles per hour than at 5 miles per hour, a speeding bullet takes a bigger hit than something that is moving more slowly.

The initial impact slows the bullet considerably, and the drag that's created as it moves through water brings it to a stop. The impact on faster-moving bullets is even greater, so they are more likely to break apart or slow to a safe speed within the first few feet of water.

It's Not Foolproof

The worst-case scenario is if someone fires a low-powered gun at you straight down into the water. In the *MythBusters* episode, one of the tests involved firing a nine-millimeter pistol directly down into a block of underwater ballistics gel. Eight feet below the surface seemed to be the safe distance—the ballistics gel showed that the impact from the bullet wouldn't have been fatal at this depth. But if a shot from the same gun were fired at a 30-degree angle (which would be a lot more likely if you were fleeing from shooters on shore), you'd be safe at just four feet down.

The problem with this escape plan is that you have to pop up sooner or later to breathe, and the shooter on shore will be ready. But if you are a proper action hero, you can hold your breath for at least ten minutes, which is plenty of time to swim to your top-secret submarine car.

What Was the Year Without a Summer?

"The Year Without a Summer" may sound like Armegeddon, but these words describe an actual year in human history—the year 1816, which Americans nicknamed "eighteen-hundred-and-froze-to-death." It was a year of floods, droughts, and unparalleled summertime frosts that destroyed crops, spread diseases, incited riots, and otherwise wrought havoc upon the world. The culprit of this global meteorological mayhem was the eruption of Tambora, a volcano on the Indonesian island of Sumbawa—the largest explosive eruption in recorded history.

✳   ✳   ✳   ✳

Monster Eruption

TAMBORA WAS CONSIDERED inactive until 1812, when a dense cloud of smoke was seen rising above its summit. But neither the smoke, which grew denser and denser over the next three years, nor the occasional rumbles heard from the mountain, could prepare the islanders for what was to come.

When Tambora exploded in April 1815, the blast was heard 1,700 miles away and so much ash was ejected into the atmosphere that islands 250 miles away experienced complete darkness. Only a couple thousand of the island's 12,000 inhabitants survived the fiery three-day cataclysm. Altogether, the eruption and its aftereffects killed more than 90,000 people throughout Indonesia, mostly through disease, pollution of drinking water, and famine. Ash rains destroyed crops on every island within hundreds of miles.

Global Cooling

Along with about 140 gigatons of magma, Tambora expelled hundreds of millions of tons of fine ash, which was spread worldwide through winds and weather systems. It is this ash that scientists now blame for the subsequent "Year Without a Summer." The sulfate aerosol particles contained in it remained in the atmosphere for years and reflected back solar radiation, cooling the globe. The effect was aggravated by the activity of other volcanoes: Soufrière St. Vincent in the West Indies (1812), Mount Mayon in the Philippines (1814), and Suwanose–Jima in Japan, which erupted continuously from 1813 to 1814. To make matters worse, all this took place during an extended period of low solar energy output called the Dalton Minimum, which lasted from about 1795 to the 1820s.

Spring of 1816 in the New World

Although the last three months of 1815 and February 1816 were all warmer than usual, the mild winter hesitated to turn into spring. Under the influence of the hot ash winds from the equator, the low-pressure system usually sitting over Iceland at this time of year shifted south toward the British Isles, and America was penetrated by polar air masses. By March, weather was becoming erratic.

On Sunday, March 17, Richmond, Virginia, was treated to

summerlike temperatures; however, the next day, there was hail and sleet, and on Tuesday morning, the flowers of apricot and peach trees were covered with icicles. At the end of May, there were still frosts and snowfall from Ohio to Connecticut.

June 1816

The first days of June were deceptively warm, with 70s, 80s, and even low 90s in the northeastern United States. But on June 6, temperatures suddenly dropped into the 40s and it began to rain. Within hours, rain turned into snow, birds dropped dead in the streets, and some trees began shedding their still unexpanded leaves. This distemper of nature continued through June 11, when the wind shifted and the cold spell was over...or so people thought.

But strange weather continued to vex the population. Gales and violent hailstorms pummeled crops. On June 27, West Chester, Pennsylvania, reportedly experienced a torrential storm where hailstones the size of walnuts fell from the sky.

July 1816

Just as the farmers were beginning to think that the damage to their crops might be minimal, another cold spell checked their hopes. On July 6, a strong northwestern wind set in, and for the next four days, winter descended upon New England and the Mid-Atlantic states once more as temperatures again dropped to the 30s and 40s. The outlook for a successful harvest was looking bleaker day by freezing day; what vegetation remained intact in New England was flavorless and languid.

August 1816

The folk wisdom that bad things come in threes proved itself before the end of the summer. On August 20, another wave of frost and snow finished off the fruit, vegetables, vines, and meager remains of the corn and bean crops. The fields were said to be "as empty and white as October." For many farmers, that spelled ruin. Even though wheat and rye yielded enough to carry the country through to the next season without mass starvation, panic and speculation drove the price of flour from $3 to nearly $20 per barrel. Animal feed became so expensive that cattle had to be slaughtered en masse. Many New England farmers, unable to cope with the disastrous season, loaded up their belongings and headed west.

Summer Overseas

Meanwhile, Europe was faring no better. Snow fell in several countries in June. Alpine glaciers advanced, threatening to engulf villages and dam rivers. In France, grapes were not ripe enough to be harvested until November, and the wine made from them was undrinkable. Wheat yields in Europe reportedly fell by 20 to 40 percent, both because of cold and water damage and because rains delayed and hampered harvesting.

Famine hit Switzerland especially hard. People began eating moss, sorrel, and cats, and official assistance had to be given to the populace to help them distinguish poisonous and nonpoisonous plants. In Rhineland, people reportedly dug through the fields for rotten remains of the previous year's potato harvest. Wheat, oats, and potatoes failed in Britain and Ireland, and a typhus epidemic swept the British Isles, killing tens of thousands. Grain prices doubled on average; in west-central Europe, they rose between three and seven times their normal price. This was a disaster for the masses of poor people, whose average expenditures for bread totaled between one-quarter and one-half of their total income.

Dearth led to hunger, and high prices led to increased poverty, which led to mass vagrancy and begging. People looted grain storages and pillaged large farms. There was a wave of emigrations to America. The European economy was still unsteady from the aftermath of the Napoleonic wars, and the crisis of 1816 led to a massive retreat from liberal ideas. By 1820, Europe was in the grip of political and economic conservatism, thanks in no small part to a volcanic eruption in Indonesia.

Who's to Blame?

Theories for why summer failed to come in 1816 abound. Many lay the blame directly on the sun. Due to volcanic particles in the air, the solar disk had been dimmed all year, which made large sunspots visible to the naked eye. Others believed that the ice persisting in the Atlantic and the Great Lakes was absorbing great quantities of heat from the atmosphere.

What Happened to the Donner Party?

Starting around 1845, hundreds of thousands of Americans migrated west, believing that it was their "manifest destiny" to claim that territory and seek their fortunes. The story of the Donner Party is one of the most tragic tales in U.S. history.

✳ ✳ ✳ ✳

A New Frontier

To reach Oregon and California, settlers had to cross the Great Plains, a journey that took weeks to complete. There was little water or shelter on this vast expanse of land, and many travelers died of dehydration, cholera, or pneumonia.

Despite such conditions, the lure of a better life was strong. In April 1846, George Donner formed a group of 33 people (mostly members of his family) to head west to Sutter's Fort, California. In May, while camped in Missouri, Donner and his group joined members from another wagon train and formed the Donner Party, named after their elected captain. Donner predicted the journey would put everyone in sunny California by June. He and 86 fellow travelers were in for a big surprise.

Trouble on the Trail

The party had gotten as far as Fort Laramie in what is now Wyoming by the end of June, when they ran into another traveler. He was headed eastbound, having used a faster, though treacherous, route from the west through the desert, one that he did not recommend. Regardless, the Donner Party took the "shortcut," which put them three weeks behind schedule. By this time, many of the travelers had fallen ill, and most of the group's animals had either died or wandered off.

In the middle of October, when the group got stuck in a monstrous mountain blizzard, it was still more than 100 miles from its destination.

Dwindling Supplies

The group was stranded in the Sierra Nevada mountain range for a few months. When the food supplies they had brought with them ran out, the oxen were slaughtered and eaten. Journals and letters from members of the party reveal that before very long the only "food" available consisted of twigs, the bones of decaying animals, and boiled leather hides.

Eventually, a small faction of the Donner Party set out to find help. The rest of the party was too weak to travel, and conditions for them only worsened.

Shocking Discoveries

The rescue group, which consisted of the few members who remained, finally found help in California. Accounts of what the first relief team saw when they arrived at the camp depict group members who were starving, freezing, and delirious. Those who were able to make the recovery trip were taken then; the rest were forced to wait for a second rescue team.

As reported by the second group of rescuers, some of the remaining members of the Donner Party had resorted to cannibalism in order to make it through the winter. The survivors eventually reached Sutter's Fort more than a year after the party's departure from Independence, Missouri, and about six months after their expected arrival. Two-thirds of the men and one-third of the women and children had died on the journey.

The Aftermath

Not surprisingly, when word got out that settlers trapped in the mountains had eaten other human beings to stay alive, migration to California slowed for a while. But when gold was discovered in 1848, images of the imperiled Donner Party were replaced by dreams of newfound wealth in the West.

Today, near the eastern shore of Donner Lake, the Donner Memorial State Park commemorates the courage and the disaster that was the Donner Party's journey. The area of nearby Alder Creek, the site of the second Donner camp, is a designated National Historic Landmark.

What Was the Peshtigo Fire?

Although the Great Chicago Fire garnered international headlines, an inferno that raged in Peshtigo, Wisconsin, burned brighter, longer, and deadlier.

✳ ✳ ✳ ✳

CONSIDER THE COLORFUL tale of Mrs. O'Leary's cow—yes, the one about the celebrated igniter of the Great Chicago Fire of 1871. Despite historical evidence that attempts to lay this fanciful tale to rest, many believe that a clumsy bovine tipped over the gas lamp that started the infamous fire. To go this myth one better, consider the "great" fire itself. Apparently, many believe that the Chicago fire was the most disastrous blaze in U.S. history.

To this misinformed if well-intentioned lot, we offer two words: Peshtigo, Wisconsin. In a bizarre twist of fate, the great Peshtigo fire happened to erupt precisely when Chicago staged its little bonfire. In total devastation and number of fatalities, the Peshtigo blaze leaves Chicago in its embers. To this day, it is the deadliest forest fire in American history. Here's the backstory to the backdraft.

From Tinderbox to Tragedy

Unlike many large fires, Peshtigo's was a conglomeration of smaller blazes that joined into a firestorm. At the time, a prolonged drought had turned the usually lush countryside into a dry thicket. Slash-and-burn land-clearing practices (the cutting and burning of woodlands to create agricultural space) were also presenting a potential problem. With a slew of these fires burning on October 8, 1871, the area around Peshtigo had become a tinderbox, with conditions ripe for disaster.

According to some accounts, the great blaze began when railroad workers touched off a brush fire. But these reports are about as reliable as the fable concerning Mrs. O'Leary's cow. No one is sure of the fire's precise origin, but one thing is certain: Once it started, the fire took on a life of its own. Survivors would compare its violent winds to those of a tornado. A firestorm had been born.

Extensive Losses

In one hour's time, Peshtigo was completely gone. Eight hundred lives were lost in the town alone. As the fire continued on its hellish mission, 16 other towns would succumb to its deadly, wind-whipped flames. The great blaze would destroy a 2,500-square-mile area (nearly 500 square miles larger than the state of Delaware) and wouldn't relent until its winds changed course, pitting the fire against itself and robbing it of its fuel source.

Damage estimates from the fire reached $169 million, which happens to be identical to the Chicago fire. But what stood out were the fatalities. The Chicago fire had snuffed out the lives of an estimated 300 people—no small number, of course—but the Peshtigo fire had claimed as many as 2,500 lives.

Since the greatest loss of life occurred in Peshtigo itself, the fire became closely associated with the town. Many wondered why the Peshtigo fire department couldn't do more to control the blaze. But the department was staffed about as well as any of that time, which is to say it was woefully understaffed. The fire company had a single horse-drawn steam-pumper designed to fight fires at its sawmill. Beyond that, it didn't have the technology to fight even the simplest structural fires, never mind an unprecedented vortex of flame. Peshtigo's citizens were reduced to "sitting ducks" as they awaited their fate amid dry wooden buildings and sawdust-strewn boulevards.

Perhaps the most troubling detail about the Peshtigo Fire is its near-anonymity. Most adults have never heard of it, and despite its well-documented impact, schools seem to overlook it. This undoubtedly speaks to Chicago's fame, which served to magnify the relative significance of its fire. But there's no need for enhancement when the fire being considered is the "Great Peshtigo Fire." Its sobering statistics say it all.

The Peshtigo Fire: What Caused the Flames?

Like many great conflagrations, the cause of the Peshtigo Fire is open to conjecture. Factors such as a prolonged and widespread drought provide reasons for the epic disaster but stop short of pinpointing its origin. What is certain is that the enormous fire (which was 10 miles wide and 40 miles long) burned for two days and claimed the lives of an estimated 1,500 to 2,500 people. When the fire reached the waters of Green Bay, it lost its fuel source, and its stormlike winds diminished. A rainstorm delivered the blaze its final deathblow. A poem published in the *Marinette Eagle* captures the tragedy's essence:

On swept the tornado, with maddening rush,

Uprooting the trees o'er the plain, thro' the brush,

And the sky-leaping flames, with hot, scorching breath,

Gathered parents and children to the harvest of death.

As years roll along and the ages have sped

O'er the charred, blackened bones of the Peshtigo dead,

And the story is told by the pen of the sage,

In letters immortal on history's page,

No fancy can compass the horror and fright,

The anguish and woe of that terrible night.

What Was America's Deadliest Natural Disaster?

Many remember Hurricane Katrina, Superstorm Sandy, or Hurricane Maria with horror, but the 1900 Galveston hurricane and flood did far more widespread damage.

✳ ✳ ✳ ✳

GALVESTON IS AN island city that basks in the sun about an hour southeast of Houston. Nearby, vacationing families enjoy the Houston Space Center, Moody Gardens, Armand Bayou Nature Center, Kemah Boardwalk, and the Forbidden Gardens. Every three years or so, Galveston can expect a brush with a major storm. Every ten years, it's likely to receive a direct hurricane hit. Usually, the city breezes through those storms with relative ease. But September 8, 1900, was another story.

Unprepared and Vulnerable

In 1900, tropical storms and hurricanes weren't assigned names. Galveston residents knew that bad weather was coming, but the U.S. Weather Bureau discouraged use of terms such as *hurricane*. In addition, geographers claimed that the slope of the sea bottom protected the city against harsh ocean conditions. Galveston, the fourth-most-populous city in the state at the time, didn't even have a seawall.

By the time the Category 4 hurricane hit the city, fewer than half its residents had evacuated. In fact, the city was busy with tourists who'd arrived to enjoy the warm gulf waters and watch the eerie, oncoming clouds.

To date, Galveston's 1900 flood, which resulted from that storm, is America's worst natural disaster, killing approximately 8,000 people with a 15-foot storm surge that destroyed roughly half of Galveston's homes and businesses and devastated the surrounding area. The flood has been the subject of books, movies, and songs. In 1904, crowds lined up to see the "Galveston Flood" attraction at New York's Coney Island. Most people don't realize, however, that the storm's damage extended far beyond Galveston.

A Wide Swath

During the 18-hour storm, the winds were so intense that telegraph lines as far away as Abilene—more than 300 miles from Galveston—were leveled. Between the Gulf of Mexico and Abilene, the 1900 storm snapped trees and crushed houses. On J. E. Dick's ranch near Galveston, 2,500 cattle drowned. Throughout East Texas, cities and towns were destroyed. Katy is just one of them.

Today, Katy is an upscale community about 25 miles west of Houston and 60 miles inland from Galveston. Before the Europeans arrived, it was a winter feeding ground for buffalo and a major hunting ground of the Karankawa. By the late 19th century, settlers had built farms and other businesses there. Katy—or "KT"—was named for the MKT (Missouri, Kansas, and Texas) railroad line that terminated in the area.

The 1900 hurricane, however, almost wiped Katy off the map. Only two houses were undamaged when the winds blew through the town's streets and swept homes and businesses from their foundations. Today, those two homes—Featherston House and Wright House—are part of Katy Heritage Park.

Houston was also in the storm's path. Much of the area's economy relied on farms and ranches that were ill prepared for the devastation that was coming. Winds and rising waters destroyed almost every barn in the hurricane's path. Waters up to ten feet deep flooded local pastures. Across East Texas, entire forests were crushed. One news reporter observed "no large timber left standing as far as the eye can see."

From there, it's not clear whether the storm headed due north or if it doubled back. Many believe it retraced its path to the Florida Keys and then continued up the East Coast. By the time it reached New York City, the winds were still raging at 65 miles per hour.

Digging Out

In the aftermath of the storm, the Galveston community dredged sand to raise the city up to 17 feet above sea level. The city also built a 17-foot-tall seawall to protect it from storm surges. Likewise, Houston and the cities around it improved drainage and created reservoirs and flood plains to absorb the water from future storms that were sure to come.

How Many Were Killed in the Triangle Shirtwaist Fire?

A horrific fire brought attention to the lives of sweatshop workers in America—and resulted in labor reform.

❋ ❋ ❋ ❋

ON A SATURDAY afternoon in March 1911, workers at the Triangle Shirtwaist Factory in New York City were getting ready to go home after a long day. They were tidying up their workspaces and brushing fabric scraps off the tables and into large bins. Someone on the eighth floor carelessly threw a match or cigarette butt into one of those bins, and within minutes, flames took over the factory floors.

Panicked workers—most of them female immigrants—rushed to evacuate, and many on the ninth floor became trapped. There were two exit doors on that floor, but one was blocked by fire and the other was locked—a precaution owners deemed necessary to prevent thefts by workers. The terrified people on that floor were faced with two choices: wait for rescue (and likely die in the fire) or jump from the windows. Many chose to jump. Overall, 146 workers died in the tragedy.

Austrian Jewish immigrant Rose Rosenfeld survived by figuring out how the executives were handling the situation. Rose hopped a freight elevator to the roof, where she was rescued by firefighters. When the bosses tried to bribe her to testify that the doors hadn't been locked, Rose refused. The tragedy brought about an investigation of the welfare and safety of sweatshop workers, which resulted in new labor laws.

Rose's anger at the needless death lasted a very long lifetime. She promoted workplace safety reform by retelling her story. Rose died February 15, 2001, at age 107, the last survivor of the Triangle Shirtwaist fire.

What Was the Eastland Disaster?

The city of Chicago has a dark history of disaster and death, with devastating fires, horrific accidents, and catastrophic events. One of the most tragic took place on July 24, 1915. On that overcast, summer afternoon, hundreds of people died in the Chicago River when the Eastland *capsized just a few feet from the dock.*

✳   ✳   ✳   ✳

Company Picnic Turns Tragic

JULY 24 WAS GOING to be a special day for thousands of Chicagoans. It was reserved for the annual summer picnic for employees of the Western Electric Company, which was to be held across Lake Michigan in Michigan City, Indiana. And although officials at the utility company had encouraged workers to bring along friends and relatives, they were surprised when more than 7,000 people arrived to be ferried across the lake on the five excursion boats chartered for the day. Three of the steamers—the *Theodore Roosevelt*, the *Petoskey*, and the *Eastland*—were docked on the Chicago River.

On this fateful morning, the *Eastland*, a steamer owned by the St. Joseph–Chicago Steamship Company, was filled to its limit. The boat had a reputation for top-heaviness and instability, and the new federal Seaman's Act, which was passed in 1915 as a result of the *Titanic* tragedy, required more lifeboats than previous regulations did. All of this resulted in the ship being even more unstable than it already was. In essence, it was a recipe for disaster.

Death and the Eastland

As passengers boarded the *Eastland*, she began listing back and forth. This had happened on the ship before, so the crew emptied the ballast compartments to provide more stability. As the boat was preparing to depart, some passengers went below deck, hoping to warm up on the cool, cloudy morning, but many on the overcrowded steamer jammed their way onto the deck to wave to onlookers on shore. The *Eastland* tilted once again, but this time more severely, and passengers began to panic. Moments later, the *Eastland* rolled to her side, coming to rest at the bottom of the river, only 18 feet below the surface. One side of the boat's hull was actually above the water's surface in some spots.

Passengers on deck were tossed into the river, splashing about in a mass of bodies. The overturned ship created a current that pulled some of the floundering swimmers to their doom, while many of the women's long dresses were snagged on the ship, tugging them down to the bottom.

Those inside were thrown to one side of the ship when it capsized. Heavy furniture onboard crushed some passengers and those who were not killed instantly drowned a few moments later when water rushed inside. A few managed to escape, but most of them didn't. Their bodies were later found trapped in a tangled heap on the lowest side of the *Eastland*.

Firefighters, rescue workers, and volunteers soon arrived and tried to help people escape through portholes. They also cut holes in the portion of the ship's hull that was above the water line. Approximately 1,660 passengers survived the disaster, but they still ended up in the river, and many courageous people from the wharf jumped in or threw life preservers as well as lines, boxes, and anything that floated into the water to the panicked and drowning passengers.

In the end, 844 people died, many of them young women and children. Officially, no clear explanation was given for why the vessel capsized, and the St. Joseph–Chicago Steamship Company was not held accountable for the disaster.

The bodies of those who perished in the tragedy were wrapped in sheets and placed on the *Theodore Roosevelt* or lined up along the docks. Marshall Field's and other large stores sent wagons to carry the dead to hospitals, funeral homes, and makeshift morgues, such as the Second Regiment Armory, where more than 200 bodies were sent.

After the ship was removed from the river, it was sold and later became a U.S. warship as the gunboat *USS Wilmette*. The ship never saw any action but was used as a training ship during World War II. After the war, it was decommissioned and eventually scrapped in 1947.

The *Eastland* may be gone, but its story and ghosts continue to linger nearly a century later.

Identifying the Bodies

At the time of the *Eastland* disaster, the only public building large enough to be used as a temporary morgue was the Second Regiment Armory, located on Chicago's near west side. The dead were laid out on the floor of the armory and assigned identification numbers. Chicagoans whose loved ones had perished in the disaster filed through the rows of bodies, searching for familiar faces, but in 22 cases, there was no one left to identify them. Those families were completely wiped out. The names of these victims were learned from neighbors who came searching for their friends. The weeping, crying, and moaning of the bereaved echoed off the walls of the armory for days.

The last body to be identified was Willie Novotny, a seven-year-old boy whose parents and older sister had also perished on the *Eastland*. When extended family members identified the boy nearly a week after the disaster took place, a chapter was closed on one of Chicago's most horrific events.

What Was Black Sunday?

Sunday April 14, 1935, began as a clear, pleasant day over much of the Midwest. But within hours, daytime would be transformed to night as a weather front with 60-mile-per-hour winds threw up a monstrous dust cloud from the barren fields of the Dust Bowl, burying homes in millions of tons of dirt.

✳ ✳ ✳ ✳

PEOPLE IN THE small towns and farms of Kansas, Oklahoma, Texas, and Colorado were used to dust storms and were ready to seal windows, doors, and every possible crack in their houses with sheets, blankets, and newspapers. But this particular storm, which came to be known as Black Sunday, was different. In Dodge City, Kansas, a strange nighttime fell for 40 minutes in the middle of the day, followed by three hours of near darkness. Inside their homes, men, women, and children huddled with handkerchiefs or wet sponges over their noses, struggling to breathe. Many believed the world was coming to an end. A few hours later in Chicago, the cloud dumped three pounds of soil for each person in the city. The next day, it blanketed New York and Washington, D.C., before sweeping out into the Atlantic Ocean.

Origin of a Disaster

The April 1935 storm was the worst of the Dust Bowl, an ecological disaster that lasted for years at the height of the Great Depression. Affecting 100 million acres of the Great Plains, it brought poverty and malnutrition to millions and spurred an exodus of poor farmers to the West Coast. For years, the Plains region had enjoyed high grain prices and phenomenal crops, but farmers had been overproducing for more than a generation. Overgrazing by cattle and sheep had further stripped the landscape. By 1930, 33 million acres of southern plains once held in place by native prairie grasses had been laid bare. The crisis began in 1931. Farmers enjoyed another bumper crop of wheat, but the resulting surplus forced prices down. Many farmers went broke. Others abandoned their fields just at the start of a severe drought that would last much of the decade.

Stormy Weather

In 1932, 14 dust storms—whipped skyward by strong, dry winds—were reported in the United States. The following year, the storms numbered 38, and a region centering on northern Texas, Oklahoma, and Kansas was dubbed the Dust Bowl. The first great storm occurred in May 1934, when high winds swirled 300,000 tons of soil from Montana and Wyoming skyward. By evening, the "black blizzard" began depositing dust like snow on the streets of Chicago. By dawn the next day, the cloud had rolled eastward over New York, Washington, D.C., and Atlanta, dimming the sun before moving out to sea and dusting ships 300 miles off shore. In the Midwest, summer temperature records were broken as thousands of livestock starved and suffocated. Hundreds of people died from heat stroke, malnutrition, and dust pneumonia.

Black Sunday

In March 1935, another big storm again blew topsoil from the fields of Kansas, Colorado, Texas, and Oklahoma all the way to the East Coast, but it was only a prelude of what was to come.

On April 14, 1935, 20 huge dust storms tore through the region, converging in a single front headed for the East. Witnesses reported that at times they could not see five feet in front of them. A pilot who encountered a dust cloud at

20,000 feet assumed it was a thunderstorm. She tried to climb above it, but could not, and had to turn back. In Oklahoma and Texas, humble homesteads were literally buried beneath feet of dust.

When the dust settled, a drastic migration began that would culminate in 15 percent of Oklahomans leaving the state. Called "Okies" in California, the uprooted people searching for a new life actually came from all the states of the Midwest affected by the continuing disaster. Working for the Farm Security Administration, photographer Dorothea Lange documented their lives, while novelist John Steinbeck immortalized their plight with *The Grapes of Wrath*.

Aftermath

Black Sunday would be an impetus for change. With dirt from the storm still falling over Washington, D.C., Hugh Hammond Bennett—a soil surveyor from North Carolina who helped found the soil conservation movement—won the support of Congress, which declared soil erosion a national menace. Later that year, President Roosevelt signed into law the Soil Conservation Act of 1935, establishing Soil Conservation Service in the Department of Agriculture. Under Bennett's direction, an aggressive campaign to stabilize the region's soil began. Roosevelt also undertook banking reforms and other agricultural policies to help rescue the Plains farmers. One of his decisions led to the planting of more than 222,000 trees.

For the next year, however, the drought continued, as summer temperatures soared to 120 degrees. Sporadic rains and floods in 1937 and 1938 joined the continuing dust storms, and wintertime brought a new kind of storm called a "snuster"—a mixture of dirt and snow reaching blizzard proportions. The fall of 1939 finally brought the rains that ended the drought. With new farming methods and increased agricultural demand due to WWII, the Plains once again became golden with wheat.

What Happened to the Hindenburg?

On May 6, 1937, when the luxury German airship Hindenburg *burst into flames, 36 people lost their lives. But it's wrong to assume that no one survived the disaster.*

✳ ✳ ✳ ✳

WHEN THE ZEPPELIN Company completed the 242-ton *Hindenburg* in 1936, the airship had the distinction of being the largest ever made. At 804 feet long and 135 feet wide, the dirigible was approximately four times larger than modern Goodyear blimps and managed a top speed of more than 80 miles per hour. On May 3, 1937, 36 passengers and a crew of 61 boarded the airship in Frankfurt, Germany, for the first transatlantic flight of the season. The craft's landing on May 6 at New Jersey's Lakehurst Naval Air Station was delayed for several hours because of a storm. When weather conditions finally improved, the *Hindenburg* began its widely publicized and highly anticipated approach for landing.

When the craft was about 200 feet above the ground, horrified onlookers noticed a small burst of flame on the ship's upper fin. Less than half a minute later, the flame had ignited the *Hindenburg's* 7 million cubic feet of hydrogen. Some passengers jumped from the windows, others fell, and the rest were trapped in the burning craft. Herbert Morrison, reporting for radio station WLS in Chicago, uttered the words "Oh, the humanity!" as he watched the fiery vessel hit the ground. The recording remains one of the most famous in broadcast history.

Despite the speed at which the airship incinerated, only 35 of the 97 passengers and crew onboard died in the disaster, along with one member of the 200-strong ground crew. The cause of the fire has never been explained with certainty, though it is believed to have been a result of the highly combustible varnish used to treat the fabric on the outside of the *Hindenburg*. Other theories have cited foreign sabotage, sparks from static electricity, and lightning strikes.

What Was the Munich Air Disaster?

On February 6, 1958, British European Airways Flight 609 crashed on its third attempt to take off from a slush-covered runway at Munich-Riem Airport in what was then West Germany. The disaster claimed the lives of twenty-three people, including eight members of the Manchester United soccer team.

* * * *

THE ILL-FATED FLIGHT was on its way back from Belgrade, Yugoslavia, where the Manchester team had just successfully advanced to the European Cup semifinals. The plane stopped in Munich to refuel. After two failed take-off attempts due to an engine power issue, the pilot made a third attempt. The plane skidded off the end of the runway, crashed through a fence and then into a house. The right side of the fuselage then struck a wooden hut, and burst into flames. Twenty people died on board, and three died later in the hospital. Among the fatalities were Manchester United players and staff, journalists, one member of the flight crew, and the copilot.

After the devastating loss of life in the Munich Air Disaster there was fear that Manchester United might fold. The team, including the eight players that perished, were known as the "Busby Babes." The name referenced their youth and their manager Matt Busby (who survived the crash).

As it turns out, Busby returned as manager the next season and built a second generation of Busby Babes. And in 1968, (ten years after the disaster) Manchester United won the European Cup, soccer's most prestigious club prize, becoming the first British team to do so.

The Munich Air Disaster is memorialized at Manchester

United's stadium, Old Trafford, with two plaques: one has the names of the players and staff who died inscribed on it, the other honors the memory of the members of the press lost in Munich. In addition, a clock permanently frozen in time at 3:04 P.M. on February 6, 1958, the time of the crash, is located on the southeast corner of the stadium with the word Munich listed below.

Has Anyone Survived a Fall from the Golden Gate Bridge?

More than two dozen people have survived their falls from the iconic bridge. That sounds like a lot—until you learn that more than 1,700 have taken the leap since it opened in 1937.

✳ ✳ ✳ ✳

A Gruesome Way to Go

THE 21-STORY DROP from the Golden Gate Bridge, which spans the opening of the San Francisco Bay, is obviously one of the more effective suicide methods. It's also one of the nastiest. After four seconds of hurtling through the air (just enough time for a change of heart), the jumper hits the water at 75 miles per hour. In most cases, the force of the impact—15,000 pounds per square inch—will break the jumper's ribs and vertebrae. The broken ribs usually pierce the lungs, spleen, and heart, and cause massive internal bleeding. If a jumper somehow survives, he or she likely will drown.

A handful of jumpers lived to tell the tale because they hit the water feet first. Kevin Hines jumped and survived in 2000, when he was 19 years old. Immediately after taking the leap, he changed his mind and prayed to survive. In the rapid fall, he managed to turn himself so that he hit feet first. Hitting vertically helped Hines's body penetrate the water, reducing the force of impact. The force was great enough to break his back and shatter his vertebrae, but none of his organs were punctured. In 1979, a man survived in good enough shape—his worst injury was several cracked vertebrae—to swim ashore and drive to a hospital.

The bridge is a suicide hotspot for two reasons: First, some people see it as romantic to leap from such a beautiful structure into the water; second, it's been incredibly easy to do. The bridge has a pedestrian walkway, and all that stands between a suicidal person and the plunge is a four-foot railing. One possible explanation for this short railing is that the chief engineer of the bridge, Joseph Strauss, was only five feet tall and wanted to be able to enjoy the view.

Building a Safer Bridge

Over the years, calls to add a barrier to the Golden Gate Bridge have been met with resistance in San Francisco. Opponents declare that the money would be better spent elsewhere; they object to compromising the beauty of the bridge to stop people from attempting suicide, since these people would likely just resort to different methods.

In October 2008, the Golden Gate Board of Directors voted to build a net system below the bridge's platform that would catch and hold jumpers. The net will be located 20 feet below the top deck on each side of the bridge and extend 20 feet outward. Fabrication of the stainless-steel netting began in May 2017. Installation is scheduled to be completed in 2021.

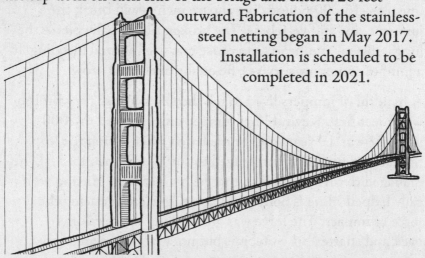

What Was the Buffalo Creek Flood?

In 1972, a calamitous flood roared through mining towns in West Virginia, leaving utter destruction in its wake. Company officials were slow to respond, which only made the disaster worse.

❋　❋　❋　❋

BUFFALO CREEK WINDS its way through 16 mining communities in West Virginia and empties into the Guyandotte River. As part of its mining operations, the Buffalo Mining Company, a subsidiary of Pittston Coal Company, dumped mine waste—consisting of mine dust, shale, clay, and other impurities—into Buffalo Creek. The company constructed its first impoundment dam in 1960. Six years later, it constructed a second dam upstream. By 1972, the mining company had built its third dam into the hillside near the Buffalo Creek communities.

The Precursors

A flood on Buffalo Creek should perhaps not have been much of a surprise. In 1967, the U.S. Department of the Interior warned West Virginia state officials that the Buffalo Creek dams were unstable and dangerous. This conclusion came as a result of a study of state dams conducted in response to a mine dam break that killed nearly 150 people—mostly children—in Wales in 1966.

In February 1971, the third impoundment dam on Buffalo Creek failed, but the second dam halted the water, preventing damage to the creek communities. The state cited Pittston Coal Company for violations but didn't follow up with inspections.

A Wall of Water

A few days before the fatal flood, a heavy, continuous rain fell, which is typical for the area at that time of year. By 8:00 A.M. on February 26, the water had risen to the crest of the third dam, which collapsed within five minutes. The force of the water then crushed the subsequent dams as the water gushed down the creek. A black wave—variously described as 10 to 45 feet high—gushed through the mining towns. The area of Buffalo Creek hollow was smothered with 132 million gallons of filthy wastewater in waves traveling at more than seven feet per second.

The flooding left 125 people dead, more than 1,100 injured, and more than 4,000 homeless.

The Aftermath

It took only three hours for the gushing waves to demolish the lives of the Buffalo Creek community. It would take years to recover from the disaster, if recovery happened at all.

Three separate commissions—federal, state, and citizen—each concluded that the Buffalo Mining Company blatantly disregarded standard safety practices. The Pittston Coal Company, in a statement from its New York office, declared the disaster "an act of God." Citizens responded by saying they never saw God building the dams in the first place.

West Virginia Governor Arch Moore Jr. banned journalists from entering the disaster site, explaining that the state was already unduly harmed and did not need any bad press. He promised to build 750 public housing units. Ultimately, 17 model homes and 90 apartments were constructed. A promised community center was never built.

With the federal disaster funds, Moore attempted to build a superhighway through the Buffalo Creek hollow. West Virginia's Department of Highways condemned and purchased hundreds of lots from flood survivors. A two-lane road was constructed, but the superhighway never was. Most property was not sold back to its original owners but instead remained held by the state.

Both state and federal mine safety agencies passed laws that improved conditions in the coalfields. In 1973, the West Virginia legislature passed the Dam Control Act, which regulated dams in the state. However, funding was never appropriated to enforce the law, and in 1992, the Division of Natural Resources estimated that state was home to at least 400 hazardous dams.

How Bad Was the Three Mile Island Nuclear Accident?

In the late 1970s, the nuclear accident at Three Mile Island in Pennsylvania gripped the country and caused panic throughout the region. It was serious, but it was no Chernobyl.

✳ ✳ ✳ ✳

NUCLEAR POWER HAS always been controversial. Advocates see it as the answer to our national energy needs, while opponents view it as an environmental disaster just waiting to happen. The latter group almost saw its nightmare come true on March 28, 1979, when a series of events led to a severe core meltdown at the Three Mile Island nuclear power plant near Middletown, Pennsylvania.

Today, four decades after the accident, many people still believe that the area around the power plant was blanketed with radioactive fallout that endangered thousands. The truth, however, is much different. Though the Nuclear Regulatory Commission (NRC) calls the accident "the most serious in the U.S. commercial nuclear power plant operating history," no lives were lost and the amount of radiation released was within safe levels.

How Safe Is "Safe"?

According to an NRC report, which followed numerous studies of and investigations into the accident, the average dose of radiation to approximately 2 million people in the area was only about 1 millirem. "To put that into context," the report explains, "exposure from a full set of chest X-rays is about

6 millirem. Compared to the natural radioactive background dose of about 100–125 millirem per year for the area, the collective dose to the community from the accident was very small. The maximum dose to a person at the site boundary would have been less than 100 millirem."

Multiple Malfunctions

The cause of the accident was a combination of mechanical problems and human error. It started when the main feedwater pumps stopped running in a secondary, non-nuclear section of the plant. This was caused either by a mechanical or an electrical failure, and it prevented the steam generators from removing heat. The turbine automatically shut down, and so did the reactor. Immediately, the pressure in the primary system—the nuclear portion of the plant—began to increase. To prevent that pressure from becoming excessive, a special relief valve opened. The valve should have closed when the pressure decreased by a certain amount, but it failed to do so. Signals to the operator did not show that the valve was still open; as a result, cooling water poured out of the valve and caused the core of the reactor to overheat.

Because the operators did not realize that the plant was experiencing a loss-of-coolant accident, they took a series of actions that made conditions worse by further reducing the flow of coolant through the core. Consequently, the nuclear fuel overheated to the point where the long metal tubes that hold the nuclear fuel pellets ruptured and the fuel pellets began to melt.

The accident at Three Mile Island was a serious cause for concern, and the plant was extremely fortunate to have avoided a catastrophic breach of the containment building and the release of massive amounts of radiation into the environment.

Chernobyl in Comparison

As bad as the Three Mile Island event was, it pales in comparison to the accident at the Chernobyl nuclear power plant just outside the town of Pripyat, Ukraine, on April 26, 1986.

Chernobyl remains the largest nuclear power plant disaster in history. That event directly killed 31 people; produced a massive plume of radioactive debris that drifted over parts of the western Soviet Union, Eastern Europe, and Scandinavia; left huge areas dangerously contaminated; and forced the evacuation of more than 200,000 people.

The accident has been the subject of countless books and films. In 2019, *Chernobyl*, a miniseries centered around the nuclear disaster and the cleanup efforts that followed, premiered on HBO to critical acclaim.

Who Has Survived Being Stranded at Sea?

Humankind has been subjected to every imaginable hostile condition, but very little beats the grueling stories of survival for days, weeks—even months—lost at sea.

✳ ✳ ✳ ✳

Hold On Tight

OCEAN-GOING TALES OF survival have a certain mythic status. They bring to mind epic travels; age-old yarns of sea monsters, mermaids; and nourishment via filtered water and the sucked bones of fish. Yet legend aside, even factually verified survival stories seem implausible. To be stranded on the sea (and to live to tell the tale) seems, well, unreal.

A hierarchy applies when gauging the relative extremity of a sea survival story. Those in cold water are the worst off, since hypothermia sets in within minutes. Survival time also depends on whether there's something to hold onto, or the person is simply treading water. Survival time is also cut short by solitude—humans have a difficult time being alone for extended periods. The best-case scenario, if such a scenario exists, is to be stranded on a boat, in warm water, along with some comrades. What follows are some true tales of survival at sea:

Juan Jesus Caamano survived 13 hours with no boat in cold waters

In 2001, a fishing boat capsized off the coast of Spain. Nine of the 16 men made it into a lifeboat, another two jumped into the frigid waters without putting on their bodysuits (and died immediately), while five others managed to get their suits on before the boat sank.

Two of those five were 36-year-old Juan Jesus Caamano and his brother-in-law. Their boat had sent out a mayday signal before sinking, so planes, helicopters, and ships from several countries were sent to look for the victims. After only four hours, the nine men in the lifeboat were saved. Experts, who estimated a man in Caamano's circumstances could survive a maximum of $3^{1}/_{2}$ hours, were surprised when, after 13 hours, Caamano was found alive, afloat in the stormy waters, tied to his dead brother-in-law. In all, six men died.

Laura Isabel Arriola de Guity survived six days; found clinging to driftwood in warm waters

In 1998, Hurricane Mitch ravished Central and Latin America, killing more than 7,000 people in Honduras alone. Isabella Arriola, 32, lived in a small coastal Honduran village that was literally swept away by the ocean. She survived for six days with no life jacket, drifting in and out of consciousness, while clinging to pieces of driftwood. Somehow, she survived through high waves and winds that climbed to 185 miles per hour. Arriola was eventually spotted by a coastguard aircraft and was rescued by helicopter. Unfortunately, she found that her husband, children, and half her village had perished in the storm.

Steven Callahan survived 76 days on a small raft

In 1982, Steven Callahan, a naval architect, was participating in a sailing race when his boat was damaged during a storm and sank in the Atlantic Ocean. Callahan managed to salvage a tiny amount of food before setting off in an inflatable rubber raft. He survived for 76 days on rainwater, fish, and seabirds before being rescued by a fishing boat. Callahan's extensive background and experience with the high seas helped him survive the ordeal.

Maralyn and Maurice Bailey survived 117 days on a small raft

In 1973, British couple Maralyn and Maurice Bailey set out on an ambitious voyage from England to New Zealand on their yacht, which was struck by a large whale and capsized off the coast of Guatemala. Maurice happened to be an expert on maritime survival skills; before they boarded their rubber raft, they collected a small amount of food, a compass, a map, an oil burner, water containers, and glue. When the Baileys ran out of food, they caught sea animals with safety pins fashioned into hooks. After two months, the raft started to disintegrate, and it needed constant care. Finally, 117 days later, a small Korean fishing boat rescued them.

How Do You Escape Quicksand?

If you happen to get trapped in one of nature's suction pits, hang loose. Your moves are the only things that can drag you down.

✳ ✳ ✳ ✳

L ET'S SAY YOU'RE running through the woods and you trip and fall. As you attempt to right yourself, you realize that the earth below you isn't really earth at all, and you find it impossible to find purchase. You are wet and covered in a granular grime, but it's not a body of water or sand pit that you've fallen into. This substance seems more like a combination of the two. In fact, it is—you have fallen into a quicksand pit. What you do from this point forth will determine whether this will be a momentary inconvenience or just a slightly longer inconvenience.

A Quicksand Primer

Quicksand is a sand, silt, or clay pit that has become hydrated, which reduces its viscosity (thickness). Therefore, when a person is "sucked" down, they are simply sinking as they would in any body of water.

So why does quicksand make people so nervous? It's probably due to the fact that it can present resistance to the person who steps in it. This is particularly true of someone who is wearing heavy boots or is laden with a backpack or other load. Obviously, the additional weight will reduce buoyancy and drag one down.

It's All in the Legs

In the human thirst for drama, quicksand has a reputation as a deadly substance. But the facts show something far different. Because quicksand is denser than water, it allows for easy floating. If you stumble into a pit, you will sink only up to your chest or shoulders. If you want to escape, all you need to do is move your legs slowly. This action will create a space through which water will flow, thereby loosening the sand's grip. You should then be able to float on your back until help arrives.

How Did Aron Ralston Survive Being Trapped Under a Boulder?

When rock climber Aron Ralston's arm was pinned by a boulder while out on a climbing trip, he did the unthinkable to survive.

✳   ✳   ✳   ✳

IN 2003, ARON Ralston went on a hiking trip in Utah's Blue John Canyon. Feeling confident and adventurous, Ralston, an experienced mountain climber, set out on the solo trip, neglecting to tell anyone he was leaving. The trip began perfectly: nice hike, beautiful day. Then, as Ralston tried to negotiate a narrow opening in the canyon, an 800-pound boulder fell and pinned his right forearm, completely crushing it.

It looked like there would be no escape. Ralston was completely trapped under the boulder and his hand and arm were deadened due to the pressure of the blow. For the next five days, Ralston concentrated on staying alive, warding off exhaustion, hypothermia, and dehydration. He knew no one would be looking for him, since no one knew of his trip. Assuming the worst, he carved his name into the rock that held him down, along with what he thought would be his death date. Using a video camera he had packed with his supplies, he taped goodbyes to his friends and family.

On the sixth day of being trapped, delirious and starving, Ralston made a hellish decision: He would cut off his own arm to escape. Bracing his arm against a climbing tool called a chockstone, Ralston snapped both his radius and ulna bones and applied a tourniquet with some rags he had on hand. Using the knife blade of his multi-tool, he then cut through the soft tissue around the broken bones and tore through tendons with the tool's pliers. The makeshift operation took about an hour.

After he was loose, Ralston still had to rappel down a 65-foot-tall cliff, then hike eight miles to his parked truck. Dehydrated and badly injured, he walked to the nearest trail and was finally discovered. A helicopter team flew Ralston to the nearest hospital where he was stabilized and sent immediately into surgery to clean up and protect what was left of his arm. He later received a prosthetic limb.

Once the press caught wind of his story, Ralston became a celebrity. His ordeal was the subject of the film *127 Hours*. These days, Ralston works as a motivational speaker, and he still goes on climbing trips, regularly setting new records.

Can People Get Sucked Out of Planes?

All sorts of objects—including human beings—can be hurled out of shattered windows, broken doors, and other holes in the skin of an aircraft. The problem in any case like this is explosive decompression, a situation in which the keys to survival include the height at which the plane is flying and the size of the aircraft cabin itself.

✳   ✳   ✳   ✳

Pressure Drop

MOST PASSENGER PLANES are pressurized to approximate an altitude of 8,000 feet or less. If there is a break in the skin of the plane at an altitude considerably higher than that—commercial jets normally fly at 30,000 feet or more—all sorts of bad things can happen. And quickly. For one thing, a lack of oxygen will render most people unconscious in little more than a minute at 35,000 feet.

As for being sucked out of the plane, this sort of tragedy generally occurs when the decompression is very sudden. The difference in pressure between the inside and outside of the plane causes objects to be pulled toward the opening. Whether or not someone survives sudden decompression depends on several things, including luck.

Fogg Nearly Disappears into the Fog

Critical care nurse Chris Fogg was almost sucked out of a medical evacuation plane on a flight from Twin Falls, Idaho, to Seattle in 2007. Fogg had not yet buckled his seat belt when a window exploded while the plane was flying at approximately 20,000 feet. His head and right arm were pulled out of the window, but Fogg held himself inside the aircraft with his left hand on the ceiling and his knees jammed against a wall.

Fogg, who weighed 220 pounds, summoned enough strength to push himself backward, which allowed air to flow between his chest and the window. This broke the seal that had wedged him in the opening. The pilot managed to get the plane to a lower altitude, and everyone aboard—including a patient who had been hooked to an oxygen device—survived the ordeal.

Tales of Terror

Not everyone has been so fortunate in cases of explosive decompression. In 1989, a lower cargo door on a United Airlines flight came loose at 23,000 feet, and the loss of pressure tore a hole in the cabin. Nine passengers were sucked out of the plane, along with their seats and the carpeting around them. A year earlier, an 18-foot portion of roof tore off an Aloha Airlines flight at 24,000 feet, hurling a flight attendant out into the sky.

Although scenes of people and debris whistling all over the place in adventure movies have been exaggerated, the threat of explosive decompression is real—even if it is rare. It's a good idea to take the crew's advice about wearing your seat belt at all times, and if there is a sudden loss of oxygen, put on that mask in a hurry. They're not kidding about the possible consequences.

How Do You Avoid a Mountain Lion Attack?

Mountain lions, also known as cougars, pumas, and panthers, are the largest cats in North America. Though mountain lions generally avoid people, attacks do occur.

✳ ✳ ✳ ✳

✳ Hike in groups. Mountain lions avoid crowds and noise, and the more people on the lookout, the better. If there are children in the group, make sure they are supervised.

✳ Be aware of your surroundings. Pay particular attention to what's behind and above you in trees and on rocks and cliffs.

✳ Don't back the animal into a corner—give it a way out. It would much rather run off and survive to hunt again.

✳ If you encounter a mountain lion, don't try to run away. Running may cause the animal to chase you, and it's much faster than you. Stand still while facing the mountain lion, but avoid looking it in the eye, which it takes as a sign of aggression. Watch its feet instead.

✳ Do things that make you appear larger and bigger than the cat, such as raising your arms over your head or holding up a jacket, a backpack, or even your mountain bike.

✳ Make loud noises. Growling can make you sound like something the cat would prefer not to mess with.

✳ Don't crouch down or bend. This makes you appear smaller and, therefore, an easy target. Don't move a lot but don't play dead. To a mountain lion, a perfectly still human looks like an entrée.

✳ Remain calm and don't act afraid. Like many animals, mountain lions can detect fear.

Chapter 10

Law and Disorder

Who Are the Non-Suspects in Police Lineups?

Appropriately enough, these "fillers" (also known as "distractors") are mostly criminals or suspected criminals. Who better to act as possible perps?

❋   ❋   ❋   ❋

IN THE TRADITIONAL "live" police lineup, in which a witness picks out the bad guy from behind a one-way mirror, the police typically present one actual suspect and four or five similar-looking inmates from the local jail. The lineup can be either simultaneous (with the suspect and fillers standing together) or sequential (with the possible perps coming out one by one). When there aren't enough suitable inmates, police officers and other station staff may participate. Occasionally, the police will even recruit people with the right look off the street and pay them a small fee for their trouble.

Nevertheless, it can be difficult to come up with five people who closely match the description of a suspected perpetrator. And even when such fillers can be found, the very nature of using people who bear similarities to the culprit can lead to false identifications—if one filler resembles the suspect much more closely than the other participants, he stands a pretty good chance of being identified by the witness as the perp. Furthermore, if the police choose fillers who don't closely match the description of the suspect, a judge might later rule that the lineup was unfair.

For this reason, many police departments have switched from using traditional lineups to utilizing photo arrays, also known as virtual lineups. With this method, the police select a series of mug shots that closely match the description of the suspected perpetrator. In the United States, the conventional virtual lineup includes two rows of three pictures and has been dubbed the "six pack." As with the live lineup, some police departments prefer to use a sequential virtual lineup, showing the witness only one picture at a time.

Some departments utilize software that automatically picks suitable faces from a large database of police pictures. So if you ever get arrested, be sure to smile for your mug shot—you never know who will be checking you out later.

What Was the Cadaver Synod?

The Cadaver Synod—or Cadaver Trial—is considered the lowest point in papal history. How low? Try six feet under.

✳   ✳   ✳   ✳

V as in Vengeance (and Stephen VII)

THE MASTERMIND BEHIND what became known as the Cadaver Synod was Italy's King Lambert, who sought revenge for Pope Formosus's actions against his father, Guido, the duke of Spoleto. Previously, Formosus's predecessor Pope Stephen VI had crowned Guido and Lambert co-Holy Roman Emperors in A.D. 892. But Formosus favored the German king Arnulf, and he convinced Arnulf to invade Italy and usurp the crown. Guido died before he was forcibly removed from office, and in February 896, Arnulf was crowned emperor.

Physical paralysis ultimately cut short Arnulf's reign; he returned to Germany, leaving Lambert to take over and exact his revenge on Formosus. The pope died before Lambert got a chance to strike, but that didn't stop Lambert: He ordered Formosus's successor Pope Stephen VII—himself a Spoletian sympathizer—to dig up the pope's body and put it on trial for perjury, violating church canons, and coveting the papacy.

A Trial of the Grotesque

No transcript of the Cadaver Synod exists, but historians agree as to how it probably went down: In January 897, the rotting corpse (it was only nine months after Formosus's death) was exhumed, carried into the courtroom, dressed in elaborate papal vestments, and propped in a chair, behind which cowered a teenage deacon, who was in charge of speaking for the dead pope. Stephen ranted and screamed at Formosus's body, who, of course, was found guilty of all charges.

As punishment, Stephen ordered that all of Formosus's papal ordinances be overturned, that the three fingers on his right hand used to give papal blessings be hacked off, and that his body be stripped of its papal vestments, dressed in peasant's clothes, and reburied in a common grave. After the sentence was carried out, the pope's body was dug up yet again and tossed in the Tiber River, from which a monk retrieved it and buried it. Again.

The Cadaver Synod caused a public rebellion and within a few months, Stephen was deposed, stripped of his vestments, and sent to prison where he was strangled to death in 897.

Return of the Synod

In 897, Pope Theodore II held a synod to annul the Cadaver Synod—one his few actions as pope, since his pontificate lasted only 20 days. Formosus's body was dug up once more and carried back to St. Peter's Basilica, where it was redressed in papal vestments and returned to its tomb. The next pope, John IX, held another synod to confirm Theodore II's decision. He also declared it illegal to put a dead body on trial.

But John's successor, Pope Sergio III, who participated in the Cadaver Synod and was a "violent hater of Formosus," held his own synod to reverse the decisions made by the previous two popes. Maybe because it was finally illegal to dig up and put dead bodies on trial, he simply had an epitaph made for Stephen's tomb that heaped insults on Formosus. Sergio's ruling was never overturned, however; it was just ignored.

* Formosus means "good-looking" in Latin.

* From A.D. 896 to 904, there were nine popes—the same number of popes throughout the entire 20th century.

* Pope Sergio III was quite the controversial figure. His papacy has been called "The Rule of the Harlots."

* Though Formosus has been unanimously vindicated and cleared of all charges, there has never been a Pope Formosus II. Cardinal Pietro Barbo apparently thought about taking the name in 1464 but was talked out of it. He took Paul II instead.

Who Was the Bloody Countess?

Born to George and Anna Bathory in August 1560, Countess Elizabeth (Erzsebet) Bathory came from one of the wealthiest families in Hungary. Of course, all families have their secrets and Elizabeth's had more than their fair share. One uncle was allegedly a devil worshipper and an aunt was believed to be a witch. So when Elizabeth herself started acting a bit odd and suffering from violent, uncontrolled fits of rage, no one really thought much about it.

✳ ✳ ✳ ✳

A Taste for Blood

AT AGE 15, with no sign of her fits subsiding, Elizabeth married Ferencz Nádasdy and moved into his castle. By most accounts, the castle's dungeon gave Bathory her first opportunities to experiment with torture. With her husband gone for long periods of time, she apparently began experimenting with black magic, often inviting people to the castle to take part in strange, sadistic rituals. Legend has it that, during this time, in a fit of rage, Bathory slapped a young servant girl across the face, drawing blood. Allegedly, Bathory looked down at her hand, which was covered in the young girl's blood, and thought the blood was causing her own skin to glow. This, according to the legend, is why Bathory believed that the blood of virginal girls would keep her young forever.

In 1604, Nádasdy died, leaving Bathory alone in the castle. For a while, she traveled abroad and, by all accounts, continued her quest to fulfill her insatiable thirst for blood. But she eventually returned and purchased her own castle. Shortly thereafter, servant girls and young girls from the neighboring villages began disappearing in the middle of the night, never to be heard from again.

Ungodly Horrors

During this time period, villagers knew better than to speak out against nobility. So when people started implying that the countess was kidnapping young girls and murdering them in her castle, the villagers kept their mouths shut. Even when Bathory's carriage would ride through town late at night with young girls in the back, villagers still kept their heads down and went about their business. Villagers were often awakened in the middle of the night by the sound of piercing screams coming from Bathory's castle. However, it wasn't until young aristocratic girls began disappearing that the decision was made to investigate. By that time, though, hundreds of young girls had already gone missing.

In December 1610, King Matthias II of Hungary sent a group of men out to Bathory's castle to investigate claims that local girls were being held there against their will. Heading up the group was a man named Gyorgy Thurzo. It would be his subsequent testimony of what the group encountered that would bring the full weight of the court down on Bathory.

Thurzo later stated that when the group arrived at the castle, the things they found inside were so horrific and gruesome that he could not bring himself to write them down.

Thurzo said that inside the door they found a young girl, dead and apparently drained of blood. A short distance away, they found another girl, alive but near death. She also appeared to have lost a large amount of blood. Advancing down into the dungeon, the group encountered several young girls who were being held captive. The group released them and then began the search for Bathory herself. In the end, Bathory and four of her servants were taken into custody. The servants were taken into the village for questioning while Bathory herself was confined to her bedroom in the castle.

Unspeakable Acts

Twenty-one judges presided over the proceedings that began on January 2, 1611. Bathory remained in her castle while her four accomplices were questioned. The things these four individuals claimed took place in the castle were almost too horrific to describe. One of Bathory's employees, a dwarf named Ficzko, said that he personally knew of at least 37 girls the countess had killed. Bathory's childhood nurse, Ilona Joo, stated that she had personally helped Bathory kill somewhere in the neighborhood of 50 girls, using such horrific devices as cages filled with spikes, fire pokers, and oily sheets that were placed between victims' legs and set on fire.

As the proceedings went on, the descriptions got worse and worse: stabbings with needles and scissors, tearing off limbs, and even sewing girls' mouths shut. The countess enjoyed whipping and beating young girls until their bodies were swollen, at which point she would use a razor to draw blood from the swollen areas. There were even rumors that she bathed in the blood of the girls in an attempt to stay young.

In the end, the countess was found guilty of killing 80 girls. However, based on the number of bodies eventually recovered at the castle, the body count could be as high as 650.

All four of Bathory's accomplices were put to death. But because the countess was a member of the nobility, she could not be executed for her crimes. Instead, she was moved to a series of small rooms in her castle and walled inside. All the doors and windows were sealed, with only a few small holes for air and one to allow food to pass though. The countess lived in her own private prison for three years before she died, still claiming she was innocent of all charges.

What's the Difference Between Mass Murders and Serial Killers?

Serial killers are made of sugar and spice and everything nice, and mass murderers are ... wait, that's not right. The distinction between the two is actually very simple.

✳ ✳ ✳ ✳

The Mass Murderer

A MASS MURDERER KILLS four or more people during a short period of time, usually in one location. In most cases, the murderer has a sudden mental collapse and goes on a rampage, progressing from murder to murder without a break. About half the time, these outbreaks end in suicides or fatal standoffs with the police.

Various school shootings over the years have been instances of mass murder, as have been famous cases of postal workers, well, "going postal." A case in which someone murders his or her entire family is a mass murder. Terrorists are lumped into this category as well, but they also make up a group of their own.

The Serial Killer

A serial killer usually murders one person at a time (typically a stranger), with a "cooling off" period between each crime. Unlike mass murderers, serial killers don't suddenly snap one day—they have an ongoing compulsion (usually with a sexual component) that drives them to kill, often in very specific ways.

Serial killers may even maintain jobs and normal relationships while going to great lengths to conceal their killings. They may resist the urge to kill for long periods, but the compulsion ultimately grows too strong to subjugate. After the third victim, an aspiring killer graduates from plain ol' murderer to bona fide serial killer.

The Rest

In between these two groups, we have the spree killer and the serial spree killer. A spree killer commits murder in multiple locations over the course of a few days. This is often part of a general crime wave. For example, an escaped convict may kill multiple people, steal cars, jaywalk, and litter as he tries to escape the police. As with a mass murderer, a spree killer doesn't plan each murder individually.

The serial spree killer, on the other hand, plans and commits each murder separately, serial-killer style. But he or she doesn't take time off between murders or maintain a double life. It is all killing, all the time. One of the best-known examples is the Washington, D.C.-area beltway snipers who killed ten people within three weeks in October 2002.

Of course, if you see any of these types of killer in action, don't worry about remembering the right term when you call the police. They're all equally bad.

How Many Tools Do You Need to Pick a Lock?

Regardless of what is portrayed in cops-and-robbers flicks, you need at least two tools to pick a lock.

✳ ✳ ✳ ✳

WHETHER YOU'RE A wannabe ruffian or a forgetful home-owner, you should know that it is nearly impossible to pick a lock with only one paper clip, one bobby pin, or one of anything else. Although you can certainly accomplish the task with simple tools, you will need two of them—one to act as a pick and a second one to serve as a tension wrench.

The simple pin-and-tumbler locks on most doors contain a cylinder and several small pins attached to springs. When the door is locked, the cylinder is kept in place by the pins, which protrude into the cylinder. When a matching key is inserted into the lock, the pins are pushed back and the cylinder turns. The key to lock-picking, then, is to push the pins back while simultaneously turning the cylinder. This is why two items are required—a pick to push the pins and a tension wrench to turn the cylinder. Professional locksmiths often use simple lock-picking techniques to avoid damaging the offending lock.

Common household items that can serve as tension wrenches include small screwdrivers and bent paper clips. Items you can use as picks include safety pins, hair fasteners, and paper clips. The determined apprentice may be happy to learn that there is a situation in which one paper clip may suffice in picking a lock: Small, inexpensive padlocks sometimes succumb to large paper clips that are bent in such a way that one end is the pick and the other end is the tension wrench. Even so, the process involves more than just jamming something into the lock and turning the doorknob. Seasoned lock-pickers rely on their senses of hearing and touch to successfully finish the job. They're anticipating a vibration accompanied by a distinct "click" that means each pin is in alignment.

What Is North America's Oldest Law Enforcement Agency?

Among the most revered of Texas's iconic institutions must be the Texas Rangers, whose rich history and daring frontier exploits have thrilled generations. These were those who could not be stampeded.

✳ ✳ ✳ ✳

THE OLDEST LAW enforcement agency in North America, the Texas Rangers has been compared with the FBI, Scotland Yard, and the Royal Canadian Mounted Police. The group's heritage began with the earliest settlements in Texas, and it became a significant part of the story of the Old West and its mythology.

Getting Off the Ground

In Mexican Tejas, the Comanche and Tonkawa raided Texian settlements on a regular basis. Stephen F. Austin, responsible for founding and developing many of these settlements from America, realized he needed a militia of some kind to ward off Native American raids, capture criminals, and patrol against intruders. He set up two such companies, which today are considered the ancestors of the modern Texas Rangers.

In 1835, in what is often considered the official founding of the Rangers, the Texas council of representatives created a Corps of Rangers and set pay at $1.25 per day. These enforcers of the law had to provide their own mounts, weapons, and equipment. As they were often outnumbered during battles, many carried multiple pistols, knives, and rifles. The most popular weapons were Spanish pistols, Tennessee and Kentucky rifles, and Bowie knives. Later, Sam Colt built his reputation on the fact that the Texas Rangers were the first to use the Colt revolver.

Like the state of Texas itself, the Texas Rangers had multicultural roots. Company rosters show that Anglos, Hispanics, and American Indians served in the ranks. In addition, a number of immigrants were also present; Ireland, Germany, Scotland, and England each contributed native sons to the Rangers.

As the cause for independence from Mexico heated up, the Rangers played a key role in protecting civilians fleeing Santa Anna's army, harassing Mexican troops, and providing intelligence to the Texas army. And it was the Rangers who responded to Colonel William Travis's last minute plea to defend the Alamo. Even so, the Rangers did not participate in actual combat as often as they may have preferred.

Texas president Sam Houston sought good relations with Native Americans, so a fighting force to be used against them was not high on his list of priorities. Texas's second president, Mirabeau B. Lamar, however, felt differently and strengthened the Rangers and their responsibilities when he got into office. He wanted them to clear the frontier of Native Americans who were in the way of Texas settlement and expansion, and the Texas Rangers rose to that call very effectively. The Cherokee War of 1839 expelled most Cherokee from Northeast Texas, and the Battle of Plum Creek moved the Comanchee farther west out of central Texas. When Houston regained the presidency in 1841, he recognized the Rangers as an effective frontier protection agency and threw his support to them.

Making Their Name

In the Mexican-American War that followed closely after Texas annexation, the Texas Rangers distinguished themselves as ferocious fighters. They supported the U.S. Army under Generals Zachary Taylor and Winfield Scott, working as scouts and extremely effective warriors. This brought them a worldwide reputation as *Los Diablos Tejanos*, the Texas Devils.

For a time after the war, however, it looked as though the Rangers might have had their best days behind them. Once

Texas became a U.S. state, the protection of its frontier was a federal issue, and there was no obvious place for the Rangers. Although it wasn't dissolved, the agency saw its purpose wither away and its best officers leave for greener pastures. There was a slight revival under Captain John S. "Rip" Ford in which the Rangers attacked and killed Comanche leader Iron Jacket, but the coming Civil War gave those interested in fighting another focus. Many Rangers and former Rangers served with the Confederacy, but there was no official connection. Reconstruction, likewise, offered little opportunity for the Texas Rangers, as their former frontier duties were handled by the Union Army.

Back in the Battle

That all changed, however, when the Democrats took back the governor's mansion in 1874. The state legislature passed a bill that year formally creating the Texas Rangers (thus making that name official). The Reconstruction government hadn't been entirely successful in maintaining order, so the Rangers had their work cut out for them. Two branches were created by the legislation: the Special Force, focusing on law enforcement, and the Frontier Battalion, protecting the western frontier and borders. The Special Force did what was necessary to get the job done. In one particular infamous incident, Rangers took the bodies of dead cattle rustlers and stacked them in the Brownsville town square as a show of force.

The Frontier Battalion, focusing on gunfighters in addition to Native Americans, had its share of high-profile captures, as well. Not bound by the borders of the state, Ranger John Armstrong captured one of Texas's deadliest outlaws, John Wesley Hardin—reputed to have killed more than 30 people—on a train in Pensacola, Florida. In the course of the capture, Hardin was knocked out, and one of his three companions was killed; the remaining two surrendered. Another famous train and bank robber, Sam Bass, was killed by four Rangers in an 1878 shoot-out at Round Rock.

By the 1890s, Texas Rangers were upholding the law in mining towns and tracking down train robbers. They were once even called upon to prevent an illegal prizefight. Records show that in one year, the Rangers scouted nearly 174,000 miles, made 676 arrests, returned 2,856 head of livestock, assisted civil authorities 162 times, and guarded jails on 13 occasions.

Into Tomorrow

The role of the Texas Rangers has continued to evolve. Today, they are part of the Texas Department of Safety, and a Ranger is far more likely to have a laptop computer than a horse. Even so, they continue to investigate cattle thefts as well as other major felony crimes. And the stories of their heyday during the early days of Texas live on to support the mythos of the officers who stand tall.

Who Founded the Mafia?

To be honest, we really didn't want to answer this question. But then our editors made us an offer we couldn't refuse.

❋ ❋ ❋ ❋

THIS IS LIKE asking, "Who founded England?" or "Who founded capitalism?" The Mafia is more of a phenomenon than an organization—it's a movement that rose from a complicated interaction of multiple factors, including history, economics, geography, and politics. Hundreds of thousands of pages have been written by historians, sociologists, novelists, screenwriters, and criminologists who have attempted to chart the history and origins of the Mafia, so it's doubtful that we'll be able to provide any real revelations in five hundred words. But we're a hardy bunch, and we'll do our best.

By all accounts, the Mafia came to prominence in Sicily during the mid-19th century. Given Sicily's history, this makes sense—the island has repeatedly been invaded and occupied, and has generally been mired in poverty for thousands of years. By the mid-19th century, Italy was in total chaos due to the abolition of feudalism and the lack of a central government or a semblance of a legitimate legal system.

As sociologists will confirm, people who live in areas that fall victim to such upheaval tend to rely on various forms of self-government. In Sicily, this took the form of what has become known as the Mafia. The fellowship, which originated in the rural areas of the Mediterranean island, is based on a complicated system of respect, violence, distrust of government, and the code of *omertà*—a word that is synonymous with the group's code of silence and refers to an unspoken agreement to never cooperate with authorities, under penalty of death. Just as there is no one person who founded the Mafia, there is no one person who runs it. The term "Mafia" refers to any group of organized criminals that follows the traditional Sicilian system of bosses, *capos* ("chiefs"), and soldiers. These groups are referred to as "families."

Although the Mafia evolved in Sicily during the 19th century, most Americans equate it to the crime families that dominated the headlines in Chicago and New York for much of the 20th century. The American Mafia developed as a result of the huge wave of Sicilian immigrants that arrived in the United States in the late 19th and early 20th centuries. These newcomers brought with them the Mafia structure and the code of *omertà*.

These Sicilian immigrants often clustered together in poor urban areas, such as Park Slope in Brooklyn and the south side of Chicago. There, far from the eyes of authorities, disputes were handled by locals. By the 1920s, crime families had sprung up all over the United States and gang wars were prevalent. In the 1930s, Lucky Luciano—who is sometimes called the father of the American Mafia—organized "The Commission," a faux-judiciary system that oversaw the activities of the Mafia in the United States.

Though Mafia families have been involved in murder, kidnapping, extortion, racketeering, gambling, prostitution, drug dealing, weapons dealing, and other crimes over the years, the phenomenon still maintains the romantic appeal that it had when gangsters like Al Capone captivated the nation. Part of it, of course, is the result of the enormous success of the *Godfather* films, but it is also due, one presumes, to the allure of the principles that the Mafia supposedly was founded upon: self-reliance, loyalty, and *omertà*.

So there you have it: a summary of the founding of the Mafia. Of course, we could tell you more, but then we'd have to... well, you know.

Who Were the Brownsville Boys?

Following the rise of the National Crime Syndicate, or what people now call the Mafia, a group of enterprising killers formed an enforcement arm that the press dubbed "Murder, Incorporated." Officially, they were known as "The Combination" or "The Brownsville Boys," since many of them came from Brooklyn's Brownsville area.

✳   ✳   ✳   ✳

THE COMBINATION BEGAN their mayhem-for-money operation around 1930 following the formation of the National Crime Syndicate. Until their demise in the mid-1940s, they enforced the rules of organized crime through fear, intimidation, and murder. Most of the group's members were Jewish and Italian gangsters from Brooklyn; remorseless and blood-thirsty, murder for money was their stock-in-trade. The number of murders committed during their bloody reign is unknown even today, but estimates put the total at more than a thousand from coast to coast. The title "Murder, Incorporated" was the invention of a fearless *New York World-Telegram* police reporter named Harry Feeney; the name stuck.

Filling a Need

The formation of the group was the brainchild of mob over-lords Johnny Torrio and Lucky Luciano. The most high-profile assassination credited to the enterprise was the murder of gang lord Dutch Schultz, who defied the syndicate's orders to abandon a plan to assassinate New York crime-buster Thomas Dewey. The job went to one of the Combination's top-echelon gunsels, Charles "Charlie the Bug" Workman, whose bloody prowess ranked alongside such Murder, Inc., elite as Louis "Lepke" Buchalter, the man who issued the orders; Albert Anastasia, the lord high executioner; Abe "Kid Twist" Reles, whose eventual capitulation led to the group's downfall; Louis Capone (no relation to Al); Frank Abbandando; Harry "Pittsburg Phil" Strauss, an expert with an ice pick; Martin "Buggsy" Goldstein; Harry "Happy" Maione, leader of the Italian faction; Emanuel "Mendy" Weiss, who is rumored to have never committed murder on the Sabbath; Johnny Dio; Albert "Allie" Tannenbaum; Irving "Knadles" Nitzberg, who twice beat a death sentence when his convictions were over-turned; Vito "Socko" Gurino; Jacob Drucker; Philip "Little Farvel" Cohen; and Sholom Bernstein, who like many of his cohorts turned against his mentors to save his own life. It was an era of infamy unequaled in mob lore.

Loose Lips

Though many of the rank and file of Murder, Inc., appeared to enjoy killing, Reles, a former soda jerk, killed only as a matter of business. Known as "Kid Twist," Reles may not have been as bloodthirsty as some of his contemporaries, but he was cursed with a huge ego and a big mouth, and he wasn't shy about doing his bragging in front of cops, judges, the press, or the public at large. The little man with the big mouth would eventually lead to the unraveling of the Combination and greatly weaken the power of the National Crime Syndicate. When an infor-mant fingered Reles and "Buggsy" Goldstein for the murder of a small-time hood, both men turned themselves in, believing they could beat the rap just as they had a dozen times before, but this one was ironclad. Reles sang loud and clear, implicating his peers and bosses in more than 80 murders and sending several of them to the electric chair, including the untouchable Buchalter. He also revealed the internal secret structure of the National Syndicate. Reles was in protective custody when he "fell" to his death from a hotel room on November 12, 1941, while surrounded by police. By the mid-1940s, Murder, Inc., was a thing of the past, and the National Crime Syndicate was in decline. When it came to singing like a canary, only Joe Valachi would surpass the performance of Reles, once the most trusted member of the Brownsville Boys.

What Did Lizzie Borden Do?

Despite the famous playground verse that leaves little doubt about her guilt, Lizzie Borden was never convicted of murdering her father and stepmother.

✳　✳　✳　✳

IT WAS A sensational crime that captured the public imagination of late-19th-century America. On the morning of August 4, 1892, in Fall River, Massachusetts, the bodies of Andrew Borden and his second wife, Abby, were found slaughtered in the home they shared with an Irish maid and Andrew's 32-year-old daughter, Lizzie. A second daughter, Emma, was away from home at the time.

Rumors and Rhyme

Although Lizzie was a devout, church-going Sunday school teacher, she was charged with the horrific murders and was immortalized in this popular rhyme: "Lizzie Borden took an ax and gave her mother 40 whacks. When she saw what she had done, she gave her father 41." In reality, her stepmother was struck 19 times, killed in an upstairs bedroom with the same ax that crushed her husband's skull while he slept on a couch downstairs. Lizzie's father was killed about an hour later. In that gruesome attack, his face took 11 blows, one of which cut his eye in two and another that severed his nose.

Andrew was one of the wealthiest men in Fall River. By reputation, he was also one of the meanest. Despite the brutality of Andrew's murder, it seems few people mourned his loss. The question wasn't why he was killed, but who did it.

Lizzie's Forbidden Romance

One of the most curious explanations for the murder involves the Bordens' servant Bridget Sullivan. Her participation has always raised questions. Like the other members of the Borden household, Bridget had suffered from apparent food poisoning the night before the murders. She claimed to have been ill in the backyard of the Borden home.

During the time Abby was being murdered, Bridget was apparently washing windows in the back of the house. Later, when Andrew was killed, Bridget was resting in her room upstairs. Why didn't she hear two people being butchered?

According to some theories, Lizzie and Bridget had been romantically involved. In this version of the story, their relationship was discovered shortly before the murders. Around this same time, Andrew was reportedly rewriting his will. His wife was now "Mrs. Borden," to Lizzie, not "Mother," as Lizzie had called her stepmother for many years. The reason for the estrangement was never clear.

Lizzie also had a strange relationship with her father and had given him her high school ring, as though he were her sweetheart. He wore the ring on his pinky finger and was buried with it.

Just a day before the murders, Lizzie had been attempting to purchase prussic acid—a deadly poison—and the family came down with "food poisoning" that night. Some speculate that Bridget was Lizzie's accomplice in the murders and helped clean up the blood afterward.

This theory was bolstered when, a few years after the murders, Lizzie became involved with actress Nance O'Neil. For two years, Lizzie and the statuesque actress were inseparable. This prompted Emma Borden, Lizzie's sister, to move out of their home.

At the time, the rift between the sisters sparked rumors that either Lizzie or Emma might reveal more about the other's role in the 1892 murders. However, neither of them said anything new about the killings.

Whodunit?

Most people believe that Lizzie was the killer. She was the only one accused of the crime, with good reason. Lizzie appeared to be the only one in the house at the time, other than Bridget. She showed no signs of grief when the murders were discovered. During questioning, Lizzie changed her story several times. The evidence was entirely circumstantial, but it was compelling enough to go to trial.

Ultimately, the jury accepted her attorney's closing argument, that the murders were "morally and physically impossible for this young woman defendant." In other words, Lizzie had to be innocent because she was petite and well bred. In 19th-century New England, that seemed like a logical and persuasive defense. Lizzie went free, and no one else was charged with the crimes.

But Lizzie wasn't the only one with motive, means, and opportunity. The most likely suspects were family members, working alone or with other relatives. Only a few had solid alibis, and—like Lizzie—many changed their stories during police questioning. But there was never enough evidence to officially accuse anyone other than Lizzie.

So whether or not Lizzie Borden "took an ax" and killed her parents, she's the one best remembered for the crime.

Who Was Jack the Ripper?

Between 1888 and 1891, he brutally murdered at least five women in London's East End. But was there really a connection between Jack the Ripper and the British royal family?

✳ ✳ ✳ ✳

T HE SERIAL KILLER known as Jack the Ripper is one of history's most famous murderers. He breathed terror into the gas-lit streets and foggy back alleys of the Whitechapel area of London and became renowned the world over. Despite the countless books and movies detailing his story, however, his identity and motives remain shrouded in mystery. One of the most popular theories, espoused by the 2001 movie *From Hell* (starring Johnny Depp), links the killer to the British royal family.

The Crimes

Five murders are definitively attributed to Jack the Ripper, and he has variously been connected to at least six other unsolved slayings in the London area. The body of the first victim, 43-year-old Mary Ann Nichols, was discovered on the morning of August 31, 1888. Nichols's throat had been cut and her abdomen mutilated. The subsequent murders, which took place over a three-year period, grew in brutality. The killer removed the uterus of his second victim, Annie Chapman; part of the womb and left kidney of Catherine Eddowes; and the heart of Mary Kelly. All of his victims were prostitutes.

The Name

A man claiming to be the murderer sent a letter (dated September 25, 1888) to the Central News Agency, which passed it on to the Metropolitan Police. The letter included the line, "I am down on whores and I shant quit ripping them till I do get buckled." It was signed, "Yours truly, Jack the Ripper." A later postcard included the same sign-off. When police went public with these details, the name "Jack the Ripper" stuck.

The Suspects

Officers from the Metropolitan Police and Scotland Yard had four main suspects: a poor Polish resident of Whitechapel by the name of Kosminski, a barrister who committed suicide in December 1888, a Russian-born thief, and an American doctor who fled to the States in November 1888 while on bail for gross indecency. Since there was little or no evidence against any of these men, the case spawned many conspiracy theories, the most popular of which links the killings to the royal family.

The Royal Conspiracy

The heir to the British throne was Prince Albert Victor, grandson of Queen Victoria and son of the man who would later become King Edward VII. The prince, popularly known as Eddy, had a penchant for hanging around in the East End, and rumors abounded that he had a daughter, Alice, out of wedlock with a shop girl named Annie Crook. To prevent major embarrassment to the Crown, Eddy sought assistance from Queen Victoria's physician, Dr. William Gull, who institutionalized Annie to keep her quiet. However, her friends, including Mary Kelly, also knew the identity of Alice's father, so Dr. Gull created the persona of Jack the Ripper and brutally silenced them one by one. A variation on this theory has Dr. Gull acting without the knowledge of the prince, instead driven by madness resulting from a stroke he suffered in 1887.

Royal involvement would certainly explain why the police were unable to uncover the identity of the Ripper or to even settle on a prime suspect. There *was* a shop girl named Annie Crook who had an illegitimate daughter named Alice, but there is nothing to connect her to either the prince or the murdered prostitutes. In fact, there is no evidence to suggest that the murdered women knew one another. Until the identity of Jack the Ripper is settled beyond doubt, these and other conspiracy theories will likely persist.

What's a Ponzi Scheme?

Do you want to get rich quick? Are you charming and persuasive? Do you lack scruples? Do you have a relaxed attitude toward the law? If so, the Ponzi Scheme may be for you!

✳ ✳ ✳ ✳

Yes, there was a real Mr. Ponzi, and here's how his scam works. First, come up with a phony investment—it could be a parcel of (worthless) land that you're sure is going to rise in value in a few months or stock in a (nonexistent) company that you're certain is going to go through the roof soon. Then recruit a small group of investors, promising to, say, double their money in 90 days. Ninety days later, send these initial investors (or at least some of them) a check for double their investment. They'll be so pleased, they'll tell their friends, relatives, neighbors, and coworkers about this sure-fire way to make a fast buck.

You use the influx of cash from these new investors to pay your initial investors—those who ask for a payout, that is. The beauty part is that most of your initial investors will be so enchanted with those first checks that they'll beg to reinvest their money with you. Eventually, of course, your new investors will start to wonder why they aren't getting any checks, and/or some government agency or nosy reporter might come snooping around . . . but by then (if you've timed it right) you'll have transferred yourself and your ill-gotten gains out of the country and out of reach of the authorities. Like related scams that include the Pyramid Scheme and the Stock Bubble, financial frauds like this one have been around for centuries, but only the Ponzi Scheme bears the name of a particular individual—Charles Ponzi.

Mr. Ambition Learns His Trade

As you might imagine—given that he was a legendary con man—Ponzi gave differing accounts of his background, so it's hard to establish facts about his early life. He was likely born Carlos Ponzi in Italy in 1882. He came to America in 1903 and lived the hardscrabble existence of a newly arrived immigrant. While working as a waiter, he slept on the floor of the restaurant because he couldn't afford a place of his own. But the handsome, suave Ponzi was determined to rise in the world—by fair means or foul. The foul means included bank fraud and immigrant smuggling, and Ponzi wound up doing time in jails in both the United States and Canada.

The Check is (Not) in the Mail

While living in Boston in 1919, the newly freed Ponzi more or less stumbled across the scheme that would earn him notoriety. It involved an easily obtained item called an International Postal Reply Coupon. In simple terms, the scam involved using foreign currencies to purchase quantities of a kind of international postal stamp, then redeeming the stamps for U.S. dollars. This brought a big profit because of the favorable exchange rate of the time, and it actually wasn't illegal. The illegal part was Ponzi's determination to bring ever-growing numbers of investors into the scheme . . . and just keep their money. Until the roof fell in, Ponzi became a celebrity. Before long, people across New England and beyond were withdrawing their life savings and mortgaging their homes to get in on the action.

The end came in the summer of 1920, when a series of investigative reports in a Boston newspaper revealed that the House of Ponzi had no foundations. By that time, he'd taken some 40,000 people for a total of about $15 million. In today's money, that's roughly $192.5 million. Ponzi spent a dozen years in prison on mail fraud charges. Upon release, he was deported and continued his scamming ways abroad before dying—penniless—in Brazil in 1948.

How Did Prohibition Get Started?

It's hard to conceive of today: Ban the sale and manufacture of alcohol! Sure, Prohibition didn't work, but a study of its roots shows why people thought an alcohol ban was feasible enough.

✳ ✳ ✳ ✳

But First...

DID YOU BRING your ax? Let's shatter a kegful of mythology! Did you know that...

... *the Prohibition movement actually began before the Civil War?* The temperance movement registered local victories as early as the 1850s.

... *one-third of the federal budget ran on ethanol?* This was before federal income tax became the main source of revenue.

... *Prohibition didn't ban alcohol consumption?* Clubs that stocked up on liquor before Prohibition legally served it throughout.

... *women's suffrage didn't affect the passage of Prohibition?* The Eighteenth Amendment enacted Prohibition. The Nineteenth Amendment gave women the vote.

... *Prohibition didn't create gangs?* The gangs were already there. They just took advantage of a golden opportunity.

... *Eliot Ness's "Untouchables" really existed?* They were agents of the Bureau of Prohibition.

Temperance

Strictly speaking, *temperance* means moderation, not abstinence. By the early 1800s, most people realized that drunkenness wasn't particularly healthy. As the industrial age gathered steam, working while intoxicated went from "bad behavior" to "asking for an industrial maiming by enormous machinery." Immigration also factored, for nativist sentiment ran high in the 1800s. Many Americans didn't like immigrants with foreign accents (many of whom saw nothing wrong with tying one on) and made alcohol an "us versus them" issue.

The XX (Chromosome) Factor

Women, logically, formed the backbone of the temperance movement. Just because you can't vote doesn't mean your brain is disconnected. With a woman's social role limited to home and family, whatever disabled the home's primary wage-earner threatened home economics. Worse still, alcohol abuse has always gone fist-in-mouth with domestic violence.

Organizations and Advances

In 1869, the Prohibition Party was formed to run antialcohol candidates. It typically polled 200,000+ popular presidential votes from 1888 to 1920 but never greatly influenced national politics in and of itself. The compressed political energy and intellect of American women—denied access to congressional seats and judgeships—found its outlet in 1873: the Woman's Christian Temperance Union (WCTU), which still exists today. By 1890, the WCTU counted 150,000 members.

Meanwhile, the male-dominated Anti-Saloon League (ASL) was founded in 1893 and achieved rapid successes due to smart campaigning. By appealing to churches and campaigning against Demon Rum's local bad guys, it drew in nonprohibitionists who disapproved of the entire saloon/bar/tavern culture. While the ASL would later hog the credit for the Eighteenth Amendment, the WCTU laid the foundation for credible temperance activism.

Only three states were "dry" before 1893. In 1913, the ASL began advocating Prohibition via constitutional amendment. By 1914, there were 14 dry states, encompassing nearly half the population; by 1917 another 12 had dried up. In that same year, the Supreme Court ruled that Americans didn't have a constitutional right to keep alcohol at home. Prohibition's ax, long in forging, now had a sturdy handle.

Eighteenth Amendment

By January 29, 1919, the necessary 36 states had ratified this amendment. In October of that year, Congress passed the Volstead Act to enforce the amendment. One year later, it would be illegal to manufacture, sell, or transport intoxicating liquors. Of course, everyone stopped drinking.

Okay, that's enough laughter.

What we got was the Roaring Twenties. Alcohol went underground, corrupting police departments and providing limitless opportunity for lawbreakers. The understaffed, oft-bought-and-paid-for Bureau of Prohibition couldn't possibly keep up. America's War on Alcohol worked no better than the later War on Drugs, which would so casually ignore history's lessons.

Enough Already

On December 5, 1933, the Twenty-first Amendment repealed the Eighteenth—the only such repeal in U.S. history. Prohibition was over.

Why Do Judges Wear Black Robes?

Because black is slimming, of course! If only it were that easy. The real reason judges wear black robes is up for debate, though only slightly. Ask any member of the Catholic Church and he or she will tell you that this practice is purely an ecclesiastical tradition. During the 1500s, priests wore black robes. And during this time, priests were—you guessed it—judges, too.

✳   ✳   ✳   ✳

BUT BLACK WASN'T the end-all back then. English court dress was quite flamboyant, to say the least. Judges would wear a black robe trimmed in fur during the winter months and a violet or scarlet robe trimmed in pink taffeta during the summer months. No wonder these robes were referred to as "costumes" in the Judges' Rules that were set forth after 1635. Judges also wore black girdles underneath their robes.

Court dress continued to evolve, and accessories were piled onto the already ornate ensemble. By the mid-18th century, judges began to take even more liberties with their costumes. For criminal trials, they wore scarlet robes with a matching hood and a black scarf. For civil trials, many judges kept it simple and wore a black silk gown. After years and years of indecisiveness and plenty of lilac and mauve, most courts settled on the simple black silk gown as a base. Ceremonial occasions were (and still are) an entirely different beast—we're talking silk stockings, leather pumps, and all kinds of shiny buckles. But that's a different story.

Today, the black robe is fairly standard in courtrooms around the world (depending on the court or level). In the United States, the black robe is definitely the garb of choice. You will never see a U.S. judge (in open court) decked out in fur trim, bright colors (definitely not pink), and, um, a girdle.

While the Catholics' explanation of why judges wear black robes makes the most sense, there are other explanations to consider: Black symbolizes a lack of favor to one side or another, and black is appropriate in a criminal trial because of the dark nature of the proceedings.

In the end, it boils down to this: The majority of judges feel that wearing a black robe during court proceedings is an unwritten rule. With the exception of the United States Solicitor General—who is usually dressed in late-19th-century attire (morning coat, gray ascot, vest, and pinstriped pants)—and the judges of the Maryland Court of Appeals—who wear scarlet robes—it is rare to see a U.S. judge in any color other than black.

Who Was H. H. Holmes?

H. H. Holmes has secured a place in history as one of the most horrifyingly prolific killers the world has ever seen.

✳ ✳ ✳ ✳

BORN IN MAY 1860 in New Hampshire, Herman Webster Mudgett was a highly intelligent child, but he was constantly in trouble. Charming, handsome, and charismatic, he nonetheless displayed traits of detachment and dispassion from an early age. As a teen, he became abusive to animals—a classic sign of a sociopath.

Fascinated with skeletons and the human body, Mudgett decided to pursue a medical degree. After marrying Clara Lovering, he enrolled in medical school. There, he had access to skeletons and cadavers. He came up with a scheme to fleece insurance companies by taking out policies for family members or friends, using stolen cadavers to fake their deaths, and collecting the insurance money.

When authorities became suspicious, he abandoned Clara and their newborn baby, moving from city to city and taking on various jobs, most likely scheming and manipulating everyone he crossed. In 1886, the charming liar and thief with murderous intentions surfaced in Chicago with a new name: H. H. Holmes. The city would become the site of his deadliest swindle of all.

A "Castle" with a Most Intriguing Floor Plan

If you lived in Chicago in the late 1800s, you were likely consumed with thoughts of the World's Columbian Exposition. Planners hoped it would make America a superstar country and put Chicago on the map as an A-list city. The Great Fire of 1871 had demolished the town, but the fair would bring the city back—and in a big way.

With new people flooding into the city every day looking to nab one of the world's fair jobs, Chicago was experiencing a population boom that made it very easy for people to simply vanish. The handsome and charismatic Holmes recognized this as an opportunity to lure women into his clutches while most people had their focus elsewhere.

He married his second wife, Myrta, in 1887, without ever securing a divorce from Lovering. Holmes quickly shipped Myrta off to live in suburban Wilmette, while he took up residence in Chicago, free to do as he pleased. He secured a position as a pharmacist at a drugstore in Englewood. He worked for the elderly Mrs. Holden, who was happy to have a handsome young doctor to help out at her store. When Mrs. Holden suddenly disappeared, Holmes told people she had moved to California, and he purchased the store.

Next, Holmes purchased a vacant lot across the street from the drugstore and began constructing a house with a floor plan he designed himself. The three-story house at 63rd and Wallace would have more than 60 rooms and 50 doors, secret passageways, gas pipes with nozzles that piped noxious fumes into windowless rooms, chutes that led down to the basement, and an airtight vault. Holmes hired and fired construction crews on a regular basis; it was said that his swindler's streak got him out of paying for most of the materials and labor used to create this "Murder Castle."

Up & Running

Advertised as a lodging for world's fair tourists, the building opened in 1892. Holmes placed ads in the newspaper to rent rooms, but also listed classified ads calling for females interested in working for a start-up company. Of course, there was no start-up company, and Holmes hired the prettiest women or those who could offer him some sort of financial gain. One by one, they inevitably succumbed to his charm. He made false promises to woman after woman, luring them deeper into his confidence. He took advantage of their naïveté to gain their trust and steal their money.

When he was done with a woman, either because she became suspicious of him or because he had simply gotten what he needed from her, Holmes got rid of her—without remorse or emotion. Sometimes he piped gas into a victim's room to kill her in her sleep; other times he locked her in his airtight vault and listened as she slowly suffocated. Evidence shows he tortured some of them before killing them. After he had brutalized the unfortunate soul, he destroyed the evidence in a vat of acid or kiln he had built expressly for that purpose, often selling his victims' bones and organs to contacts in the medical field.

The End of "Doctor Death"

After the world's fair ended, creditors put pressure on Holmes, and he knew it was time to flee. Strange as it seems, when Holmes was finally brought to justice, it wasn't initially for homicide; it was for one of his many financial swindles. But as clues about missing women emerged, investigators became suspicious of him for other reasons.

Detective Frank Geyer began to follow the trail of this mysterious man whose identity changed with the weather. Geyer had traced many missing world's fair women back to Holmes's lodging house. He was particularly interested in the whereabouts of three children—Howard, Nellie, and Alice Pietzel. Geyer followed their tracks across the Midwest and into Canada. In Toronto he finally found a house where Holmes had allegedly stayed with several children in tow. Buried in a shallow grave in the backyard, stuffed in a single traveling trunk, he discovered the bodies of the two Pietzel girls. Geyer found the boy's remains several months later in an oven in an Indianapolis home.

When the evidence was brought back to court, Geyer got full clearance to investigate every inch of Holmes's Chicago dwelling. The investigation turned up a lot more than detectives anticipated, and one of America's most chilling stories of murder and crime officially broke.

Inside his heavily guarded cell, Herman Webster Mudgett admitted his crimes. He officially confessed to 27 murders, six attempted murders, and a whole lot of fraud. What he didn't confess to, however, were any feelings of remorse.

Holmes was executed by hanging in 1896. He was buried in Holy Cross Cemetery near Philadelphia in a coffin lined with cement, topped with more cement, and buried in a double grave—per his own request. Was he ready to rest eternally after a life of such monstrosity? Or was he afraid that someone would conduct experiments on him as he had done to so many hapless victims?

"I was born with the devil in me. I could not help the fact that I was a murderer, no more than the poet can help the inspiration to sing."

—H. H. HOLMES

What Are Some of History's Coldest Cases?

They were gruesome crimes that shocked us with their brutality. But as time passed, the cases went cold. Yet the files remain open. Here are some of the world's most famous cold cases.

✳ ✳ ✳ ✳

Elizabeth Short

ELIZABETH SHORT, ALSO known as the Black Dahlia, was murdered in 1947. Like thousands of others, Elizabeth wanted to be a star. Unlike the bevy of blondes who trekked to Hollywood, this 22-year-old beauty from Massachusetts was dark and mysterious. She was last seen alive outside the Biltmore Hotel in Los Angeles on the evening of January 9.

Short's body was found on a vacant lot in Los Angeles. It had been cut in half at the waist and both parts had been drained of blood and then cleaned. Her body parts appeared to be surgically dissected, and her remains were suggestively posed. Despite receiving a number of false confessions and taunting letters that admonished police to "catch me if you can," the crime remains unsolved.

Dorothy Arnold

After spending most of December 12, 1910, shopping in Manhattan, American socialite Dorothy Arnold told a friend she was planning to walk home through Central Park. She never made it. Fearing their daughter had eloped with her one-time boyfriend George Griscom Jr., the Arnolds immediately hired the Pinkerton Detective Agency, although they did not report her missing to police until almost a month later. Once the press heard the news, theories spread like wildfire, most of them pointing the finger at Griscom. Some believed he had murdered Arnold, but others thought she had died as the result of a botched abortion. Still others felt her family had banished her to Switzerland and then used her disappearance as a cover-up. No evidence was ever found to formally charge Griscom, and Arnold's disappearance remains unsolved.

The Zodiac Killer

The Zodiac Killer was responsible for several murders in the San Francisco area in the 1960s and 1970s. His victims were shot, stabbed, and bludgeoned to death. After the first few kills, he began sending letters to the local press in which he taunted police and made public threats, such as planning to blow up a school bus. In a letter sent to the *San Francisco Chronicle* two days after the murder of cabbie Paul Stine in October 1969, the killer, who called himself "The Zodiac," included in the package pieces of Stine's blood-soaked shirt. In the letters, which continued until 1978, he claimed a cumulative tally of 37 murders.

Swedish Prime Minister Olof Palme

On February 28, 1986, Swedish Prime Minister Olof Palme was gunned down on a Stockholm street as he and his wife strolled home from the movies unprotected around midnight. The prime minister was fatally shot in the back. His wife was seriously wounded but survived.

In 1988, a petty thief and drug addict named Christer Petterson was convicted of the murder because he was picked out of a lineup by Palme's widow. The conviction was later overturned on appeal when doubts were raised as to the reliability of Mrs. Palme's evidence. Despite many theories, the assassin remains at large.

Bob Crane

In 1978, Bob Crane, star of TV's *Hogan's Heroes,* was clubbed to death in his apartment. Crane shared a close friendship with John Carpenter, a pioneer in the development of video technology. The two shared an affinity for debauchery and sexual excesses, which were recorded on videotape. But by late 1978, Crane was tiring of Carpenter's dependence on him and had let him know that the friendship was over.

The following day, June 29, 1978, Crane was bludgeoned to death with a camera tripod in his Scottsdale, Arizona, apartment. Suspicion immediately fell on Carpenter, and a small spattering of blood was found in Carpenter's rental car, but police were unable to connect it to the crime. Examiners also found a tiny piece of human tissue in the car. Sixteen years after the killing, Carpenter finally went to trial, but he was acquitted due to lack of evidence.

Tupac Shakur

On September 7, 1996, successful rap artist Tupac Shakur was shot four times in a drive-by shooting in Las Vegas. He died six days later. Two years prior to that, Shakur had been shot five times in the lobby of a Manhattan recording studio the day before he was found guilty of sexual assault. He survived that attack, only to spend the next 11 months in jail. The 1994 shooting was a major catalyst for an East Coast-West Coast feud that would envelop the hip-hop industry and culminate in the deaths of both Shakur and Notorious B.I.G. (Christopher Wallace).

On the night of the fatal shooting, Shakur attended the Mike Tyson-Bruce Seldon fight at the MGM Grand in Las Vegas. After the fight, Shakur and his entourage got into a scuffle with a gang member. Shakur then headed for a nightclub, but he never made it. No one was ever arrested for the killing.

Jimmy Hoffa

In 1975, labor leader Jimmy Hoffa disappeared on his way to a Detroit-area restaurant. Hoffa was the president of the Teamsters Union during the 1950s and 1960s. In 1964, he went to jail for bribing a grand juror investigating corruption in the union. In 1971, he was released on the condition that he not participate in any further union activity. Hoffa was preparing a legal challenge to that injunction when he disappeared on July 30, 1975. He was last seen in the parking lot of the Machus Red Fox Restaurant.

Hoffa had strong connections to the Mafia, and several mobsters have claimed that he met a grisly end on their say so. Although his body has never been found, authorities officially declared him dead on July 30, 1982. In November 2006, the FBI dug up farmland in Michigan hoping to turn up a corpse. So far, no luck.

JonBenét Ramsey

In the early hours of December 26, 1996, Patsy Ramsey reported that her six-year-old daughter, JonBenét, had been abducted from her Boulder, Colorado, home. Police rushed to the Ramsey home where, hours later, John Ramsey found his little girl dead in the basement. She had been battered, sexually assaulted, and strangled.

Police found several tantalizing bits of evidence—a number of footprints, a rope that did not belong on the premises, marks on the body that suggested the use of a stun gun, and DNA samples on the girl's body. The ransom note was also suspicious. Police found that it was written with a pen and pad of paper belonging to the Ramseys. The amount demanded, $118,000, was a surprisingly small amount, considering that John Ramsey was worth more than $6 million. It is also interesting to note that Mr. Ramsey had just received a year-end bonus of $118,117.50.

A number of suspects were considered, but one by one they were cleared. Finally, the police zeroed in on the parents. For years, the Ramseys were put under intense pressure by authorities and the public alike to confess to the murder. However, a grand jury investigation ended with no indictments. In 2003, a judge ruled that an intruder had killed JonBenét. Then, in August 2006, John Mark Karr confessed, claiming that he was with the girl when she died. However, Karr's DNA did not match that found on JonBenét.

In 2008, Boulder County District Attorney Mary Lacy formally apologized to the family in a letter, saying that neither the parents nor the son were considered suspects. Lacy added that DNA evidence not available in 1996 pointed to an unknown male as the killer. The case remains unsolved.

How Do You Make a Citizen's Arrest?

Nearly every state allows an ordinary person to make a citizen's arrest, but this doesn't mean that you should convert your garage into a jail and start rounding up suspected criminals. Perpbusting is best left to professionals.

❋ ❋ ❋ ❋

THE CONCEPT OF a citizen's arrest dates to medieval England, where it was standard practice for ordinary people to help maintain order by apprehending and detaining anyone who was observed committing a crime. This remained part of

English common law, and over the years, the concept spread to other countries. Standards of exactly what citizens could and couldn't do to detain suspected criminals were modified over the years, as well.

Today, laws governing citizen's arrests vary from country to country; in the U.S., they vary from state to state. The intent is to give citizens the power to stop someone from inflicting harm when there's no time to wait for authorities. It's considered a last resort and is only meant for dire emergencies.

Every state except North Carolina explicitly grants citizens (and, generally, other residents) the power to arrest someone who is seen committing a felony. Some states extend this to allow a citizen's arrest when the citizen has probable cause to believe that someone has committed a felony.

"Arrest" in this context means stopping and detaining the suspect until law enforcement arrives. Kentucky law kicks it up a notch—it grants citizens the right to use deadly force to stop a fleeing suspected felon.

The general guidelines for a citizen's arrest in the United States break down like this: In most cases, you can arrest someone during or immediately following the commission of a criminal act. First, you tell the suspect to stop what he or she is doing, and then you announce that you're making a citizen's arrest. As long as the suspect stays put, you don't have the right to physically restrain him or her.

Don't notify the suspect of his or her constitutional rights; this would be considered impersonating an officer. Typically, you don't have the right to search or interrogate a suspect, either. If the suspect resists, you have the right to use enough force to detain him or her until law enforcement arrives. It's illegal to use excessive force or to imprison someone extendedly if either is due to your failure to notify law enforcement immediately.

Even if you follow the law to the letter, making a citizen's arrest is risky business because, among other reasons, the law doesn't grant you the same legal protection it gives a police officer. In most cases, the suspect could sue you personally for false arrest or false imprisonment, especially if he or she ends up being acquitted of the charges. In other words, if you see a fishy-looking character running down the street, think twice before you spring into action and yell, "Stop!"

What's the Point of Multiple Life Sentences?

No, the justice system isn't secretly Buddhist. There are good reasons for multiple life sentences, and they don't have anything to do with reincarnation.

✳ ✳ ✳ ✳

LOGICALLY ENOUGH, JUDGES hand down multiple sentences in order to punish multiple criminal offenses. Multiple charges may be decided in the same trial, but they are still considered separate crimes and often yield separate punishments. Even in cases of life imprisonment, multiple sentences can end up being very important in the rare instances in which convictions are overturned on appeals.

Let's say a jury finds a man guilty of killing five people. The judge might sentence him to five life sentences to address the five charges. Even if any one of the convictions is overturned (or even if four of them are overturned), the murderer still has to serve a life sentence. To walk free, he would have to be exonerated of all five murders.

Furthermore, "life" doesn't always mean an entire lifetime. Depending on the sentencing guidelines of the state, the judge may sentence a man to life imprisonment with the possibility of parole. In this instance, life is the maximum length of the sentence, meaning that the defendant could conceivably go free if a parole board releases him after he's served the minimum time (thirty years, for example).

If, however, a defendant is convicted on multiple charges, the judge may hand down multiple life sentences with the possibility of parole—but the judge can also specify that those sentences are to be served consecutively rather than concurrently. This way, the prisoner will not get a parole hearing until the minimum time for all the sentences put together has been served.

Consider multiple life sentences to be a safeguard, a way to ensure that the bad guys never see the light of day.

How Are a Copyright, a Patent, and a Trademark Different?

Think of it this way: You patent your design for self-cleaning underpants, you trademark the name TidyWhities, and you copyright your TidyWhities spin-off cartoon.

✳   ✳   ✳   ✳

THE DIFFERENCE BETWEEN copyrights, patents, and trademarks is that each protects a different type of intellectual property. Normally, when we think of property, we think of houses or cars or pieces of land—things that exist in the physical world. A piece of intellectual property, on the other hand, is a product of the mind, like a song or a slogan or an invention. And in order to encourage innovation, our laws protect this kind of property, as well. After all, why would you bother putting in the countless hours of R&D necessary to perfect your TidyWhities if you knew that Hanes could swoop in and rip off your design whenever it wanted?

Copyrights

Copyrights cover what the law calls "original works of authorship," any unique and tangible creation. As soon as you paint a picture, write a song, film a movie, scribble out a blog post, etc., it's automatically copyrighted. (Although it's a good idea to stamp your masterwork with the copyright symbol, your name, and the year, just to stake your claim.) You can register copyrighted works with the U.S. Copyright Office to firmly establish your authorship, but the copyright exists whether you do this or not.

It's important to remember that copyrights only apply to the form of the creation, not to any of the information that it may contain. For example, the facts in this book are not subject to copyright. But the way in which we've woven these facts together to create a stunning tapestry of knowledge is totally copyrighted. (Bootleggers, get to steppin'.) If you create something and copyright it yourself, the protection lasts for your lifetime plus 70 years.

Patents

Unlike a copyright, which covers the material form of an idea, a patent covers an idea itself. It can't be just any brainwave, though; only ideas for inventions and designs can be patented. The most common type of patent protection is the utility patent, which applies to ideas for machines, processes (like a manufacturing process), compositions of matter (like a new fabric), and new uses for any of these things.

Another difference between patents and copyrights is that patents aren't granted automatically. To get one, you have to file an application with the U.S. Patent and Trademark Office, including a thorough written description of your idea, typically with supporting diagrams. Patent examiners review every application to determine if its idea is sufficiently different from previous inventions, actually doable (no time-machine concepts, please), and "non-obvious." The non-obvious requirement prevents inventors from patenting easy tweaks to existing inventions (making a giant spatula, for example).

Although the utility patent is the most commonly issued type of patent protection, there are others worth noting. Plant patents are similar, but cover original plant species that are engineered by humans. Design patents, on the other hand, cover only non-functional designs for products (the exact shape of your TidyWhities, for example).

When a patent is approved, the inventor has the legal right to stop others from making or selling the invention for a period of 20 years. The inventor can make money by selling the invention exclusively or by licensing the idea to a company that can manufacture and market the product.

Trademarks

This brings us to the trademark. This is the narrowest form of intellectual property protection—it covers names and symbols that indicate the source of a product or service. For example, Apple has trademarked its little apple icon, as well as the words "Apple" and "Macintosh" when applied to computers and electronics. When the U.S. Patent and Trademark Office grants you a trademark, it remains yours for as long as you keep using the name or symbol. Hmm…wonder if TidyWhities is taken.

What Are the Finer Points of an Insanity Plea?

No, judges don't keep a "You must be this nuts to get out of jail" sign hidden behind their benches. But you can be found not guilty by reason of insanity if you're crazy in just the right way.

✳   ✳   ✳   ✳

A Murky Defense

CRIMINAL INSANITY DOESN'T refer to any specific mental disorder, but it is related to mental illness. The reasoning behind the insanity defense is that some mental disorders may cause people to lose the ability to understand their actions or to differentiate between right and wrong, leaving them unable to truly have criminal intent. Intent is an important element of crime. If you intentionally burn down a house by dropping a lit cigarette in a trash can, we'd call you an arsonist. But if you do exactly the same thing accidentally, we'd probably just call you an inconsiderate (and perhaps a criminally negligent) jerk.

Similarly, the reasoning goes, you shouldn't be punished if a mental illness leads you to break the law without really comprehending your actions. Now, this doesn't apply to just any run-of-the-mill murderer with an antisocial personality disorder. A lack of empathy may lead someone to commit crimes, but if he understands what he's doing and he realizes that what he's doing is wrong, he's not insane.

How to Be Considered Legally Insane

You can only be found not guilty by reason of insanity in two cases: if mental illness keeps you from understanding your actions and deprives you of the ability to tell right from wrong; or if mental illness leaves you unable to control your actions and you experience an irresistible impulse to commit a crime. Details vary from state to state (and some states don't recognize the insanity defense at all), but these are the general criteria.

Some form of the insanity defense seems to date back to the 16th century, but early versions were awfully hazy. The 1843 trial of Daniel M'Naghten helped to clear things up. Thinking that the pope and English Prime Minister Robert Peel were out to get him, M'Naghten went to 10 Downing Street to kill Peel but ended up killing Peel's secretary. Witnesses claimed that M'Naghten was delusional, and the jury found him not guilty by reason of insanity. Queen Victoria was none too pleased, so a panel of judges was convened to clarify the rules governing the insanity defense as it involved the inability to distinguish right from wrong.

The definition has been controversial ever since, and every high-profile case in which it is invoked seems to throw the idea into question. Patty Hearst and Jeffery Dahmer both tried to use the insanity defense unsuccessfully, while David Berkowitz (Son of Sam) and Ted Kaczynski (the Unabomber) seemed ready to pursue the defense but ultimately decided against it. But a jury did acquit John Hinckley Jr. of all charges related to his assassination attempt on President Reagan after it determined that he was insane.

It's No Sure Thing

A successful insanity plea is rare. In the 1990s, a study funded by the National Institute of Mental Health found that defendants pleaded insanity in less than 1 percent of cases, and that only a quarter of those pleas were successful. Those who are successful hardly ever get off scot-free—they're simply committed to mental institutions rather than sent to prisons. On average, those who are found insane end up spending more time confined to an institution than they would have in prison if they had been found guilty.

Who Murdered the Clutters?

If you ever find yourself in northwestern Kansas looking for the village of Holcomb, don't blink or you'll miss it. It's the kind of place where nothing ever seems to happen. And yet, back in 1959, Holcomb became one of the most notorious locations in the history of American crime.

✳ ✳ ✳ ✳

"Everyone Loved the Clutters..."

IN THE 1940s, successful businessman Herb Clutter built a house on the outskirts of town and started raising a family with his wife, Bonnie. The Clutters quickly became one of the most popular families in the small village, due largely to their friendly nature. People would be hard-pressed to find someone who had a bad word to say about them.

On the morning of Sunday, November 15, 1959, Clarence Ewalt drove his daughter Nancy to the Clutter house so she could go to church with the family as she did every week. She was a good friend of the Clutters' teenage daughter, who was also named Nancy. Nancy Ewalt knocked on the door several times but got no response. She went around to a side door, looked around and called out, but no one answered. At that point, Mr. Ewalt drove his daughter to the Kidwell house nearby and picked up Susan Kidwell, another friend. Susan tried phoning the Clutters, but no one answered. So the three drove back to the Clutter house. The two girls entered the house through the kitchen door and went to Nancy Clutter's room, where they discovered her dead body.

Unspeakable Acts

Sheriff Robinson was the first officer to respond. He entered the house with another officer and a neighbor, Larry Hendricks. According to Nancy Ewalt, the three men went first to Nancy Clutter's room, where they found the teenager dead of an apparent gunshot wound to the back of the head. She was lying on her bed facing the wall with her hands and ankles bound. Down the hallway in the master bedroom, the body of Bonnie Clutter was discovered. Like her daughter, Bonnie's hands and feet were also bound, and she appeared to have been shot point-blank in the head.

In the basement of the Clutter home, police found the bodies of Herb Clutter and his 15-year-old son, Kenyon. Like his mother and sister, Kenyon had been shot in the head; his body was tied to a sofa.

As atrocious as the other three murders were, Herb Clutter appeared to have suffered the most. Like the others, he had been shot in the head, but there were slash marks on his throat, and his mouth had been taped shut. And although his body was lying on the floor of the basement, there was a rope hanging from the ceiling suggesting that, at some point, he may have been hung from the rope.

Dewey's Task Force

Alvin A. Dewey of the Kansas City Bureau of Investigation (KBI) was put in charge of the investigation. Even though

Dewey was a police veteran and had seen his fair share of violent murders, the Clutter murders hit him hard. Herb Clutter was a friend, and their families had attended church together.

At his first press conference after the bodies were discovered, Dewey announced that he was heading up a 19-man task force that would not rest until they found the person or persons responsible for the horrific murders. But he knew it was going to be a tough case. For one, the amount of blood and gore at the scene suggested that revenge might have been the motive. But the Clutters were upstanding members of the community and loved by all, as evidenced by the nearly 600 mourners who showed up for the family's funeral service. The idea that the murders were the result of a robbery gone bad was also being pursued, but Dewey had his doubts about that, as well. For him, it just didn't fit that the entire Clutter family would have walked in on a robbery and then been killed the way they had. For that reason, Dewey began to believe that there had been more than one killer.

A Secret Clue

There was not a lot of evidence left behind at the crime scene. Not only was the murder weapon missing, but whoever pulled the trigger had taken the time to pick up the spent shells. However, Dewey did have an ace up his sleeve, and it was something not even the press was made aware of. Herb Clutter's body had been found lying on a piece of cardboard. On that cardboard were impressions from a man's boot. Both of the victims found in the basement, Herb and Kenyon Clutter, were barefoot, which meant the boots may have belonged to the killer. It wasn't much to go on, but for Dewey, it was a start. Still, as Christmas 1959 crept closer, the case was starting to come to a standstill. Then, finally, a big break came from an unlikely place: Lansing Prison.

A Break in the Case

The man who would break the case wide open was Lansing

Prison inmate Floyd Wells. Earlier in the year, Wells had been sentenced to Lansing for breaking and entering. His cellmate was a man named Richard Hickock. One night, the two men were talking, and Hickock mentioned that even though he was going to be released from prison soon, he had nowhere to go. Wells told him that back in the late 1940s, he had been out looking for work and stumbled across a kind, rich man named Clutter who would often hire people to work around his farm. Once he mentioned Herb Clutter, Hickock seemed obsessed with the man. He wouldn't stop asking Wells to tell him everything he knew about Clutter. How old was he? Was he strong? How many others lived in the house with him?

One night, Hickock calmly stated that when he was released, he and his friend Perry Smith were going to rob the Clutters and murder anyone in the house. Wells said that Hickock even went so far as to explain exactly how he would tie everyone up and shoot them one at a time. Wells further stated that he never believed Hickock was serious until he heard the news that the Clutters had been murdered in exactly the way Hickock had described.

Captures and Confessions

On December 30, after attempting to cash a series of bad checks, Hickock and Smith were arrested in Las Vegas. Among the items seized from the stolen car they were driving was a pair of boots belonging to Hickock. When confronted with the fact that his boots matched the imprint at the crime scene, Hickock broke down and admitted he had been there during the murders. However, he swore that Perry Smith had killed the whole family and that he had tried to stop him.

When Smith was informed that his partner was putting all the blame on him, he decided it was in his best interest to explain his side. Smith gave a very detailed version of how Hickock had devised a plan to steal the contents of a safe in Herb Clutter's home office. The pair had arrived under cover of darkness at approximately 12:30 A.M. Finding no safe in the office, the pair went up into the master bedroom, where they surprised Herb Clutter, who was sleeping alone in bed. When told they had come for the contents of the safe, Herb told them to take whatever they wanted, but he said there was no safe in the house. Not convinced, Smith and Hickock rounded up the family and tied them up, hoping to get one of them to reveal the location of the safe. When that failed, Smith and Hickock prepared to leave. But when Hickock started bragging about how he had been ready to kill the entire family, Smith called his bluff, and an argument ensued. At that point, Smith said he snapped and stabbed Herb Clutter in the throat. Seeing the man in such pain, Smith said he then shot him to end his suffering. Smith then turned the gun on Kenyon. Smith ended his statement by saying that he'd made Hickock shoot and kill the two women.

The Verdict

The murder trial of Richard Hickock and Perry Smith began on March 23, 1960, at Finney County Courthouse. Five days later, the case was handed over to the jury, who needed only 40 minutes to reach their verdict: Both men were guilty of all charges. They recommended that Hickock and Smith be hanged for their crimes.

Sitting in the front row when the verdicts were read was Truman Capote, who had been writing a series of articles about the murders for *The New Yorker*. Those articles would later inspire his best-selling novel *In Cold Blood*.

After several appeals, both men were executed at Lansing Prison, one right after the other, on April 14, 1965. Richard Hickock was the first to be hanged, with Perry Smith going to the same gallows roughly 30 minutes later. Agent Alvin Dewey was present for both executions.

Several years after the murders, in an attempt to heal the community, a stained-glass window at the First Methodist Church in Garden City, Kansas, was posthumously dedicated to the memory of the Clutter family. Despite an initial impulse to bulldoze the Clutter house, it was left standing and today is a private residence.

What Exactly Is Money Laundering?

You knock over an armored car and suddenly your mattress is overflowing with cash. But if you enjoy your ill-gotten gains by treating yourself to something big—a solid-gold yacht, say—the Feds will want to know where the money came from. And if you can't point to a legitimate source, it's off to prison with you.

✳   ✳   ✳   ✳

WHEN FACED WITH this dilemma, criminals turn to money laundering, the process of making "dirty" money look "clean"—in other words, making it appear that the money is legitimate income. For relatively small amounts of dirty cash, the go-to trick is to set up a front: a business that can record the cash as profit. For example, Al Capone owned laundromats all over Chicago so that he could disguise the income from his illegal liquor business as laundry profits (how appropriate). There wasn't any way to know how much money people really spent at the laundromat, so all the profit appeared to be legitimate.

On a larger scale—like when drug traffickers take in millions—the laundromat scheme doesn't really work, and things get more complicated. But no matter how elaborate the scheme, you can usually break it down into three basic steps: placement, layering, and integration.

In the placement stage, the goal is to get the hard cash into the financial system, which usually means depositing it into accounts of some kind. In the U.S., banks report any transaction greater than ten thousand dollars to the authorities, so one placement strategy is to deposit money gradually, in smaller increments, across multiple bank accounts. Another option is to deposit the money in a bank in a country that has lax financial monitoring laws.

The goal of the next stage—layering—is to shift the money through the financial system in such a complicated way that nobody can follow a paper trail back to the crime. In other words, the criminals are trying to disguise the fact that they are the ones who put the money into the financial system in the first place. Every time launderers move money between accounts, convert it into a different currency, or buy or sell anything—particularly in a country with lax laws—the transaction adds a layer of confusion to the trail.

Finally, in the integration stage, the criminals get the money back by some means that looks legitimate. For example, they might arrange to have an offshore company hire them as generously paid consultants; this way, the money that they earned from their crimes enters their bank accounts as legitimate personal income.

Money laundering is big business, and it's a key foundation for drug trafficking, embezzling, and even terrorism. Many nations have enacted stricter laws and boosted enforcement in order to crack down on money laundering, but they can't put a stop to it unless everyone is vigilant. As long as there are countries with lax financial regulations that trade in the world economy, criminals will have a way to launder their funds.

So, if you've been scrubbing your ill-gotten cash in the sink and hanging it on the line to dry, stop it now. You're doing it wrong.

Why Do Cops Say You Have the Right to Remain Silent?

The violation of one man's rights becomes a warning to us all.

✳ ✳ ✳ ✳

MOST OF US have never heard of Ernesto Miranda. Yet in 1963, this faceless man would prompt the passage of a law that has become an integral part of all arrests. Here's how it came to pass.

You Have the Right to Remain Silent

In 1963, following his arrest for the kidnapping and rape of an 18-year-old woman, Ernesto Miranda was arrested and placed in a Phoenix, Arizona, police lineup. When he stepped down from the gallery of suspects, Miranda asked the officers about the charges against him. The police implied that he had been positively identified as the kidnapper and rapist of a young woman. After two hours of interrogation, Miranda confessed.

Miranda signed a confession that included a typed paragraph indicating that his statement had been voluntary and that he had been fully aware of his legal rights.

But there was one problem: At no time during his interrogation had Miranda actually been advised of his rights. The wheels of justice had been set in motion on a highly unbalanced axle.

Anything You Say Can and Will Be Used Against You in a Court of Law

When appealing Miranda's conviction, his attorney attempted to have the confession thrown out on the grounds that his client hadn't been advised of his rights. The motion was over-ruled. Eventually, Miranda would be convicted on both rape and kidnapping charges and sentenced to 20 to 30 years in prison. It seemed like the end of the road for Miranda—but it was just the beginning.

You Have the Right to an Attorney

Miranda requested that his case be heard by the U.S. Supreme Court. His attorney, John J. Flynn, submitted a 2,000-word petition [for a writ of *certiorari* (judicial review), arguing that Miranda's Fifth Amendment rights had been violated. In November 1965, the Supreme Court agreed to hear Miranda's case. The tide was about to turn.

A Law Is Born

After much debate among Miranda's attorneys and the state, a decision in Miranda's favor was rendered. Chief Justice Earl Warren wrote in his *Miranda* v. *Arizona* opinion, "The person in custody must, prior to interrogation, be clearly informed that he has the right to remain silent, and that anything he says will be used against him in court; he must be clearly informed that he has the right to consult with a lawyer and to have the lawyer with him during interrogation, and that, if he is indigent, a lawyer will be appointed to represent him."

Aftermath

In the wake of the U.S. Supreme Court's ruling, police departments across the nation began to issue the "Miranda warning." As for Miranda himself, his freedom was short-lived. He would be sentenced to 11 years in prison at a second trial that did not include his prior confession as evidence. Miranda was released in 1972, and he bounced in and out of jail for various offenses over the next few years. On January 31, 1976, Miranda was stabbed to death during a Phoenix bar fight. The suspect received his Miranda warning from the arresting police officers and opted to remain silent. Due to insufficient evidence, he would not be prosecuted for Ernesto Miranda's murder.

Who Are Some of the 20th Century's Worst Criminals?

Our TV screens are saturated with bizarre slayings and murderous mayhem. Makes you wonder how far-fetched those scriptwriters will get. After all, real people don't commit those types of crimes, right? Wrong. In fact, the annals of history are crammed with crimes even more gruesome than anything seen on television. Here are some of the 20th century's worst criminals.

✳   ✳   ✳   ✳

Ed Kemper

ED KEMPER HAD a genius IQ, but his appetite for murder took over at age 15 when he shot his grandparents because he wanted to see what it felt like. Nine years later, he'd done his time for that crime, and during 1972 and 1973, Kemper hit the California highways, picking up pretty students and killing them before taking the corpses back to his apartment, having sex with them, then dissecting them. He killed six women in that manner and then took an ax to his own mother, decapitating and raping her, then using her body as a dartboard. Still not satisfied, he killed one of his mother's friends as well.

Upset that his crimes didn't garner the media attention he thought they warranted, Kemper confessed to police. He gleefully went into detail about his penchant for necrophilia and decapitation. He asked to be executed, but because capital punishment was suspended at the time, he got life imprisonment and remains incarcerated in California.

Andrei Chikatilo

Andrei Chikatilo was Russia's most notorious serial killer. The Rostov Ripper, as he came to be called, began his rampage in 1978 in the city of Shakhty, where he started abducting teenagers and subjecting them to unspeakable torture before raping and murdering them, and, often, cannibalizing their bodies.

Authorities gave the crimes little attention, but as the body count grew, police were forced to face the facts—Russia had a serial killer.

Chikatilo was actually brought in for questioning when the police found a rope and butcher knife in his bag during a routine search, but he was released and allowed to continue his killing spree. In the end, he got careless and was arrested near the scene of his latest murder. Under interrogation, he confessed to 56 murders. During the trial, he was kept in a cage in the middle of the court, playing up the image of the deranged lunatic. It didn't help his cause, though. He was found guilty and executed on February 14, 1994.

Cameron Hooker

With the assistance of his wife, Janice, in May 1977 Cameron Hooker snatched a 20-year-old woman who was hitchhiking to a friend's house in northern California. He locked her in a wooden box that was kept under the bed he shared with Janice, who was well aware of what lay beneath. During the next seven years, Hooker repeatedly tortured, beat, and sexually assaulted the young woman. Eventually, she was allowed out of the box to do household chores, but she was forced to wear a slave collar. As time went by, Hooker allowed his prisoner more and more freedom, even letting her get a part-time job. Janice's conscience finally got the best of her, and she helped the young woman escape. After seven years of hell, the prisoner simply got on a bus and left. Hooker was convicted and sentenced to 104 years in a box of his own.

Andras Pandy

Andras Pandy was a Belgian pastor who had eight children by two different wives. Between 1986 and 1989, his former wives and four of the children disappeared. Pandy tried to appease investigators by faking papers to show that they were living in Hungary. He even coerced other children into impersonating the missing ones. Then, under intense questioning, Pandy's daughter Agnes broke down. She told authorities that she had been held by her father as a teenage sex slave and then was forced to join him in killing her family members, including her mother, brothers, stepmother, and stepsister. The bodies were chopped up, dissolved in drain cleaner, and flushed down the drain. Pandy was sentenced to life in prison, while Agnes received 21 years as an accomplice. Pandy died in prison on December 23, 2013.

Harold Shipman

The most prolific serial killer in modern history was British doctor Harold Shipman, who murdered up to 400 of his patients between 1970 and 1998. Shipman was a respected member of the community, but in March 1998, a colleague became alarmed at the high death rate among his patients. She went to the local coroner, who in turn went to the police. They investigated, but found nothing out of the ordinary. But when a woman named Kathleen Grundy died a few months later, it was revealed that she had cut her daughter Angela out of her will and, instead, bequeathed £386,000 to Shipman. Suspicious, Angela went to the police, who began another investigation. Kathleen Grundy's body was exhumed and examined, and traces of diamorphine (heroin) were found in her system. Shipman was arrested and charged with murder. When police examined his patient files more closely, they realized that Shipman was overdosing patients with diamorphine, then forging their medical records to state that they were in poor health.

Shipman was found guilty and sentenced to 15 consecutive life sentences, but he hung himself in his cell in January 2004.

Fred and Rose West

In the early 1970s, a pattern developed in which young women were lured to the home of Fred and Rose West in Gloucester, England, subjected to sexual depravities, and then ritually slaughtered in the soundproof basement. The bodies were then dismembered and disposed of under the cellar floor. As the number of victims increased, the garden became a secondary burial plot. This became the final resting place of Fred and Rose West's own daughter, 16-year-old Heather, who was butchered in June 1983.

Police became increasingly concerned about the whereabouts of Heather. One day they decided to take the family joke that she was "buried under the patio" seriously. When they began excavating the property in June 1994, the number of body parts uncovered shocked the world. With overwhelming evidence stacked against him, Fred West committed suicide while in custody in 1995. Rose received life imprisonment.

John Wayne Gacy

In the mid-1960s, John Wayne Gacy was, by all outward appearances, a happily married Chicago-area businessman who doted on his two young children. But when Gacy was convicted of sodomy in 1968, he got ten years in jail, and his wife divorced him.

Eighteen months later, Gacy was out on parole. He started a construction company, and in his spare time, he volunteered as a clown to entertain sick children. He also began picking up homeless male prostitutes. After taking them home, Gacy would beat, rape, and slaughter his victims before depositing the bodies in the crawl space underneath his house.

In 1978, an investigation into the disappearance of 15-year-old Robert Piest led police to Gacy, following reports that the two had been seen together on the night the boy disappeared. Suspicions were heightened when detectives uncovered Gacy's sodomy conviction, and a warrant was issued to search his home. Detectives found a piece of jewelry belonging to a boy who had disappeared a year before. They returned to the house with excavating equipment and made a gruesome discovery.

Gacy tried to escape the death penalty with a tale of multiple personalities, but it didn't impress the jury. It took them only two hours to convict him of 33 murders. On May 10, 1994, he was put to death by lethal injection.

Ed Gein

Ed Gein was the son of an overbearing mother who taught him that sex was sinful. When she died in 1945, he was a 39-year-old bachelor living alone in a rundown farmhouse in Plainfield, Wisconsin. After his mother's death, he developed a morbid fascination with the medical atrocities performed by the Nazis during World War II. This fascination led him to dig up female corpses from cemeteries, take them home, and perform his own experiments on them, such as removing the skin from the body and draping it over a tailor's dummy. He was also fascinated with female genitalia, which he would fondle and, on occasion, stuff into women's panties and wear around the house.

He soon tired of decomposing corpses and set out in search of fresher bodies. Most of his victims were women around his mother's age. He went a step too far, however, when he abducted the mother of local sheriff's deputy Frank Worden. Learning that his missing mother had been seen with Gein on the day of her disappearance, Worden went to the Gein house to question the recluse. What he found there belied belief. Human heads sat as prize trophies in the living room along with a belt made from human nipples and a chair completely upholstered in human skin. But for Worden, the worst sight was in the woodshed. Strung up by the feet was the headless body of his mother. Her front had been slit open and her heart was found on a plate in the dining room.

Gein confessed but couldn't recall how many people he'd killed. He told detectives that he liked to dress up in the carved out torsos of his victims and pretend to be his mother. He spent ten years in an insane asylum before he was judged fit to stand trial. He was found guilty, but criminally insane, and died of heart failure in 1984, at age 77.

Jeffrey Dahmer

Jeffrey Dahmer looked like an all-American boy, but as a child, he performed autopsies on small animals, including neighborhood dogs. At age 18, he graduated to humans, picking up a 19-year-old boy and taking him home to drink beer. Dahmer attacked him with a barbell, dismembered his body, and buried it in the backyard. More abductions and murders followed, and Dahmer also began to eat his victims.

In 1989, Dahmer was sentenced to eight years in jail for child molestation but only served ten months. After his release, he immediately resumed the slaughter. In May 1991, Dahmer picked up a 14-year-old boy, gave him money to pose for suggestive photos, and then plied him with alcohol and sleeping pills. While the boy slept, Dahmer went to the store. Waking up alone, the boy fled but ran straight into Dahmer. When they were approached by police, Dahmer convinced the officers that the two were lovers. Upon returning to the apartment, Dahmer slaughtered the boy and then had sex with his corpse.

Two months later this scenario was virtually reenacted when a 31-year-old man escaped from the apartment. With handcuffs dangling from one arm, he approached a nearby police officer. This time the officer decided to check out the apartment. What the officer and his partner saw horrified them. Dismembered bodies, skulls, and internal organs littered the place, and a skeleton hung in the shower. When they opened the refrigerator, they were confronted with a human head. Three more heads were wrapped up in the freezer, and a pan on the stove contained human brains.

During the ensuing trial, another gruesome fact emerged—Dahmer had drilled holes into the skulls of some of his victims and poured in acid in an attempt to keep them alive as zombie-like sex slaves. He was given 15 life terms, but in November 1994, he was beaten to death in prison.

Around the World

Where Is the Highest Point on Earth?

Think you're at the top of the world when you climb Mt. Everest? Think again. You'll need to scale Ecuador's Mt. Chimborazo to make that claim.

✳ ✳ ✳ ✳

Y OU'VE SCALED MT. Everest and are marveling at the fact that you're getting your picture taken at the highest point on the planet. You're as close to the moon as any human being can be while standing on the surface of the earth. Actually, you're not. To achieve that, you'd have to climb back down and travel to the other side of the world—Ecuador, to be exact—so you can schlep to the summit of Mt. Chimborazo.

It's true that Everest, at 29,035 feet, is the world's tallest mountain—when measured from sea level. But thanks to Earth's quirky shape, Chimborazo, which rises only 20,702 feet from sea level, is about a mile and a half closer to the moon than Everest's peak.

Earth is not a perfect sphere. Rather, it's an oblate spheroid. Centrifugal force from billions of years of rotating has caused the planet to flatten at the poles and bulge out at the equator.

In effect, this pushes the equator farther from the earth's center than the poles—about 13 miles closer to the moon. The farther you move from the equator, the farther you move from the moon. Chimborazo sits almost at the equator, while Everest lies about 2,000 miles north—enough to make it farther from the moon than Chimborazo, despite being more than 8,000 feet taller.

Are the Pyramids of Egypt the Oldest Man-made Structures on Earth?

Ask most people what they consider the oldest, most magnificent architecture in the world, and the pyramids of Egypt are sure to be part of the answer. Magnificent, yes. Oldest, no.

✳   ✳   ✳   ✳

THE PYRAMIDS OF Giza are the most famous monuments of ancient Egypt and the only structures remaining of the original Seven Wonders of the Ancient World. Originally about 480 feet high, they are also the largest stone structures constructed by humans. They are not, however, the oldest.

What's Older Than the Pyramids?

That glory goes to the prehistoric temples of Malta—a small island nation south of Sicily. The temples date from 4000 to 2500 B.C. At approximately 6,000 years old, they are a thousand years older than the pyramids. Not much is known about the people who built these magnificent structures, but they were likely farmers who constructed the temples as public places of worship.

Because the Maltese temples were covered with soil from early times and not discovered until the 19th century, these megalithic structures have been well preserved. Extensive archaeological and restorative work was carried out in the early 20th century archaeologists to further ensure the temples' longevity.

The major temple complexes are now designated as UNESCO World Heritage Sites.

Which Pyramid Is the Oldest?

That would be the Step Pyramid at Saqqara, Egypt. It was built during the third dynasty of Egypt's Old Kingdom to protect the body of King Djoser, who died around 2649 B.C. It was this architectural feat that propelled the construction of the gigantic stone pyramids of ancient Egypt on a rocky desert plateau close to the Nile. These pyramids, known as the Great Pyramids, were built around 2493 B.C. The largest structure served as the tomb for Pharaoh Khufu.

What Are Ziggurats?

Everybody's heard of the pyramids of Egypt, but what about the ziggurats of Mesopotamia? Starting in the fourth millennium B.C., more than 2,000 years before the Egyptians built the Great Pyramid of Cheops, the Sumerians in Mesopotamia were busy constructing mighty towers in attempts to reach all the way up to heaven. Or at least that's what the Bible tells us.

✳   ✳   ✳   ✳

THE WORD ZIGGURAT comes from Akkadian, one of the earliest languages of the Near East. It means "to build on a raised area." Ziggurats resembled huge wedding cakes made of brick and clay. The tallest towers consisted of seven layers.

How tall were these ziggurats? Not very, according to our standards. The temple of Borsippa, one of the largest ziggurats that has been excavated by archaeologists, is estimated to have stood 231 feet high at completion. That's only a little less than a fifth as tall as the Empire State Building (1,250 feet) and less than a quarter of the height of the Eiffel Tower (984 feet). But on the relatively flat terrain of the Tigris-Euphrates valley, it's easy to see how that height would have impressed the locals.

Joseph Campbell, a famous scholar of world mythology,

believed the ziggurats were regarded by the Sumerians as connectors between the earth and heaven. The lowest layers represented the original mound from which the earth was created, and the top layer served as a temple where the gods could dwell and look out over the land.

Did the Tower of Babel, a type of ziggurat, actually exist? About 50 to 60 miles south of contemporary Baghdad lie the remains of what archaeologists think is the ancient city of Babylon. There, they have uncovered the first layer of a temple whose name is Etemenanki, according to cuneiform tablets, which translates to "the foundation between heaven and earth." This temple must have been important because it was reconstructed several times over the centuries, most notably by King Nebuchadnezzar II around 600 B.C.

King Neb, as you may recall, is one of the great villains of the Bible. Dubbed the "Destroyer of Nations" by the prophet Jeremiah, he conquered Jerusalem in 587 B.C., demolishing King Solomon's Temple and dragging the Hebrews off into slavery and exile in Babylon. After witnessing the destruction of their house of worship, the Hebrews had ample reason to resent Babylon and its seven-story ziggurat.

Babylon itself fell to Alexander the Great in 331 B.C. After that, any attempt to repair Etemenanki always seemed to end in disaster, and it eventually crumbled into a single, low mound. Its story, however, lives on, and with it our fascination with the ancient people whose towers once tried to join the earth with the sky.

Did Troy Exist?

Sure. Troy Aikman, Troy Donahue, Troy, Michigan—which one do you want to read about? Oh, you're thinking about Troy, the site of the Trojan War? Yup, that existed too.

* * * *

IF YOU REMEMBER your history classes—or if you saw the movie—you know that Troy was the walled city of the Trojans. Troy's Prince Paris stole the beautiful Helen from her husband in Sparta and carried her back to Troy. The disgruntled husband and all his kingly friends began a war that lasted ten years and ended with Troy's destruction. This was chronicled in *The Iliad*, Europe's oldest epic poem. How old? Perhaps 3,000 years old.

The Greeks and Romans never doubted that Troy had been a real place, situated near the Dardanelles—today, a part of Turkey. In 1870, a German-born archaeologist named Heinrich Schliemann announced that he'd discovered the ruins of Troy. Schliemann dug into a mound called Hisarlik and found layers of ancient cities, each built on the ruins of earlier settlements. He found (or possibly faked) gold treasures, but it was his assistant—Wilhelm Dörpfeld—who later realized that no fewer than nine separate cities had been built on that spot. Conveniently, they're labeled Troy I through Troy IX.

Troy I began as a Stone Age village around 3600 B.C. Over the millennia, it evolved into a royal city. Schliemann assumed that remains near the bottom of his excavation—Troy II—were from the real Troy, because Troy II was destroyed by fire. That fortified city, though, dates back to 2300 B.C.—far too early to be the Troy of legend. Scholars today believe that *The Iliad's* Troy is probably Troy VIIa, built on the ruins of a richer city that was destroyed by an earthquake in the 12th century B.C.

How much of *The Iliad* is based on fact? We will probably

never know, partly because very little evidence can survive for 3,000 years, but mostly because Schliemann's excavation methods destroyed more than they saved.

From 1982 until his death in 2005, German archaeologist Manfred Korfmann made more discoveries near the site of Troy. He found that a 50-foot-high burial mound, long called the Tomb of Achilles, did indeed date from the time of Troy VIIa. Korfmann also excavated a cemetery with more than 50 Greek graves from the same period. Swords and pottery imply that Greek aristocrats were buried there, along with women and children. What's more, Korfmann may have found the ancient harbor and camp where most of *The Iliad's* action took place. Although not every scholar and archaeologist accepts this site as ancient Troy, it was declared a UNESCO World Heritage Site in 1998.

Is Australia a Continent or an Island?

Why is Australia considered a continent instead of an island?

✳ ✳ ✳ ✳

I N GRAMMAR SCHOOL, some of us were far more interested in the "social" aspect of social studies than the "studies" part. Nevertheless, everyone can recite the continents: Africa, Asia, Europe, South America, North America, Australia, and . . . some other one. What gives with Australia? Why is it a continent? Shouldn't it be an island?

It most certainly is an island (the world's largest) and so much more. Australia is the only land mass on Earth to be considered an island, a country, and a continent.

Australia is by far the smallest continent, leading one to wonder why it is labeled a continent at all when other large islands, such as Greenland, are not. The answer lies in plate tectonics, the geologic theory explaining how Earth's land masses got to where they are today. According to plate tectonic theory, all of Earth's continents once formed a giant land mass known as Pangaea. Though Pangaea was one mass, it actually comprised several distinct pieces of land known as plates.

Over millions of years, at roughly the speed of your hair growth, these plates shifted, drifting apart from one another until they reached their current positions. Some plates reconnected, such as South America and North America, while others moved off into a remote corner like a punished child, such as Australia. (It's no wonder Australia was first used by the British as a prison colony.) Because Australia is one of these plates—while Greenland is part of the North American plate—it gets the honor of being called a continent.

All of this debate might ultimately seem rather silly. Some geologists maintain that in 250 million years, the continents will move back into one large mass called Pangaea Ultima. Australia will merge with Southeast Asia—and social studies tests will get a whole lot easier.

Who Got to Pick the Seven Wonders of the World?

Humans love their lists—to-do, grocery, pros and cons—so it makes sense that we would obsessively list cool stuff to see. There is a "wonder list" for every kind of wonder imaginable. The most famous is the Seven Wonders of the Ancient World.

❋　❋　❋　❋

ONE OF THE earliest references to "wonders" is in the writings of Greek historian Herodotus from the fifth century B.C. Herodotus wrote extensively about some of the impressive wonders he had seen and heard about. However, the concept of the Seven Wonders didn't really catch on until the second century B.C.

For the next 1,500 or so years, six of the seven were a lock, often appearing on compiled lists, with the seventh spot being a rotating roster of hopefuls. By the time the list became the accepted seven of today (around the Renaissance), the Lighthouse of Alexandria had taken up the seventh spot.

No one person actually got to pick the seven; it was more of a generally accepted concept based on the frequency with which certain wonders landed on different lists. Furthermore, by the time the Middle Ages rolled around, most of the wonders couldn't be seen in their full glory because of damage or destruction, so the selections were based primarily on reputation. The Seven Wonders of the Ancient World were the Pyramids of Giza in Egypt, the Hanging Gardens of Babylon in Iraq, the Statue of Zeus at Olympia in Greece, the Mausoleum of Maussollos at Halicarnassus in Turkey, the Colossus of Rhodes, the Temple of Artemis at Ephesus, and the Lighthouse of Alexandria in Egypt.

The Pyramids of Giza were the oldest when the lists began, and they are the only wonder still standing. The Colossus of Rhodes was big in size (107 feet high) but not big on longevity—the statue stood for only 54 years, but was impressive enough to stay in the minds of list-makers.

In 2001, the New 7 Wonders Foundation was established by a Swiss businessman. The foundation's intention was to create a new list of seven wonders of the world based on an online vote. (Notably, users could vote more than once.) In 2007, the wonders chosen were Chichén Itzá in Mexico, Christ the Redeemer in Brazil, the Colosseum in Rome, the Great Wall of China, Machu Picchu in Peru, Petra in Jordan, and the Taj Mahal in India. The Pyramids of Giza were given honorary finalist status after Egypt protested that these great historical structures shouldn't have to compete against such young whippersnappers.

Where Is Petra?

In the wilds of southern Jordan lies one of antiquity's most beautifully preserved sights: what survives of Petra, the ancient Nabataean capital.

✳ ✳ ✳ ✳

Where exactly is Petra?

Petra lies within the Hashemite Kingdom of Jordan, perhaps 80 miles south of Amman in the Naqab Desert, about 15 miles east of the Israeli border. It is a World Heritage Site and a Jordanian national treasure, cared for accordingly.

Why settle out in the desert?

Petra was a key link in the trade chain connecting Egypt, Babylon, Arabia, and the Mediterranean. It had water (if you knew how to look) and was quite defensible.

When was it founded?

In 600 B.C., the narrow red sandstone canyon of Petra housed a settlement of Edomites: seminomadic Semites said to descend from Biblical Esau. Egypt was still rich but declining. Rome was a young farming community dominated by its Etruscan kings. The rise of classical Athens was decades away. Brutal Assyria had fallen to Babylonian conquerors. With the rise of the incense trade, Arab traders began pitching tents at what would become Petra. We know them as the Nabataeans.

Did they speak Arabic?

The answer is as fluid as a Petra incense broker's sales pitch. Nabataean history spanned a millennium. They showed up speaking early Arabic in a region where Aramaic was the business-speak. The newcomers thus first wrote their Arabic in a variant of the Aramaic script. But Petra's trade focus meant a need to adopt Aramaic as well, so Nabataeans did—many words crossed the Arabic/Aramaic linguistic fence at Petra. By the end (about 250 years before the rise of Islam), Nabataean "Arabaic" had evolved into classical (Koranic) Arabic.

What were these Nabataeans like?

The Swiss or Swedes of the biblical world. They weren't expansionists, but defended their homeland with shrewd diplomacy and obstinate vigor. Despite great wealth, they had few slaves. Despite monarchical government, Petra's Nabataeans showed a pronounced democratic streak. Empires rose and fell around them; business was business.

The trade must have been lucrative indeed.

Vastly. The core commodity was incense from Arabia, but many raw materials and luxuries of antiquity also passed through Petra—notably bitumen (natural asphalt), useful in waterproofing and possibly in embalming.

Speaking of religion, were they religious?

Religious, yes; fanatical, no. Most Nabataeans were pagan, worshipping benevolent fertility and sun deities. Jews were welcome at Petra, as were Christians in its later days.

What of Nabataean women's roles?

Nabataean women held a respected position in society, including property and inheritance rights. While no major ancient Near Eastern culture was truly egalitarian, the women of Petra participated in its luxuriant prosperity.

Take me to Petra in its heyday. What do I experience?

It is 70 B.C., and you walk the streets of Petra, home to about 20,000 people. Ornate homes and public buildings rivaling Athenian and Roman artistry are carved into the high red sandstone walls of the canyon. A camel caravan arrives from Arabia loaded with goods; white-robed traders dismount with elegant gifts for their buying contacts. The wealthy aroma of frankincense constantly reminds your nostrils why Petra exists. Most people wear robes and cloaks, often colored by exotic dyes. Petra is luxurious without being licentious.

You overhear conversations in Aramaic and Arabic: A new cistern is under construction in the nearby hills. Workers are shoring up a building damaged by a recent earth tremor. Old-timers grouse that reigning King Aretas III wishes he were Greek. A modestly robed vendor walks past with dates for sale; you fish out a thick silver coin to offer her. Along with your bronze change and the delicious dates, she wishes you the favor of al-Uzza, the Nabataean goddess identified with Aphrodite and Venus.

You ask a passing water-bearer: Who's that guy in the outland-ish robe draped over one shoulder, followed by servants? A man of faraway Rome, says she. You've heard of this Rome, a dynamic market for Petra's goods, with domains beginning to rival Alexander the Great's once-mighty empire. Only time will tell how Petra will reckon with this next tide of power.

No one lives at Petra now. When and why did it decline?

Petra's last king, Rabbel II, willed his realm to Rome. When he died in A.D. 106, Nabataea became the Roman province of Arabia Petraea. Again the Nabataeans adjusted and kept up the trade. In the second and third centuries A.D., the caravans began using Palmyra (in modern Syria) as an alternate route, starting a long, slow decline at Petra. An earthquake in 363 delivered the knockout punch: damage to the intricate water system sus-taining the city. By about 400, Petra was a ghost town.

How might I see this for myself?

Thousands do it daily. If you can travel to Jordan, you can travel to Petra—either with an organized tour booked through a travel agent or on your own if that's your style. Nearby hotels and restaurants offer modern accommodations. The site charges a daily entrance fee.

Is Timbuktu an Actual Place?

The city of Timbuktu lives in modern English vocabulary as a somewhat mythical place remembered for its unique, lyrical name. If someone were actually to travel to Timbuktu, what (if anything) would they find there?

✳ ✳ ✳ ✳

THE REAL TIMBUKTU is a small city in northwestern Africa. It is located in central Mali about 500 miles from the Atlantic coast on the Niger River. Its roughly 30,000 inhabitants are mostly of Tuareg, Songhai, Fulani, or Moorish heritage. Most of Timbuktu's residents are Sunni Muslims.

The Name

The Tuaregs, a nomadic Berber people of the Sahara region, founded Timbuktu sometime around A.D. 1000. The story goes that a well-respected elderly lady named Buktu lived near a well ("tin" in Tuareg). Nomads who needed to leave things behind for safekeeping entrusted them to Buktu and said they had left their possessions at "Tin Buktu." Ms. Buktu is long gone, but her name has endured through Timbuktu. Even today, there is a well in Timbuktu, said to be that of Buktu herself.

The Place

Timbuktu began as an encampment and grew into a town, becoming an important stop on the trans-Saharan trade route. Salt mined from the Sahara went south and west; slaves and gold went north toward the Mediterranean. Even though Timbuktu changed hands among African empires, it developed into a prestigious Islamic cultural and religious center.

In its peak era beginning in about 1330, Timbuktu had 100,000 residents, including an astonishing 25,000 students. The prized turban of a Timbuktu scholar proclaimed its wearer to be a devout Muslim steeped in Islamic learning. In order to receive the lowest of four degrees conferred in Timbuktu, the student had to memorize the entire Koran. Learned scholars coming to Timbuktu from afar required extra teaching to bring their knowledge up to Timbuktu standards. In terms of prestige, it might be fair to call Timbuktu the Oxford or Harvard of the medieval Islamic world.

The golden era ended in 1591, when Moroccans armed with the latest gunpowder weapons conquered the Songhai Empire. The Moroccan conquest didn't kill Timbuktu, but the city was mortally wounded as trade routes shifted after the year 1600. Carrying goods across the sea became safer and faster than hauling everything across the Sahara. The city became somewhat of a back-water, yet remained an important destination for dedicated students seeking immersion in Islam.

By the 1800s, Timbuktu was only known as a legend to Europeans. A French exploration society offered a handsome bounty to anyone who visited Timbuktu and returned to describe it. At least one explorer perished in the attempt to locate Timbuktu, but an intrepid Frenchman named René-Auguste Caillé finally returned with an account of the contemporary city. His report would have made a lousy tourist brochure, as he found only a collection of mud huts threatened by the rising sands of the Sahara. The only remarkable aspects of Timbuktu, Caillé said, were its centers of Islamic learning.

The French captured Timbuktu in 1893, incorporating it into their immense West African domain. In 1960, the Republic of Mali achieved independence. At that time Timbuktu hadn't changed a lot since Caillé's visit. However, Timbuktu's prominence has risen in subsequent years. Today, Timbuktu is sometimes called "The Mecca of Africa" for the prestigious Islamic study courses offered at the city's Sankore Mosque. Additionally, hundreds of thousands of priceless historical documents can still be found in Timbuktu. Refusing to be erased and forgotten again, the city has even successfully managed to keep the Sahara's drifting sands at bay.

How Was the Ancient City of Angkor Lost and Found Again?

For hundreds of years, rumors of the lost city of Angkor spread among Cambodian peasants. On a stifling day in 1860, Henri Mahout and his porters discovered that the ancient city was more than mere legend.

✳   ✳   ✳   ✳

FRENCH BOTANIST AND explorer Henri Mahout wiped his spectacles as he pushed into the Cambodian jungle clearing. Gasping for breath in the rain forest's thick mists, he gazed down weed-ridden avenues at massive towers and stone temples wreathed with carvings of gods, kings, and battles. The ruins before him were none other than the temples of Angkor Wat.

Although often credited with the discovery of Angkor Wat, Mahout was not the first Westerner to encounter the site. He did, however, bring the "lost" city to the attention of the European public when his travel journals were published in 1868. He wrote: "One of these temples—a rival to that of Solomon, and erected by some ancient Michelangelo—might take an honorable place beside our most beautiful buildings."

Mahout's descriptions of this "new," massive, unexplored Hindu temple sent a jolt of lightning through Western academic circles. Explorers from western Europe combed the jungles of northern Cambodia in an attempt to explain the meaning and origin of the mysterious lost shrine.

The Rise of the Khmer

Scholars first theorized that Angkor Wat and other ancient temples in present-day Cambodia were about 2,000 years old. However, as they began to decipher the Sanskrit inscriptions, they found that the temples had been erected during the 9th through 12th centuries. While Europe languished in the Dark

Ages, the Khmer Empire of Indochina was reaching its zenith.

The earliest records of the Khmer people date back to the middle of the 6th century. They migrated from southern China and settled in what is now Cambodia. The early Khmer retained many Indian influences from the West—they were Hindus, and their architecture evolved from Indian methods of building.

In the early 9th century, King Jayavarman II laid claim to an independent kingdom called Kambuja. He established his capital in the Angkor area some 190 miles north of the modern Cambodian capital of Phnom Penh. Jayavarman II also introduced the cult of devaraja, which claimed that the Khmer king was a representative of Shiva, the Hindu god of chaos, destruction, and rebirth. As such, in addition to the temples built to honor the Hindu gods, temples were also constructed to serve as tombs when kings died.

The Khmer built more than 100 stone temples spread out over some 40 miles. The temples were made from laterite (a material similar to clay that forms in tropical climates) and sandstone. The sandstone provided an open canvas for the statues and reliefs celebrating the Hindu gods that decorate the temples.

Home of the Gods

During the first half of the 12th century, Kambuja's King Suryavarman II decided to raise an enormous temple dedicated to the Hindu god Vishnu, a religious monument that would subdue the surrounding jungle and illustrate the power of the Khmer king. His masterpiece—the largest temple complex in the world—would be known to history by its Sanskrit name, "Angkor Wat," or "City of Temple."

Pilgrims visiting Angkor Wat in the 12th century would enter the temple complex by crossing a square, 600-foot-wide moat that ran some four miles in perimeter around the temple grounds. Approaching from the west, visitors would tread the moat's causeway to the main gateway. From there, they would follow a spiritual journey representing the path from the outside world through the Hindu universe and into Mount Meru, the home of the gods. They would pass a giant statue of an eight-armed Vishnu as they entered the western gopura, or gatehouse, known as the "Entrance of the Elephants." They would then follow a stone walkway decorated with nagas (mythical serpents) past sunken pools and column-studded buildings once believed to house sacred temple documents.

At the end of the stone walkway, a pilgrim would step up to a rectangular platform surrounded with galleries featuring six-foot-high bas-reliefs of gods and kings. One depicts the Churning of the Ocean of Milk, a Hindu story in which gods and demons churn a serpent in an ocean of milk to extract the elixir of life. Another illustrates the epic battle of monkey warriors against demons whose sovereign had kidnapped Sita, Rama's beautiful wife. Others depict the gruesome fates awaiting the wicked in the afterlife.

A visitor to King Suryavarman's kingdom would next ascend the dangerously steep steps to the temple's second level, an enclosed area boasting a courtyard decorated with hundreds of dancing apsaras, female images ornamented with jewelry and elaborately dressed hair.

For kings and high priests, the journey would continue with a climb up more steep steps to a 126-foot-high central temple, the pinnacle of Khmer society. Spreading out some 145 feet on each side, the square temple includes a courtyard cornered by four high conical towers shaped to look like lotus buds. The center of the temple is dominated by a fifth conical tower soaring 180 feet above the main causeway; inside it holds a golden statue of the Khmer patron, Vishnu, riding a half-man, half-bird creature in the image of King Suryavarman.

Disuse and Destruction

With the decline of the Khmer Empire and the resurgence of

Buddhism, Angkor Wat was occupied by Buddhist monks, who claimed it as their own for many years. A cruciform gallery leading to the temple's second level was decorated with 1,000 Buddhas; the Vishnu statue in the central tower was replaced by an image of Buddha. The temple fell into various states of disrepair over the centuries and is now the focus of international restoration efforts.

Why Does the Leaning Tower of Pisa Lean?

To understand why the tower leans, one should know the history of this remarkable crooked edifice, including where it was built. At the turn of the first century A.D., Pisa was a vibrant seaport city on the northwestern coast of Italy. In 1063, the Pisans attacked the city of Palermo. They were victorious and returned home with treasures.

✳ ✳ ✳ ✳

THE PISANS, BEING a proud people, wanted to show the world how important their city was, and decided to erect a great cathedral complex, called the Field of Miracles; the complex included a cathedral, cemetery, baptistery, and bell tower.

Pisa was originally named Poseidonia in 600 B.C., from a Greek word meaning "marshy land." Bonanno Pisano, the original architect of the bell tower, did not think this was important information when he began the project. In 1173, Bonanno decided that since there was a good deal of water under the ground, he'd build a shallow foundation, one that was about three meters deep.

Five years later, when third-floor construction was about to begin, Bonanno realized that his structure was sinking on one side; this was because he built upon a bed of dense clay. But being a proud Pisan, he continued to go skyward. To attempt to solve the problem, he added two inches to the southern columns and thought no one would notice. People noticed. The third floor reached completion, and the job was halted indefinitely.

In 1272, construction of the bell tower resumed under the guidance of architect Giovanni di Simone. He completed four more floors, built at an angle to compensate for the listing. But not only did his remedy cause the tower to tilt in the other direction, but it also created a curve. In 1284, the job was once again halted. In 1319, the Pisans picked up their tools and completed the seventh floor. The bell tower was added in 1372, and then it was left to lean in peace until the 19th century.

In 1838, the foundation was dug out so visitors could see how it was built, which caused the tower to lean even more. Then in 1934, Benito Mussolini ordered the foundation to be reinforced with concrete. The concrete was too heavy, however, and it sunk the tower further into the clay.

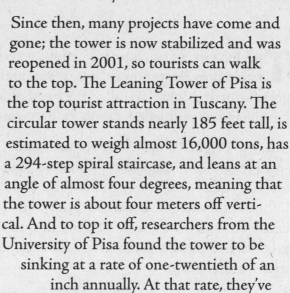

Since then, many projects have come and gone; the tower is now stabilized and was reopened in 2001, so tourists can walk to the top. The Leaning Tower of Pisa is the top tourist attraction in Tuscany. The circular tower stands nearly 185 feet tall, is estimated to weigh almost 16,000 tons, has a 294-step spiral staircase, and leans at an angle of almost four degrees, meaning that the tower is about four meters off vertical. And to top it off, researchers from the University of Pisa found the tower to be sinking at a rate of one-twentieth of an inch annually. At that rate, they've predicted, the tower will collapse in fewer than three hundred years.

Where Is No Man's Land?

For a place so seemingly desolate, remote, and forlorn, this place sure pops up a lot.

✳ ✳ ✳ ✳

Take a look at a map and you will find a No Man's Land in the Caradon district of southeast Cornwall, England; a No Man's Land on East Falkland Island; and a Nomans Land Island (also charted No Man's Land or No Man's Island) in Chilmark, Massachusetts. And that's just to name a few.

Some of these places are indeed uninhabited, but that's probably for good reason. In the case of the Falkland Island No Man's Land, the terrain is extremely rough due to a craggy chain of mountains known as Wickham Heights. And the No Man's Land in Massachusetts? It is located only three miles off the quaint coast of Martha's Vineyard, but this island was once used as a practice range for bombing.

In more general terms, No Man's Land is a phrase that has been around since at least the 14th century. It's often used to reference an unoccupied area between the front lines of opposing armies, or to designate land that is unowned, undesirable, or otherwise under dispute.

A good example: Following the Louisiana Purchase between the United States and Spain, an area called No Man's Land (aka the Neutral Strip or Sabine Free State) was designated neutral ground because the two governments could not agree on a boundary. From 1806 to 1819, both countries claimed ownership of this tract, but neither enforced any laws or control. No wonder it became a haven for outlaws and renegades.

In its earliest use, No Man's Land likely referred to a plot of land just outside the north walls of London. In the early 1300s, this No Man's Land was a place where criminals were executed and left out in the open for public view.

Is Yellowstone About to Explode?

About 3.8 million people visit Yellowstone National Park each year. They do a little hiking, maybe some fishing. They admire the majesty of the mountains. And, of course, they visit the geysers. Hordes of tourists sit and wait patiently for Old Faithful to do its thing every 90 minutes or so.

✳ ✳ ✳ ✳

FEW OF THESE tourists give much thought to what is going on below their feet while they are at Yellowstone. Geologists, however, have known for years that some sort of volcanic activity is responsible for the park's strange, volatile, steamy landscape. Just one problem: They couldn't find evidence of an actual volcano, the familiar cone-shaped mountain that tells to us in no uncertain terms that a huge explosion once took place on that spot.

In the 1960s, NASA took pictures of Yellowstone from outer space. When geologists got their hands on these pictures, they understood why they couldn't spot the volcano: It was far too vast for them to see. The crater of the Yellowstone volcano includes practically the entire park, covering about 2.2 million acres. Obviously, we're not talking about your typical, garden-variety volcano. Yellowstone is what is known as a supervolcano.

There is no recorded history of any supervolcano eruptions, so we can only use normal volcanic activity as a measuring stick. Geologists believe that Yellowstone has erupted about 140 times in the past 16 million years. The most recent blast was about one thousand times more powerful than the 1980 eruption of Mount St. Helens in Washington, and it spread ash over almost the entire area of the United States west of the Mississippi River. Some of the previous Yellowstone eruptions were many times more destructive than that.

And here's some interesting news: In the past twenty years or so, geologists have detected significant activity in the molten rock and boiling water below Yellowstone. In other words, the surface is shifting.

Nearby, the Teton Range has gotten a little shorter. Scientists have calculated that Yellowstone erupts about every 600,000 years. And get this: The last Yellowstone eruption took place about 640,000 years ago.

Before you go scrambling for the Atlantic Ocean, screaming and waving your arms in the air, know that the friendly folks who run Yellowstone National Park assure us that an eruption is not likely to happen for at least another thousand years. And even then, any eruption would be preceded by weeks, months, or perhaps even years of telltale volcanic weirdness.

So don't worry. It's safe to go to Yellowstone. For now.

Which Hawaiian Island Has the State's Most Unusual Waterfall?

Hawaii's third largest island, Oahu, touts the state's most unusual waterfall—one that defies gravity.

✳ ✳ ✳ ✳

Tears in the Mist

THE LUSH NU'UANU Valley on the eastern coast of Oahu stretches from Honolulu to the Ko'olau Range and ends quite suddenly in steep cliffs, called the Pali.

Here, on only the rainiest and windiest of days, visitors can see the famous Upside-Down Waterfall, so called because water cascading from the 3,150-foot summit of Mount Konahuanui falls only a few feet before strong trade winds blow it back up in the air. The water dissipates into mist, creating the illusion of water slowly falling upward.

Natives call the waterfall *Waipuhia*, or "blown water."
According to one legend, Waipuhia was named for a young
girl who lived in the hills of the Nu'uanu Valley and whose
bright eyes pleased the gods. One tragic day, the girl's true love
was lost in a storm, and when she wept for him, her tears were
caught halfway down the cliff by the god of wind and tossed
into the spray by the god of mist.

Lookout Lore

Weather permitting, the best view of the waterfall is from
the 1,186-foot Nu'uanu Pali Lookout, itself an infamous
spot in Hawaiian lore. As the legend goes, in 1795, King
Kamehameha I drove the Oahu warriors up the Nu'uanu
Valley to the Pali, where thousands of them were driven over
the cliffs to their deaths.

While scholars pooh-pooh the story, natives say that at night
the cries of long-dead warriors can be heard echoing through
the valley. Others tell of seeing a ghostly white figure—perhaps
the king—on the Pali Highway leading up to the Lookout, as
well as ghost warriors falling from cliffs.

What eventually became the Pali Highway was built in
1898 by Honolulu native (and future mayor) John Wilson.
Apparently, Wilson's workers encountered several bones during
the project—and simply laid the road right over them.

What Sunken Civilizations Have Been Discovered?

Researchers have discovered the tantalizing remains of what appears to be advanced Mesolithic and Neolithic civilizations hidden for millennia under water or sand. But are the ancient cities real, or is it just wishful thinking?

✳ ✳ ✳ ✳

La Marmotta: Stone Age Lakefront

WHAT IS NOW the bottom of Italy's six-mile-wide Lake Bracciano was once a lovely and fertile river floodplain. In 1989, scientists discovered a lost city, which they renamed La Marmotta. Dive teams have recovered artifacts ranging from ancient timbers to uneaten pots of stew, all preserved under ten feet of mud.

The site dates back to about 5700 B.C. around the late Stone Age or Neolithic era. Though not much is known about the people who lived there, scientists do know that the city's residents migrated from the Near East or Greece in 35-foot-long, wooden dugout boats with their families. They had domesticated animals, pottery, religious statues, and even two species of dogs. They laid out their village with large wooden houses. Items such as obsidian knives and greenstone ax blades show that La Marmotta was a busy Mediterranean trade center. But after 400 years of occupation, it seems the village was hastily abandoned. Why they fled still puzzles researchers.

Atlantis Beneath the Black Sea

Ever since the Greek writer Plato described the lost island of Atlantis in the fourth century B.C., scholars have searched for the its location. One oft-suggested candidate is a grouping of underwater settlements northwest of the Black Sea. Researchers claim this advanced Neolithic population center was once situated on shore along a freshwater lake that was engulfed by seawater by 5510 B.C. Ancient landforms in the area seem to have centered around an island that roughly fits the description of Atlantis. Similarities between the lore of Atlantis and this settlement include the use of a form of early writing, the existence of elephants (from eastern trade routes), obsidian used as money, and circular observatory structures.

Japan, Gateway to Mu

According to Japanese geologist Masaaki Kimura, a legendary lost continent called Mu may have been discovered off the coast of Japan. Kimura says underwater formations that were found in 1985 at Yonaguni Island indicate that they were handmade and that they possibly once resembled a Roman city complete with a coliseum, a castle, statues, paved streets, and plazas. Although photos show sharp, step-like angles and flat surfaces, skeptics still argue these "roads" were actually created by forces such as tides or volcanoes. Nevertheless, Kimura maintains his belief that the ruins are the proof of a 5,000-year-old city.

Ancient Alpine Lake Towns

Today, most people would associate the Alps, the mountain region that borders Germany, Switzerland, and Italy, with skiing. But in late Stone Age or Neolithic period (6000–2000 B.C.), the region's lakes dominated the action. A dry spell in the mid-1800s lowered water levels and allowed evidence of ancient villages to surface within many lakes in the region. One site at the Swiss town of Obermeilen yielded exciting finds such as wooden posts, artifacts made from antlers, Neolithic clay objects, and wooden utensils. It is now believed that the posts supported large wooden platforms that sat over the water, serving as docklike foundations for houses and other village structures.

Hamoukar: City of Commerce

Until the mid-1970s, when the ancient settlement of Hamoukar was discovered in Syria, archaeologists believed the world's oldest cities—dating back to 4000 B.C.—were in present-day Iraq. But the massive, 750-acre Hamoukar, surrounded by a 13-inch-thick wall and home to an estimated 25,000 people, was already a prosperous and advanced city by 4000 B.C.

Situated in the land between the Tigris and Euphrates rivers, Hamoukar was sophisticated enough to support commercial bakeries and large-scale beer breweries. People used clay seals as "brands" for mass-produced goods, including delicate pottery, jewelry, and stone goods. The city was also a processing area for obsidian and later, copper. The settlement was destroyed in a fierce battle around 3500 B.C., leaving more than 1,000 slingshot bullets in the city's ruins.

The Great Danes

They sure ate a lot of shellfish—that much is known about the Mesolithic European culture that lived along the coast of what is now Denmark between 5600 and 4000 B.C. The now-underwater cities were investigated in the 1970s; the first is known as Tybrind Vig and its people are called the Ertebölle. The Ertebölle skeletons resemble those of modern Danes, but some also show Cro-Magnon facial features such as protruding jaws and prominent brow ridges. Archaeologists have found implements made of antler, bone, and stone sticking out of the Danish sea floor. They also found large piles of shellfish at the oldest sites, indicating that the inhabitants loved seafood. Preserved remains of acorns, hazelnuts, and other plants showed their diet was well rounded.

The Ertebölle made clever use of local materials. They lived in wattle or brush huts; "knitted" clothing from plant fibers; made ceramic pots decorated with impressions of grains, cord, and bones; and created art from polished bone and amber. Eventually, it is assumed, the Ertebölle hunter-gatherers either evolved into or were replaced by people with farming skills.

Why Isn't Scotland Yard in Scotland?

British nomenclature is loaded with misleading terms. For example, plum pudding is not pudding, nor does it contain plums. Given this legacy of verbal imprecision, it's not surprising that the headquarters of the famous police force that patrols London is called Scotland Yard.

❋ ❋ ❋ ❋

IT STARTED IN 1829, when Charles Rowan and Richard Mayne were charged with organizing a citywide crime-fighting force in London. At the time the two men lived together in a house at 4 Whitehall Place, and they ran their fledgling outfit out of their garage, using the back courtyard as a makeshift police station. "Rowan and Mayne's Backyard" wasn't an appropriate name for the headquarters of a police force. Instead, it was called Scotland Yard.

Why? After years of research, word sleuths have narrowed the origin of the name to two likely possibilities. According to the first explanation, Scotland Yard sits on the location of what was once the property of Scottish royalty. The story goes that back before Scotland and England unified in 1707, the present-day Scotland Yard was a residence used by Scottish kings and ambassadors when they visited London on diplomatic sojourns. The other, less regal possibility is that 4 Whitehall Place backed onto a courtyard called Great Scotland Yard, named for the medieval landowner—Scott—who owned the property.

Regardless of the name's true origin, the Metropolitan police have moved on—sort of. In 1890, they decided that they needed new digs and moved to a larger building on the Victoria Embankment. Given a chance to redeem themselves and give their headquarters a name that actually made sense, what did the London police choose? New Scotland Yard.

What's Become of the Most Famous Ancient Cities?

In the ancient world, it took far fewer people to make a great city. Some didn't survive; some have flourished; and others have exploded. With the understanding that ancient population estimates are necessarily approximate, here are the fates of some great metropolises:

✳   ✳   ✳   ✳

Memphis (now the ruins of Memphis, Egypt): By 3100 B.C., this Pharaonic capital bustled with an estimated 30,000 people. Today it has none—but modern Cairo, 12 miles north, is home to an estimated 20 million people.

Ur (now the ruins of Ur, Iraq): Sumer's great ancient city once stood near the Euphrates with a peak population of 65,000 around 2030 B.C. The Euphrates has meandered about ten miles northeast, and Ur now has a population of zero.

Alexandria (now El-Iskandariya, Egypt): Built on an ancient Egyptian village site near the Nile Delta's west end, Alexander the Great's city once held a tremendous library. In its heyday, it may have held 250,000 people; today an estimated 5.2 million people call it home.

Babylon (now the ruins of Babylon, Iraq): Babylon may have twice been the largest city in the world, in about 1700 B.C. and 500 B.C.—perhaps with up to 200,000 people in the latter case. Now, it's windblown dust and faded splendor.

Athens (Greece): In classical times, this powerful city-state stood miles from the coast but was never a big place—something like 30,000 residents during the 300s B.C. It now reaches the sea with about 3 million residents.

Rome (Italy): With the rise of its empire, ancient Rome became a city of more than 500,000 and the center of Western civilization. Though that mantle moved on to other cities, Rome now has around 2.8 million people.

Xi'an (China): This longtime dynastic capital, famed for its terra-cotta warriors but home to numerous other antiquities, reached 400,000 people by A.D. 637. Its 12 million people make it as important a city now as then.

Constantinople (now Istanbul, Turkey): First colonized by Greeks in the 1200s B.C., this city of fame was made Emperor Constantine the Great's eastern imperial Roman capital with 300,000 people. As Byzantium, it bobbed and wove through the tides of faith and conquest. Today, it is Turkey's largest city with around 15 million people.

Baghdad (Iraq): Founded around A.D. 762, this center of Islamic culture and faith was perhaps the first city to house more than 1,000,000 people. It has sometimes faded but never fallen. Today it has a population of over 5 million.

Tenochtitlán (now Mexico City, Mexico): Founded in A.D. 1325, within a century, this island-built Aztec capital had more than 200,000 inhabitants. Most of the surrounding lake has been drained over the years. A staggering 21 million souls call metro Mexico City home.

Carthage (now the ruins of Carthage, Tunisia): Phoenician seafarers from the Levant founded this great trade city in 814 B.C. Before the Romans obliterated it in 146 B.C., its population may have reached 700,000. Today, it sits in empty silence ten miles from modern Tunis—population 638,000.

When Was the Colosseum Built?

With recently deceased dictator Nero out of the picture, Rome's new ruler, Vespasian, sought to show the ravaged populace that he wasn't like his self-serving predecessor. He proved to be the ruler who could finally bring the people out of their long-lasting troubles—all it took was an architectural triumph designed to house 50,000 roaring Romans thirsty for an entertainingly gruesome battle.

* * * *

DURING HIS REIGN as emperor in the first century A.D., Nero had repeatedly proved himself a ruthless ruler, stealing everything he could from the Roman people and killing anyone who got in his way. In the year between Nero's forced suicide and the rise of Vespasian (born Titus Flavius Vespasianus), three other emperors took brief turns ruling Rome, but Vespasian became the man who mattered. He chose to launch his reign with a monumental gesture meant to cause the people to forget Nero. He initiated construction of the most substantial arena of the time, a structure that became the cultural nucleus of Rome—and remained so for the next 450 years.

Putting a Bad Ruler Behind Them

During Nero's reign, which marked the end of the long-running and brutal Julio-Claudian dynasty, land and resources were absorbed into his extravagant estate, the Domus Aurea. Set in the heart of Rome, Nero's grandiose property featured a lake, a mansion with more than 300 rooms, and hundreds of acres of land. The opulent interior of the house showcased unrivaled luxuries, from expansively marbled floors to a slave-driven revolving dome ceiling that would intermittently release mists of perfume and flutters of rose petals over the frequent assemblages of partygoers. Ever the egotist, Nero commissioned a towering bronze statue in his own image, the

Collossus Neronis, and ordered it to be erected at the palace steps to greet—or perhaps intimidate—visitors.

As an apt show of goodwill to the Roman people, Vespasian confiscated the land for his building project from Nero's lavish estate. The great Flavian Amphitheater eventually resided beside the lake Nero had built to complete his posh property. Historians suggest that it is from Nero's statue that the Flavian Amphitheater drew its eventual name, the Colosseum.

A Massive Undertaking

The arena was built with a multitude of materials and mirrored Greek architecture, despite the lack of experience the Romans had with such technology. Adapting to the task, the Romans used travertine stone to make up much of the exterior of the elliptical building; wooden floors covered in sand (which was good for absorbing blood) spread across the entirety of the interior. Tiers of seats allowed for massive seating capacity, and mazes beneath the main floor kept wild animals contained in preparation for events. Trapdoors to surprise gladiators, as well as a retractable roof to provide shade for patrons, completed the structure. Upon its opening, the Colosseum was the perfect meeting place for the Roman community.

The construction of the Colosseum lasted ten years and extended through two reigns. Upon Vespasian's death, his son Titus ascended to the position of emperor in A.D. 79 and sought to finalize the arena's creation. Titus brought thousands of slaves from Jerusalem to speed up completion of the arena, and the Romans celebrated in A.D. 80 with inaugural games that included the slaying of 9,000 wild animals, noonday executions, and gladiatorial brawls that usually ended in death. This introductory series marked the beginning of a 450-year stretch of ongoing community celebrations and the creation of traditional Roman-style entertainment.

What Are the Seven Wonders of the Natural World?

Each of the following sites captures the imagination with its natural power and beauty. And they have one thing in common: Nothing made by humans can approach their majestic dignity.

✻　✻　✻　✻

1. Grand Canyon

The Grand Canyon in northwestern Arizona was formed by the erosive power of the weather and the Colorado River and its tributaries as they scoured away billion-year-old rocks. Although known to Native Americans for thousands of years, the vast gorge was not discovered by the first Spanish explorers until 1540. Grand Canyon National Park was established in 1919, preserving the more than 1.2 million acres of colorful cliffs and waterways that are home to 75 species of mammals, 50 species of reptiles and amphibians, 25 species of fish, and more than 300 species of birds.

The canyon stretches 277 miles, with some sections reaching a mile deep and 18 miles across. More than five million visitors view the canyon annually, often hiking or riding mules down to the canyon floor, while the more adventurous opt for boating or rafting the Colorado River through the canyon.

2. Aurora Borealis (Northern Lights)

The aurora borealis (also called the northern lights) consists of awe-inspiring twirls of light in the sky, caused by "solar wind"—electrically charged particles interacting with Earth's magnetic field. The aurora borealis can be up to 2,000 miles wide, but it fluctuates in size, shape, and color, with green being the most common color close to the horizon while purples and reds appear higher.

Named after Aurora, Roman goddess of dawn, and Boreas, Greek god of the north wind, these ribbons of color are best viewed in northern climates like Alaska, but have been seen as far south as Arizona.

3. Mount Everest

Mount Everest, part of the Himalayan Mountains, was formed about 60 million years ago due to the shifting of Earth's rocky plates. Named after Sir George Everest, a British surveyor-general of India, Everest is the highest mountain on Earth, looming some 29,035 feet high and growing a few millimeters every year. Climbing Everest isn't easy, due to avalanches, strong winds, and thin air. Nevertheless, in 1953, Edmund Hillary and Sherpa Tenzing Norgay were the first climbers to reach the peak. More than 800 others have done so since.

4. Paricutin

Paricutin provides one of nature's best lessons in how volatile Earth is. Exploding out of a Mexican cornfield in 1943, Paricutin was the first known volcano to have witnesses at its birth. Within a year, the cone had grown to more than 1,100 feet high. The flow eventually spread over 10 square miles, engulfing the nearby towns of Paricutin and San Juan Parangaricutiro. The eruptions ceased in 1952, and the cone now soars 1,345 feet high.

5. Victoria Falls

Victoria Falls, originally called Mosi-oa-Tunya ("smoke that thunders"), was named after Queen Victoria of England in 1855. The raging waters of the Zambezi River pour 19 trillion cubic feet of water per minute into a gorge that is 1.25 miles wide and 328 feet deep, making this the largest curtain of falling water in the world. Located between Zambia and Zimbabwe, Victoria Falls is flanked by national parks and is now one of the world's greatest tourist attractions, with resorts, hiking trails, and observation posts around it. White-water rafting at the foot of the falls makes for a thrilling adventure.

6. Great Barrier Reef

The Great Barrier Reef blankets 137,600 square miles and extends a dramatic 1,242 miles along Australia's northeastern coast, making it the largest group of reefs in the world. The reef began forming more than 30 million years ago and is made up of the skeletons of marine polyps. Four hundred species of living polyps can also be found there, along with 1,500 species of fish, as well as crabs, clams, and other sea life. The area is an Australian national park and is visited by around two million tourists a year.

7. Giant Sequoia Trees

Ancient giant sequoia trees are nature's ever-growing wonders. Giant sequoias grow naturally on the western slopes of California's Sierra Nevada Mountains at elevations from 5,000 to 7,000 feet. Some are as tall as a 26-story building, with their trunks spanning up to 100 feet and the bark on the older specimens reaching two to four feet thick. California's Sequoia National Park is home to several noteworthy giants,

including the General Sherman, which is the world's largest tree by volume, measuring 274.9 feet high, almost 103 feet around, and comprising 52,508 cubic feet of wood. Giant sequoia trees are estimated to be between 1,800 and 2,700 years old. Depending on the tree and where it is situated, giant sequoias can grow up to two feet in height every year, producing almost 40 cubic feet of additional wood each year.

Do Countries Get Paid for Delivering Mail from Other Countries?

Yes, but luckily, countries work out the tab amongst themselves.

✳ ✳ ✳ ✳

IMAGINE HAVING TO buy stamps from every country that handled your letter as it went around the world. This is how people did it in the early days of mail, and it was a real pain.

In 1874, a bunch of nations got together and formed an international organization to sort it all out. The goals were to eliminate the need for countries to establish individual postal treaties with one another and to allow people to buy stamps from whatever country they were in. The organization is now a United Nations agency called the Universal Postal Union (UPO).

Over the years, the UPO has adjusted its formula to make certain that every country receives a fair share of the dough. Initially, the UPO assumed that almost every letter would get a reply, meaning that any two countries would spend about the same amount of time and money delivering mail from the other. As a result, participating countries kept all the money for mail leaving their shores. But with the rise of magazine delivery, mail-order business, and the like, some countries (including the United States) ended up getting the short end of the stick, receiving more mail than they sent. So the UPO instituted terminal dues: payments from the country of origin to the destination country to cover the costs associated with foreign mail.

Today, terminal dues are based on a complex formula that factors in the total weight of the mail and the total number of pieces going from one nation to another, as well as the quality of service in the destination country. For industrialized countries, the formula takes into account the cost of delivering mail in the destination country. For developing countries, the formula uses an average world rate instead of an individual rate.

The math is complicated, and the UPO seems to be forever tweaking its formula. Just be glad the United Nations figures it all out so that you don't have to.

Why Is America Called America?

Weren't you paying attention in your eighth-grade world history class? As you were undoubtedly told, the Americas are named for the Italian explorer Amerigo Vespucci. But what did he do that was so great? The only fact about his life that anyone seems to remember is that, well, America is named after him. How did a dude who's otherwise forgotten by history manage to stamp his name on two entire continents?

✳ ✳ ✳ ✳

WHILE HE DIDN'T make the lasting impression of his contemporary Christopher Columbus, Vespucci was no slouch. As a young man, he went to work for the Medici family of Florence, Italy. The Medicis were powerbrokers who wielded great influence in politics (they ran the city), religion (some were elected to be bishops and popes), and art (they were the most prominent patrons of the Renaissance, commissioning some of the era's most memorable paintings, frescos, and statues).

Like many of the movers and shakers of that age, the Medici family had an interest in exploration, which is where Vespucci came in. Under their patronage, he began fitting out ships in Seville, where he worked on the fleet for Columbus's second voyage. Vespucci evidently caught the exploration bug while hanging around the port—between 1497 and 1504 he made as many as four voyages to the South America coast, serving as a navigator for Spain and later Portugal. On a trek he made for

Portugal in 1501, Vespucci realized that he wasn't visiting Asia, as Columbus believed, but a brand-spankin' new continent. This "ah-ha" moment was his chief accomplishment, though he also made an extremely close calculation of Earth's circumference (he was only 50 miles off).

Vespucci's skills as a storyteller are what really put his name on the map. During his explorer days, Vespucci sent a series of letters about his adventures to the Medici family and others. Vespucci livened up ho-hum navigational details with salacious accounts of native life, including bodice-ripping tales of the natives' sexual escapades. Needless to say, the dirty letters were published and proved to be exceedingly popular. These accounts introduced the term "The New World" to the popular lexicon.

German cartographer Martin Waldseemüller was a fan, so he decided to label the new land "America" on a 1507 map. He explained his decision thusly: "I do not see what right any one would have to object to calling this part after Americus, who discovered it and who is a man of intelligence, [and so to name it] *Amerige*, that is, the Land of Americus, or *America*: since both Europa and Asia got their names from women."

But there are those who believe that Vespucci's forename wasn't the true origin of the name. Some historians contend that the term "America" was already in use at the time and that Waldseemüller incorrectly assumed it referred to Vespucci. Some have suggested that European explorers picked up the name Amerrique—"Land of the Wind" in Mayan—from South American natives. Others say it came from a British customs officer named Richard Ameryk, who sponsored John Cabot's voyage to Newfoundland in 1497 and possibly some pre-Columbian explorations of the continent. Yet another theory claims that early Norse explorers called the mysterious new land *Ommerike*, meaning "farthest outland."

In any case, the name ended up on Waldseemüller's map in

honor of Vespucci. The map proved to be highly influential; other cartographers began to use "America," and before long it had stuck.

Keep this story in mind the next time you're composing a heart-stoppingly boring e-mail—if you spruce it up a bit, you might get a third of the world named after you.

Why Was the Taj Mahal Built?

Known as one of the Wonders of the World, the Taj Mahal was a shrine to love and one man's obsession. Today an average of three million tourists a year travel to see the UNESCO World Heritage site.

✳ ✳ ✳ ✳

Taj Mahal: Foundations

THE MUGHAL (OR "Mogul") Empire occupied India from the mid-1500s to the early 1800s. At the height of its success, this imperial power controlled most of the Indian subcontinent and much of what is now Afghanistan, containing a population of around 150 million people.

During this era, a young prince named Khurram took the throne in 1628, succeeding his father. Six years prior, after a military victory Khurram was given the title Shah Jahan by his emperor father. Now, with much of the subcontinent at his feet, the title was apt: *Shah Jahan* is Persian for "King of the World." (17th-century emperors were nothing if not modest.)

When Khurram Met Arjumand

Being shah had a lot of fringe benefits—banquets, treasures, and multiple wives, among other things. Shah Jahan did have several wives, but one woman stood out from the rest. When he was age 15, he was betrothed to 14-year-old Arjumand Banu Begam. Her beauty and compassion knocked the emperor-to-be off his feet; five years later, they were married. The bride took the title of *Mumtaz Mahal*, which means, according to various translations, "Chosen One of the Palace," "Exalted One of the Palace," or "Beloved Ornament of the Palace." You get the point.

Court historians have recorded the couple's close friendship, companionship, and intimate relationship. The couple traveled extensively together, Mumtaz often accompanying her husband on his military jaunts. But tragedy struck in 1631, when on one of these trips, Mumtaz died giving birth to what would have been their 14th child.

Breaking Ground

Devastated, Shah Jahan began work that year on what would become the Taj Mahal, a palatial monument to his dead wife and their everlasting love. While there were surely many hands on deck for the planning of the Taj, the architect who is most often credited is Ustad Ahmad Lahori. The project took until 1648 to complete and enlisted the labor of 20,000 workers and 1,000 elephants. This structure and its surrounding grounds covers 42 acres. The following are the basic parts of Mumtaz's giant mausoleum.

The Gardens: To get to the structural parts of the Taj Mahal, one must cross the enormous gardens surrounding it. Following classic Persian garden design, the grounds to the south of the buildings are made up of four sections divided by marble canals (reflecting pools) with adjacent pathways. The gardens stretch from the main gateway to the foot of the Taj.

The Main Gateway: Made of red sandstone and standing approximately 100 feet high and 150 feet wide, the main gateway is composed of a central arch with towers attached to each of its corners. The walls are richly adorned with calligraphy and floral arabesques inlaid with gemstones.

The Tomb: Unlike most Mughal mausoleums, Mumtaz's tomb is placed at the north end of the Taj Mahal, above the river and in between the mosque and the guesthouse. The tomb is entirely sheathed in white marble with an exterior dome that is almost 250 feet above ground level. The effect is impressive: Depending on the light at various times of the day, the tomb can appear pink, white, or brilliant gold.

The Mosque and the Jawab: On either side of the great tomb lie two smaller buildings. One is a mosque, and the other is called the *jawab*, or "answer." The mosque was used, of course, as a place of worship; the jawab was often used as a guesthouse. Both buildings are made of red sandstone so as not to take away too much from the grandeur of the tomb. The shah's monument to the love of his life still stands, and still awes, more than 370 years later.

Where Is the World's Largest Library?

The Library of Congress, located in Washington, D.C., is the world's largest library with more than 168 million items.

✳   ✳   ✳   ✳

THE LIBRARY OF Congress was established on April 24, 1800. Founding Father James Madison came up with the proposal for a congressional library in 1783, and an act of Congress signed by President John Adams made it a reality nearly a quarter century later. The original collection had 740 books and three maps.

The library was destroyed on August 24, 1814, when invading British troops burned the Capitol building (where the library was housed) during the War of 1812. The collection was replaced when Thomas Jefferson sold his personal library of 6,487 books to Congress later that year for $23,950. Another massive fire in December 1851 destroyed about two-thirds of the library's 55,000 volumes, including most of Thomas Jefferson's personal library. Many of the volumes have since been replaced.

Expansion

After the Civil War, the library was greatly expanded under the direction of Librarian of Congress Ainsworth Rand Spofford, who changed it from merely a congressional resource to a national institution. Spofford was also instrumental in establishing the copyright law of 1870, which placed the U.S. Copyright Office in the Library of Congress and required anyone seeking a copyright to provide two copies of the work to the library.

Facilities

The library's burgeoning collection soon outgrew its space in the Capitol. Congress approved the construction of a separate building and the new "Congressional Library" opened in 1897. The Italian Renaissance-style building was later named for Thomas Jefferson to honor his role in the library's history. The John Adams Building was built in Art Deco style and completed in 1939. The James Madison Memorial Building, completed in 1981, more than doubled the library's available space. In addition to its three Capitol Hill buildings, the Library of Congress now has a storage facility in Fort Meade, Maryland, and the Packard Campus for Audio Visual Conservation Center in Culpeper, Virginia.

Collections

Today, the Library of Congress is the world's largest library. Its collections of more than 168 million items include over 39 million cataloged books and other print materials in 470 languages; the largest rare book collection in North America; and the world's largest collection of legal materials, maps, films, sheet music, and sound recordings.

One of the library's greatest treasures is the Gutenberg Bible. Produced in the mid-1450s, the Gutenberg Bible is the first book printed using movable metal type in Western Europe. The work is one of three perfect copies on vellum in the world. The book is displayed at the Thomas Jefferson Building.

By the Numbers

The Library of Congress's collections contain more than:

* 72.5 million manuscripts

* 39 million books and other print materials

* 14.9 million photographs

* 8.2 million pieces of sheet music

* 5.6 million maps

* 4 million sound recordings

* 1.8 million moving images

What Was Oklahoma's Great Land Lottery?

They trekked in by the tens of thousands to Oklahoma, by horse and by foot, under the blazing July sun. Hungry for land, they formed great lines, with hundreds sleeping in place. During this great 1901 migration, thousands of people camped out in one valley alone.

* * * *

THIS WAS NOT the pell-mell, anything-goes 1889 land rush that gave Oklahoma Territory land to the "Sooners." No, this was quite the reverse. So contentious and confused had been the five land races between 1889 and 1895 that, to divvy up Oklahoma's remaining land, the federal government had opted for a civilized approach: a lottery. Vast crowds came from across the nation to register for it.

Some groups were opposed to the giveaway. Ranchers wanted to continue grazing their stock on the lottery lands. Kiowa Chief Lone Wolf sued the Interior Department to keep the Indian lands settler-free.

Oklahoma Before the Lottery

From the end of the Civil War, the Indian Territory, later known as Oklahoma, had come under irresistible pressure for land. In 1866, the federal government coaxed the local Indian tribes into ceding two million acres. Soon, Anglo leaders such as William Couch were leading expeditions of "Boomers" (prospective settlers) into these "Unassigned Lands." In 1889, a group of Creek Indians—in defiance of the opposition of the "Five Civilized Tribes"—sold the government three million more acres. That same year, the Indian Appropriations Act opened 160-acre blocks of Oklahoma land to homesteaders on a first-come basis.

A multitude—50,000 on the first day—swarmed into Kickapoo country on horse, foot, and wagon. Many of the arrivals were former slaves. Thousands more—the Sooners—sneaked into the territories before the official start date. Gunfights broke out between Boomers and Sooners. Lawsuits between claimants dragged on for decades. Of every 14 Boomers, only one wound up with an irrefutable land claim. Four other land rushes through 1895 had similar woes. When the time came to redistribute the remainder of Oklahoma's turf, Washington resolved to find a better way.

A Better Way?

On July 4, 1901, President McKinley proclaimed that 4,639 square miles of land from the Comanche, Apache, Wichita, and Kiowa reservations would be parceled out on the basis of a vast lottery.

Registration for a chance to own a block of land took place at Fort Sill and in the town of El Reno, between July 10 and 26. Tens of thousands of would-be settlers swarmed in from Texas, Kansas, and, most of all, from settled parts of Oklahoma.

Under the arrangement, 480,000 acres of pasture were reserved for the Indian tribes, though most of this was leased to ranchers for pennies an acre. Thousands of Indians did receive homesteads; many Native Americans leased most of their acreage to farmers for a yearly per-acre fee of $1.50. Off-limits to the land rush were the War Department's Fort Sill and the Wichita Mountain Forest Reserve.

At the registration offices, each applicant filled out a card with his or her name, birthdate, height, and other identifying information. The cards were placed in large, wheellike containers for mixing and selection. Land parcels were divided into two huge swaths of territory around Lawton and El Reno.

As vast crowds waited to apply in heat over 100 degrees, trouble broke out. A Mexican was taken out and killed for trying to jump to the front of a registration line. People were required to notarize their applications: A mob almost lynched a fake notary, and lawmen arrested another notary who used an outdated seal. In the meantime, grifters and gamblers taking advantage of the bored multitudes waiting in line were banished from the streets. More welcome were painted Cheyenne Indians who offered spectators war dances for 25 cents.

Most registrants were farmers of limited income. No one owning more than 160 acres in another state was permitted to register. One registration card per person was the rule; hundreds trying to game the lottery with multiple applications were barred.

Single-day registration peaked at 16,700. In all, approximately 160,000 hopefuls signed up for a chance at 13,000 homesteads.

The Winners Are Revealed

Drawings began on July 29 in El Reno in front of 50,000 witnesses, whose tents and booths packed the dusty streets. From a platform on the grounds of a school, officials pulled the lucky registrations out of twin containers, representing the El Reno and Lawton parcels.

At 1:30 P.M., to a great hurrah, Commissioner Colonel Dyer called out the first name from the El Reno bin—Stephen A.

Holcomb of Pauls Valley in Indian Territory.

The first lottery winner for Lawton was James R. Wood, a hardware clerk. The second was Miss Mattie Beal, a telephone operator from Wichita. After Commissioner Dyer read out her description—5-foot-3, 23 years old—the crowd cried: "They must get married!"

On August 6, winners began filing claims for their new properties at a land district office. There they got to choose the shape of their new 160 acres: a narrow strip, a square, or even the shape of a Z. In an unlucky stroke, 1,362 winners who failed to show up for the filings forfeited their claims for good.

The land rush immediately led to the creation of new Oklahoma counties—Comanche, Caddo, and Kiowa. Lots in the county seats were sold to raise some $664,000 to build roads, bridges, and a courthouse.

On November 16, 1907, boosted by the growing number of settlers and the economic growth that followed, Oklahoma became the 46th state.

What Are Some Top-Secret Locations You Can Visit?

There are plenty of stories of secret government facilities hidden in plain sight. Places where all sorts of strange tests take place, far away from the general public. Many of the North American top-secret government places have been (at least partially) declassified, allowing average Joes to visit. We've listed some locations where you can play Men in Black.

✳ ✳ ✳ ✳

Titan Missile Silo

JUST A LITTLE south of Tucson, Arizona, lies the Sonoran Desert, a barren, desolate area where nothing seems to be happening. That's exactly why, during the Cold War, the U.S.

government hid an underground Titan Missile silo there.

Inside the missile silo, one of dozens that once littered the area, a Titan 2 Missile could be armed and launched in just under 90 seconds. Until it was finally abandoned in the 1990s, the government manned the silo 24 hours a day, with every member being trained to "turn the key" and launch the missile at a moment's notice. Today, the silo is open to the public as the Titan Missile Museum. Visitors can take a look at one of the few remaining Titan 2 missiles in existence, still sitting on the launch pad (relax, it's been disarmed). Folks with extra dough can also spend the night inside the silo and play the role of one of the crew members assigned to prepare to launch the missile.

Peanut Island

You wouldn't think a sunny place called Peanut Island, located near Palm Beach, Florida, could hold many secrets. Yet in December 1961, the U.S. Navy came to the island on a secret mission to create a fallout shelter for then-President John F. Kennedy and his family. The shelter was completed, but it was never used and was all but forgotten when the Cold War ended. Today, the shelter is maintained by the Palm Beach Maritime Museum, which gives weekend tours of the space.

Wright-Patterson Air Force Base

If you believe that aliens crash-landed in Roswell, New Mexico, in the summer of 1947, then you need to make a trip out to Ohio's Wright-Patterson Air Force Base. That's because, according to legend, the UFO crash debris and possibly the aliens (both alive and dead) were shipped to the base as part of a government cover-up. Some say all that debris is still there, hidden away in an underground bunker beneath the mysterious Hangar 18.

While most of the Air Force Base is off-limits to the general public, you can go on a portion of the base to visit the National Museum of the U.S. Air Force, filled with amazing artifacts tracing the history of flight. But don't bother to ask any of the museum personnel how to get to Hangar 18—the official word is that the hangar does not exist.

Los Alamos National Laboratory

Until recently, the U.S. government refused to acknowledge the Los Alamos National Laboratory's existence. But in the early 1940s, the lab was created near Los Alamos, New Mexico, to develop the first nuclear weapons in what would become known as the Manhattan Project.

Back then, the facility was so top secret it didn't even have a name. It was simply referred to as Site Y. No matter what it was called, the lab produced two nuclear bombs, nicknamed Little Boy and Fat Man—bombs that would be dropped on Hiroshima and Nagasaki, effectively ending World War II. Today, tours of portions of the facility can be arranged through the Lab's Public Affairs Department.

Fort Knox

It is the stuff that legends are made of: A mythical building filled with over 4,700 tons of gold, stacked up and piled high to the ceiling. But this is no fairytale—the gold really does exist, and it resides inside Fort Knox.

Since 1937, the U.S. Department of the Treasury's Bullion Depository has been storing the gold inside Fort Knox on a massive military campus that stretches across three counties in north-central Kentucky. Parts of the campus are open for tours, including the General George Patton Museum. But don't think you're going to catch a glimpse of that shiny stuff—visitors are not permitted to go through the gate or enter the building.

Nevada Test Site

If you've ever seen one of those old black-and-white educational films of nuclear bombs being tested, chances are it was filmed at the Nevada Test Site, often referred to as the Most Bombed Place in the World.

Located about an hour north of Las Vegas, the Nevada Test

Site was created in 1951 as a secret place for the government to conduct nuclear experiments and tests in an outdoor laboratory that is actually larger than Rhode Island. Out there, scientists blew everything up from mannequins to entire buildings.

Those curious to take a peek inside the facility can sign up for a daylong tour. Of course, before they let you set foot on the base, visitors must submit to a background check and sign paperwork promising not to attempt to photograph, videotape, or take soil samples from the site.

Where Is the Road of Death?

You're packed on an ancient bus, fog obscuring the mountainous road. The hairpin turns and the bus fishtailing on the muddy road make you queasy. Through the windshield, you see a coffee truck coming toward you. As the vehicles inch past each other, the bus's tires slip in the mud, and it goes careening down the mountain. Not exactly how you imagined your summer vacation, right?

✳ ✳ ✳ ✳

A Dangerous Drive

EACH YEAR, HUNDREDS of people die on Bolivia's Yungas road, earning it the title of "most dangerous highway in the world." Built in the 1930s, it runs between La Paz and Coroico, and is the main connection between coffee plantations in the highlands and a third of the country. It starts in La Paz, at an altitude of 11,900 feet. The road winds its way through the Andes mountains where it reaches a peak of 16,500 feet, then drops 15,000 feet to the tropical rainforest lowlands.

If It Ain't Broke, Don't Pave It

The 43-mile drive takes four hours, on average; that is, if there are no heavy rains, mist, mudslides, or accidents blocking the road. With soaring cliffs on one side, steep drops on the other, blind turns, and no guardrails to speak of, this road is not for the faint of heart. For most of its length, the one-lane, two-way road is only ten feet across. Alongside the road are makeshift memorials of crosses and flowers.

In 2006, a Yungas bypass was opened. The Bolivian government and foreign investors financed this wide, paved highway for the purpose of opening up trade in the region. The $500 million, 20-year project was touted as a life-saving alternative for commercial trucks and tourist buses. However, Bolivian drivers have rejected it so far because the new route is considerably longer.

The deadly Yungas road is now one of Bolivia's most popular tourist attractions. It is especially popular with mountain bikers who enjoy the nearly 40-mile-long stretch of continuous downhill riding and challenge each other to see how fast they can go. Meanwhile, locals report hearing the tourists' screams as they plunge over the cliff.

Chapter 12

Intriguing Individuals

Who Was Nefertiti?

In establishing the identity of the Egyptian queen Nefertiti, scholars find themselves up to their necks in conflicting info.

✳ ✳ ✳ ✳

LIKE CLEOPATRA, NEFERTITI is one of the most famous queens of ancient Egypt. She's also often referred to as "The Most Beautiful Woman in the World," largely due to the 1912 discovery of a painted limestone bust of Nefertiti depicting her stunning features: smooth skin, full lips, and a graceful swanlike neck—quite the looker! Now housed in Berlin's Neues Museum, the likeness has become a widely recognized symbol of ancient Egypt and one of the most important artistic works of the pre-modern world. But the bust, like almost everything about the famous queen, is steeped in controversy.

Conflicting Accounts

It wasn't until the bust surfaced in the early 20th century that scholars began sorting out information about Nefertiti's life. Her name means "the beautiful one is come," and some think she was a foreign princess, not of Egyptian blood. Others believe she was born into Egyptian royalty, that she was the niece or daughter of a high government official named Ay, who later became pharaoh. Basically, no one knows her origins for sure.

When the beautiful one was age 15, she married Amenhotep IV, who later became king of Egypt. Nefertiti was thus promoted to queen. No one really knows when this happened—other than it was in the 18th Dynasty—but it's safe to say that it was a really long time ago (as in, the 1340s B.C.). Nefertiti appears in many reliefs of the period, often accompanying her husband in various ceremonies—a testament to her political power.

An indisputable fact about both Nefertiti and Amenhotep IV is that they were responsible for bringing monotheism to ancient Egypt. Rather than worship the vast pantheon of Egyptian gods—including the supreme god, Amen-Ra—the couple devoted themselves to exclusively worshipping the sun god Aten. In fact, as a sign of this commitment, Amenhotep IV changed his named to Akhenaten. Similarly, Nefertiti changed her name to Neferneferuaten-Nefertiti, meaning, "The Aten is radiant of radiance [because] the beautiful one is come." (But we're guessing everyone just called her "Nef.") Again, it's unclear as to why the powerful couple decided to turn from polytheism. Maybe there were political reasons. Or perhaps the two simply liked the idea of one universal god.

Disappearance/Death?

In studying Egyptian history, scholars discovered that around 14 years into Akhenaten's reign, Nefertiti seems to disappear. There are no more images of her, no historical records. Perhaps there was a conflict in the royal family, and she was banished from the kingdom. Maybe she died in the plague that killed half of Egypt. A more interesting speculation is that she disguised herself as a man, changed her named to Smenkhkare, and went on to rule Egypt alongside her husband. But—all together now—*no one knows for sure!*

During a June 2003 expedition in Egypt's Valley of the Kings, an English archeologist named Joann Fletcher unearthed a mummy that she suspected to be Nefertiti. But despite the fact that the mummy probably is a member of the royal family from the 18th Dynasty, it was not proven to be female. Many Egyptologists think there is not sufficient evidence to prove that Fletcher's mummy is Nefertiti. So, that theory was something of a bust.

In 2009, Swiss art historian Henri Sierlin published a book suggesting that the bust is a copy. He claimed that the sculpture was made by an artist named Gerard Marks on the request of Ludwig Borchardt, the German archeologist responsible for discovering the bust in 1912. Despite the mysteries surrounding Nefertiti, there's no question that she was revered in her time. At the temples of Karnak are inscribed the words: "Heiress, Great of Favours, Possessed of Charm, Exuding Happiness . . . Great King's Wife, Whom He Loves, Lady of Two Lands, Nefertiti."

Julius Caesar: Oppressor or Enlightened Leader?

Julius Caesar is one of the most recognized figures in all of human history. However, most people don't know as much about him as they think.

❋ ❋ ❋ ❋

CAESAR WAS NOT the first Roman emperor; indeed, he was never an emperor at all. He was a dictator, but in his time that word had a reasonable and legitimate political connotation. As history suggests, Caesar was able in many areas. He led men into battle with courage and skill and was also a brilliant administrator and politician who instituted reforms that benefited the common people of Rome.

Rising Out of Chaos

Caesar's birth in 100 B.C. (sometimes listed as 102 B.C.) coincided with great civil strife in Rome. Although his parents' status as nobles gave him advantages, Caesar's childhood was spent in a politically volatile Rome marked by personal hatreds and conniving. As an adult, he learned to be wary in his dealings with other powerful people. By the time Caesar was 20, a patrician named Sulla had been the Roman dictator for about 20 years. Although Caesar and Sulla were friends, Sulla later became enraged when Caesar refused to divorce his wife, Cornelia, who was the daughter of a man Sulla loathed (and murdered), Cinna. In order to save his neck, Caesar promptly left Rome for Asia.

When Sulla died in 78 B.C., Caesar returned to Rome and took up the practice of law. Caesar had everything necessary for success: He had received the best possible education, developed impressive oratorical skills, and made himself an outstanding writer. He also spent huge sums of money, most of which he had to borrow. The money went to bribes and sumptuous parties for the influential and bought Caesar access to power. Leading politicians looked on him favorably and rewarded him with a series of increasingly important political positions in Spain and Rome. Caesar's time in Spain was especially useful, as he used his position there to become very wealthy.

Coming Out on Top

In 59 B.C., Caesar, who was by now a general, made a successful bid for power in concert with Marcus Licinius Crassus, the richest man in Rome; and Pompey, another ambitious general who was known, to his immodest pleasure, as Pompey the Great. These three Type-A personalities ruled Rome as the First Triumvirate, with Caesar becoming first among equals as consul. Caesar had always been popular among the common people and with Rome's soldiers, and he aimed to cement that loyalty with reforms that would benefit them. Soon, Caesar was made governor of Gaul and spent the next 11 years conquering all of what is now France, with a couple of profitable trips to Britain for good measure. While on campaign, he wrote an account of his actions, called *Commentaries*, which is among the finest of all military literature.

Old Friends and New

To leave Rome, even for military glory, was always risky for any of the empire's leaders. While Caesar was abroad, Crassus was killed in battle. This void encouraged Pompey, who made it clear that Caesar was no longer welcome in Rome. Caesar and his army responded by crossing the Rubicon River in 49 B.C. to seize control of the city. Within a year of the civil war that followed, Caesar defeated Pompey. He also began a torrid affair with Egypt's Queen Cleopatra. After a few other actions against Rome's enemies, Caesar was acclaimed by all of Rome as a great hero. In turn, he pardoned all who had opposed him.

Hail, Caesar

Mindful of the fleeting nature of popularity, Caesar continued to promote a series of important reforms:

* Some of the land that had been held by wealthy families was distributed to common people desperate to make a living. As one might expect, this didn't go over well with the wealthy.

* Tax reforms insisted upon by Caesar forced the rich to pay their fair share. This innovation didn't win Caesar many new friends among the powerful.

* Retired soldiers were settled on land provided by the government. Because this land was in Rome's outlying territories, it became populated with a happy, well-trained cadre of veterans meant to be Rome's first line of defense, if needed. Unemployed citizens were also given the opportunity to settle in these areas, where jobs were much more plentiful. This reduced the number of poor people in Rome and decreased the crime rate.

* As he had done earlier, Caesar made residents of the provinces, such as people living in Spain, citizens of Rome. This idea proved quite popular. Many years later, some of the Roman emperors actually came from Spain.

* Working people are happy people (so it's said). In a clever move, Caesar instituted a massive public works program that provided both jobs and a sense of pride among the citizens of Rome.

Beware the Ides of March

All these reforms notwithstanding, Caesar's enemies feared he would leverage his great popularity to destroy the Roman Republic and institute in its place an empire ruled by one man. So, in one of those moments of violence that turns the wheel of history, Caesar was assassinated by people he trusted on March 15, 44 B.C.—the Ides of March, for those of you who remember your Shakespeare. The civil war that followed was ultimately won by Caesar's nephew, Octavian, who changed his name to Caesar Augustus . . . and who replaced the republic and instituted in its place an empire ruled by one man! Augustus was the first of a long succession of emperors who ruled virtually independent of the Roman Senate. It was the rulers who followed Caesar, then, and not Caesar himself, who proved the undoing of the system so cherished by Caesar's enemies.

Was There a Real Pied Piper?

It's an intriguing story about a mysterious piper and more than 100 missing children. Made famous by the eponymous Brothers Grimm, this popular fairy tale has captivated generations of boys and girls. But is it actually more fact than fiction?

✳   ✳   ✳   ✳

THE LEGEND OF The Pied Piper of Hameln documents the story of a mysterious musician who rid a town of rats by enchanting the rodents with music from his flute. The musician led the mesmerized rats to a nearby river, where they drowned. When the townsfolk refused to settle their debt, the rat catcher returned several weeks later, charmed a group of 130 children with the same flute, and led them out of town. They disappeared—never to be seen again.

It's a story that dates back to approximately A.D. 1300 and has its roots in a small German town called Hameln. Several accounts written between the 14th and 17th centuries tell of a stained-glass window in the town's main church. The window pictured the Pied Piper with hands clasped, standing over a group of youngsters. Encircling the window was the following verse (this is a rough translation): "In the year 1284, on John's and Paul's day was the 26th of June. By a piper, dressed in all kinds of colors, 130 children born in Hameln were seduced and lost at the calvarie near the koppen."

The verse is quite specific: precise month and year, exact number of children involved in the incident, and detailed place names. Because of this, some scholars believe this window, which was removed in 1660 and either accidentally destroyed or lost, was created in memory of an actual event. Yet, the verse makes no mention of the circumstances regarding the departure of the children or their specific fate. What exactly happened in Hameln, Germany, in 1284? The truth is, no one actually knows—at least not for certain.

Theories Abound

Gernot Hüsam, the current chairman of the Coppenbrügge Castle Museum, believes the word "koppen" in the inscription may reference a rocky outcrop on a hill in nearby Coppenbrügge, a small town previously known as Koppanberg. Hüsam also believes the use of the word "calvarie" is in reference to either the medieval connotation of the gates of hell—or since the Crusades—a place of execution.

One theory put forward is that Coppenbrügge resident Nikolaus von Spiegelberg recruited Hameln youth to emigrate to areas in Pomerania near the Baltic Sea. This theory suggests the youngsters were either murdered, because they took part in summertime pagan rituals, or drowned in a tragic accident while in transit to the new colonies.

But this is not the only theory. In fact, theories concerning the fate of the children abound. Here are some ideas about what really happened:

* They suffered from the Black Plague or a similar disease and were led from the town to spare the rest of the population.

* They were part of a crusade to the Holy Land.

* They were lost in the 1260 Battle of Sedemünder.

* They died in a bridge collapse over the Weser River or a landslide on Ith Mountain.

* They emigrated to settle in other parts of Europe, including Maehren, Oelmutz, Transylvania, or Uckermark.

* They were actually young adults who were led away and murdered for performing pagan rituals on a local mountain.

Historians believe that emigration, bridge collapse/natural disaster, disease, or murder are the most plausible explanations.

Tracing the Piper's Path

Regardless of what actually happened in Hameln hundreds of years ago, the legend of the Pied Piper has endured. First accounts of the Piper had roots to the actual incident, but as time passed, the story took on a life of its own.

Earliest accounts of the legend date back to 1384, at which time a Hameln church leader, Deacon von Lude, was said to be in possession of a chorus book with a Latin verse related to the legend written on the front cover by his grandmother. The book was misplaced in the late 17th century and has never been found.

The oldest surviving account—according to amateur Pied Piper historian Jonas Kuhn—appears as an addition to a 14th-century manuscript from Luneburg. Written in Latin, the note is almost identical to the verse on the stained-glass window and translates roughly to:

"In the year of 1284, on the day of Saints John and Paul on the 26th of June 130 children born in Hamelin were seduced By a piper, dressed in all kinds of colors, and lost at the place of execution near the koppen."

Sixteenth-century physician and philosopher Jobus Fincelius believed the Pied Piper was the devil. In his 1556 book, *Concerning the Wonders of His Times*, Fincelius wrote: "It came about in Hameln in Saxony on the River Weser ... the Devil visibly in human form walked the lanes of Hameln and by playing a pipe lured after him many children ... to a mountain. Once there, he with the children ... could no longer be found."

In 1557, Count Froben Christoph von Zimmern wrote a chronicle detailing his family's lineage. Sprinkled throughout the book were several folklore tales including one that referenced the Pied Piper. For some unknown reason, the count introduced rats into his version of the story: "He passed through the streets of the town with his small pipe ... immediately all the rats ... collected outside the houses and followed his footsteps." This first insertion of rodents into the legend led other writers to follow suit.

In 1802, Johan Wolfgang Goethe wrote "Der Rattenfanger," a poem based on the legend. The monologue was told in the first person through the eyes of the rat catcher. Goethe's poem made no direct reference to the town of Hameln, and in Goethe's version the Piper played a stringed instrument instead of a pipe. The Piper also made an appearance in Goethe's literary work *Faust*.

Jacob and Wilhelm Grimm began collecting European folktales in the early 1800s. Best known for a series of books that documented 211 fairy tales, the brothers also published two volumes between 1816 and 1818 detailing almost 600 German folklore legends. One of the volumes contained the story of Der Rattenfanger von Hameln.

The Grimm brothers' research for The Pied Piper drew on 11 different sources, from which they deduced two children were left behind (a blind child and a mute child); the piper led the children through a cave to Transylvania; and a street in Hameln was named after the event.

No End in Sight

While the details of the historical event surrounding the legend of The Piped Piper have been lost to time, the mystique of the story endures. Different versions of the legend have even appeared in literature outside of Germany: A rat catcher from Vienna helped rid the nearby town of Korneuburg of rats. When he wasn't paid, he stole off with the town's children and sold them as slaves in Constantinople. A vagabond rid the English town of Newton on the Isle of Wight of their rats, and when he wasn't paid, led the town's children into an ancient oak forest where they were never seen again. A Chinese version had a Hangchow district official use magic to convince the rats to leave his city.

The legend's plot has been adapted over time to fit whichever media is currently popular and has been used as a story line in children's books, ballet, theatre, and even a radio drama. The intriguing story of the mysterious piper will continue to interest people as long as there is mystery surrounding the original event.

Who Was Mansa Musa?

History's epic gold rushes were generally characterized by masses of people trekking to the gold. But in 1324, the legendary Mansa Musa bucked the trend by trekking masses of gold to the people—which severely depressed the Egyptian gold market.

✳ ✳ ✳ ✳

IF YOU COULD talk to a gold trader from 14th-century Cairo, he might say that the worst time of his life occurred the day Mansa Musa came to town.

Musa, king of the powerful Mali Empire, stopped over in Cairo during his pilgrimage to Mecca. Arriving in the Egyptian metropolis in 1324, Musa and his entourage of about 60,000 hangers-on were anything but inconspicuous. Even more conspicuous was the 4,000-pound hoard of gold that Musa hauled with him.

While in Cairo, Musa embarked on a spending and gift-giving spree unseen since the pharaohs. By the time he was finished, Musa had distributed so much gold around Cairo that its value plummeted in Egypt. It would be more than a decade before the price of gold recovered from the Mali king's extravagance.

A Fool and His Money?—Not Musa

Musa's story conjures the old adage about fools and their money soon parting—especially when you consider he had to borrow money for the trip home. But Musa was no fool.

Musa ruled Mali from 1312 until 1337, and ushered in the empire's golden age. He extended Mali's power across sub-Saharan Africa from the Atlantic coast to western Sudan. Mali gained tremendous wealth by controlling the trans-Sahara trade routes, which passed through Timbuktu and made the ancient city the nexus of northwest African commerce.

During Musa's reign, Mali exploited the Taghaza salt deposits to the north and the rich Wangara gold mines to the south, producing half the world's gold.

Musa's crowning achievement was the transformation of Timbuktu into one of Islam's great centers of culture and education. A patron of the arts and learning, Musa brought Arab scholars from Mecca to help build libraries, mosques, and universities throughout Mali. Timbuktu became a gathering place for Muslim writers, artists, and scholars from Africa and the Middle East. The great Sankore mosque and university built by Musa remain the city's focal point today.

Musa's *Hajj* Puts Mali on the Map

Musa's story is seldom told without mention of his legendary pilgrimage, or *hajj*, to Mecca.

The *hajj* is an obligation every Muslim is required to undertake at least once in their life. For the devout Musa, his *hajj* would be more than just a fulfillment of that obligation. It would also be a great coming-out party for the Mali king.

Accompanying Musa was a flamboyant caravan of courtiers and subjects dressed in fine Persian silk, including 12,000 personal servants. And then there was all that gold. A train of 80 camels carried 300 pounds of gold each. Five hundred servants carried four-pound solid-gold staffs.

Along the way, Musa handed out golden alms to the needy in deference to one of the pillars of Islam. Wherever the caravan halted on a Friday, Musa left gold to pay for the construction of a mosque. And don't forget his Cairo stopover. By the time he left Mecca, the gold was all gone.

But one doesn't dish out two tons of gold without being noticed. Word of Musa's wealth and generosity spread like wildfire. He became a revered figure in the Muslim world and inspired Europeans to seek golden kingdoms on the Dark Continent.

Musa's journey put the Mali Empire on the map—literally. European cartographers began placing it on maps in 1339. A 1375 map pinpointed Mali with a depiction of a black African king wearing a gold crown and holding a golden scepter in his left hand and a large gold nugget aloft in his right.

Who Was the Original Dracula?

Most people are aware of Bram Stoker's Dracula *and the many cultural reincarnations that the title character has gone through. But the fictional character of Dracula was based on a human far more frightening than his fictional avatar.*

✳ ✳ ✳ ✳

Background

THE LATE 1300s and early 1400s were a dramatic time in the area now known as Romania. Three sovereign states—Transylvania, Moldavia, and Wallachia—held fast to their independence against the Ottoman Empire. Wallachia was an elective monarchy, with much political backstabbing between the royal family and the boyars, the land-owning nobles.

Vlad III, known after his death as Vlad the Impaler, was born in the latter half of 1431 in the citadel of Sighisoara, Transylvania. His family was living in exile when he was born, ousted from their native Wallachia by pro-Turkish boyars. He was the son of a military governor who himself was a knight in the Order of the Dragon, a fraternity established to uphold Christian beliefs and fight Muslim Turks. Vlad II was also known as Vlad Dracul—Dracul meaning devil in Romanian. The *a* at the end of Dracul means "son of."

The throne of Wallachia was tossed from person to person, much like a hot potato, but with a lot more bloodshed. In 1436, Vlad Dracul took over the throne of Wallachia, but two years after that, he formed an alliance with the dreaded Turks, betraying his oath to the Order of the Dragon. He was assassinated in 1447 for his treachery.

Unfortunately for Vlad the Impaler, while his father was nego-
tiating deals with the sultan of the Ottoman Empire, he traded
his sons as collateral for his loyalty. While in captivity, Vlad the
Impaler was frequently beaten and tortured.

Battleground

Released by the Turks after his father was killed, Vlad the
Impaler showed up in Wallachia and defeated the boyars who
had taken over the throne. He ruled for a brief time during
1448, but Vlad was quickly kicked out when the man who
assassinated his father appointed someone else to fill the kingly
duties. Vlad the Impaler bided his time, and in 1456, he not
only took back the throne of Wallachia but also killed his
father's murderer. He ruled Wallachia until 1462, but he was
not a happy monarch.

Vlad the Impaler had a habit of killing huge numbers of
people—slaves who didn't work hard enough, weak people
who he felt were wasting space in his kingdom, and of course,
criminals—you really did not want to be a criminal in Vlad's
kingdom. Mostly, as might be guessed from his nickname, Vlad
liked impaling people and then perching them in circles around
town, an example of what would happen if citizens stepped
out of line. In addition, he was rumored to drink the blood of
those he had killed. On the upside, however, the crime rate in
Wallachia was impressively low.

Breakdown

In 1461, Vlad the Impaler took on the Turks but was
run out of Wallachia the next year. He lost the throne to
Sultan Mehmed II's army and eventually sought refuge in
Transylvania. The sultan installed Vlad's brother Radu on
the throne of Wallachia. Once again, Vlad the Impaler was
not happy. In 1476, with help from his Transylvanian pals, he
launched a campaign to take back the throne of Wallachia, and
he succeeded, impaling up a storm along the way. The Turks

retaliated, and even though Vlad tried to organize an army to fight them, he couldn't raise a battalion large enough to defeat the Turks permanently. In his final battle, Vlad was killed, though the manner of his death is unknown. Some say that he was mistakenly killed by his own army, while others say that he was killed and decapitated by the Turks. One thing is known, however: Unlike the hundreds of thousands he killed, Vlad the Impaler was never one of the impalees.

Who Was the Real Humpty Dumpty?

Humpty Dumpty sat on a wall,

Humpty Dumpty had a great fall,

All the king's horses, And all the king's men,

Couldn't put Humpty together again.

✳ ✳ ✳ ✳

Fans of lewis Carroll's *Alice's Adventures in Wonderland* and *Through the Looking Glass* will recall that Alice meets Humpty Dumpty during her adventures. In Carroll's tales, Humpty Dumpty is a giant egg with spindly legs and arms who waxes rhetorical about the meaning of "Jabberwocky." But the Humpty rhyme predates Carroll's stories by hundreds of years. Who was the original Humpty? And why is he depicted as an egg?

Nursery-rhyme scholars have several theories regarding the origin of the Humpty Dumpty nursery rhyme, which dates back to the 15th century, according to some estimates. The first candidate is Richard III, the Plantagenet king who was dumped from his horse at the Battle of Bosworth Field on August 22, 1485, and was promptly carved into pieces by his Tudor enemies. Shakespeare's depiction of Dick as a hunchback further supports the idea that he is the egghead featured in the rhyme.

Unfortunately, there is no evidence anywhere outside of the Bard's imagination that Richard III had a hump on his back.

A second, more common explanation is that Humpty Dumpty refers not to a person but a thing—an enormous cannon. At the Battle of Colchester in 1648, during the English Civil War, a giant cannon was mounted atop a tower at St. Mary's by the Wall Church to defend the royalist stronghold from the upstart Roundheads, the Puritan supporters of Parliament. The tower was struck by Roundhead cannon fire and the great cannon plummeted to the ground, where it broke apart. Despite the best efforts of the king's horses and the king's men, nobody could put the cannon together again.

So why is Humpty depicted as a giant egg? In the original print version, the Humpty rhyme doubled as a riddle. What object might fall and be unable to be put back together again? An egg, obviously. Well, perhaps it was obvious to people in the 19th century, when the rhyme first appeared in print. As for why Humpty would appear in Lewis Carroll's stories to debate semantics with little Alice, we're not sure. But we suspect that the enormous amounts of opium that Carroll was reported to have enjoyed might have had something to do with it.

Who Was Montezuma, and Why Did He Want Revenge?

As Fred Willard's character puts it in the movie Waiting for Guffman, *"Montezuma's revenge is nothing more than good old-fashioned American diarrhea." Specifically, it's a general term for the diarrhea that afflicts about half of the tourists who visit Mexico and Central America, and it's caused by contaminated food and water.*

✳ ✳ ✳ ✳

THE NICKNAME, WHICH became popular in the 1960s, refers to Montezuma II, a 16th-century Aztec emperor. From

1502 to 1520, Montezuma ruled the Aztec Empire in what is now southern Mexico, greatly expanding its reach and wealth by conquering other indigenous tribes. Everything was going swimmingly for Montezuma until the Spanish conquistador Hernán Cortés and his men showed up in 1519. According to some accounts, Montezuma and others believed that the Spaniards were gods whose coming was foretold by prophecy. But the Spaniards may have started this legend themselves after the fact. Anyway, Montezuma welcomed Cortés and his men as honored guests and showered them with gifts.

Before long, Cortés had set his sights on claiming the Aztec land and the civilization's considerable gold for Spain. His first step was to capture Montezuma and hold him as a sort of hostage. By manipulating Montezuma, Cortés attempted to subdue the Aztecs and persuade them not to resist the Spanish.

But many in the Aztec capital resented the Spanish and began to look down on Montezuma. When the Aztec people revolted against the conquistadors, Cortés commanded Montezuma to address the crowd and convince them to submit. Instead, they pelted Montezuma with stones. The emperor died three days later, though it's not clear whether the stoning was to blame or the Spanish executed him.

The revolt pushed the Spanish out of the capital, and eventually a new leader, Cuauhtemoc, spearheaded the resistance against Cortés. In the spring of 1521, the Spanish laid siege to the capital; Cuauhtemoc and his people surrendered several months later. In just a few years, Cortés brought the Aztec Empire to an end.

So if the spirit of Montezuma is still lurking in Mexico, it makes sense that it might exact vengeance on foreign visitors. But if you're ever south of the border, it's best not to joke about Montezuma's revenge. Jimmy Carter made that mistake on an official visit in 1979, sparking a minor international incident that hurt already strained relations with Mexican President

José López Portillo. President Carter didn't mean anything by the comment, but the reaction was understandable. What nation wants to be known for inducing diarrhea?

Who Was Suleiman the Magnificent?

Suleiman the Magnificent was a warrior-scholar who lived up to his billing. A Turkish Sultan who reigned from 1520 to 1566, Suleiman led the Ottoman Empire to its greatest heights.

✳ ✳ ✳ ✳

NOT ONLY WAS Suleiman a brilliant military strategist, he was also a great legislator, a fair ruler, and a devotee of the arts. During his rule, he expanded the country's military empire and brought cultural and architectural projects to new heights. For all this and more, Suleiman is considered one of the finest leaders of 16th-century Europe.

Under Suleiman's leadership, his forces conquered Mesopotamia (now Iraq), fending off the Safavid's Iran. The Ottomans would then successfully occupy Iraq until the First World War. Suleiman annexed or made allies of the Barbary Pirate states of North Africa, who remained a thorn in Europe's underbelly until the 1800s. He also led an army that went deep into Europe itself, crushing the Hungarian King Louis II at the great Battle of Mohács in 1526, which led to the Siege of Vienna.

An accomplished poet, Suleiman was gracious in victory, saying of the young Louis: "It was not my wish that he should be thus cut off while he scarcely tasted the sweets of life and royalty." To his favorite wife Hurrem, a harem woman and daughter of a Ukrainian Orthodox priest, he wrote: "My springtime, my merry faced love, my daytime, my sweetheart, laughing leaf... My woman of the beautiful hair, my love of the slanted brow, my love of eyes full of mischief..."

While Shari'ah, or sacred law, ruled his farflung land's religious life, Suleiman reformed the Ottomans' civil law code. In fact, the Ottomans called him Kanuni, or "The Lawgiver." The final form of Suleiman's legal code would remain in place for more than 300 years.

Who Were the Wives of Henry VIII?

England's Henry VIII is famous for having six wives. But how much do you know about those ladies themselves?

✳ ✳ ✳ ✳

A TRUE RENAISSANCE MAN and child of privilege, Henry VIII spent his youth enjoying life's finer pursuits, learning about music, languages, the arts, sports, poetry, and architecture. During these years, he also picked up a penchant for vice, earning a steadfast reputation as a gambler and, most notably, a womanizer. Although Henry was second in line to succeed his father as King of England and Lord of Ireland, his elder brother's death left the position open. Henry took over the monarchy just shy of his 18th birthday, but he was more interested in entertainment than politics. The new king took a few years to get settled into the business of running England, but he was quickly thrust into his first marriage. Undeserved as his lecherous reputation might be—monarchs were expected to play the part of the playboy—Henry certainly did run up quite a collection of wives: a total of six by the time of his death in 1547 at age 55.

Catherine of Aragon

Marriage to wife number one, Catherine of Aragon, was an arrangement pushed by her father, King Ferdinand II of Spain, and Henry's own father, Henry VII. Catherine had been married to Henry's older brother Arthur for only a few months, and upon his passing, Henry was betrothed to the widow. In this way, the fathers were guaranteeing an ongoing union between England and Spain. It took Henry nearly a quarter of a century to end this marriage of convenience, but he was finally granted an annulment on the grounds that Catherine had once been married to his brother. The pope refused to grant this annulment, so Henry arranged to receive it from the archbishop of Canterbury. This severely damaged Henry's—and England's—relationship with the Roman Catholic Church. Three years later, Henry closed Catholic monasteries and abbeys.

Anne Boleyn

Anne Boleyn, marchioness of Pembroke, was a lady-in-waiting who became the other woman. Anne was an English noble, educated in France, who provided reputable servitude to Queen Catherine. During her period of personal assistance, Anne and Henry began their affair, with Henry proposing marriage roughly six years prior to his annulment from Catherine. An argument has been made that the pair did not consummate their affair until Henry's annulment was final (although others claim she was pregnant when she married). According to the theory, Anne was not so moralistic that she wouldn't engage with a married man—she had simply seen the fate that befell her sister Mary when she carried on with Henry. When Mary Boleyn finally gave in and consummated her affair with the king, she was rewarded with a pink slip and sent packing. It turns out that Mary was the luckier of the two, being simply sent away. Anne, on the other hand, after failing to produce a male heir, was beheaded on trumped-up charges of adultery and witchcraft.

Jane Seymour

Apparently, Henry viewed his wives' ladies-in-waiting as his own personal marriage buffet. Upon Queen Anne's passing, he plucked his third wife, Jane Seymour, from Anne's group of attendants. Of course, it has been suggested that Henry's interest in Jane was the true reason he had Anne killed—not the six fingers he accused her of having (which was seen as the mark of the devil). Unfortunately, Jane only lasted a year as Henry's wife. Although she finally brought Henry a legitimate male heir, Edward, Jane succumbed to a fever caused from complications of childbirth.

Anne of Cleves

On the market yet again, Henry once more tried his hand at an arranged marriage. Following his chancellor's advice, Henry agreed to marry Anne of Cleves for her family's advantageous political ties to both the Catholic Church and the Protestant Reformation. With the nuptials already scheduled, Henry was said to have voiced his misgivings upon finally meeting his bride-to-be. Although striking in personality, Anne was not as agreeable in appearance as the king had hoped: He likened Anne's visage to that of a horse. Although he followed through with the vows, Anne—dubbed "Flanders Mare" by Henry—was released from her role as queen through an annulment. But at least she got a generous settlement for her troubles.

Catherine Howard

The tables were turned on the adulterous King Henry by his fifth wife, Catherine Howard, a woman who was known to engage in illicit affairs of her own. Even before settling down with the king, Catherine—who was Anne Boleyn's first cousin—was intimately involved with many men about town. Soon after they wed, the king discovered that his bride was still sowing her oats with other suitors. Apparently, what's good for the gander was most certainly not good for the goose, for Henry said, "Off with her head!" and Catherine was no more.

Catherine Parr

Henry's sixth and final wife, Catherine Parr, was famous for her own lengthy list of marriages. With two marriages before Henry and one after, Catherine holds the record for the most-married queen in English history. She is also the only one of Henry's six brides to make it out of her marriage alive and without an annulment. Only four years after their wedding, Henry died at age 55 from obesity-related complications.

Catherine escaped the fates of Henry's first five wives and survived as a widow free to marry one last time—to Thomas Seymour, Jane Seymour's brother.

Who Were Henry VIII's Tower of London Victims?

✳ Queen Catherine Howard, Henry's fifth wife, was beheaded for adultery on the Tower Green. With her went her lovers, Thomas Culpepper and Francis Dereham, and her lady-in-waiting Jane Rochford.

✳ Jane Rochford was instrumental in the downfall of two queens. She arranged trysts for Catherine Howard, for which both were executed, and she had previously testified against her husband, George Boleyn, and sister-in-law Queen Anne, helping them to their graves by accusing them of incest.

✳ Desperate to marry Jane Seymour, Henry had his second queen, Anne Boleyn, executed on trumped-up charges of adultery and witchcraft. Accused and killed with her were her brother George, as well as Henry Norris, Francis Weston, and William Brereton, who had been close friends with the king. Anne's musician, Mark Smeaton, was also executed for supposed adultery with the queen.

✳ The royal House of Plantagenet nearly became extinct under Henry's rule. The Plantagenets were descended from earlier kings of England, primarily the profligate Edward III, and possibly had a better claim to the throne than the Tudors. Those who made this assertion publicly were often executed on petty or unfounded charges.

✳ Edward Stafford, Third Duke of Buckingham, was beheaded for being the leader of nobles who were openly resentful of Henry's reliance on lowborn ministers such as Cardinal Wolsey, the son of a butcher. Many historians believe he was also killed because he was part of the royal Plantagenet family and had bragged that his family was more royal than Henry's.

* King Henry's paranoia grew as he edged closer to death, and Henry Howard, Earl of Surrey and son of the Duke of Norfolk, was one of those who paid the price. The king became convinced that Norfolk and Surrey were planning to grab the throne from Henry's son Edward when he died, so both were sent to the Tower. Surrey was beheaded, but his father was saved, only because Henry died the day before he was to be executed.

* Thomas Howard, Third Duke of Norfolk, narrowly avoided losing his head when Henry VIII died the day before he was to sign the duke's death warrant. He was released in 1553 by Mary I.

* Margaret Pole, the 67-year-old Countess of Salisbury, suffered one of the most gruesome beheadings on record. She refused to put her head on the block, saying that she was no traitor, and therefore had to be forced down. The executioner's first blow struck her shoulder. According to some accounts, she then jumped up and ran from the executioner, who struck her 11 times before she finally died.

* The longest-serving prisoner of the Tudor reign was Sir William de la Pole, who sat in the Tower of London for 37 years. Sir William was arrested by Henry VII for suspicion of treason because he was a Plantagenet and he and his brother were Yorkist heirs, the leading contenders for the English throne. Henry VIII had Sir William executed in 1513.

* Being Henry's most trusted minister provided no protection from the executioner. Thomas Cromwell rose to power in 1532 and was a major figure in the English Reformation. Like many of Henry's advisors, his fall was caused by his

support for one of Henry's wives—in this case, his arrangement of the king's marriage to Anne of Cleves, whom Henry despised. Cromwell was sent to the block in 1540.

* Anne Askew's execution proved that Henry considered Protestants to be heretics. She had been arrested for preaching Protestant views and was cruelly racked to get the names of other prominent reformists. Queen Catherine Parr was nearly arrested after pleading for mercy for Anne, but her plea was rejected and Anne burned at the stake.

How Terrible Was Ivan the Terrible?

The first all-powerful Russian ruler, Tsar Ivan the Terrible, was terrible indeed.

* * * *

THE TERRIBLE ONE had an unhealthy dose of paranoia. It must have been his upbringing. As a child prince in Moscow, Ivan was under the thumb of boyars, or Russia's nobles. Feuding noble families such as the Shuiskis would break into young Ivan's palace, robbing, murdering, and even skinning alive one of the boy's advisors. The orphan (his mother had been poisoned) took out his frustrations on animals, poking out their eyes or tossing them off the palace roof. In 1543, at age 13, Ivan took some personal revenge, and had Andrei Shuiski thrown to the dogs—literally. After other vile acts, he'd sometimes publicly repent—by banging his head violently on the ground.

When his beloved wife Anastasia died in 1560 (Ivan beat his head on her coffin), the boyars refused allegiance to his young son Dmitri. Then Ivan really became terrifying. He set up the Oprichniki, a group of hand-picked thugs. After his forces sacked the city of Novgorod in 1570, he had its "archbishop sewn up in a bearskin and then hunted to death by a pack of hounds." Women and children fared no better; they were tied to sleds and sent into the freezing Volkhov River.

Over time, Ivan had the lover of his fourth wife impaled and had his seventh wife drowned. Perhaps afflicted by encephalitis, and likely by syphilis, his behavior grew ever stranger. He beat up his son's wife, who then miscarried, and later beat his son Ivan to death with a royal scepter (then beat his head on the coffin).

Ivan the Terrible may well have been mad as a hatter, and by the same cause that drove 19th-century hatmakers insane—mercury poisoning. When his body was exhumed in the 1960s, his bones were found to have toxic levels of the metal.

Who Was Button Gwinnett?

His invasion of Florida was a disaster and he may have plagiarized his most lasting composition, but Button Gwinnett still managed to get his signature on the Declaration of Independence.

✳ ✳ ✳ ✳

From England to Georgia to Pennsylvania

IN 1762, BUTTON Gwinnett emigrated from England to the colonies, where he dabbled in trade before borrowing a large sum to establish a plantation. He served as a representative to the colony's House of Commons until 1773. After losing his land and slaves, Gwinnett allied himself with the burgeoning revolutionary cause, but his English birth made him politically unpopular, so Gwinnett's rival, Lachlan McIntosh, was given the honor of leading Georgia's Continental battalion. Denied the laurels of military leadership, Gwinnett went to Philadelphia as one of the state's representatives to the Continental Congress. It was in this role that he signed the Declaration of Independence in 1776.

Elected to the Georgia legislature, Gwinnett used a pamphlet given to him by John Adams as the basis for the new state's constitution. When the governor died in early 1777, Gwinnett was appointed to the post. At a time when the struggling nation could ill afford intrigue, he worked to undermine his old rival General McIntosh by spreading dissent among his officers, devising a questionable plan for invading Florida, and then appointing one of McIntosh's subordinates to lead the ill-fated expedition. After a mere two months in office, Gwinnett lost the governorship.

Lachlan's Loose Tongue

Like Gwinnett, McIntosh was a boastful man who delighted in the embarrassment of his rivals. In the days following Gwinnett's defeat, McIntosh publicly derided the ex-governor. Finally, Gwinnett challenged him to a duel. On May 16, 1777, the two Georgians stood 12 paces apart and discharged pistols. Both men were wounded; McIntosh survived, but Gwinnett succumbed to gangrene. He died days later at age 42.

How Did Franz Mesmer Transfix Europe?

The Age of Enlightenment saw the explosion of new ideas. One of these was the possibility of tapping into a person's subconscious, causing them to enter a dreamlike state where they might find relief from various ailments, whether through actual effect or merely by the power of a hypnotist's suggestion. One early practitioner of this technique became so famous that his very name became synonymous with the ability to send his patients into a trance—the art of mesmerism.

✳   ✳   ✳   ✳

FRANZ ANTON MESMER was a late bloomer. Born in Germany in 1734, Mesmer had difficulty finding a direction in life. He first studied for the priesthood, then drifted into astronomy and law before finally graduating at age 32 from the University of Vienna with a degree in medicine. He set up practice in Vienna and married a well-to-do widow, becoming a doctor to the rich and famous and using his connections to cater to an upper-crust clientele. He lived comfortably on a Viennese estate and counted among his friends Wolfgang Amadeus Mozart, who wrote a piece for Mesmer to play on the glass harmonica, an instrument lately arrived from America.

At first, Mesmer's medical prescriptions were unremarkable; bleeding and purgatives were the order of the day, and Mesmer followed accepted medical convention. But Mesmer's attention was also drawn to the practice of using magnets to induce responses in patients, a technique much in vogue at the time. Mesmer experimented with magnets to some effect and came to believe that he was successfully manipulating tides, or energy flows, within the human body. He theorized that illness was caused by the disruption of these flows, and health could be restored by a practitioner who could put them back in order. He also decided that the magnets themselves were an unnecessary prop and that he was performing the manipulation of the tides himself, because of what he termed his animal magnetism—the word "animal" merely stemming from the Latin term for "breath" or "soul." He would stir the tides by sitting in a chair opposite a patient, knees touching, gazing unblinkingly into their eyes, making passes with his hands, and massaging the areas of complaint, often continuing the treatment for hours until the patient felt the magnetic flows moving inside their body.

Europe Becomes Mesmerized

Mesmer gained notoriety as a healer, his fame growing to the point where he was invited to give his opinion in other famous cases of the day. He investigated claims of unusual cures and traveled around Switzerland and Germany, holding demonstrations at which he was able to induce symptoms and their subsequent cures by merely pointing at people, much to the amazement of his audience. He also took on more challenging cases as a doctor, but a scandal involving his treatment of a blind piano player—he temporarily restored her sight, only to have her lose her audiences because the novelty of watching her play was now gone—caused Mesmer to decide that 1777 was an opportune year to move to Paris.

France would prove to be a fertile ground for Mesmer. He resumed seeing patients, while at the same time seeking approval from the scientific community of Paris for his techniques. The respect and acknowledgment he felt he deserved from his peers was never to come, but his popular reputation soared; Marie Antoinette herself wrote Mesmer and begged him to reconsider when he once announced that he intended to give up his practice.

His services were in such demand that he could no longer treat patients individually; he resorted to treating groups of patients with a device he called a baquet, a wooden tub bristling with iron rods around which patients would hold hands and collectively seek to manipulate their magnetic tides. Mesmer himself would stride back and forth through the incense-laden room, reaching out and tapping patients with a staff or finger. For a complete cure, Mesmer believed the patients needed to undergo a convulsive crisis—literally an experience wherein they would enter a trancelike state, shake and moan uncontrollably, and be carried to a special padded chamber until they had come back to their senses. The treatment proved particularly popular with women, who outnumbered men 8–1 as patients of Mesmer. This statistic did not go unnoticed by the monitors of public decency, who drew the obvious conclusion that something immoral was taking place, though they were unable to produce much more than innuendo in support of their accusations.

When I Snap My Fingers...

Unfortunately, Mesmer's incredible popularity also made him an easy target for detractors. Mesmerism became such a fad that the wealthy even set up baquets in their own homes. But, as with many trends, once over they are held up for popular ridicule. As a result, Mesmer saw his client base decline and even found himself mocked in popular theater.

Copycats emerged to the extent that in 1784, the king set up a commission—including representatives from both the Faculty of Medicine and the Royal Academy of Science—to investigate all claims of healing involving animal magnetism. Benjamin Franklin, in Paris as an ambassador at the time, was one of the investigators. In the end, the commission determined that any treatment benefits derived from Mesmerism were imagined. This rejection by the scientific community combined with the erosion of his medical practice drove Mesmer from Paris in 1785. He kept an understandably low profile after that, spending some time in Switzerland, where he wrote and kept in touch with a few patients. He died in 1815.

Mesmer's legacy remains unresolved. Some still view him as a charlatan of the first order. Others see in his techniques the foundation of modern hypnotherapy, which has become a well-recognized practice in modern psychiatry. Regardless, it is indisputable that Franz Anton Mesmer's personal animal magnetism continues to capture our imagination even today.

Was Johnny Appleseed a Real Person?

Johnny Appleseed is often depicted as a happy-go-lucky farmer who roamed the American frontier barefoot, wearing a pan on his head and scattering apple seeds. Although this image fits comfortably with folklore, Johnny Appleseed was actually a real person.

✳   ✳   ✳   ✳

JOHNNY APPLESEED WAS born John Chapman on September 26, 1774, in Leominster, Massachusetts. He made his name by moving west ahead of the first pioneers, mainly in and around western Pennsylvania, Indiana, and Ohio. He traveled with a supply of apple seeds that he used to plant orchards (some of which exist to this day). By the time the first settlers arrived, he had fully grown apple trees ready to sell to them, along with nutritious fruit and that intoxicating beverage of choice among weary travelers—hard cider. Chapman quickly became known for his friendly, outgoing nature, and settlers welcomed him into their homes both for his liquid refreshments and his entertaining stories. They nicknamed him Johnny Appleseed, and along with his popularity, legends about him began to spread.

Although there's no evidence to support the idea that Johnny Appleseed wore a cooking pot on his head, he was known to remain barefoot—even in ice and snow. He preached a liberal Christian theology called Swedenborgianism, befriended Native Americans, and espoused a deep love of nature. He believed it was a sin to chop down trees or kill animals, and he often used his apple-tree profits to buy lame horses and save them from slaughter.

Johnny Appleseed died in 1845, but his reputation continued to grow. In 1871, a story about his life appeared in *Harper's New Monthly Magazine*, and the depiction served to elevate him from eccentric tree planter to "patron saint of horticulture."

Aaron Burr: Hero or Villain?

Mention the name Aaron Burr and the thing most people remember is his famous duel with Alexander Hamilton. That may have been the high point of his life, because by the time Burr passed away in 1836, he was considered one of the most mistrusted public figures of his era.

✳ ✳ ✳ ✳

How to Make Friends...

BURR SEEMED TO have a knack for making enemies out of important people. George Washington disliked him so much from their time together during the Revolutionary War that as president, he had Burr banned from the National Archives, didn't appoint him as minister to France, and refused to make him a brigadier general.

After the war, Burr became a lawyer in New York, frequently opposing his future dueling partner Alexander Hamilton. But it wasn't until Burr beat Hamilton's father-in-law in the race for a Senate seat that the problems between them really started.

In 1800, Burr ran for president against Thomas Jefferson. Back then, the candidate with the most votes got to be president; whoever came in second became vice president—even if they were from different parties. When the election ended in a tie in the Electoral College, it was thrown to the House of Representatives to decide. After 35 straight tie votes, Jefferson was elected president, and Burr became vice president.

Like Washington, Jefferson didn't hold Burr in high regard. So in 1804, Burr decided to run for governor of New York. When he lost, he blamed the slandering of the press in general and the almost constant criticism from Hamilton in particular.

Hamilton later shot off at the mouth at a dinner party, and Burr decided he'd had enough. After giving Hamilton a chance to take his comments back (Hamilton refused), Burr challenged him to the famous duel.

I Challenge You to a Duel

On July 11, 1804, Burr and Hamilton met at Weehawken, New Jersey. Some say that Hamilton fired first, discharging his pistol into the air; others say that he just missed. Burr, on the other hand, didn't miss, shooting Hamilton. He died the following day.

After the duel, Burr fled to his daughter's home in South Carolina until things cooled down. He was indicted for murder in both New York and New Jersey, but nothing ever came of it, and he eventually returned to Washington to finish his term as vice president. But his political career was over.

King Burr?

After his term as vice president, Burr decided to head west, to what was then considered Ohio and the new lands of the Louisiana Purchase. It seemed that Burr had things on his mind other than the scenery, however. According to some (mostly his rivals), Burr intended to create a new empire with himself as king. As the story goes, he planned to conquer a portion of Texas still held by Mexico, then convince some of the existing western states to join his new confederacy. Called the Burr Conspiracy, it got the attention of President Jefferson, who issued arrest orders for treason. Eventually, Burr was captured and in 1807 was brought to trial.

But Burr caught a break. The judge was Chief Justice John Marshall. Marshall and Jefferson didn't get along, and rather than give his enemy an easy victory, Marshall demanded that the prosecution produce two witnesses that specifically heard Burr commit treason. The prosecution failed to come up with anybody, and Burr was set free.

Burr left the United States to live in Europe. Returning to New York in 1812, he quietly practiced law until his death in 1836.

Who Was Sojourner Truth?

Freed slave Sojourner Truth was a vocal advocate of social justice, and her love of God carried her through trying times.

✳ ✳ ✳ ✳

SOJOURNER TRUTH WAS unique among 19th-century preachers—she was a former slave who fought for women's rights and other social causes, and she steadfastly refused to back down in the face of adversity. Her life was rife with abuse and heartache, but she always found comfort in the Bible.

Truth was born into slavery as Isabella Baumfree in 1797, in a

Dutch enclave in upstate New York. She was sold around age 9 for $100 (which also included a flock of sheep) and endured physical abuse at the hands of her new master because she spoke limited English, her first language being Dutch. It was during this period that Truth first sought solace in religion, praying loudly whenever she was frightened or hurt.

Finding Freedom

Truth was sold several more times in the ensuing years. She married another slave in 1817 and bore four children. Freedom seemed at hand when the State of New York enacted legislation that called for the end of slavery within the state on 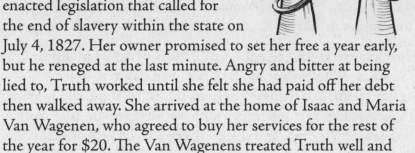 July 4, 1827. Her owner promised to set her free a year early, but he reneged at the last minute. Angry and bitter at being lied to, Truth worked until she felt she had paid off her debt then walked away. She arrived at the home of Isaac and Maria Van Wagenen, who agreed to buy her services for the rest of the year for $20. The Van Wagenens treated Truth well and insisted she call them by their given names.

It was while working for the Van Wagenens that Truth experienced a religious epiphany that inspired her to become a preacher. She began attending a local Methodist church, and in 1829, she left to travel in the company of a white female evangelical teacher. Truth began preaching at regional churches and developed a reputation as an inspiring speaker. She later joined a religious reformer named Elijah Pierson, who became her mentor until his death in 1834.

Truth moved to New York City, where she decided to become a traveling minister. She changed her name to Sojourner Truth and set out on the road, relying on the kindness of strangers to make her way. In 1844, Truth joined a Massachusetts commune known as the Northampton Association of Education and Industry, which had been founded by a group of abolitionists who espoused women's rights and religious tolerance. She left when the collective disbanded in 1846.

Literary Success

Truth began dictating her autobiography, *The Narrative of Sojourner Truth: A Northern Slave,* shortly after, and renowned abolitionist William Lloyd Garrison privately published the book in 1850. The memoir was a success and brought Truth both a needed income and promotion as a public speaker. Soon, Truth found herself in great demand, speaking about women's rights and the evils of slavery, often turning to her own experiences as illustration. In 1854, she gave one of her most famous lectures, titled "Ain't I A Woman?" at the Ohio Woman's Rights Convention in Akron.

Through everything, religion was Truth's personal mainstay. She was very active during the Civil War, enlisting black troops for the Union and helping runaway slaves. In 1864, she worked at a government refugee camp for freed slaves on an island off the coast of Virginia, and she even met President Abraham Lincoln. Following the war, she continued her efforts to help newly freed slaves through the Freedman's Relief Association.

Truth pursued her work on behalf of freed blacks until her death on November 26, 1883, from complications related to leg ulcers. She was buried next to her grandson, Sammy Banks, in Oak Hill Cemetery in Battle Creek, Michigan.

A Lasting Legacy

Sojourner Truth's legacy of spiritual pursuit and social activism resulted in numerous honors in the decades following her death. Among them were a memorial stone in the Stone History Tower in downtown Battle Creek; a portion of Michigan state highway M-66 designated the Sojourner Truth Memorial Highway; induction into the national Women's Hall of Fame in Seneca Falls, New York; and a commemorative postage stamp.

How Did Dr. David Livingstone and Henry Morton Stanley Meet?

The improbable meeting of Dr. David Livingstone and Henry Morton Stanley in 1871 was perhaps the greatest celebrity interview of all time, a high point in African exploration that would leave as its legacy one of the most brutal colonial empires in history.

✳   ✳   ✳   ✳

I T HAD BEEN five years since Scottish missionary David Livingstone disappeared into central Africa to find the source of the Nile, and he was presumed dead by his sponsor, Britain's Royal Geographical Society. New York newspaper magnate James Gordon Bennett Jr. saw the potential for a great story in Livingstone's disappearance. He dispatched young war correspondent Henry Morton Stanley to find him.

Dr. Livingstone, I Presume?

Stanley led a large party of guards and porters into uncharted territory in March 1871. Within a few days, his stallion was dead from tsetse flies, and dozens of his carriers were deserting with valuable supplies. Over the months that followed, his party was decimated by tropical disease. They endured encounters with hostile tribes—and at one point were pursued by cannibals chanting, "Meat! Meat!" Finally, on November 10, 1871, Stanley found the ailing Livingstone at a settlement on Lake Tanganyika in present-day Tanzania, supposedly greeting him with "Dr. Livingstone, I presume?"

Though most of his party had perished and he had won only a handful of converts to Christianity, Livingstone had become the first European to see Victoria Falls. Stanley's dispatches to the *New York Herald,* which told the world of Livingstone's discoveries as well as Stanley's own adventures, were the media sensation of the age.

Fame and Misfortune

Upon his return to Great Britain, Stanley was met with public ridicule by scientists and the press, who doubted his claim that he found Livingstone and questioned the veracity of his other accounts as well. Though his book, *How I Found Livingstone*, was a best seller, Stanley was deeply wounded by his detractors.

Indeed, Stanley was an unlikely hero. Born John Rowland, he was the illegitimate child of a disinterested mother who gave him up to a workhouse. He left Britain at the age of 17 to work as a deckhand on a merchant vessel. However, he jumped ship in New Orleans and took the name of an English planter, who he claimed had adopted him. Contemporary historians doubt that Stanley ever met the man.

Stanley's adult life was an improbable series of adventures and lies. He served, unremarkably, on both sides during the Civil War and worked unsuccessfully at a variety of trades before trying his hand at journalism, reporting on the Indian wars in the West and the Colorado gold rush. Stanley came to the attention of newspaper magnate Bennett while reporting for the *New York Herald* on a British military expedition into Abyssinia. His colorful writing won him the assignment to find Livingstone.

The Greatest African Explorer

Stanley may have found in Livingstone the father figure he never had. His accounts of the missionary created a portrait of a saintly doctor who, inspired by his opposition to Africa's brutal slave trade, had opened the continent to Western civilization and Christianity. When Livingstone died in 1873, Stanley served as a pallbearer at his funeral in Westminster Abbey. A year later, he set out on another epic expedition to complete Livingstone's work. Over the next three years, Stanley established Lake Victoria as the source of the Nile and led his party down the uncharted Congo River—a 2,900-mile course that transversed the continent.

Though acclaimed as the greatest of African explorers, Stanley's accounts of his brutal methods—such as whipping African porters and gunning down tribespeople with modern weaponry—brought public outrage in Britain. After examining his original notes and letters, however, some contemporary historians believe that he often exaggerated his exploits, including the numbers of Africans supposedly killed, to elevate his own legend.

"The Horror!"

Unable to persuade the British government to employ him, Stanley undertook a third journey in 1879 under the sponsorship of Belgium's King Leopold II. He established 22 trading posts along the Congo River, laying the foundation for a vast colonial empire that would exploit the rubber and ivory trades at the expense of millions of African lives.

Stanley earned the African nickname Bula Matari, or "breaker of rocks," on account of his ruthless determination to build roads linking the Congo's waterways. Natives were beaten, tortured, and killed under his command. This third expedition led to the scramble for Africa among European nations, culminating in the Berlin Conference of 1885, which divided the continent among colonial powers. Leopold II established his rights to the so-called Congo Free State, his private enterprise encompassing most of the Congo Basin. Historians estimate that as many as 10 million Congolese were murdered or died from disease or overwork under Leopold's regime, inspiring Joseph Conrad's novel *Heart of Darkness*.

A final African expedition between 1887 and 1889 further tarnished Stanley's name. Sent to rescue a dubious ally in southern Sudan, he left behind a rear column whose leaders—former British army officers and aristocrats—degenerated into sadism. Though most of his party perished and much more African blood was shed, Stanley helped establish British territorial claims in East Africa and opened a path to further colonization.

Finally marrying and adopting the grandchild of a Welsh nun, Stanley retired from exploration to write books and conduct lecture tours. He won a seat in Parliament in 1895 and was knighted by Queen Victoria in 1899. He died in 1904 at the age of 63. Although he was considered a national hero, he was denied burial next to Livingstone at Westminster Abbey due to his mixed reputation.

Who Was the First Woman to Run for President?

When Victoria Woodhull ran for president in 1872, some called her a witch, others said she was a prostitute. In fact, the very idea of a woman casting a vote for president was considered scandalous—which may explain why Woodhull spent election night in jail.

❋   ❋   ❋   ❋

KNOWN FOR HER passionate speeches and fearless attitude, Victoria Woodhull became a trailblazer for women's rights. But some say she was about 100 years before her time. Woodhull advocated revolutionary ideas, including gender equality and women's right to vote. "Women are the equals of men before the law and are equal in all their rights," she said. America, however, wasn't ready to accept her radical ideas.

Woodhull was born in 1838 in Homer, Ohio, the seventh child of Annie and Buck Claflin. Her deeply spiritual mother often took little Victoria along to revival camps where people would speak in tongues. Her mother also dabbled in clairvoyance, and Victoria and her younger sister Tennessee believed they had a gift for it as well. With so many chores to do at home (washing, ironing, chipping wood, and cooking), Victoria only attended school sporadically and was primarily self-educated.

Soon after the family left Homer, a 28-year-old doctor named Canning Woodhull asked the 15-year-old Victoria for her hand in marriage. But the marriage was no paradise for Victoria—she soon realized her husband was an alcoholic. She experienced more heartbreak when her son, Byron, was born with a mental disability. While she remained married to Canning, Victoria spent the next few years touring as a clairvoyant with her sister Tennessee. At that time, it was difficult for a woman to pursue divorce, but Victoria finally succeeded in divorcing her husband in 1864. Two years later she married Colonel James Blood, a Civil War veteran who believed in free love.

In 1866, Victoria and James moved to New York City. Spiritualism was then in vogue, and Victoria and Tennessee established a salon where they acted as clairvoyants and discussed social and political hypocrisies with their clientele. Among their first customers was Cornelius Vanderbilt, the wealthiest man in America.

A close relationship sprang up between Vanderbilt and the two attractive and intelligent young women. He advised them on business matters and gave them stock tips. When the stock market crashed in September 1869, Woodhull made a bundle buying instead of selling during the ensuing panic. That winter, she and Tennessee opened their own brokerage business. They were the first female stockbrokers in American history, and they did so well that, two years after arriving in New York, Woodhull told a newspaper she had made $700,000.

Woodhull had more far-reaching ambitions, however. On April 2, 1870, she announced that she was running for president. In conjunction with her presidential bid, Woodhull and her sister started a newspaper, *Woodhull & Claflin's Weekly*, which highlighted women's issues including voting and labor rights. It was another breakthrough for the two since they were the first women to ever publish a weekly newspaper.

That was followed by another milestone: On January 11, 1871, Woodhull became the first woman ever to speak before a congressional committee. As she spoke before the House

Judiciary Committee, she asked that Congress change its stance on whether women could vote. Woodhull's reasoning was elegant in its simplicity. She was not advocating a new constitutional amendment granting women the right to vote. Instead, she reasoned, women already had that right. The Fourteenth Amendment says that, "All persons born or naturalized in the United States . . . are citizens of the Unites States." Since voting is part of the definition of being a citizen, Woodhull argued, women, in fact, already possessed the right to vote. Woodhull, a persuasive speaker, actually swayed some congressmen to her point of view, but the committee chairman remained hostile to the idea of women's rights and made sure the issue never came to a floor vote.

Woodhull had better luck with the suffragists. In May 1872, before 668 delegates from 22 states, Woodhull was chosen as the presidential candidate of the Equal Rights Party; she was the first woman ever chosen by a political party to run for president. But her presidential bid soon foundered. Woodhull was on record as an advocate of free love, which opponents argued was an attack on the institution of marriage (for Woodhull it had more to do with the right to have a relationship with anyone she wanted). Rather than debate her publicly, her opponents made personal attacks.

That year, Woodhull caused an uproar when her newspaper ran an exposé about the infidelities of Reverend Henry Ward Beecher. Woodhull and her sister were thrown in jail and accused of publishing libel and promoting obscenity. They would spend election night of 1872 behind bars as Ulysses Grant defeated Horace Greeley for the presidency.

Woodhull was eventually cleared of the charges against her (the claims against Beecher were proven true), but hefty legal bills and a downturn in the stock market left her embittered and impoverished. She moved to England in 1877, shortly after divorcing Colonel Blood. By the turn of the century she had become wealthy once more, this time by marriage to a British banker. Fascinated by technology, she joined the Ladies Automobile Club, where her passion for automobiles led Woodhull to one last milestone: In her sixties, she and her daughter Zula became the first women to drive through the English countryside.

Who Were the Women's Suffrage Leaders?

The following are a few prominent women's suffragists whose efforts helped lead to the U.S. Constitution being amended in 1920 to grant women the right to vote.

✳ ✳ ✳ ✳

✳ Lucretia Mott (died 1880) was an abolitionist and women's rights activist. She helped organize the Seneca Falls Woman's Rights Convention. She refused to use cotton cloth, cane sugar, and other goods produced through slave labor, and she often sheltered runaway slaves in her home.

✳ Sojourner Truth (died 1883) was a former slave and prominent abolitionist and women's rights activist. She was famed for her simple yet powerful oratory, especially her 1851 "Ain't I a Woman?" speech.

✳ Lucy Stone (died 1893) recruited many (Susan B. Anthony and Julia Ward Howe, for instance) to the cause of women's suffrage. After her marriage, she and her husband put their house in her name. She refused to pay property taxes on it at one point, claiming she should not have to pay taxes because she did not have the right to vote.

✳ Amelia Bloomer (died 1894) was a suffragist, editor, temperance leader, and tireless volunteer. She also became known for wearing "bloomers" (trousers underneath a skirt).

* Frances E. Willard (died 1898) served as president of the Woman's Christian Temperance Union from 1879 to 1898 and lectured across the country on prison, education, and labor reform.

* Elizabeth Cady Stanton (died 1902) helped organize the Seneca Falls convention and worked to liberalize divorce laws and other laws that made it difficult for women to leave abusive relationships.

* Susan B. Anthony (died 1906) helped found the Equal Rights Association. In 1872, she voted in a presidential election in an attempt to show that under the Constitution, women should already have the right to vote. She was arrested, tried, convicted, and ordered to pay a fine. She never paid the fine, and the authorities did not pursue the case.

* Emmeline Pankhurst (died 1928) was a British suffragist who founded the Women's Franchise League and the Women's Social and Political Union. She went to jail 12 times in 1912.

* Carrie Chapman Catt (died 1947) founded the League of Women Voters.

How Did Annie Oakley Become a Sharpshooter?

Despite being neglected as a child and suffering an accident later in life, Oakley rose to personal triumph and inspired young girls all over the country.

* * * *

ANNIE OAKLEY BECAME a star in Buffalo Bill Cody's "Wild West" show in the late 19th century as a female sharpshooter. Her lasting image as a self-reliant, hearty, and highly skilled shooter represented the best values of the Old West just as that era was fading. Oakley was not born in the West, nor had she been part of its settlement—but she embodied ideals that were important to Americans.

A Quick Study

Born Phoebe Ann Mosey in 1860 in the remote farmland of Darke County, Oakley endured a horrible childhood. Her father died after a protracted illness, leaving her mother with eight mouths to feed. To help, little Phoebe took her father's rifle into the woods and taught herself how to shoot, bringing home game for the family to eat. Despite her daughter's growing skills with the gun, her mother could not provide for the family, and eight-year-old Phoebe was sent to live at the Darke County Infirmary—put simply, the poorhouse. She would be in and out of this establishment, between living with abusive farming families, running back home, and eventually returning to her family after her twice-widowed mother's third marriage.

Phoebe became a professional hunter to help with the household expenses, killing game birds to sell to local hotels. Within a few years, she had paid off the mortgage on her mother's farm. Phoebe's mother then sent her to Cincinnati to live with an older sister and attend school, but the young girl preferred the shooting galleries where she could hone her skills.

When Phoebe was 15, she was asked to participate in a public sharpshooting match with a man named Frank Butler. To the crowd's delight, the tiny teenager bested the tall, broad-shouldered Butler. Despite the defeat, Butler began to correspond with the little girl with the big gun while he toured the vaudeville circuit. The two were married the following year. From Butler, Phoebe learned about show business, and by 1882, she had changed her name to Annie Oakley and joined him onstage.

More Than Just Sharpshooting

When it became obvious that Oakley was the act's main attraction, Butler became her manager. Around 1884, they approached Buffalo Bill Cody about a position with his traveling western show. After an impressive audition, she joined the extravaganza. The legendary Sioux leader Sitting Bull, who was also part of Cody's show, called her "Little Sure Shot" and legally adopted her. Cody merely called her "Missie."

Oakley's act was more than just shooting at a target: She could shoot glass balls while galloping around the arena on a horse; with a gun in each hand, she could hit two targets at once; and she could shoot upside down and backward while looking in a mirror. Annie stayed with Buffalo Bill Cody's Wild West Show for 17 years, longer than any other performer. After a train accident left her with a slight paralysis in 1901, she quit the show but continued performing as a shooter for 20 more years.

Rather than resting on her laurels, Oakley used her celebrity to help young women become self-reliant. She taught young girls to shoot (a skill still mostly associated with men at that time), and never forgetting her own turbulent childhood, she used her wealth to support and educate 18 orphan girls. Oakley died on November 3, 1926. Never separated from Annie in life, Butler joined her in death 18 days later.

Was Einstein Really a C Student?

Could it be that the world's most famous genius didn't do his homework or was never ready for a pop quiz? Let's put it this way: Are most average students teaching themselves advanced physics instead of attending class? Yeah, didn't think so. If Einstein was an average student, he was no average average student.

✳   ✳   ✳   ✳

ALBERT EINSTEIN WAS born in 1879 and had speech difficulties. His verbal development was slow, but his mind certainly wasn't. When he went to Catholic school, it wasn't so much that he didn't get good grades (although he was not an academic star)—it was more that he just hated school. He was a distraction in the class, he didn't pay attention, and, most importantly, he did not respect the authority of his teachers. When he was in class, he acted out, but when he cut class, he taught himself what he wanted to learn as opposed to goofing off all day.

When Einstein was in high school in Munich, his family moved to Italy. He left school to be with his family again. Many people use phrases like, "He didn't finish high school" or "He dropped out of school," but this was for a very specific reason, and he didn't stop his education. C'mon—it was Einstein. He tried to avoid going back to high school by getting accepted to college. Because he didn't finish high school, he had to take a qualification test, which he failed. So back to high school he went, where he graduated just fine, and then went to college and got his degree in physics.

He had the same issues in college—his teachers did not like his classroom demeanor. He was no valedictorian, but his college grades were above average. Of course, it can be hard to get stellar grades in other subjects when you're busy reading everything you can find about physics.

Einstein said he didn't like traditional curricula and teaching methods. He hated rote learning, saying that such structure stifled creativity. There's no question he loved learning; he just didn't like to do it at school.

After having a hard time finding work as a professor, Einstein took a job in the Swiss patent office. He worked there full-time, and in his spare time in 1905, he developed his special theory of relativity and published five papers, one introducing $e=mc^2$, which changed the world of science forever. What a slacker.

What Happened to Van Gogh's Ear?

Vincent van Gogh is remembered as a brilliant, temperamental artist who sliced off his left ear in a fit of insanity. But like the ear itself, the veracity of this story is only partial.

❊ ❊ ❊ ❊

A Tortured Soul

THROUGHOUT HIS LIFE, the great Dutch artist was plagued by a wide range of physical and mental ailments, including epilepsy, lead poisoning, bipolar disorder, and depression. As a child, he was withdrawn and suffered from social paralysis, and his anxiety increased greatly after he was sent away to boarding school.

Van Gogh did indeed take a whack at his left ear, but he only severed part of the earlobe. This act of self-mutilation happened when he was spending time with his friend and fellow artist Paul Gauguin in Paris. Actually, the word *friend* may be imprecise here—van Gogh and Gauguin often drank heavily together and ended up in heated arguments. On the Parisian social and artistic scene, absinthe was a popular libation, and van Gogh had a particular fondness for it. At the time, it was thought that people who consumed too much of the powerful liquor were prone to violent behavior.

Fighting Dirty

During a spat with Gauguin on Christmas Eve in 1888, van Gogh attacked him with a razor. When he failed to cause Gauguin any harm, van Gogh filled the emotional void by razoring off a piece of his own earlobe. He gave the bloody chunk to his prostitute friend Rachel, advising her to keep it as something precious. (Laugh if you wish. What would it be worth today?)

The incident happened about two years before van Gogh shot himself to death. It's reasonable to assume that his suicide was connected to a general and final psychological collapse—another irrational, self-harming act.

Who Were the First to Reach the North Pole?

Who were the first two men to reach the North Pole? Many people can identify Robert E. Peary, but the other explorer is not nearly as well known.

✳ ✳ ✳ ✳

"I Can't Get Along Without Him"

MATTHEW HENSON WAS born in Maryland on August 6, 1866, one year after the Civil War ended. At the age of 13, the young African American began working aboard a ship, and it was there that he learned to read, write, and navigate.

In 1887, Henson met explorer Robert Peary. Peary hired Henson as a valet, but quickly found him indispensible. "I can't get along without him," Peary said.

Henson joined Peary in 1890 to help the explorer achieve his dream of being the first to reach the North Pole. Over the next 18 years the two men repeatedly tried to reach the pole, only to be thwarted every time. Henson's worth and value to the expeditions grew, and Peary gave him more and more responsibility. In 1910, Peary wrote, "Matthew A. Henson, my Negro assistant, has been with me in one capacity or another…on each and all of my northern expeditions except the first. He has shared all the physical hardships of my Arctic work. [He] can handle a sled better, and is probably a better dog driver than any other man living…except some Eskimo hunters…"

On Top of the World

In August 1908, Peary and Henson set out once again for the

North Pole. By the following April, they were closing in at last on their elusive goal. On April 6, 1909, the group—Henson, Peary, and four native Inuits—drove farther than they had ever gone before. Henson arrived at camp 45 minutes before Peary. By dead reckoning, he figured that the Pole had been reached. When Peary arrived, Henson greeted him by saying, "I think I'm the first man to sit on top of the world."

As Henson recalled, Peary was furious. Peary soon determined that the Pole was still three miles away, but he left to cover the final distance on his own (without longitudinal coordinates, so knowing which direction to go was problematic), without waking the sleeping Henson. "It nearly broke my heart," Henson recalled of Peary's actions.

"From the moment I declared to Commander Peary that I believed we stood upon the Pole he apparently ceased to be my friend," Henson wrote in 1910.

Upon his return, Peary was widely hailed as the first one to reach the North Pole. (Today his claim is hotly disputed.) He received awards and honors galore for this achievement. But for Henson, the disappointment had just begun.

Was Race a Factor?

Peary spent the rest of his life being feted as the first man to reach the North Pole. He died in 1920, but not before some waves of controversy emerged. At first, Henson's contributions were not only overlooked, but ignored. He settled into a desk job working as a clerk in a customs house in New York City.

But in 1912, Henson wrote a book about his experiences, which enraged Peary. A debate exploded, with some people speculating that a large reason Peary had chosen Henson to join him on the expeditions was due to his race—that he figured because Henson was African American, that he would not dare contradict Peary's claims, and if he did, people would not believe him.

In a 1939 magazine interview, Henson was stoic, and even philosophical. "Mr. Peary was a noble man," he said. "He was always my friend. I have not expected much, and I have not been disappointed."

Gradually, because it was clear Henson's contributions had been so vital, public opinion began to turn around. In 1944, Congress awarded Henson a duplicate of the silver medal Peary had received. Presidents Truman and Eisenhower both honored him. Henson died in 1955, and in 1988 his coffin was reinterred in Arlington National Cemetery.

Finally, in 2000, the National Geographic Society posthumously awarded Henson its highest honor: the Hubbard Medal—the same award Peary had received in 1906.

Who Was Typhoid Mary?

There were hundreds, if not thousands, of typhoid carriers in New York at the turn of the 20th century. But only one of them was labeled a menace to society and banished to an island for life.

✳ ✳ ✳ ✳

THE POPULAR IMAGE of Typhoid Mary in the early 1900s— an image enthusiastically promoted by the tabloids of the day—was of a woman stalking the streets of New York, infecting and killing hundreds of hapless victims. In truth, Mary Mallon, the woman who came to be recognized as Typhoid Mary, is known to have infected 47 people, three of whom died.

Mary Mallon immigrated to the United States from Ireland in 1883 at age 15. For a time, she lived with an aunt in New York City, but soon began working as a domestic servant, one of the few avenues of gainful employment open to a poor young woman of the day.

Sometime before the turn of the century, she must have contracted and then recovered from a mild case of typhoid. Since a mild case of typhoid can mimic the symptoms of the flu, it is quite possible that Mallon never even knew she had contracted the disease.

Mallon, an excellent cook, was working in the kitchens of the city's wealthiest families. In August 1906, she was hired by banker Charles Warren to cook for his family at their rented summer home on Long Island. After 6 of the 11 people in the house fell ill with typhoid, George Soper, a sanitary engineer, was hired by Charles Warren's landlord to pinpoint the source of the outbreak. Soper's attention eventually focused on the cook. After months of tracing Mary Mallon's job history, Soper discovered that typhoid had struck seven of the eight families for whom she'd cooked.

In March 1907, Mallon was working at a home on Park Avenue when George Soper paid a visit. Soper told Mary that she was a possible typhoid carrier and requested samples of her blood, urine, and feces for testing.

The idea that a healthy person could pass a disease on to others was barely understood by the general public at the time. For someone like Mary Mallon, who prided herself on never being sick, Soper's requests seemed particularly outrageous. Believing herself falsely accused, she picked up a carving fork and angrily forced Soper out of the house.

Because Mallon refused to submit voluntarily to testing, the New York Health Department called in the police. Officers dragged her into an ambulance and, with the city health inspector sitting on top of her, took her kicking and screaming to the Willard Parker Hospital. Tests revealed high concentrations of typhoid bacilli in her blood.

Quarantine

Declaring her a public menace, the health department moved Mallon to an isolation cottage on the grounds of the Riverside Hospital on North Brother Island in the East River. She had broken no laws and had not been given a trial, but she remained in quarantine for nearly three years.

In 1909, Mallon sued the health department for her freedom, insisting that she was healthy and that her banishment was illegal and unjustified. The judge ruled against Mallon, and she was sent back to Brother Island. In 1910, a new health department inspector freed her on the condition that she never work as a cook again. Mallon kept her promise for a time, but eventually returned to the only profession she knew that could offer her a decent income.

A 1915 typhoid outbreak at Sloane Maternity Hospital in New York City killed 2 people and infected 25 others. An investigation revealed that a recently hired cook named "Mary Brown" was in fact Mary Mallon. Mallon was immediately returned to her lonely cottage on Brother Island, where she remained quarantined until her death in 1938.

Historians have debated why Mallon was treated so differently than hundreds of other typhoid carriers. At the time of her first arrest, there were 3,000–4,500 new cases of typhoid each year in New York City. Approximately three percent of typhoid fever victims became carriers, which translated to roughly 100 new carriers per year. The city would have gone bankrupt had it tried to quarantine even a handful of them as it did Mallon.

Why Mary?

Typhoid Mary was not even the deadliest carrier. A man named Tony Labella was responsible for 122 cases and 5 deaths in the 1920s. Despite the fact that he handled food and was uncooperative with authorities, he was isolated for only two weeks and then released. A bakery and restaurant owner named Alphonse Cotils was also a carrier. In 1924, Cotils was arrested after officials discovered him inside his restaurant after being warned to stay away from food. Cotils was released after promising to conduct his business by phone.

So why was Mary Mallon forced into a life of quarantine when others were not? For one thing, Mallon was the first discovered healthy carrier of typhoid. At the time, Mallon, like most people, didn't understand that a healthy person could be a carrier of the disease, so she saw no reason to change her behavior. Mallon's use of an assumed name in the Sloane Maternity Hospital case was also seen by the public as a deliberate act, maliciously designed to put others at risk.

Some historians suspect that Mallon's fate was tied to the fact that she was a single female and an Irish immigrant. Prejudice against the Irish still ran high at the time, and it was considered unnatural—if not immoral—for a woman to remain single all her life. Another strike against Mary Mallon was her work as a domestic servant. Diseases like typhoid fever were associated with the unclean habits of the "lower classes." These factors combined to transform Mary Mallon from a simple woman into the menacing, legendary Typhoid Mary—a threat that had to be contained.

How Did Houdini Die?

Ehrich Weiss, better remembered as Harry Houdini, was the master escape artist and illusionist of his time—perhaps of all time. Contrary to rumor, though, he did not die at the hands of angry spiritualists.

✳   ✳   ✳   ✳

SEVERAL OF HOUDINI'S stunts almost did him in, especially if sabotage or malfunction affected the gear. He finished numerous escapes bleeding, bruised, or otherwise broken. But he was always a "show must go on" performer, and that's ultimately what caused his death.

Houdini was a consummate showman, but he was also a trifle odd. He developed the macho habit of encouraging people to test his stony abs by slugging him in the gut. In 1926, while visiting Houdini backstage before a performance in Montreal, a college student asked to give the famous abs the punch test. The eager recruit hit him before the magician could brace himself for the repeated blows, and a terrible pain shot through Houdini's side. Despite his agony, that night's performance went on.

Later that evening, still in severe pain, Houdini was reading a newspaper while waiting for a train to his next gig, in Detroit. A burly "fan" approached him and drove a fist straight through the paper and into the performer's stomach, worsening matters considerably.

In Detroit, Houdini finished his show by sheer will before finally checking into a hospital. Doctors found that he had an abnormally long appendix that spanned his pelvis, and as a result of the blows, it had ruptured. Rumors began to swirl that the student who had punched Houdini was actually an offended member of a group of spiritualists whom Houdini often spoke against and attempted to expose. The truth isn't quite so sensational. Houdini died of peritonitis six days after he was hospitalized—quite fittingly, on Halloween.

Who Was the White Rose of Stalingrad?

The most feared fighter pilot over Stalingrad was a woman. Lily Litvak, the "White Rose of Stalingrad," terrorized German pilots and helped inspire a nation to a monumental victory.

✳ ✳ ✳ ✳

IN THE UKRAINE city of Krasy Luch, there stands a tall marble monument with 12 gold stars ascending its column, capped with a large, striking bust of a woman crowned in an aviator's cap and glasses.

The monument is dedicated to Lily Litvak, the celebrated

Soviet fighter ace who struck fear into German pilots in the skies over Stalingrad. The 12 gold stars on her monument commemorate the 12 solo and 3 shared kills she recorded in her brief but illustrious career.

A Deadly Flower

Litvak was affectionately called the "White Rose of Stalingrad" for the white lily (which was mistaken for a rose) painted on each side of the cockpit of her Yak-1 fighter plane. Her skill and tenacity as a fighter pilot became so well-known that German pilots would allegedly peel away when they saw the white flowers coming.

A licensed flying instructor by her 18th birthday, Litvak volunteered for an aviation unit after Germany invaded the Soviet Union, but she was rejected because of her lack of flying time. After embellishing her experience, she joined the famed all-female 586th Fighter Regiment, where she honed her fighter-pilot skills.

Initially, Litvak faced more of a challenge from chauvinistic attitudes than from enemy pilots. When she transferred to an all-male air unit at Stalingrad in September 1942, her commander refused to let her fly. After continual pleading, she was finally given a plane and quickly made believers of her male comrades after scoring her first two kills on her second combat mission.

A Timely Inspiration for a Beleaguered Nation

For the next 11 months, the stunning beauty with golden blonde hair and captivating gray eyes outwitted and outfought German pilots, who often couldn't believe that they had been shot down by a woman. A German fighter ace who was shot down by Litvak refused to believe that he had been bested by a woman until they were introduced, and she herself described to him minute details of their dogfight that only the two of them could have known.

Through the course of 168 combat missions, Litvak was shot

down two or three times, once sustaining serious injury to her legs. She bounced back each time with a more determined will to fight that was further hardened following the death of her fighter-pilot husband. Her luck finally ran out on August 1, 1943, when eight German fighters ganged against her and sent her crashing to her death 17 days shy of her 22nd birthday.

Although her remains weren't found until 1979, Litvak's heroics in the skies over Stalingrad were never forgotten by the Soviet people. Her bravery and achievements provided a timely inspiration to a nation facing defeat and desperate for something from which to draw hope. In recognition of her contribution to her nation's monumental victory, Litvak was posthumously awarded its highest honor, the Hero of the Soviet Union, in 1990.

Who Were the Women in Hitler's Life?

Adolf Hitler's personality stands in the shadows of his historic legacy—much as he expected most women to stand in his own shadow. But since Hitler generally found women nonthreatening and more loyal than men, women saw parts of Adolf Hitler's inner self that few men ever did.

✳ ✳ ✳ ✳

His Mother Klara

THE FIRST WOMAN in Hitler's world, of course, gave him life. Klara Hitler (née Pölzl) was the young wife of a much older husband when she brought "Adi" into the world on April 20, 1889. But their home would always be tinted with mourning, for Adi and his little sister Paula were the only two of Klara's six babies to survive to adulthood. Small wonder Klara spoiled her only surviving son, especially after his father died when Adi was only 13.

Hitler was devoted to his mother. He was about 19 when she

died from breast cancer—Adolf had spent months by her side caring for Klara as her condition worsened. Her loss severed a crucial strand binding him to humanity.

His Sister Paula

With Paula, Adolf had friendly relations but little in common. After their mother's death, Adolf moved to Vienna and lost contact with his sister until the early 1920s. He did, however, assign her his share of the orphan's pension from the state. Beyond that, Paula and Adolf were in only sporadic contact for many years as their paths in life diverged.

His Half Sister Angela and Her Daughter Geli

By 1928, Adolf Hitler was a bachelor nearing 40 and chieftain of a rising political party. He lived in a rented house in Bavaria. His half sister Angela Raubal (née Hitler, long since widowed) came to run the household, bringing her daughters Geli and Friedl. At about 20 years old, Geli Raubal was lovely, charming, and flirtatious—and Adolf fell hard for her. The fact that Geli was his niece and young enough to be his daughter did not seem to have bothered him; he behaved more like a jealous boyfriend than an uncle, restricting her from social and creative activities. Any time she showed interest in other men, as saucy Geli often did, her uncle went into a rage. After a bitter argument with Adolf one fall day in 1931, Geli was found dead with a bullet through her heart, an apparent suicide. Hitler was so distraught he considered following suit. His brief and stormy relationship with Geli brought his controlling nature and fierce jealous streak to the fore.

Eva Braun

Even while Hitler was getting angry with Geli over her independent behavior, he had begun seeing Eva Braun, a receptionist/assistant in the shop of Hitler's official photographer. This would be his last and most enduring romance—but it was only on his terms. Hitler made Germany his first priority, often neglecting Eva. In the early years, when he had not yet consolidated his power, she was a well-kept secret and grew so lonely she tried twice to commit suicide. Later, their relationship became better known, but he resisted marriage until the Third Reich was beyond saving; she became Hitler's bride mere hours before the two of them committed suicide on April 30, 1945. Eva was presumably everything Hitler wanted in a lover: German, beautiful, much younger, loyally devoted to him, disinterested in politics, and content with mundane pastimes.

His Secretary Traudl Junge

In the professional sphere, Hitler mostly encountered women as secretaries. One secretary who shared her recollections was Traudl Junge (née Humps), who served Hitler until the last days in the bunker. Traudl described Hitler as a self-deprecating, considerate boss who tried hard to put her at ease. When her young husband died in combat at the front, Hitler took time out from the war to console her. The wives of Hitler's lieutenants also found him compassionate and charming at most times: He always asked about their children, and if they were along, he would talk to the boys and girls themselves.

Leni Riefenstahl

Hitler knew one woman who was nobody's stenographer: Leni Riefenstahl. Riefenstahl was already well-known in cinema as an actress when Hitler first asked her to produce a documentary. Lacking confidence, she initially delegated the project to a subordinate. Hitler found out, yet wasn't angry or harsh, simply persuasive as only Hitler could be. Riefenstahl reconsidered and poured herself into making the film. When Hitler suggested some changes to the film to placate certain politicians who felt slighted, she angrily refused, citing artistic principles. Not even his chilling reply "Are you forgetting whom you're talking to?" could bend her will. Hitler gave in, and Leni Riefenstahl did it her way. The result was her vision of the 1934 Nazi Party Congress in Nuremberg. *Triumph Des Willens* ("Triumph of the Will") has become one of the best-known examples of propaganda in film history.

Chapter 13

The Arts

Who Was the Tenth Muse?

In a literary canon that is almost exclusively male, Sappho, the captivating poet from the Greek island of Lesbos (modern Lesvos) stands out as a female author whose works achieved popular acclaim in antiquity.

✳   ✳   ✳   ✳

BORN AROUND 630 B.C., Sappho belonged to an aristocratic Lesbian family at a time when colonization, the creation of pan-Hellenic festivals (such as the Olympic Games), and the works of Homer (the *Iliad* and *Odyssey*) fueled the growth of a common aristocratic Greek culture. Within this culture, Greek aristocrats used lyric poetry to reflect on politics, values, and personal experience. Sappho's poetry addresses all these issues, but it is most famous for capturing the powerful, poignant—yet playful—sincerity of desire, longing, and affection.

An intriguing and sometimes controversial element of Sappho's poetry is that many poems are directed toward other women. It is, in fact, from these poems that the term "lesbian" was coined in the 19th century to mean "homosexual." However, though Sappho's world fostered intense and even erotic relationships among social peers, the relationships she wrote about would not have neatly corresponded to modern terms.

Despite these ambiguities, the continued popularity of her

poetry remains a testament to its universality and to her talent and insight. Sappho's language and unique meter (which came to be known as "Sapphic stanza") have influenced many other poets and authors since her time. Plato, writing nearly 200 years after her death, called Sappho the "tenth Muse," and writers from the Roman poets Catullus and Horace, to contemporary authors such as Erica Jong and Guy Davenport, have been inspired to evoke her character or poetry in their own work.

Today, only one complete Sappho poem survives.

What Makes Something Art?

If you want to see a name-calling, hair-pulling intellectual fight (and who doesn't?), just yell this question in a crowded coffee shop. After centuries of debate and goatee-stroking, it's still a hot-button issue.

✳ ✳ ✳ ✳

BEFORE THE 14TH century, the Western world grouped painting, sculpture, and architecture with decorative crafts such as pottery, weaving, and the like. During the Renaissance, Michelangelo and the gang elevated the artist to the level of the poet—a genius who was touched by divine inspiration. Now, with God as a collaborator, art had to be beautiful, which meant that artists had to recreate reality in a way that transcended earthly experience.

In the 19th and 20th centuries, artists rejected these standards of beauty; they claimed that art didn't need to fit set requirements. This idea is now widely accepted, though people still disagree over what is and isn't art.

A common modern view is that art is anything that is created for its own aesthetic value—beautiful or not—rather than to serve some other function. So, according to this theory, defining art comes down to the creator's intention. If you build a chair to have something to sit on, the chair isn't a piece of art. But if you build an identical chair to express yourself, that chair *is* a piece of art. Marcel Duchamp demonstrated this in 1917, when he turned a urinal upside down and called it "Fountain." He was only interested in the object's aesthetic value. And just as simply as that: art.

This may seem arbitrary, but to the creator, there is a difference. If you build something for a specific purpose, you measure success by how well your creation serves that function. If you make pure art, your accomplishment is exclusively determined by how the creation makes you feel. Artists say that they follow their hearts, their muses, or God, depending on their beliefs. A craftsperson also follows a creative spirit, but his or her desire for artistic fulfillment is secondary to the obligation to make something that is functional.

Many objects involve both kinds of creativity. For example, a big-budget filmmaker follows his or her muse but generally bends to studio demands to try to make the movie profitable. (For instance, the movie might be trimmed to ninety minutes.) Unless the director has full creative control, the primary function of the film is to get people to buy tickets. There's nothing wrong with making money from your art, but purists say that financial concerns should never influence the true artist.

By a purist's definition, a book illustration isn't art, since its function is to support the text and please the client—even if the text is a work of art. The counter view is that the illustration *is* art, since the illustrator follows his or her creative instincts to create it; the illustrator is as much an artistic collaborator as the writer.

Obviously, it gets pretty murky. But until someone invents a handheld art detector, the question of what makes something art will continue to spark spirited arguments in coffee shops the world over.

When Was Oil Paint First Used?

The unique characteristics of oil paint contributed to the accomplishments of the Renaissance—and still inspire artists.

✳   ✳   ✳   ✳

PAINTINGS ARE AMONG the most ancient of artworks. More than 30,000 years ago, Neolithic painters decorated caves with patterns and images of animals. All paints include two elements: pigment and a liquid binder. Pigments from charred wood and colored minerals are ground into a fine powder. Then they are mixed into the binder; linseed oil is the most popular, but other oils, including walnut oil, are common.

The idea of using oil as a binder for pigment is very old, but oil paints as we know them are relatively modern. In the 12th century, a German monk named Theophilus wrote about oil paint in his "Schoedula Diversarum Artium" and warned against paint recipes using olive oil because they required excessively long drying times. The Italian painter and writer Cennino Cennini described the technique of oil painting in his encyclopedic *Book of Art*. Oil paints came into general use in northern Europe, in the area of the Netherlands, by the 15th century and, from there, spread southward into Italy. Oils remained the medium of choice for most painters until the mid-20th century.

Oil paintings are usually done on wood panels or canvas, although paintings on stone and specialty paper are not uncommon. In any case, the support material is usually prepared with a ground to which oil paint easily adheres. Oil paints dry slowly, an advantage to artists, who adjust their compositions as they work. When the painting is done, a protective layer of varnish is often applied. In the 19th century, oil paint in tubes simplified the painter's work. A rainbow of innovative, synthetic colors contributed to the emergence of new approaches to art and, in particular, modern abstract painting.

Who Was the Real Mona Lisa?

It's been one of history's great mysteries: Who posed for Leonardo da Vinci when he painted art's most famous face, the Mona Lisa, in the early 1500s?

✳   ✳   ✳   ✳

The Possibilities

YOU WOULD THINK that the missing eyebrows would be a dead giveaway as to the identity of the woman who posed for the *Mona Lisa*. How many eyebrow-less ladies could have been wandering around Italy back then? As it turns out, quite a few—it was a popular look at the time. Those crazy Renaissance women.

The leading theory has always been that Lisa is Lisa Gherardini, the wife of wealthy Florentine silk merchant Francesco del Giocondo. Sixteenth-century historian Giorgio Vasari made this claim in *The Lives of the Artists*, noting that the untitled painting was often called "La Gioconda," which literally means "the happy woman" but can also be read as a play on the name Giocondo. (If you're wondering what the more popular title means, "Mona" is simply a contraction of *ma donna*, or "my lady," in Italian; the title is the equivalent of "Madam Lisa" in English.)

Vasari was infamous for trusting word of mouth, so there's a possibility that he got it wrong. Therefore, historians have proposed many alternative Lisas, including Leonardo da Vinci's mom, various Italian noblewomen, a fictitious ideal woman, and a prostitute. Some have believed that the painting is a disguised portrait of Leonardo himself, noting that his features in other self-portraits resemble Lisa's. Hey, maybe the guy wanted to see what he would look like as a woman—nothing wrong with that.

Lisa Gherardini

In 2005, Armin Schlecter, a manuscript expert at Heidelberg University Library in Germany, closed the case. While looking through one of the books in the library's collection—a very old copy of Cicero's letters—Schlecter discovered notes in the margin that were written in 1503 by Florentine city official Agostino Vespucci. Vespucci, who knew Leonardo, described some of the paintings on which the artist was working at the time. One of the notes mentions a portrait of Lisa del Giocondo, aka Lisa Gherardini, which proves fairly conclusively that Vasari had the right Lisa.

Historians know a bit about Lisa's life. She was Francesco's third wife; she married him when she was 16 and he was 30, a year after his second wife had died. They lived in a big house, but it was in the middle of the city's red-light district. She likely sat for the portrait soon after the birth of her third child, when she was about 24. She had five children altogether and died at age 63.

Did Someone Else Write Shakespeare's Plays?

"What's in a name? That which we call a rose, by any other name, would smell as sweet." But would that which we call prose, by any other name, read as neat?

✳   ✳   ✳   ✳

For someone so famous, William Shakespeare remains a mysterious figure. Here's what we know:

He was born in Stratford-upon-Avon, England, in 1564 and died in 1616. He married when he was 18, his wife bore three children, and he lived apart from his family in London. Shakespeare left behind scant personal correspondence, but he gave the world 38 plays, 154 sonnets, and two narrative poems.

Thirty-six of the plays were published seven years after his death in what is now called the *First Folio*. He wrote romances, histories, comedies, tragedies, and "problem plays" (which can't really be characterized by any of the previous categories). The man was incredibly talented.

Or was he? Conspiracy theorists have alleged through the years that Shakespeare didn't write any of his plays and that they were really penned by, among others, Edward de Vere (also known as the Earl of Oxford), Sir Francis Bacon, Christopher Marlowe, or even Queen Elizabeth I. One prominent theory is that there are anagrams in the plays that, when decoded, reveal an author other than Shakespeare. Another is that Shakespeare was too uneducated to have written so wonderfully and that he was merely a front for a female or noble author. (It was considered uncouth in those days for such an esteemed person to write plays.)

So we ask: Did Shakespeare write his own material? The answer is yes . . . and no.

Upon arriving in London sometime around 1588, Shakespeare joined a theater company called Lord Chamberlain's Men, later renamed the King's Men. Shakespeare's plays were performed almost exclusively by this company. He was an actor, too, and appeared in his own and in other company members' plays. The creation of a play was (and still is) a collaborative effort. Copies of scripts were shared, commented upon, and edited. Once rehearsals began, scenes were deleted and changed. Even after a play premiered, it was subject to change.

Plays were the best entertainment available to the public in an era without video games, movies, and television, but a company couldn't survive without constantly updating its offerings. As a result, there was enormous pressure for new material. And the plays were not actually owned by the playwright in the way we use a copyright today—the company owned the play. Shakespeare made his living by being a member of the company, not by writing any individual piece (although he was listed as the company's house playwright).

The point is, a number of people in the company would have provided input on Shakespeare's plays. That, however, is about as far as the conspiracy goes. Almost all academics today reject the notion that Shakespeare didn't write his plays, but as with shooters on the grassy knoll and UFOs in New Mexico, rumors persist in the popular mind. It's a plot device worthy of, well, Shakespeare.

Who Wrote the First American Novel?

Steeped in controversy, the plot of the first American novel—with its themes of seduction, incest, and suicide—would be more readily accepted in today's culture than it was in late 18th-century America.

✳ ✳ ✳ ✳

WILLIAM HILL BROWN wrote *The Power of Sympathy*, the first American novel, in 1789. Printer Isaiah Thomas was contracted to publish a limited run of the book and to sell it through his two bookshops. In an ironic twist—given the historical significance the book later assumed—*The Power of Sympathy* was presented as the work of an anonymous author.

Even if the book had been properly credited at the outset, few readers outside of upper-crust Boston would have been familiar with the author. When *The Power of Sympathy* appeared, William Hill Brown was a reasonably prolific but little-known playwright; he later wrote a comic opera, poetry, essays, and two more novels.

The son of a respected clockmaker, Brown was born in Boston in November 1765. He attended the Boston Boy's School, where he pursued creative writing, a craft encouraged by his step-aunt. Brown spent his formative years in an upper-class Boston neighborhood, living across the street from a married, politically active lawyer named Perez Morton.

A Story Born in Scandal

In 1788, rumors of a romantic scandal involving Morton and his sister-in-law, Frances Apthorp, circulated among Boston's elite. The rumor turned out to be true, and rather than face public ridicule, the mortified Frances committed suicide. Perez, on the other hand, continued with his life as though nothing had happened. The public apparently went along with this tactic; Morton was later elected speaker of the lower house in the General Court of Massachusetts in 1806 and was named attorney general in 1810.

Writer (and former neighbor) William Brown was naturally well aware of the Morton-Apthorp scandal and published his book just a year later.

Following a novelistic style popular during the period, *The Power of Sympathy* unfolds via letters exchanged by central and secondary characters. The stinger is that the protagonists, Thomas Harrington and Harriot Fawcett, are about to unknowingly embark on an incestuous relationship.

In the novel, Harriot is Thomas's half-sister, born out of wedlock to a mistress of Thomas's father. For obvious reasons of propriety, the pregnancy and birth had been kept secret from the community and the rest of the family. When Harriot discovers the truth, she commits suicide. The facts soon become clear to Thomas as well, and he elects to follow his half-sister in suicide.

Credit Where Credit Is Due

Pressure from the Morton and Apthorp families, as well as from other prominent citizens, forced Brown to remove his book from circulation. Many copies were subsequently destroyed, and few exist today. In an odd twist, when the novel was reissued in the 19th century—nearly 100 years later—it was attributed to a deceased, once-popular Boston poet named Sarah Apthorp Morton, who happened to be the wife of Perez Morton—the man whose indiscretion helped inspire the novel in the first place! A correction issued by William Brown's aged niece not long after the book's republication led to proper attribution at last. Brown would finally be recognized as the author of the first novel written and published in America.

What Book Got Its Author Charged with Offending Morality and Religion?

The publication of Gustave Flaubert's Madame Bovary *offended national sensibility and caused Flaubert to be charged with offending morality and religion.*

✳   ✳   ✳   ✳

The Case

WHEN MADAME BOVARY was first published serially in the *Revue de Paris* in 1851, the *Revue's* editor, Leon Laurent-Pichat; the work's author, Gustave Flaubert; and the publisher, Auguste-Alexis Pillet, were charged with "offenses to public morality and religion" by the conservative Restoration Government of Napoleon III. Many, including Flaubert, believed that his work was being singled out because of the regime's distaste for the notoriously liberal *Revue*.

Prosecutor Ernest Pinard based his case upon the premise that adultery must always be condemned as an affront to the sanctity of marriage and society at large. In this, Pinard had a point. The novel conspicuously lacks any voice reminding the reader that adultery is reprehensible and simply tells the tale of Emma Bovary's gradual but inevitable acceptance of her need for sexual satisfaction outside the confines of a provincial marriage. Other works of the period, notably the popular plays of Alexandre Dumas, commonly featured adulterous characters. But in these, there was a voice of reason reminding the audience that the character's actions were wrong and worthy of punishment. That *Madame Bovary* lacked such perspective was certainly unprecedented and—according to the government—worthy of censure.

The Defense

Defense attorney Antoine Marie Jules Sénard (a close friend of Flaubert's and one of the people to whom the work was dedicated) argued that literature must always be considered art for art's sake and that Flaubert, in particular, was a consummate artist whose intentions had nothing to do with affecting society at large.

Whether or not Flaubert intended to undermine any aspect of French society is debatable. As the son of a wealthy family, he could afford to sit in his ivory tower and decry what he perceived as the petty hypocrisies of the emerging middle class. Certainly, Gustave Flaubert was a perfectionist who spent weeks reworking single pages of prose. In *Madame Bovary*, he sought to create a novel that was stylistically beautiful above all else. To test his craft, Flaubert would shout passages out loud to test their rhythm. It took the author five years of solitary toil to complete the work. The literary elite, notably Sainte-Beuve, Victor Hugo, and Charles-Pierre Baudelaire, immediately recognized the novel's genius, but the general public largely ignored the work when it was first published.

The Verdict

In the end, the judges agreed with Sénard and acquitted all of the accused but not before the sensational trial had sparked public interest in a work that might otherwise have gone unnoticed by the very society—the emerging middle class of France's provinces—the trial was meant to protect.

Who Were the Impressionists?

How did a group of painters come to be called "Impressionists"? Read on to find out.

✳ ✳ ✳ ✳

HEADS WILL NOD in synchronous unison when you comment on a painting's Impressionistic aspects. Impressionism began in France in the mid-1800s. A group of artists, including Claude Monet and Pierre-Auguste Renoir, joined together after their works were repeatedly rejected for exhibition at the prestigious Salon in Paris. The artists staged their own exhibition in 1874.

Impression: Sunrise, a painting of Monet's that was exhibited at the separate exhibition, garnered particular scorn from critics; they derided its "unfinished" appearance. The artists were gratified by this scorn because they felt that what they were doing was new, different, and exciting. They began to call themselves "Impressionists" (after the Monet painting) to show that they were going to continue to innovate rather than give in to the critics.

Instead of describing a scene precisely, Impressionists tended to focus on the sensation the scene conveyed. In short, Impressionists broke all the rules of the day. Some instructors of Impressionistic painting teach the acronym ELBOW:

✳ E: Everyday life—no contrived or ornate scenes

✳ L: Light—specifically, sunlight

✳ B: Brushstrokes—small and subtle, in primary colors

✳ O: Outdoor—Impressionists painted outside to capture L and W

✳ W: Weather and atmosphere—these elements create the overall *impression*, hence the name

The last living Impressionist was Claude Monet, who died on December 5, 1926, outliving Mary Cassatt by fewer than six months.

The following artists are also considered major Impressionists:

* Edouard Manet (1832–83)

* Berthe Morisot (1841–95)

* Alfred Sisley (1839–99)

* Camille Pissarro (1830–1903)

* Edgar Degas (1834–1917)

* Pierre-Auguste Renoir (1841–1919)

* Mary Cassatt (1844–1926)

* Claude Monet (1840–1926)

Where and What Was Tin Pan Alley?

A place that was once synonymous with songwriting is long gone, yet the popular music it produced will last forever.

✳   ✳   ✳   ✳

I F YOU'RE A student of classic popular music, you'll hear these in your head as soon as you read the titles: "In the Good Old Summertime," "Give My Regards to Broadway," "Shine on Harvest Moon," "By the Light of the Silvery Moon," "Let Me Call You Sweetheart." And try these: "Alexander's Ragtime Band," "Swanee," "Baby Face," "Ain't She Sweet," "Happy Days Are Here Again," "Take Me Out to the Ball Game," "God Bless America." These and many, many more hit songs of the late 19th and early 20th centuries sprang from the West 28th Street district in lower Manhattan between Fifth and Sixth avenues, which was once known as Tin Pan Alley.

Why *Tin Pan Alley?* Well, legend has it that newspaper writer Monroe Rosenfeld coined the name after hearing the dissonant sound of multiple composers simultaneously pounding pianos in music publishers' offices that were located practically on top of each other. Others attribute the name to Roy McCardell's May 1903 article in *The World*, titled "A Visit to Tin Pan Alley, Where the Popular Songs Come From."

Beauty and Business

Although the "tin pan" racket may have given some neighbors plenty of headaches, the music itself often provided a lot more pleasure, since it was created by such legends as Irving Berlin, Hoagy Carmichael, George M. Cohan, Scott Joplin, Jerome Kern, Cole Porter, and Fats Waller, as well as the songwriting teams of George and Ira Gershwin; Al Dubin and Harry Warren; Buddy DeSylva, Lew Brown, and Ray Henderson; Gus Kahn and Walter Donaldson; Bert Kalmar and Harry Ruby; and Arthur Freed and Nacio Herb Brown.

Until the latter part of the 19th century, major publishers of American music were scattered throughout the country, with particular concentrations in New York, Chicago, Boston, Philadelphia, St. Louis, Cincinnati, Baltimore, Cleveland, Detroit, and New Orleans. However, when a post-Civil War boom in the purchase of pianos resulted in a massive increase in demand for sheet music of songs to play on them, the industry began to assemble in the city that was already the main center for the performing arts: New York. There, at 51 West 28th Street, M. Witmark & Sons initially led the way by providing new music for free to established performers as a means of plugging its song catalog. Soon others followed suit, including the Robbins Music Corporation, the Remick Music Company, the E. B. Marks Music Company, and Shapiro, Bernstein & Company, as well as the firms headed by Irving Berlin and fellow composer Harry Von Tilzer.

Writing to Order

During these early years, composers and lyricists of proven ability usually signed exclusive contracts with a particular company and then wrote to order, producing songs to suit current trends. These were often created for Broadway and vaudeville—escapist entertainment required upbeat numbers with catchy melodies. The music publishers were happy to oblige, especially in the wake of Charles K. Harris's 1892 waltz song, "After the Ball," which sold more than two million copies of sheet music during that year alone. This was big business, and pop songs of both commercial and—in many cases—long-lasting appeal were churned out to satisfy the public's appetite for romantic ballads, novelty songs, and dance tunes, as well as ragtime, jazz, and blues.

By 1907, most of the major publishers had relocated from West 28th Street to the West 30s and beyond, yet the Tin Pan Alley moniker prevailed until sheet music sales declined in line with the ascent of radio and the record player during the early 1930s. Thereafter, the Tin Pan Alley style and business model became anachronisms, and the scene was long gone by the time rock 'n' roll rose to prominence a quarter-century later.

Who Was the King of Ragtime?

Scott Joplin was the most famous ragtime composer of all time. He became known as the King for compositions including "The Entertainer" written in 1902, although he may have gained his greatest fame and renown more than 50 years after his death as composer of the music in The Sting.

✳   ✳   ✳   ✳

DESPITE HIS ENDURING musical legacy, the details of much of Scott Joplin's early life remain imprecise. His birth date is often recorded as November 24, 1868, although it seems likely that it may have been as much as a year before that. He was born near Linden, where Jiles Joplin, his father and a former slave, worked as a laborer. It appears as though Mr. Joplin boasted at least a rudimentary knowledge of music that he delighted in passing on to his son.

By the time that he was seven years old, Scott Joplin was already an experienced banjo player, and when his family moved to the Texas/Arkansas border town of Texarkana, he was introduced to the instrument that would make him famous. His mother, Florence, did domestic work for a neighboring attorney, who allowed young Scott to experiment on his piano.

The Father of Ragtime

The elder Joplin saved enough money to buy his son a used piano, and Scott's talent quickly blossomed. At age 11, Joplin began taking free lessons from Julius Weiss, a German-born piano teacher who helped shape Joplin's musical influences, including European opera. As a teen, Joplin formed a vocal quartet and performed in the dance halls of Texarkana before venturing out as a pianist on the saloon and honky-tonk circuit that stretched from Texas to Louisiana, Missouri, Illinois, and Kentucky.

In St. Louis, Joplin encountered a style of music that featured abbreviated melody lines called "ragged time," or "ragtime" for short. Joplin adopted the principles of ragtime into longer musical forms including a ballet—*The Ragtime Dance*, written in 1899—and two operas—*The Guest of Honor* in 1903 and *Treemonisha* in 1910. While the orchestration scores for both operas were sadly lost during the copyright process, a piano-vocal score for *Treemonisha* was later published. It was, however, Joplin's shorter compositions that earned him the title "The King of Ragtime."

From the Maple Leaf to New York

One of his first compositions to be published, "Maple Leaf Rag" in 1899, went on to sell more than one million copies of sheet music. The piece was named after one of the music clubs

Joplin enjoyed playing in Sedalia, Missouri—the Maple Leaf Club. Joplin occasionally returned to Texarkana to perform, but by 1907 he was living in New York City. It was here that he wrote his instructional manual, *The School of Ragtime*. In 1916, Joplin's health deteriorated in part due to syphilis, which he'd contracted a few years before. His playing became inconsistent, and he was eventually forced to enter the Manhattan State Hospital, where he died on April 1, 1917. Joplin was married and divorced twice. His only child, a daughter, died in infancy.

Legacy

It wasn't until years after his death that Scott Joplin achieved the full recognition his work deserved. In 1971, the New York Public Library published his collected works, but his music found a whole new audience with the release of the popular 1973 Paul Newman and Robert Redford movie, *The Sting*. Joplin's work, adapted by Marvin Hamlisch, was featured heavily in the film's score, which won an Academy Award. "The Entertainer," released as a single from the movie, became a bona fide top ten hit.

Joplin himself was posthumously awarded a Pulitzer Prize in 1976 for *Treemonisha*, which has been recognized as the first grand opera by an African American composer. Today, a large mural on Texarkana's Main Street depicts the life and accomplishments of one of the town's most famous sons.

What Ballet Premiere Caused Riots?

Ah, the ballet. The grace. The beauty. The fistfights?

✳   ✳   ✳   ✳

WHEN IGOR STRAVINSKY'S *Rite of Spring* premiered at the Théâtre des Champs-Élysées in Paris on May 29, 1913, spectators—so displeased with the discordant nature of the music, the experimental choreography, and the nontraditional costume of the cast—exploded into a full-blown riot.

Although Stravinsky was well-known for his diverse styling, the pre-Modernist audience apparently didn't have any hint of what was to come. Classical ballet, which most people were accustomed to, is tulle and temperance, not sexuality, barbarism, and bassoon. From the start, the audience in attendance at *Rite of Spring* was turned off by the innovations of all the major components: music, dance, story, and costume. The catcalls that erupted moments after the ballet began were a testament to their hatred of the whole darned thing!

What Part Did They Like?

The music, composed by Stravinsky, was riddled with a cacophony of new sounds and rhythms. Where typical scores felt light and even springlike themselves, the music in *Rite of Spring* was bumpy, angular, and full of haphazard staccatos.

Reflecting the music, the dance moves, choreographed by Vaslav Nijinsky, featured jerky twists and pelvic thrusts more indicative of Elvis than of a graceful ballet. The dancers' arms and legs flailed wildly in angles depicting the primitive movements of fertility rites in pagan Russia. Struck by the incongruity between this performance and the ballet they thought they knew, the audience hissed with such furor that the performers couldn't hear one another.

The story of *Rite of Spring* includes, in addition to the dance of fertility, an abduction, a virgin sacrifice, and paganism. A tad bit racier than *Swan Lake* and, apparently, an overload to the genteel sensibilities of the audience.

In the spirit of the story, the costumes reflected the tribal culture in which it was set. Thus, the dancers were adorned in heavy woolen smocks, decorated with geometrics, which created a furnacelike effect for the mocked and—now sweating—performers. Their elaborately painted faces peering out at the audience topped off the atrocity of the sacrificial ritual to the god of spring uncomfortably unfolding before them.

Intermission at Last

Even with the intermission intervention of the Paris police, the spectators were still so overloaded by the ballet's brashness that their rioting carried on through the entire performance.

Stravinsky hid backstage embarrassed, perplexed, and angered by the reception. In later reflection, Stravinsky would blame the premiere's failure, in part, on Nijinsky's mistranslation of the music, suggesting he was a fine dancer but had been overwhelmed by the choreographic task he'd been handed.

Over the Years

Rite of Spring ran through its scheduled performances without further uproar. The Nijinsky choreography has since been lost, but similar angular dance moves have replaced them in the continued versions performed as a mainstay by troupes worldwide. In addition, the music was used in the Disney classic *Fantasia* to enhance the depiction of the cosmos creation, a true homage to Stravinsky's intent for the music to portray life in its most primitive form.

Stravinsky never attempted such audience-accosting innovation again, continuing his career without evidence of such bizarre scandal. Though Stravinsky might have given up his visionary take on the future of music, his *Rite of Spring* score had already done its magic. Musicologists consider it one of the great masterpieces of the 20th century. Stravinsky successfully achieved his goal of a harmonious juxtaposition of rhythm, pitch, and—somehow—dissonance.

What Is Art Deco?

The Art Deco style perfectly captured the excitement and energy of a new century.

✳   ✳   ✳   ✳

T HE PERIOD BETWEEN the two world wars was one of dramatic social, political, and technological change throughout the Western world. The old empires and aristocracies of the preceding five centuries had all but fallen away, replaced by democratic governments and a much looser, more egalitarian social order. The chasm between rich and poor narrowed dramatically, as the middle class grew and as entry to the wealthiest upper circles became easier through success in business and industry. New inventions allowed more leisure time for everyone; population centers shifted rapidly from rural areas to fast-paced urban settings; and prudish Victorian notions of morality were replaced by the fast and easy lifestyle of the Jazz Age. It was almost as if the entire world had been completely reinvented in a radical and exciting new way.

A Breath of Fresh Air

Inspired by this dizzying, liberating change, artists and designers attempted to reflect and represent their new, distinctly modern world while retaining what they found of value from the past. They embraced sleek, clean designs that combined geometric patterns and machine-tooled lines with traditional motifs, such as the female form and floral patterns. Artists combined natural materials such as jade, ivory, and chrome with new materials such as plastic, ferroconcrete, and vita glass. They merged elements of cutting-edge art movements such as Cubism and Bauhaus with traditional Greek, Roman, Egyptian, and Native American styles. And they applied their creation to all areas of this new modern world: buildings, fashion, posters, advertising, appliances, and furniture. The result was a sleek, elegant, sophisticated, and luxurious style now known as Art Deco.

Exposition Internationale des Arts Décoratifs

The trend toward this modern new world—and the graphic style that so perfectly represented it—developed gradually in the first two decades of the 20th century. Art Deco saw its formal debut in 1925 at an exhibit held in Paris called the *Exposition Internationale des Arts Décoratifs et Industriels Moderne*. Designers and crafters from 23 countries displayed a breathtaking array of artifacts that together captured all that was innovative and exciting about the 20th century. At the time, the movement was generally referred to as *style moderne*; it wasn't until decades later that the term "Art Deco"—derived from the name of the Paris exhibition—came into use.

The Movement Hits the States

Though the United States did not participate in the 1925 show, the country quickly became an influential force in the Art Deco movement. The style swept across America and figured prominently in Hollywood movies. Studios were quick to see that Art Deco offered an ideal visual shorthand for conveying sophistication, wealth, and elegance. Through the efforts of costumers, set designers, and prop masters, the movement soon became a familiar backdrop against which Greta Garbo, Bette Davis, William Powell, and Fred Astaire played out the fantasies of the nation on the silver screen. Even the grand movie palaces built in the 1920s and '30s fully embraced the style, and the few that remain today offer excellent examples of the movement's influence on interior design. While Hollywood stars did little to define and shape the Art Deco style, they likely did more than anyone to popularize it, not only in the United States but also in Europe, where American films were screened regularly.

Art Deco has had a lasting influence on architecture. Most major urban areas in the United States and Europe still have buildings constructed in this style, though the most famous and representative examples can be found in these New York City landmarks: the Chrysler Building, the Empire State Building, Rockefeller Center, and the interior of Radio City Music Hall.

What Classic American Film Starred Refugees from Hitler's Europe?

European cinematic talents found a new home in California and made one of the best films in movie history.

✳ ✳ ✳ ✳

FANS OF CLASSIC American cinema might be surprised to learn that many of their favorite films from the 1930s and '40s benefited from a wave of emigration sparked by the rise of Nazis in Europe. Such leading lights from the period, including Peter Lorre, Marlene Dietrich, Billy Wilder, Jean Renoir, Otto Preminger, and Fritz Lang, had come to Hollywood not only to ply their craft but also to escape Nazi Europe. Many, such as Max Reinhardt, Erich von Stroheim, and Ernst Lubitsch, had been lured to California in the 1920s by the wealth and technical sophistication of the Hollywood system. After the rise of the Nazis, however, some of those who had previously been employed by the European cinematic industry sought safety as well as employment in Hollywood.

Searching for a Safe Haven

The 1938 Anschluss, in which Germany annexed Austria, convinced many Europeans that Nazism would not be averted. Then in March 1938, 70,000 Austrians, including many prominent members of Vienna's cinematic community, were arrested and questioned closely about their racial heritage. Following the 1938 Kristallnacht, or "Night of Broken Glass," in which Nazis destroyed Jewish property and sent as many as 30,000 to prison camps, the fervor to find a safe haven abroad increased. Sadly, the world had not yet recognized the true threat of Nazi Germany, and no country, including the United States, was ready to welcome the flood of Jewish emigrants. Hollywood was no different, and most members of Tinsel Town's artistic community saw the refugees as unwelcome competition.

Proving that money trumped morality, nearly all of the Hollywood studios continued dealings with the Fascist regime until the start of the war. In many cases, studios altered films that might offend the Nazis rather than risk losing the valuable German and Austrian markets. The one exception, Warner Brothers, was headed by the firmly anti-Nazi brothers Harry and Jack Warner, whose family had left Germany at the turn of the century. In 1939, the studio released the highly controversial film *Confessions of a Nazi Spy*, which starred Edward G. Robinson and was allegedly based on accounts by former FBI agent Leon G. Turrou, who had investigated Nazi spies in the United States before the war. As a result, studio head Jack Warner, producer Robert Lord, and many members of the cast and crew received death threats from Fascist organizations operating in the United States.

A Cinematic Classic Is Born

Although scores of intellectuals and artists who fled Nazi Europe abandoned their artistic talents during their exile in the United States, others prospered and through their efforts changed the course of American cinema. Nowhere is this more apparent than in the enduring Warner Brothers classic film, *Casablanca* (1942). Though much of the film's storyline and setting are complete fantasy (for example, there weren't any Nazis in Casablanca during World War II), the romanticized story of Europeans seeking refuge in the United States featured a cast and crew largely comprised of refugees from Hitler's Europe. In fact, 11 of the 14 names that appear in the film's opening credits are European.

The film's director, Michael Curtiz, had left his native Hungary before the rise of Hitler, and his sensibilities were still deeply rooted in the Viennese cinema where he first made his mark. Technical advisor Robert Aisner had fled France using the same route outlined in the film's opening narration. A few of the film's stars—Conrad Veidt, Peter Lorre, and Paul Henreid—as well as many of the bit players had also fled the Nazis. Veidt, who played the villainous Nazi Major Strasser, was a German refugee who had already garnered critical attention by playing menacing Nazis in other films. Indeed, the vehemently anti-Nazi Veidt reportedly agreed to play Nazi characters only if they were thoroughly detestable. The Hungarian Lorre, who played the short-lived Ugarte in the film, was a refugee from Austria and had starred in fellow refugee Fritz Lang's *M*, which had been filmed while both were still in Germany. Lorre moved to Hollywood after narrowly escaping occupied France. In Hollywood, he and Humphrey Bogart became close friends and worked on *The Maltese Falcon* before being cast together in *Casablanca*. Austrian-born Paul Henreid, who played the French resistance leader Victor Laszlo, was a real-life refugee from the Nazis and was extremely critical of the film's numerous plot flaws (for example, why would a man who wanted to remain unnoticed strut around in an all-white suit?) and equally disapproving of Humphrey Bogart's acting abilities.

Other refugees from Hitler's Europe who acted in *Casablanca* include Curtis Bois, who played a pickpocket; Marcel Dalio, cast as a croupier; Helmut Dantine, who played a desperate husband trying to win enough money to purchase freedom for himself and his refugee wife; and S. Z. "Cuddles" Sakall, who played the lovably loose-jowled headwaiter, Carl. The contributions of these actors and numerous extras, technicians, and crew of European extraction lent *Casablanca* a credibility that has made it one of the most beloved films in movie history.

Did Elvis Really Invent Rock and Roll?

We appreciate the skepticism implied by the "really" in this question. Can any single person have invented rock? And even if so, would Elvis Presley be that person? Gallons of intellectual blood have been spilled on this question, and we're going to spill a few more right here.

✳   ✳   ✳   ✳

ELVIS DID INVENT rock and roll... sort of... maybe... in a way. If you define rock as a peculiarly American form of pop music that combines blues and country structures and riffs with aggressive—even distorted—guitars and edgy topics like love, lust, cars, and parties, then he definitely did not. Lots of folks were playing that tune several years before Elvis—a fact that Elvis himself happily acknowledged.

Queue up Jackie Brenston's "Rocket 88," and you'll see what we mean. Lots of folks consider that 1951 tune—written by Ike Turner—the birth of rock. Or you can go back to 1948 and Arthur Smith's "Guitar Boogie"—the first national hit to feature an electric guitar—as a watershed. Or it could have been Fats Domino's 1949 tune "The Fat Man," which historian Piero Scaruffi refers to as "certainly... a new kind of boogie." All of these songs have an indisputable rockin' quality that seems to differ from previous rhythm-and-blues or "race" music (so-called because of its black practitioners). They are fast, aggressive, rockin'—and Elvis was barely 13 when the first of them came out.

But if you do not define rock in purely musical terms—if you define it as a cultural phenomenon that was an amalgam of black and white influence and interest—then you can call Elvis the inventor. Better yet, let's call him "the right talent at the right time."

Certain critics excoriate Elvis and his handlers for this. Starting with his 1954 version of Arthur Crudup's "That's All Right Mama," historians have hammered Elvis for doing what popular musicians have done since the beginning of time: borrow from each other in an effort to be, well, popular. Scaruffi calls Elvis "the ultimate white robber of black hits," as if something as freewheeling as American roots music should respect vague, unwritten, idealistic, and narrow-minded notions of intellectual property.

Elvis himself never claimed to have invented rock, as historians have pointed out, and his cover of the Crudup tune was all in a day's work. In fact, Elvis was a devoted student of black gospel and R&B from childhood, and he combined his deep knowledge of those styles with his own spectacular (admit it!) talent to create a tune that's fantastic, no matter what your politics.

If you want to pinpoint when black and white first came together in a way that truly rocked—and defined the multicultural element of rock—then Elvis is your man, and "Mama" is your tune.

Who Put Pop Art on the Map?

The tomato soup cans. The portrait of Marilyn Monroe. That banana. There are some images in popular culture that are so ubiquitous, it's easy to forget who created them in the first place.

✳ ✳ ✳ ✳

Andy warhol is the guy behind some of the most recognizable art of the latter half of the 20th century. In fact, his pop art helped shape pop(ular) culture in general. Read on to discover more about the life and times (and art) of Andy Warhol.

Mama Warhola

Warhol (born Andrew Warhola in 1928) had a close relationship with his mother, who immigrated to the United States from Slovakia. She lived with him in New York City from 1952 to 1971. She sometimes created art with her son, credited as simply "Andy Warhol's Mother."

Warhol's Big Break

After attending college at Carnegie Mellon University in Pennsylvania, Warhol got work as an illustrator in New York City at magazines such as *Glamour*. Throughout the 1950s, he made a name for himself as one of the most sought-after illustrators in the industry. Warhol's extensive client list included *The New York Times*, *Harper's Bazaar*, Tiffany & Co., Fleming-Joffe leather company, Bonwit Teller department store, Columbia Records, *Vogue*, and NBC.

Those Soup Cans

Beginning in the 1960s, Warhol dedicated more time to art. He painted a series of pictures based on comics and advertisements, including the now-iconic Campbell's Tomato Soup can in 1962. The paintings were an instant megahit, and Warhol's career as a pop art icon was launched.

Short Films, Long Films

Warhol wasn't just a painter—he was a publisher, writer, music producer, and film director, as well. As an auteur, Warhol created more than 600 films, many of them just under five minutes. His longest work was a 25-hour-long piece called *Four Stars*, made in 1967–68.

The Fabulous Factory

By 1964, Warhol had his "Factory" in the city, a warehouse space entirely decked out in silver. Parties for the glitterati were thrown at the Factory, where the art world at large, cross-dressers, and folks on the fringe of society were eager to attend. When it wasn't packed with guests, Warhol used it for studio space.

In 1966, Andy also opened the Gymnasium, a nightclub in New York that featured exercise equipment on the dance floor.

Avant-Garde

Warhol was the first artist to exhibit video footage as art, essentially creating the "multi-media" medium in 1965. Warhol also regularly taped conversations with others or dictated his ideas into a tape recorder. There are approximately 3,400 of these audiotapes.

Plastic and Velvet

For a time, Warhol tried his hand at performance art. He had a multi-media show called "The Exploding Plastic Inevitable." Featured on the bill was the prefame (but now iconic) rock band The Velvet Underground.

I Shot Andy Warhol

In June of 1968, Valerie Solanas, a writer who had appeared in one of Andy's films, shot Warhol in the chest while in his studio. After a five-hour operation, the artist recovered. A movie about the event, called I Shot Andy Warhol, was released in 1996.

Most Famous Quote

Even if people don't know his body of artwork that well, they've probably heard Warhol's most famous line: "In the future, everybody will be world famous for fifteen minutes." It's now common to hear the phrase, "15 minutes of fame."

Who Was Basquiat?

Neo-expressionist artist Jean-Michel Basquiat first achieved fame in the late 1970s as part of the informal graffiti duo SAMO. His paintings were being exhibited in galleries and museums internationally by the 1980s.

* * * *

Early Life

JEAN-MICHEL BASQUIAT WAS born in Brooklyn in 1960 to a Haitian father and Puerto Rican mother. At the age of six he became a junior member of the Brooklyn Museum. Basquiat attended an arts-oriented private school during his pre-teen years and an alternative high school, ultimately dropping out and leaving home at age 17.

SAMO

To survive, Basquiat lived with friends and made money selling t-shirts and postcards with his drawings on them. Basquiat had begun to gain notoriety as a graffiti artist and tagger. Along with his friend Al Diaz, Basquiat created a tag, "SAMO," pronounced same-oh. They combined the SAMO calling card with poetic/cryptic phrases and social commentary spray-painted all over lower Manhattan. Basquiat and Diaz's SAMO tag was omnipresent and led to them selling the story of SAMO to the *Village Voice* in 1978 for $100. By 1980, the friends had a falling out and SAMO was retired with tags declaring "SAMO is dead."

Solo Career

Next would come Basquiat's solo career. Early on he created art using discarded doors and windows as his canvas. He made his public debut in a multi-artist exhibition called The Times Square Show. The positive media from that show led to Basquiat landing his first solo show, which sold out. In 1982, Basquiat had a prolific year, painting and living in Modena, Italy, and Los Angeles.

Heads and skulls were recurring images in many of Basquiat's paintings. He also used a crown motif in much of his work. The crowns were a way of honoring African American heroes as kings and saints. Basquiat depicted athletes, writers, musicians, and even himself wearing crowns. Basquiat also used his art as a platform to comment on race relations, social injustice, slavery, and colonialism.

Between 1983 and 1985, Basquiat collaborated with pop artist Andy Warhol, producing works that were generally not well received by art critics.

Warhol's death in 1987 was cited as a contributing factor in Basquiat's downward spiral and untimely death at age 27. Basquiat had turned to Warhol when struggling with drug abuse and Warhol had been able to rein him in. But on August 12, 1988, Jean-Michel Basquiat overdosed on heroin, joining the infamous 27 club.

In 2017, one of Basquiat's 1982 paintings of a skull, *Untitled*, sold for a record-breaking $110.5 million—the highest amount ever paid at auction for a work by an American artist.

What Is EGOT?

EGOT is an acronym used to describe the accomplishment of winning all four of the major American entertainment awards— the Emmy, Grammy, Oscar, and Tony Award. The awards honor performances in television, music, film, and theater, respectively.

❋ ❋ ❋ ❋

THE ORIGIN OF the term is a bit surprising. EGOT was coined in 1984 by actor Phillip Michael Thomas, best known for his role as Tubbs on the 1980s TV series *Miami Vice*. He told the Associated Press that he aspired to win all four awards within five years. Unfortunately, Mr. Thomas has never won, nor been nominated for, any of the EGOT awards.

To date, only 15 performers have achieved an EGOT, and of that number, two of them carry a bit of controversy. Whoopi Goldberg and Robert Lopez's Emmys were won as Daytime rather than Primetime Emmys, which carry less prestige.

Below is a list of performers that have an EGOT, along with the year they achieved it:

1. Richard Rogers, composer (1962)

2. Helen Hayes, actress (1977)

3. Rita Moreno, actress (1977)

4. John Gielgud, actor (1991)

5. Audrey Hepburn, actress (1994) *posthumously

6. Marvin Hamlisch, composer (1995)

7. Jonathan Tunick, music director and composer (1997)

8. Mel Brooks, performer, writer, and director (2001)

9. Mike Nichols, performer, director, and producer (2001)

10. Whoopi Goldberg, performer and producer (2002)

11. Scott Rudin, producer (2012)

12. Robert Lopez, composer (2014)

13. John Legend, songwriter and producer (2018)

14. Andrew Lloyd Webber, composer and producer (2018)

15. Tim Rice, lyricist and producer (2018)

There are currently more than 40 living people who are only one award away from achieving an EGOT. A few of the performers seen as having the best odds are Cyndi Lauper, Helen Mirren, Kate Winslet, and Lin-Manuel Miranda.

Chapter 14

Food and Drink

Do Poppy Seeds Cause Positive Drug Tests?

The next time you enjoy a slice of poppy-seed cake with ice cream, you can say, "This will go straight to my hips . . . and perhaps straight from my urine to a positive drug test in a lab."

✳ ✳ ✳ ✳

DEPENDING ON WHEN you take the test, simply eating one poppy-seed bagel can lead to a positive result. Such a finding is often referred to as a "false positive." This term, however, is false in itself: The test comes back "positive" because you do have morphine in your system. But the reason you test positive is what your employer or parole officer cares about: Were you chasing the dragon or chasing the complete breakfast?

Poppy seeds contain morphine, but after being gobbled up, they don't have any drug-related effect on the body. However, the morphine is detectable in your urine, and there's no way to tell from a basic urine test whether the morphine came from heroin or a muffin.

To address this curious problem, the legal threshold for a positive drug-test result was raised in 1998. The Mandatory Guidelines for Federal Workplace Drug Testing Programs adjusted the point at which a test is considered "positive" from 300 nanograms per milliliter to 2,000 nanograms per milliliter. This revised threshold does miss a few drug abusers, but it filters out most of the positive results that are caused by the munchies. Additionally, hair testing can help to clarify which type of morphine is detected.

What's the Difference Between Brandy and Cognac?

Cognac is to brandy what champagne is to sparkling wine. Does that help? If not, try this: More than anything, the distinction between cognac and brandy is geographical.

* * * *

COGNAC IS A type of brandy that is made exclusively from the grapes that grow in a specific region of France. Connoisseurs say that cognac is perhaps the finest of all brandies. The clerk at the corner liquor store, meanwhile, is more concerned about the fact that it's the most expensive brandy you can buy; it's behind the counter, so please ask nicely.

Brandy is no more nor less than distilled, fermented fruit juice. Anything that's simply called "brandy" is made from fermented grapes, like wine. When brandy is made from other fruits, it's indicated in the name. An example is apple brandy, which is produced from cider.

As one of the earliest forms of distilled wine, brandy has a distinguished place in the history of spirits. Distilled wine was the original hard liquor, and it was popularized by the court physicians of Renaissance-era Europe (who thought it had medicinal properties). They got the idea of distillation—which purifies the drink and increases its alcohol content—from Arab alchemists.

The word "brandy" itself derives from the Dutch *brandewijn* ("burnt wine"). It has been widely enjoyed for more than 500 years, and it really was carried around by Saint Bernard dogs in tiny kegs in the Swiss Alps. But you don't need to be snow-bound to enjoy its warming properties.

Did the Egyptians Brew Beer?

The ancient Egyptians most definitely brewed and drank beer. It was actually a source of nutrition, motivation, and sometimes a form of payment for work.

✳   ✳   ✳   ✳

ALTHOUGH THE EGYPTIANS are not credited with inventing beer (that claim goes to the Sumerians of present-day Iran), the Egyptians did perfect the brewing process. Egyptian beer improved on the Sumerian brews by creating a smoother, lighter drink that has more in common with modern-day brews than the Mesopotamian. According to legend, the god Osiris taught Egyptians the art of brewing.

Ancient Egyptian beer used a simpler method than exists today. Egyptian brews started in a bakery with cooked loaves of bread. The cooked loaves of bread were mixed with water and then placed in heated ceramic jars to ferment. These beers notably lacked hops. On occasion, dates, honey, or herbs may have been added to the brews to add sweetness and increase flavor.

In ancient Egypt, beer was traditionally brewed by women and provided a means for them to earn money. Beer was consumed by both adults and children as a source of nutrition, as well as an intoxicant. There were five different kinds of beer in ancient Egypt. The average brew carried an alcohol content of three to four percent, while stronger brews were served at religious festivals and celebrations.

Beer was also essential to laborers. The workers that built the pyramids of Giza were provided with a daily ration of beer as payment. Records indicate that these workers received four to five liters of beer a day.

Another area in which beer was used was medicine. It was used to treat stomach ailments, coughs, and constipation. Over 100 medicinal recipes from ancient Egypt call for beer as an ingredient. Even when beer was not included in the ingredients, it was suggested that a patient take the prescription with a cup of beer which was thought to "gladden the heart."

What Is Head Cheese?

The name of this delicacy is deceptive, because head cheese has absolutely nothing in common with your favorite mozzarella or cheddar. Head cheese isn't a dairy product at all—it's a jellied loaf of sausage. If you want to get fancy, you can even call it a terrine.

✳   ✳   ✳   ✳

A S FOR THE head part, that's right on. Head cheese is made with meaty bits from the head of a calf or pig, or sometimes even a sheep or cow. That's the traditional recipe, anyway; today's head cheese might include other edible animal parts, including feet, tongues, and hearts.

Getting back to that head, it's usually split or quartered and simmered in a large stockpot until the meat becomes tender and falls off the bone. Any meat remaining on the skull is picked off, and then it's all chopped up.

At this point, seasonings are added. Ingredients vary by culture, region, or even butcher. In Denmark, head cheese (*sylte*) is spiced with thyme, allspice, and bay leaves. In southern Louisiana, where it's also known as "souse," head cheese is traditionally flavored with vinegar and hot sauce.

What really makes head cheese come together is the cooking liquid in the stockpot. As the calf or pig or sheep head simmers, the collagen from the skull cartilage and marrow leeches into the broth. This collagen-infused stock is added to the chopped, seasoned meat, and the whole mixture is poured into a pan or mold. From there, the head cheese is cooled in the refrigerator, and *voilà*—the collagen causes the mixture to set and solidify into a gelatin.

At this point, the head cheese is ready to be removed from the mold. Usually served at room temperature, it can be thinly sliced and eaten with crackers, or cubed like cheese for a tasty appetizer. Look for it ready-made at your neighborhood deli or market—and be sure to serve it to your most deserving guests.

Why Does Swiss Cheese Have Holes?

Rumors continue to run rampant about this age-old question.

✳ ✳ ✳ ✳

SOME SAY MANUFACTURERS allow mice to nibble on Swiss before packaging the cheese. Others insist crafty deli owners cut the holes by hand with their carving knives. However, both of these conspiracy theories have more holes than, well, Swiss cheese.

Truth be told—and it's a bit embarrassing—Swiss cheese has holes because it has bad gas. Those holes in your sweet, nutty Swiss are actually popped bubbles of carbon dioxide gas.

Where do these gassy bubbles come from? Well, all cheese begins with a combination of milk and starter bacteria. The type of bacteria used helps determine the flavor, aroma, and texture of the finished cheese product. In the case of Swiss, cheese-makers use a special strain of bacteria called *Propionibacter shermani*. During the curing process, when the cheese ripens, this *P. shermani* eats away at the lactic acid in the cheese curd, tooting carbon dioxide gas all the while.

Swiss cheese is a densely packed variety with a thick, heavy rind, so this built-up gas has nowhere to go. Trapped inside, the gas forms into bubbles. These bubbles eventually pop, leaving behind the characteristic holey air pockets.

In formal cheese lingo, these holes are referred to as "eyes." And the art of cheese making is such that their sizes can be controlled. By adjusting acidity, temperature, and curing time, dairies can create a mild baby Lorraine Swiss with lacy-looking pinholes or a more assertive Emmentaler Swiss with eyes the size of walnuts.

Oddly, in the United States, the size of Swiss cheese holes is subject to United States Department of Agriculture regulation. Every wheel of Grade A Swiss that is sold in America must have holes with diameters that are between three-eighths and thirteen-sixteenths of an inch.

All of this goes to show that sometimes, it's best not to over-think your cheese. Just slap it on a cracker, pour a glass of wine, and enjoy.

Is There a Killer Sushi?

If you're planning to have a dignitary from Japan over for dinner, there's one delicacy from his homeland you may want to avoid preparing: pufferfish.

✳   ✳   ✳   ✳

THE PUFFERFISH, ALSO known as blowfish or fugu, is a homely creature that, when threatened, inflates itself and displays protective spikes that are filled with tetrodotoxin, a neurotoxin that is about 1,200 times more deadly than cyanide. The average pufferfish has enough of it in its three-foot-long body to kill 30 people.

Believe it or not, pufferfish is served raw as sushi, after the tetrodotoxin has been removed. This is, however, an inexact science; about 100 people die every year in Japan from puffer-fish that have been improperly prepared. The initial symptom of pufferfish poisoning is paralysis of the lips and face, which can appear from ten minutes to several hours after ingestion. The cause of death is respiratory paralysis. There is no known antidote to tetrodotoxin, but the treatment of symptoms includes aggressive measures to keep the airways open.

Sushi chefs who want to work with pufferfish go through an intensive program of study at the Harmonious Fugu Association in Tokyo. They're taught how to prepare the creature for consumption, including how to cut and separate the toxic parts from the edible ones. Last, but certainly not least, they're taught first aid.

Why would someone eat pufferfish? Well, it's akin to mountain climbing, bungee jumping, or skydiving—the thrill of trying to cheat death. When a person at a sushi bar orders pufferfish, it is traditional to offer many toasts to his or her health. This person, this gastronomic renegade, becomes the center of attention.

While the pufferfish is an extreme example, sushi in general is a relatively high-risk food. Raw fish is full of bacteria, and mercury levels—particularly in tuna—have become an issue. The traditional accompaniments to sushi are meant to help. Vinegar is added to the rice to heighten the pH level and potentially kill bacteria; wasabi and pink pickled ginger also have bacteria-killing properties.

Nevertheless, you might want to consider introducing that Japanese dignitary to a dish called pizza.

What Is Sake?

Most Americans consider sake a Japanese rice wine, but it is actually more akin to beer. Furthermore, a look back in time suggests that sake may have originated in China, not Japan.

✳   ✳   ✳   ✳

What Is Sake?

THE JAPANESE WORD for sake, *nihonshu*, literally means "Japanese alcoholic beverage" and does not necessarily refer to the specific rice-based beverage that foreigners exclusively call sake. What differentiates sake from other alcoholic beverages is its unique fermentation process. Although all wines are the result of a single-step fermentation of plant juices, sake requires a multiple-step fermentation process, as does beer. The requisite ingredients are rice, water, yeast, and an additional substance that will convert the starch in the rice to sugar. People have always found ways to make alcohol with whatever ingredients are available, so it is likely that beverages similar to sake emerged soon after rice cultivation began. The most popular theory holds that the brewing of rice into alcohol began around 4000 B.C. along the Yangtze River in China, and the process was later exported to Japan.

The Many Ways to Ferment Rice

The sake of yore was different from the sake that's popular today. At one time it was fermented with human saliva, which reliably converts starch to sugar. Early sake devotees chewed a combination of rice, chestnuts, millet, and acorns, then spit the mixture into a container to ferment. This "chew and spit" approach to alcohol production has been seen the world over in tribal societies. Subsequent discoveries and technological developments allowed for more innovative approaches to fermentation. Sometime in the early centuries A.D., a type of mold called *koji-kin* was discovered to be efficient in fermenting rice. In the 1300s, mass sake production began in Japan, and it soon became the most popular national beverage.

How Do They Salt Peanuts in the Shell?

No, bioengineers haven't created a super breed of naturally salty peanut plants (yet). The method isn't nearly that complicated.

* * * *

To salt peanuts while they're still in the shell, food manufacturers soak them in brine (salty water). In one typical approach, the first step is to treat the peanuts with a wetting agent—a chemical compound that reduces surface tension in water, making it penetrate the shell more readily. Next, the peanuts are placed into an enclosed metal basket and immersed in an airtight pressure vessel that is filled with brine. The pressure vessel is then depressurized to drive air out of the peanut shells and suck in saltwater.

Peanuts may go through several rounds of pressurization and depressurization. Once the peanuts are suitably salty, they are rinsed with clean water and spun on a centrifuge in order to get rid of the bulk of the water. Finally, they are popped into an oven so that the drying process can be completed.

Now, if they could just figure out how to cram some chocolate into those peanuts.

What's the Shelf Life of a Twinkie?

Can Twinkies really stay fresh for 50 years or more? If you were around during the Cold War, when a nuclear attack from the Soviet Union seemed possible, you might believe they do.

* * * *

At the height of the Cold War in the 1950s and 1960s, Twinkies were staples of the survival foods people stocked in household bomb shelters. This helped spawn the notion that the spongy snacks could withstand not only a nuclear holocaust, but also the ravages of time.

Truth is, a Twinkie's shelf life is about 25 days. If even that seems like a lot of stay-fresh time for a baked product, consider that Twinkies are a processed, packaged food and contain no dairy ingredients that can go bad in a hurry. Like many other commercially baked goods, they're tweaked with preservatives and stabilizing trans fats.

Check the label and you'll find such ingredients as vegetable and/or animal shortening and partially hydrogenated soybean, cottonseed, or canola oil. These artificially produced fats are more solid than clear liquid oils and, thus, are less likely to spoil. They help Twinkies stay soft and tasty, though not for years or decades.

The Cold War is history, but Twinkies are still plenty popular.

Is Chinese Food from China?

What we're getting at here is whether the modern idea of Chinese takeout is less East and more West. In that context, Chinese food is definitely a product of the United States.

❊   ❊   ❊   ❊

I N NEARLY EVERY case, so-called "American Chinese" foods were inspired by counterparts from China. Not surprisingly, the American versions of Chinese foods are more meat-based and less dependent on vegetables than dishes that originate in the Far East. General Tso's chicken, sesame chicken, Chinese chicken salad, chop suey, chow mein, crab rangoon, fried rice, and Mongolian beef are among the many items at Chinese restaurants that are essentially American derivatives of staples from the motherland.

The origin of nearly every menu item at a typical American Chinese establishment is hotly contested. However, perhaps the most popular staple of these restaurants, the fortune cookie, is indisputably American—or more specifically, was created by a Chinese immigrant in the United States.

As with any great invention, several parties have been credited with thinking up the fortune cookie, including a Japanese landscape architect named Makota Hagiwara, who some say distributed the treat in San Francisco in the early 1900s. However, it is widely thought that Los Angeles baker and Chinese immigrant David Jung, later the founder of the Hong Kong Noodle Company, first handed out cookies containing encouraging words (the fortunes) to homeless Californians in 1918. Since Jung was a Presbyterian minister, the strips of paper he inserted in his cookies featured Bible scripture.

By the 1930s, several fortune-cookie factories were in production. The paper-filled treats were folded by hand and inserted using chopsticks until 1964. Today, fortune cookies are a hit everywhere. Even in China. Fortune cookies first began surfacing in Asia simply because American tourists asked for them.

What Makes Popcorn Pop?

Heating kernels of popcorn causes them to eventually explode into fluffy, crunchy, edible flakes that have volumes about 40 times greater than the original kernels. Almost nothing else in nature behaves this way, including most other varieties of corn. What makes popcorn so special?

❋ ❋ ❋ ❋

THE MOST IMPORTANT factor that allows popcorn to pop is the pericarp. Also referred to as the hull, the pericarp is the outer shell of the kernel. The pericarp of popcorn is strong and nearly impermeable to water. Inside the pericarp are water and starch, the two other keys to the popping equation.

When you heat popcorn, the water inside becomes superheated, which means that it's hot enough to boil but can't become steam because the pericarp holds it in. Meanwhile, the starch also heats up and becomes fluid, like a gelatin. As this moisture gets hotter and hotter, the pressure builds until the pericarp can't take the strain. Eventually, the pericarp bursts.

When this happens, a bunch of things occur within a fraction of a second. As the pericarp explodes, the superheated moisture can expand and turns to steam. The gelatinous starch is also sent outward by the explosion, but it cools quickly. As it cools, it solidifies, and the foam turns into a light, fluffy solid. As such, the shape of the popped kernel is basically a frozen starch explosion.

If popcorn is heated too slowly, the moisture gradually seeps out as steam. (The pericarp isn't totally watertight.) If it's heated too quickly, the kernel pops before the starch is hot enough. Another important factor is moisture content. Popcorn must be dried until it only has about 14 percent moisture. Too much moisture results in chewy popcorn, while too little leaves unpopped kernels. Field corn, sweet corn, and most wild corns won't pop because their pericarps aren't tough enough to withhold the pressure and let moisture escape too easily.

Some food for thought for the next time you're waiting for the movie to begin ...

What Is Meatless Meat?

The popularity and availability of meatless meat has been steadily rising in the U.S. Dare we say it's gone mainstream?

✳ ✳ ✳ ✳

WHAT'S DIFFERENT ABOUT the next generation of plant-based meat alternatives is the attempt to make them taste more like meat. And not only that, they were designed to look like and have a texture akin to meat. The aim is to appeal to meat-eating consumers who want a substitute for red meat occasionally, as well as flexitarians who primarily eat vegetarian, but eat meat or fish from time to time.

One of the largest players, Beyond Meat, makes products that are non-GMO and made from gluten-free pea protein. Their "Beyond Beef" is a plant-based product meant to mimic ground beef in taste, feel, and smell. Beyond Meat products are found in over 15,000 restaurants, hotels, universities, and institutions, including Yankee Stadium. Some of the largest fast food chains have recognized the demand for meatless meat products. Carl's Jr. sells a Beyond Famous Star burger, Del Taco offers a Beyond taco, and Dunkin' serves a Beyond Sausage breakfast sandwich. The next foray for Beyond is a partnership with KFC for Beyond Fried Chicken.

Impossible Foods has also made a big impact selling meatless meat products at restaurants and fast food chains. Their patties are made of potato protein and soy-protein and use heme to replicate beef's properties. Red Robin sells an Impossible burger, White Castle an Impossible Slider, Qdoba has Impossible tacos, Little Caesars offers Impossible meatless sausage, and perhaps the largest rollout, Burger King's Impossible Whopper.

Eating meat alternatives is potentially good for human health and may also benefit the planet. Meatless meat products are lower in cholesterol, sodium, and fat than their beef counterparts. They also contain a broader range of vitamins and minerals than beef. Environmentally, raising cows contributes to global warming through greenhouse gas emissions, land use, and water use.

Why Do Doughnuts Have Holes?

The saga of how doughnuts came to have holes in the middle remains a bit unclear.

✳ ✳ ✳ ✳

THE ORIGIN OF doughnuts most likely can be traced to Northern Europe during medieval times. Called *olykoeks* ("oily cakes"), the pastries came to America with the Pilgrims, who had picked up the recipe in Holland, their first refuge from England, which they abandoned for America in the early 1600s. The dough in the middle of these pastries rarely got cooked, so that area often was filled with apples, prunes, or raisins.

By the mid-1800s, the pastries were being made with a hole in the middle—and this is where the plot thickens. Two stories about the origin of the hole involve Hanson Crockett Gregory, a sea captain from Rockport, Maine. One says that he poked out the middle of one of his wife's homemade doughnuts by plunging it into a spoke on the ship's wheel. That eliminated the uncooked middle, and it enabled Gregory to eat and keep his boat at an even keel at the same time.

A second story—this one slightly more plausible—involves Gregory eating doughnuts with other crew members. Tired of the raw dough in the middle, he took a tin off the ship's pepper box and used it to push out the middle, leaving only the cooked edges. He tasted it and exclaimed that it was the best doughnut he had ever eaten. Years later, in 1916, Gregory recounted this story in the *Washington Post*.

There is no real proof that backs up either account involving Gregory, but this much is certain: A plaque commemorating his culinary claim stands at the house in Maine where he lived. And perhaps not coincidentally, doughnuts did indeed have holes by the mid-1800s, making them easier to cook and improving their taste.

Once they started coming with holes in them, doughnuts soared in popularity. During World War I, the French gave doughnuts to American soldiers to remind them of home. In the 1920s, doughnuts were the snack of choice in movie theaters. At the 1934 World's Fair in Chicago, they were called, "The food hit of the Century of Progress."

What Are the World's Most Revolting Foods?

Turning our attention briefly to some of the most curious delicacies of the world, from maggot-infested cheese to mouse-flavored liquor, we present the following culinary adventures.

✳   ✳   ✳   ✳

Baby Mice Wine

THOSE BRAVE MEN and women who enjoy eating the worm from the bottom of a tequila bottle and want to advance to spirit-soaked vertebrates might be interested in baby mice wine, which is made by preserving newborn mice in a bottle of rice wine. This traditional health tonic from Korea is said to aid the rejuvenation of one's vital organs. Anecdotal evidence, however, suggests that the sight of dead baby mice floating helplessly in liquor is more likely to break your heart than rejuvenate it.

Balut

Balut are eaten in the Philippines, Cambodia, and Vietnam. They are duck eggs that have been incubated for 15 to 20 days (a duckling takes 28 days to hatch) and then boiled. The egg is then consumed—both the runny yolk and the beaky, feathery, and veiny duck fetus. Balut are usually sold on the streets for the equivalent of about 25 cents each; one can have them with coarse salt or vinegar, or just plain. Those who are trying balut for the first time are strongly advised to keep their eyes tightly closed.

Casu Marzu

The Sardinian delicacy casu marzu is a hard sheep's milk cheese infested with *Piophila casei*, the "cheese fly." The larvae eat the cheese and release an enzyme that triggers a fermentation process, causing their abode to putrefy. The cheese is not considered true casu marzu until it becomes a caustic, viscous gluey mass that burns your mouth and wriggles on your tongue when you eat it. *Nota bene:* The cheese fly is also called "the cheese skipper," because its larvae have the amazing ability to leap up to six inches in the air when disturbed. Since the larvae rightfully consider it disturbing to be eaten, it is suggested that consumers of casu marzu make use of protective eye gear during the repast.

Cobra Heart

This Vietnamese delicacy delivers precisely what it promises: a beating cobra heart, sometimes accompanied by a cobra kidney and chased by a slug of cobra blood. Preparations involve a large blade and a live cobra. If you find yourself in the uncomfortable situation where the snake has already been served but you feel your courage failing, ask for a glass of rice wine and drop the heart into it. Bottoms up!

Escamoles

Escamoles are the eggs, or larvae, of the giant venomous black *Liometopum* ant. This savory Mexican chow, which supposedly has the consistency of cottage cheese and a surprisingly buttery and nutty flavor, can be found both in rural markets and in multi-star restaurants in Mexico City. A popular way to eat escamoles is in a taco with a dollop of guacamole, but it is said that they are also quite delicious fried with black butter or with onions and garlic.

Hákarl

Hákarl, an Icelandic dish dating back to the Vikings, is putrefied shark meat. Traditionally, it has been prepared by burying a side of shark in gravel for three months or more; nowadays, it might be boiled in several changes of water or soaked in a large vat filled with brine and then cured in the open air for two months. This is done to purge the shark meat of urine and trimethylamine oxide. Sharks have an extra concentration of both to maintain essential body fluid levels, but the combination makes the meat toxic. Since rancid shark meat is not considered all that tasty, native wisdom prescribes washing it down with a hearty dose of liquor.

Lutefisk

If the idea of rotten shark meat does not appeal, consider lutefisk, or "lye fish"—possibly the furthest from rotten that food can get. This traditional Scandinavian dish is made by steeping pieces of cod in lye solution. The result is translucent and gelatinous, stinks to the high heavens, and corrodes metal kitchenware. Enjoy it covered with pork drippings, white sauce, or melted butter, with potatoes and Norwegian flatbread on the side. (As a side note: The annual lutefisk-eating contest in Madison, Minnesota, is scheduled right before an event called the Outhouse Race. This might not be entirely a coincidence.)

Pacha

This dish can be found everywhere sheep can be found, especially in the Middle East. To put it simply, pacha, which is the Iraqi name for it, is a sheep's head stewed, boiled, or otherwise slow-cooked for five to six hours together with the sheep's intestines, stomach, and feet. Other meats might also be added to the broth. Something to keep in mind: If you are served this dish in Turkmenistan, where it is called *kelle-bashayak*, this means two things—one, you're the guest of honor at the gathering, and two, you will be expected to help consume the head or else risk offending the hosts.

Spiders

Spiders are popular fare in parts of Cambodia, especially in the town of Skuon; however, they are not part of the traditional cuisine and were not widely eaten until the horror years of the bloody Khmer Rouge regime in the late 1970s, when food became scarce. After the country was rebuilt, the villagers' taste for spiders did not recede entirely. Today, tarantulas are sold on the streets for about ten cents per spider and are said to be very good fried with salt, pepper, and garlic.

Is Jell-O Made from Horses?

Could this fun, wiggly dessert be the final resting place for the likes of Black Beauty and Mister Ed? Sure. But let's not be too picky—any creature with bones can become Jell-O. It's an equal opportunity dessert.

✳ ✳ ✳ ✳

JELL-O IS MADE from gelatin, which is processed collagen. Collagen makes your bones strong and your skin elastic and stretchy (there's that jiggly wiggle). To make gelatin, you take bones, skin, tendons, and whatnot from animals (primarily cows or pigs), grind everything up, wash and soak it in acid (and also lime, if cow parts are used), and throw it in a vat to boil. The acid or lime breaks down the components of the ground animal pieces, and the result is gelatin, among other things. The gelatin conveniently rises to the top of this mixture of acid and animal parts, creating an easy-to-remove film.

In the Victorian era, when gelatin was really catching on, it was sold in the film state. People had to clarify the gelatin by boiling it with egg whites and eggshells, which took a lot of time. In 1845, a crafty inventor patented a powdered gelatin, which was to be extracted from the bones of geese. In 1897, this powdered gelatin was named Jell-O and went on to become the line of dessert products that, to this day, we always have room for.

Why does the list of ingredients in Jell-O include gelatin and not cow and pig pieces? Because the U.S. federal government does not consider gelatin an animal product, since it is extensively processed. Gelatin is also found in gummy bears candy, cream cheese, marshmallows, and other foods.

If you like Jell-O, cream cheese, and marshmallows, but would rather not eat the boiled bones and skin of animals, there are alternatives. Agar and carrageenan are made from seaweed and can be used to create delicious gelatin-like goodies.

So while it's unlikely your Jell-O contains traces of Mister Ed or Black Beauty, it could test positive for Wilbur or Elsie.

What Causes Food Cravings?

Got a hankering for some steamed carrots and Brussels sprouts? Didn't think so. Most cravings are of the sweet, salty-crunchy, super-high-fat varieties. But just what is it that prompts us to make a mad dash to the 7-Eleven for Funyuns and Ding Dongs in the middle of the night?

✳ ✳ ✳ ✳

RESEARCHERS AREN'T EXACTLY sure, but one theory that is gaining acceptance speculates that food cravings are actually addictions. How so? Brain image studies conducted by Marcia Pelchat, a sensory psychologist at the Monell Chemical Senses Center in Philadelphia, show that food cravings activate parts of the brain that are typically involved with habit formation. Known as the caudate nucleus, this is the same region of the brain that's affected by cocaine, alcohol, and cigarettes. "Think of food cravings as a sensory memory," says Pelchat. "You remember how good it felt the last time you had that food."

Happy Chomping

It all has to do with a food's biological and emotional resonance. Brian Wansink, a food psychology expert and the author of *Mindless Eating: Why We Eat More Than We Think*, agrees that people crave foods that connect them to pleasant experiences.

Men, he says, are drawn toward hearty meals—such as barbecue ribs, burgers, meat loaf, pasta, pizza—because they associate those foods with a nurturing wife or mother. Women, on the other hand, connect those same savory meals to long hours spent in the kitchen. Wansink notes that chocolate and ice cream don't involve any prep work or cleanup, which may help to explain why women are drawn to those types of sweets. That's right, ladies—just flip the lid off that pint of Häagen-Dazs and you've got one quick euphoria fix.

But what about the "wisdom of the body" theory, which states that our bodies simply crave what we nutritionally need? Pelchat says that wisdom doesn't apply, unless you're a sodium-deficient rodent: "When rats are salt deprived, they show a sodium appetite; they seem to be able to detect amino acids when they're protein deprived. But there's actually very little evidence for that in people. A lot of people in our society crave salty foods, but very few are actually salt deficient."

So that sudden urge to hit the A&W drive-thru isn't exactly motivated by nutritional necessity. You're really just addicted to the chili cheese fries.

Why Do Fruits and Vegetables Change Colors as They Ripen?

Brilliant color is one way to tell if your bananas, apples, tomatoes, and berries are sweet, juicy, and ready to eat. Ever bite into a green banana? That's bitter, brother!

✳　✳　✳　✳

How and why do fruits and vegetables change color? Well, you know how every autumn the leaves turn from green to rich shades of yellow, red, and brown? Aging—or ripening—fruits and vegetables go through a similar process.

Most unripe fruits and veggies are hard, sour, and—you guessed it—green. That green color is largely due to the presence of chlorophyll. (Quick flashback to science class: That's the green pigment found in all green plants. It's vital for photosynthesis, which allows plants to get energy from sunlight.) As growing fruits and vegetables mature, rising levels of acid and enzymes cause the green chlorophyll pigments to break down.

That's when your produce begins to show its true hues.

Bananas and certain varieties of apples have vivid skins of yellow and red, respectively, waiting to emerge from underneath that green layer of chlorophyll. Other fruits, like tomatoes, make brand-new color compounds (in their case, glossy red-orange ones) as their chlorophyll begins to wane.

As for peppers, their final coloration depends on their degree of ripeness. No, those aren't different varieties of bell peppers at the grocery store—it just so happens that peppers are vegetables that are good to eat at any stage. They change from green (unripe) to yellow and orange (semi-ripe) to red (fully ripe). That's why green peppers are slightly bitter, while the red ones taste sweet.

What does this all have to do with the autumn leaves? The changing colors of falling leaves and ripening fruits and vegetables is simply a sign of plant senescence (a fancy term biologists use to describe the natural process of deterioration with age). The brilliant tints that are found on ripe fruit and vegetable peels are comprised of active and healthy antioxidants. Eat some every day—preferably before they turn brown and mushy.

What Is Major League Eating?

It is a competitive world in which we live. And Major League Eating (MLE) is the self-described "governing body of all stomach centric sport worldwide."

✳   ✳   ✳   ✳

EATERS COMPETE IN approximately 70 Major League Eating-sanctioned events annually. There are contests for eating the most oysters, chicken wings, tamales, cabbage, cannoli, matzo balls, tacos, cheesecake, peas, pizzas, asparagus, waffles, jalapeños, funnel cake, kimchi, bacon, and cheese curds in a specified time. And while this is not an exhaustive list, it shows the breadth of items that are competitively eaten.

The highest profile and signature event of Major League Eating is Nathan's Famous Fourth of July Hot Dog Eating Contest in Coney Island, New York. The winner takes home a purse of $40,000, as well as the bejeweled championship Mustard Yellow Belt. ESPN has broadcast Nathan's Hot Dog Eating Contest live since 2004 with a play-by-play announcer and color commentator.

The Nathan's Hot Dog Eating Contest tabulates the number of hot dogs and buns consumed within a ten-minute period. There are multiple techniques employed by contestants. The most prominent one, "dunking," involves soaking the buns in water or fruit punch to make them easier to swallow.

The early 2000s saw the rise of Takeru Kobayashi of Japan, who ate 50 hot dog and buns in 2001, doubling the previous record of 25 hot dogs consumed. Kobayashi became a legend of sorts and went on to win a streak of Nathan's contests from 2001 to 2006.

Kobayashi was taken down in 2007 by Joey Chestnut of San Jose, California. Chestnut would go on to win Nathan's Hot Dog Eating Contest an impressive eight years in a row from 2007 to 2014. He later continued his dominance from 2016 to 2019. Chestnut set the world record for hot dog eating in 2018 with an astonishing 74 hot dogs and buns consumed in ten minutes. According to Major League Eating's website, Joey Chestnut is "the greatest eater in history."

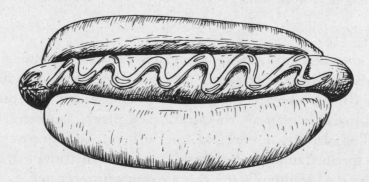

Chapter 15

Myths and Legends

Who Built the Pyramids?

The Great Pyramids of Egypt have maintained their mystery through the eons, and there's still a lot we don't know about them. But we do know this: Slaves, particularly the ancient Hebrew slaves, did not build these grand structures.

✳   ✳   ✳   ✳

IT'S EASY TO see why people think slaves built the pyramids. Most ancient societies kept slaves, and the Egyptians were no exception. And Hebrew slaves did build other Egyptian monuments during their 400 years of captivity, according to the Old Testament. Even ancient scholars such as the Greek historian Herodotus (fifth century B.C.) and the Jewish historian Josephus (first century A.D.) believed that the Egyptians used slave labor in the construction of the pyramids.

Based on the lifestyles of these ancient builders, however, researchers have discredited the notion that they were slaves (Nubians, Assyrians, or Hebrews, among others) who were forced to work. They had more likely willingly labored, both for grain (or other foodstuffs) and to ensure their place in the afterlife. What's more, we now know that the Great Pyramids were built more than a thousand years before the era of the Hebrews (who actually became enslaved during Egypt's New Kingdom).

Archaeologists have determined that many of the people who built the pyramids were conscripted farmers and peasants who lived in the countryside during the Old Kingdom. Archaeologist Mark Lehner of the Semitic Museum at Harvard University has spent more than a decade studying the workers' villages that existed close to the Giza plateau, where the pyramids were built. He has confirmed that the people who built the pyramids were not slaves—rather, they were skilled laborers and "ordinary men and women."

Did Atlantis Exist?

Did the legendary island of Atlantis ever really exist? Or did Plato make the whole thing up?

✳   ✳   ✳   ✳

IT'S HARD TO believe that Plato, an early Greek philosopher, was the type to start rumors. But in two of his dialogues, *Timaeus* and *Critias*, he refers to what has become one of the most famous legends of all time: the doomed island of Atlantis.

In *Timaeus*, Plato uses a story told by Critias to describe where Atlantis existed, explaining that it "came forth out of the Atlantic Ocean, for in those days the Atlantic was navigable; and there was an island situated in front of the straits which are by you called the Pillars of Heracles; the island was larger than Libya and Asia put together, and was the way to other islands . . ."

Plato also divulges the details of its fate: "afterwards there occurred violent earthquakes and floods; and in a single day and night of misfortune all your warlike men in a body sank into the earth, and the island of Atlantis in like manner disappeared in the depths of the sea. For which reason the sea in those parts is impassable and impenetrable, because there is a shoal of mud in the way; and this was caused by the subsidence of the island." In *Critias*, the story revolves around Poseidon, the mythical god of the sea, and how the kingdom of Atlantis attempted to conquer Athens.

Although many ascribe Plato's myth to his desire for a way to emphasize his own political theories, historians and writers perpetuated the idea of the mythical island for centuries, both in fiction and nonfiction. After the Middle Ages, the story of the doomed civilization was revisited by such writers as Francis Bacon, who published *The New Atlantis* in 1627. In 1870, Jules Verne published his classic *Twenty Thousand Leagues Under the Sea*, which includes a visit to sunken Atlantis aboard Captain Nemo's submarine *Nautilus*. And in 1882, *Atlantis: The Antediluvian World* by Ignatius Donnelly was written to prove that Atlantis did exist—initiating much of the Atlantis mania that has occurred since that time. The legendary Atlantis continues to surface in today's science fiction, romantic fantasy, and even mystery stories.

Santorini: A True Atlantis?

More recently, historians and geologists have attempted to link Atlantis to the island of Santorini (also called Thera) in the Aegean Sea. About 3,600 years ago, the Minoa, or Thera, eruption—one of the largest eruptions in history—occurred on Santorini. This eruption caused the volcano to collapse, creating a huge caldera or "hole" at the top of the mountain. Historians believe the eruption caused the end of the Minoan civilization on Thera and the nearby island of Crete, most likely because a tsunami resulted from the massive explosion. Since that time, most of the islands grew from subsequent volcanic eruptions around the caldera, creating what is now the volcanic archipelago of islands called the Cycladic group.

Could this tourist hot spot truly be the site of the mythological island Atlantis? Some say that Plato's description of the palace and surroundings at Atlantis were similar to those at Knossos, the ceremonial and cultural center of the Minoan civilization. On the scientific end, geologists know that eruptions such as the one at Santorini can pump huge volumes of material into the air and slump other parts of a volcanic island into the ocean. To the ancient peoples, such an event could literally be translated as an island quickly sinking into the ocean. But even after centuries of study, excavation, and speculation, the mystery of Atlantis remains unsolved.

Did Nero Fiddle While Rome Burned?

Over the ages, the phrase "Nero fiddled while Rome burned" has become a euphemism for heedless and irresponsible behavior in the midst of a crisis. But as a matter of historical fact, legend has it wrong.

❋ ❋ ❋ ❋

IN A.D. 64, much of Rome burned to the ground in what is known as the Great Fire. According to legend, the reigning emperor, Nero, purposely set the blaze to see "how Troy looked when it was in flames." From atop a palace tower, he played his fiddle and sang as the fire raged and consumed two-thirds of the empire's capital.

Nero, a patron of the arts who played the lyre, wrote poetry, and fancied himself a great artist, often performed in public, challenging the beliefs of Rome's political class who believed such displays were beneath the dignity of an emperor. But music was, in fact, the most dignified of Nero's interests. Under the influence of a corrupt adviser who encouraged his excesses, his life became a series of spectacles, orgies, and murders. A few months after his first public performance, the Great Fire ravaged Rome for five days. Roman historian Suetonius, who hadn't even been born at the time of the fire, describes Nero singing from the Tower of Maecenas as he watched the inferno. Dio Cassius, a historian who lived a hundred years later, places him on a palace roof, singing "The Capture of Troy."

However, the historian Tacitus, who actually witnessed the fire, ascertained that the emperor was at his villa in Antium, 30 miles away. Many contemporary historians agree that Nero was not in Rome when the fire broke out. According to Tacitus, Nero rushed back to Rome to organize a relief effort and, with uncharacteristic discipline and leadership, set about rebuilding and beautifying the city he loved.

Will Cracking Your Knuckles Cause Arthritis?

Scare tactics can sometimes get people to give up annoying habits—and that may be the origin of the misconception that cracking one's knuckles will cause arthritis.

✳   ✳   ✳   ✳

EXPERTS INSIST THAT there is no medical evidence that frequent knuckle-cracking leads to the development of arthritic hands, but that doesn't mean it's a good habit to have. Many people find those knuckle-cracking noises highly annoying—a lot like fingernails on a chalkboard.

That distinctive sound is created by a fairly complicated sequence of events. Our joints are covered by connective-tissue capsules. Inside them is a thick, clear substance called synovial fluid, which lubricates our joints and supplies nutrients to our bones. The fluid also contains gases, including carbon dioxide. When a knuckle-cracker goes into pre-pop mode and extends the fingers, the capsule around the knuckles gets stretched out and its volume increases. This, in turn, lowers the pressure of the synovial fluid inside the joints and causes carbon dioxide bubbles to form, a process known as cavitation. The popping or cracking sound is created when the bubbles burst. It takes about half an hour before the gases are reabsorbed into the synovial fluid. Until that happens, the knuckles cannot be cracked again.

Although knuckle-crackers are not at increased risk for arthritis, a long-term cracking habit can cause injury to the ligaments around the finger joints. One study found that habitual knuckle-crackers might also end up with decreased grip strength, swelling of the hands, and soft-tissue damage.

Many people who repeatedly crack their knuckles claim it relieves finger stiffness and gives them greater finger mobility, especially after typing on a keyboard for an extended period. A better, if less noisy, solution is a simple stretch of the hands.

Did Lady Godiva Really Ride in the Nude?

Imagine a beautiful, long-haired woman riding a horse through the center of town—in the nude. It's quite an image. But is the ride of Lady Godiva just a legend?

✳ ✳ ✳ ✳

INDEED, THERE WAS a Lady Godiva. She was the wife of Leofric, Earl of Mercia, and she lived in the 11th century near the town of Coventry, England. She supposedly was extremely pious, a patron of the church, and instrumental in the building of several abbeys.

Some writings portray Leofric as equally religious, though not very generous toward "the little people." At one point, he levied a huge tax on the citizens of Coventry. Godiva felt awful for the townspeople and begged her husband to repeal the tax. Leofric said he would remove the tax if Godiva stripped naked and rode her horse through the streets of Coventry. Godiva declared the streets be cleared, let down her long hair to cover her body, and did the deed while accompanied by two knights. Leofric kept his word and rolled back the tax.

In another version of the story, Godiva was a patron of the arts. Leofric, who was not, convinced his wife to go on her ride by pointing out the Greek and Roman celebrations of the nude form as a work of art.

There's really no way to know for certain if Godiva's ride happened. The chronicler at the abbey in nearby Evesham didn't mention it in his 11th-century writings about Leofric and Godiva. No contemporaries wrote of it either. It wasn't written about until much later—in the 13th century—by Roger of Wendover. However, Roger's writings are known to be full of exaggerations and biases rather than historical facts.

Later writers, such as Matthew of Westminster in the 14th century, implied that a miracle kept the townspeople from seeing Godiva in the nude. Some later writers said Leofric was a persecutor of the church but underwent a religious conversion because of this miracle. So although there is no proof of the ride, the legend lives.

Colleges and chocolate companies employ Godiva logos. And in Coventry, her ride is commemorated each year as part of a festival. Not usually in the nude, though.

Is There a Fountain of Youth?

It's been an obsession of explorers for centuries, but no one has been able to find the magic elixir.

✳   ✳   ✳   ✳

SPANISH EXPLORER JUAN Ponce de León was supposedly searching for the fabled fountain of youth when he discovered Florida. However, it wasn't until after his death in 1521 that he became linked with the fountain.

The first published reference associating Ponce de León with the fountain of youth was the *Historia General y Natural de las Indias*, by Gonzalo Fernandez de Oviedo in 1535. The author cited the explorer's search for a fountain of restorative water to cure his impotence, but the veracity of this account is questionable since Ponce de León had children at the time of his 1513 voyage and didn't even mention the fountain in his travel notes.

Moreover, the fountain of youth legend predates Ponce de León. In Arabic versions of the *Alexander Romance*, a collection of myths about Alexander the Great, the Macedonian king and his troops cross a desert and come to a fountain in which they bathe to regain strength and youth. This story was translated to French in the 13th century and was well known among Europeans.

If a fountain of youth actually exists, no one has found it in it in any of its supposed locations, which are most typically cited as Florida, the Bahamas, or the Bay of Honduras. It may turn out, however, that a fountain of youth exists in science. David Sinclair, a Harvard University professor and the founder of Sirtris Pharmaceuticals, discovered in 2003 that the molecule resveratrol could extend the lifespan of worms and fruit flies. In 2006, Italian researchers prolonged the life of the fish *Nothobranchius furzeri* with resveratrol. It's not quite eternal life—but it's more than Ponce de León found.

Do People Really Go Mad During a Full Moon?

The story goes that if you ask emergency-room workers or police officers, they'll tell you that the number of disturbed individuals who come to their attention rises dramatically during a full moon. What's the truth behind the story?

✳   ✳   ✳   ✳

IT'S A LONG-HELD belief that a lunar effect causes "lunacy" in susceptible people—resulting in an increase in homicides, traffic accidents, suicides, kidnappings, crisis calls to emergency services, admissions to psychiatric institutions, and all kinds of other nutty things. The rationale: The earth is 80 percent water, and so is the human body. Theoretically, then, since the moon has such a dramatic effect on the tides, it could move the water in our bodies in some similar way, causing strange behavior.

Are the stories true? Most evidence says no.

In 1996, scientists Ivan Kelly, James Rotton, and Roger Culver did a thorough examination of more than one hundred studies of lunar effects. Perhaps surprisingly, they found no significant correlation between the state of the moon and people's mental and physical conditions. When all of the statistical wrinkles had been smoothed out, there was no evidence of a rise in violence, accidents, disasters, or any other kind of strange behavior.

A study by C. E. Climent and R. Plutchik, written for *Comprehensive Psychiatry*, showed that psychiatric admissions are lowest during a full moon, and an examination conducted at the University of Erlangen–Nuremberg in Germany indicated no connection between suicide rates and phases of the moon. So why the myths? Perhaps people just want to believe the spooky tales, and lunar effects are tossed into movies and literature simply because they're compelling drama. Who doesn't love a good werewolf tale?

The constant reinforcement of the "full moon" message makes it much more likely that the public will accept it as proven fact. Myths also tend to stay alive if you pick and choose the data to fit the story. One murder that occurs during a full moon creates a story that can be told over and over, yet the ten homicides that happen at any other time of the month just disappear into a pile of statistics.

Renowned UCLA astronomer George O. Abell consistently dismissed claims that the moon could have a strong enough effect on the water in a human body to cause any behavioral changes. Abell pointed out that a mosquito would exert more gravitational pull on a human arm than the moon ever might.

So, is that arm-biting mosquito spooked by the moon? That's

not entirely a joke, because it seems animals actually are affected by lunar activity. It might be a bit scary to read a study in the *British Medical Journal* that appears to prove there's a significant increase in bites by cats, rats, horses, and dogs when the moon is full.

Suddenly, the image of a dog howling at the moon might give you a little shiver. But a man baying at the moon? Most likely he'd be someone who's goofy all month long.

Were Witches Burned?

Contrary to popular belief, no witches were burned at the stake during the Salem witch trials, and men (and even dogs!) were not immune from punishment.

✳   ✳   ✳   ✳

Blame it on Tituba

IN THE EYES of 17th-century colonists in Salem, Massachusetts, Satan was constantly seeking to tempt God-fearing locals into witchcraft. In 1692, the town pastor owned a slave from Barbados named Tituba, who entertained the local children with fortune- and story-telling. No one knows the actual reason, but the girls among the group soon began to claim that they were being spiritually tormented. They also began to exhibit such strange behaviors as hysteria, seizures, and apparent hallucinations. Some people identified the "illnesses" as a toxic condition known as ergotism, which is caused by a rye fungus. But the more likely explanation is much simpler. These were just children being children—eager for attention, imitating one another, and aware that the attention ends once the charade does.

Nonetheless, Tituba was quickly identified as the source of the beguiling "spells," and she ultimately confessed under pressure. But rather than being burned at the stake, her punishment was that she was indentured for life to pay the costs of her jailing.

Her arrest was the snowball behind an avalanche of accusations. Those subsequently charged with being witches were either "proven guilty" or "soon to be proven guilty."

Witches Take Many Forms

Approximately 150 people (and two dogs) were arrested during the Salem witch trials, and 19 people (including six men) were hanged. One gent who refused to enter a plea was subjected to "pressing," a form of torture in which rocks are slowly placed atop a person's body until he or she finally suffocates—a process that can take as long as three days. Suddenly, incineration doesn't look so bad.

Does Lightning Strike the Same Place Twice?

The adage "lightning never strikes the same place twice" seems nearly as old as lightning itself, but it's about as accurate as your average seven-day forecast. The truth is, lightning can—and often does—strike the same place twice.

✳ ✳ ✳ ✳

Debunking a Myth

To understand why this belief is an old wives' tale, we need a quick refresher course on how lightning works. As Ben Franklin taught us, lightning is pure electricity. (Electricity is a result of the interplay between positive and negative charges.) During a thunderstorm, powerful winds create massive collisions between particles of ice and water within a cloud; these encounters result in a negatively charged electrical field. When this field becomes strong enough—during a violent thunderstorm—another electrical field, this one positively charged, forms on the ground.

These negative and positive charges want to come together, but like lovers in a Shakespearean tragedy, they need to overcome the resistance of the parental atmosphere. Eventually, the attraction grows too strong and causes an invisible channel—known as a "stepped leader"—to form in the air. As the channel reaches toward the ground, the electrical field on the earth creates its own channels and attempts to connect with the stepped leader. Once these two channels connect, electricity flows from the cloud to the ground. That's lightning.

Lightning is an amazing phenomenon. The average bolt is about 50,000 degrees Fahrenheit, or about ten times the temperature of the sun's surface. During a typical thunderstorm, nearly 30,000 lightning bolts are created. The National Oceanic and Atmospheric Administration estimates that more than 25 million bolts of lightning strike the earth each year.

Given that huge number, it's hard to believe that lightning doesn't strike the same place twice. In fact, it does—especially when the places in question are tall buildings, which can be struck dozens of times a year. According to the National Lightning Safety Institute, the Empire State Building is hit an average of 23 times a year.

The Human Lightning Rod

But tall buildings aren't the only objects that attract multiple lightning strikes. Consider park ranger Roy Cleveland Sullivan. For most of his career, Sullivan roamed the hills of Virginia's Shenandoah National Park, watching for poachers, assisting hikers, checking on campers—and being struck by lightning.

From 1942 to 1977, Lightnin' Roy was struck by lightning seven times. His eyebrows were torched off, the nail on one of his big toes was blown off, his hair was set aflame, and he suffered various burns all over his body.

How Short Was Napoleon?

Napoleon Bonaparte, one of the most successful and brutal military leaders of all time, had a short fuse and was often shortsighted. But he was not, contrary to popular belief, short in stature.

✳ ✳ ✳ ✳

Slighted by History

IT TURNS OUT that an error in arithmetic contributed to history's perception of Napoleon as a small man. The only known measurement of Bonaparte came from his autopsy, which reported a height of 5'2". But it was not taken into account that this measurement was calculated in French units. Translating to slightly more than 168 centimeters, his height was actually 5'6" by the English Imperial system. This was above average for a 19th-century Frenchman.

Another possible reason for this misconception is the fact that Napoleon kept himself surrounded by a group of relatively tall guardsmen. Napoleon was never seen in public without his "imperial guard." These soldiers averaged six feet in height and would have towered over Napoleon.

A Napoleon Complex

Napoleon wasn't short, but his temper was. Over time, the notion that the general's irascible, aggressive personality stemmed from his small size has been applied to any small-statured man who uses his temper to compensate for his height. This is referred to as a "Napoleon Complex," and though psychologists regard it as a negative social stereotype, it also proves to be a myth. In 2007, researchers at the University of Central Lancashire studied the effect of height on aggression in men. Using heart monitors to gauge reactions, scientists found that *taller* men were more likely to respond to provocation with aggressive behavior.

As Napoleon himself said, "History is the version of past events that people have decided to agree upon." It turns out that history cut Napoleon about four inches short.

Is a Dog's Mouth Cleaner Than a Human's?

Smooch your pooch at your own risk. It's not man's best friend that could kiss and kill.

✳ ✳ ✳ ✳

MOST DOG OWNERS will tell you that their dog's mouth is much cleaner than a human's. In fact, this old wives' tale has been touted so loudly and for so long that most people assume it's true. Most veterinarians, however, disagree. They'll tell you it's a stalemate—both human and canine mouths are rife with bacteria.

One of the biggest reasons people believe the myth is the fact that dogs lick their wounds, and those wounds tend to heal very quickly. But it's not as though a dog's saliva has amazing antibacterial properties. Dogs' cuts and scrapes get better fast because their tongues help get rid of dead tissue and stimulate circulation, which in turn facilitates the healing process.

You Know Where It's Been

If you still think a dog's tongue is more antiseptic than your own, just take a look at what your pet's tongue touches over the course of a day. Dogs use their tongues for eating and drinking, as well as for activities such as bathing and exploring garbage cans and weird dead things in the yard.

A dog bite, like a human bite, can cause infection if it breaks the skin. But the bacteria transmitted in each are fairly species-specific. In other words, a bug that's harmful to humans likely won't be transmitted to your pooch if you give him a big, slobbery kiss on the mouth, and vice versa.

✳ The one critter you don't want to kiss is the Komodo dragon, which is indigenous to Indonesia. The mouth of this giant, carnivorous lizard is a veritable petri dish of disgusting bacteria, many of which can result in an agonizing, often fatal infection.

Did Betsy Ross Really Stitch the First American Flag?

Schoolchildren are taught numerous things about the American Revolution that aren't necessarily supported by history. Among the debated stories is the one about Betsy Ross stitching the first American flag.

✳ ✳ ✳ ✳

WHO WAS BETSY Ross? Elizabeth (Betsy) Griscom was born in 1752 to a Quaker family, the eighth of 17 children. When she turned 21 in 1773, she eloped with an Episcopalian named John Ross, and because of their union she was expelled from her congregation. Before they met, John and Betsy had both worked as apprentice upholsterers, so they decided to start their own business. Sadly for young Betsy, John died in January 1776 while serving with the Pennsylvania militia. The patriotic seamstress continued to run the business, and she soon expanded her efforts, making and mending gear for the Continental Army (a receipt exists that shows she made flags for the Pennsylvania State Navy in 1777).

So she *could* have sewn the first flag. Yes, but there's no proof that she actually did. In 1870, at a meeting of the Historical Society of Pennsylvania, Betsy's grandson, William Canby, insisted that George Washington had sought out Betsy and asked her to design and create a flag for the new country. Other Canby relatives swore out affidavits in agreement.

Suppose Washington had indeed asked her to make the first flag. When he became the first president, why didn't he do something to honor her? Why did her contribution never come up during her lifetime? Betsy Ross died in 1836, yet her family waited 34 years to announce her accomplishment. It could be that the family legend embellishes a grain of truth. Betsy Ross did make flags for the war effort, so she could have lived her life believing she had made the first American flag.

Are Cockroaches Nuke-Proof?

We've all heard that cockroaches would be the only creatures to survive a nuclear war. But unless being exceptionally gross is a prerequisite for withstanding such an event, are cockroaches really that resilient?

✳   ✳   ✳   ✳

COCKROACHES ARE INDEED that resilient. For one thing, they've spent millions of years surviving every calamity the earth could throw at them. Fossil records indicate that the cockroach is at least 300 million years old. That means cockroaches survived unscathed whatever event wiped out the dinosaurs, be it an ice age or a giant meteor's collision with Earth.

The cockroach's chief advantage—at least where nuclear annihilation is concerned—is the amount of radiation it can safely absorb. During the Cold War, a number of researchers performed tests on how much radiation various organisms could withstand before dying. Humans, as you might imagine, tapped out fairly early. Five hundred Radiation Absorbed Doses (or rads, the accepted measurement for radiation exposure) are fatal to humans. Cockroaches, on the other hand, scored exceptionally well, withstanding up to 6,400 rads.

Such hardiness doesn't mean that cockroaches will be the sole rulers of the planet if nuclear war breaks out. The parasitoid wasp can take more than 100,000 rads and still sting the heck out of you. Some forms of bacteria can shrug off more than one million rads and keep doing whatever it is that bacteria do.

Clearly, the cockroach would have neighbors.

Not all cockroaches would survive, anyway—definitely not the ones that lived within two miles of the blast's ground zero. Regardless of the amount of radiation a creature could withstand, the intense heat from the detonation would liquefy it. Still, the entire cockroach race wouldn't be living at or near ground zero—so, yes, at least some would likely survive.

Is It Dangerous to Awaken a Sleepwalker?

This is yet another old wives' tale that has been shredded by science. In fact, it's more dangerous not to awaken a sleepwalker.

✳ ✳ ✳ ✳

An Unsolved Puzzle

W E'VE ALL HAD the experience of waking up in the middle of the night to find ourselves drinking a Slurpee and singing Barry Manilow's "Copacabana" on the back porch of the neighbor's house. Wait, everybody has, right? Er, we meant that metaphorically.

Sleepwalking, or somnambulism, is one of the great medical mysteries. Anyone who has encountered a sleepwalker wandering around the house—or singing naked on the back porch—can attest that it is an eerie experience. Sleepwalking is listed in a group of sleep disorders known as parasomnia, and researchers aren't sure what causes it. They know that stress and irregular sleep patterns may contribute to episodes, and that children are far more likely to suffer from the condition than adults. They also know that the old wives' tale warning that a person awakened from a somnambulist daze may die is just that—an old wives' tale.

Some experts trace this myth back to the beliefs of various indigenous cultures that thought when a person slept, his or her soul left the body, and that if you woke up a sleepwalker, the soul would be lost forever. Others argue that the myth arose simply due to the distress and shock sleepwalkers sometimes experience when woken up.

Just Don't Use Cold Water

Though it is true that a sleepwalker may be distressed and disoriented upon being roused from a midnight stroll, there are no documented cases of sleepwalkers expiring from it. Indeed, sleep experts argue that not waking a sleepwalker can lead to more harm than waking one, especially if he or she is engaged in certain activities at the time (climbing, jumping, handling a knife, driving, etc.). In most cases, specialists suggest that it is best to gently guide the somnambulist back to bed.

There might be another reason to wake a sleepwalker. In 1982 an Arizona man named Steven Steinberg went on trial for killing his wife, who was stabbed 26 times with a kitchen knife. Despite overwhelming evidence and Steinberg's own admission that he had committed the crime, the defendant was unable to answer the simplest questions about the circumstances of his wife's death. Why? The man had killed his wife while sleepwalking. Steinberg was acquitted of the charges.

Do Lemmings Commit Mass Suicide?

A bit of fraudulent filmmaking and a popular video game have done much to uphold the long-standing misconception that lemmings commit mass suicide.

❋　❋　❋　❋

THE IMAGE OF lemmings hurtling over cliffs to certain doom is entrenched in our culture to the point where "lemming" has become a metaphor for any sort of collective self-destruction. But, come on: Lemmings don't commit suicide. No animal does, with the exception of human beings. Lemmings, unlike people, do not mindlessly follow crowds at their own peril, but they do engage in one behavior en masse, and that is mating.

Numbers Are Up, Numbers Are Down

These fuzzy Arctic rodents mate only a few weeks after being born and birth litters of as many as 13 pups three weeks after mating. Lemmings can give birth multiple times in one summer, leading to an exponential boom in population. Every four years, there is what is known as a "lemming year," when the critters' numbers reach a critical mass that can no longer be sustained by their surroundings. Violence among the animals increases, and they begin to disperse over large distances in search of food. Contrary to popular belief, they do not move together as one single pack but instead go in all directions, following one another in randomly formed lines. They often end up at riverbanks or cliffs and will enter the water and swim as far as they can in an attempt to reach land or an ice patch. Of course, some end up drowning—but that's purely accidental.

Curiously, "lemming years" are followed by a crash in population numbers, with the next year's crowd dwindling to practically nothing. What happens to all of the lemmings after a boom year? Scientists have settled on increased predation as the explanation. When the lemming population surges, owls, foxes, and seabirds gorge themselves on the rodents, which in turn gives rise to a boom in their own populations. The next summer there are so many more predators that they bring the lemming population down to near extinction. That's where the furious mating comes in handy—in no time, the cycle starts all over again.

Another Disney-Made Myth

So how did the popular theory about lemming mass suicides come to be? Most sources point to the 1958 Disney movie *White Wilderness*. This film depicts a collection of lemmings scurrying across a cliff until they reach the edge of a precipice overlooking the Arctic Ocean. The lemmings then leap over the cliff to sad and certain oblivion. But a bit of creative license was taken to create this shot—it was filmed in Alberta, Canada, which is landlocked. (Lemmings aren't even native to Canada. All of the creatures used in the film were imported.) In order to give the illusion that the lemmings were migrating in large groups, the filmmakers covered a turntable with snow and put a few lemmings on it, filming as the animals went around and around. To show the lemmings landing in the water, the film-makers herded a group over a riverbank. Once in the water, the little guys had just a short, safe swim to shore.

✳ Those who missed the Disney nature film can witness (and manipulate) a version of a lemming mass suicide in the video game *Lemmings*, released in 1991. *Lemmings* has players rescuing lemmings as they follow one another aimlessly off ledges and into a host of treacherous death traps, many involving lava or acid. Suddenly, a plunge into a cool pool of water doesn't look so bad.

Did Feminists Really Burn Bras?

In the late 1960s, the media reported that feminists were burning their bras at organized protests. The initial reports weren't true, but the label "bra-burning feminists" stuck.

✳ ✳ ✳ ✳

Fiery Feminists

IN 1968, ROBIN Morgan and other influential feminist activists organized a protest of that year's Miss America beauty pageant. The demonstrators had considered burning bras and other symbols of the female beauty culture, but they decided this would be a fire hazard. Instead, they threw bras, girdles, handbags, and cosmetics into trash cans.

The mainstream media, however, got wind of the initial plan and inaccurately portrayed the hypothetical bra-burning incident as though it had actually happened. Doubtlessly titillated by the word *bra* and all it brings to mind, the male-dominated media began to report on bra burnings as though they were central to the feminist movement. Before long, "bra burners" became a catchphrase for radical feminists.

A Stereotype Goes Down in Flames

Historians and researchers have gone to great lengths to prove that there were no bra burnings at the famed protests. Many have interpreted the obsession with the idea as an attempt to reduce feminist politics into snide remarks about silly girls who torch their unmentionables. Although such bra-burning reductionism is sure to be found in many reports on the feminist movement, recent feminists have since taken up the media's reports and burned their own bras as the radical symbolic statement it was meant to be. Thus, though the famous bra burnings that the media reported never occurred, the spirit of creative destruction as a form of protest is not a myth.

Can You Tickle Yourself?

Go ahead and try. Your brain is expecting your attempts at self-tickling, so they won't work. When someone else tickles you, however, the contact is unexpected, and the shock contributes to the effect.

✳   ✳   ✳   ✳

WHEN THE NERVES of your skin register a touch, your brain responds differently depending on whether you're responsible for it. MRI scans show that three parts of the brain—the secondary somatosensory cortex, the anterior cingulated cortex, and the cerebellum—react strongly when the touch comes from an external source. Think of it like this: When you see a scary movie for the first time, you jump when the maniac suddenly appears and kills someone. The second time you see the movie, it isn't a surprise, so you don't jump. The same goes for tickling: It's the element of surprise that causes the giddy laughter of the ticklish.

Why do we laugh hysterically when other people tickle us? Scientists believe that it's an instinctual defense mechanism—an exaggerated version of the tingle that goes up your spine when an insect is crawling on you. This is your body's way of saying, "You may want to make sure whatever is touching you won't kill you." The laughter is a form of panic due to sensory overload.

If you're in desperate need of tickling but have no friends or family willing to help, you can invest in a tickling robot. People do respond to self-initiated remote-control tickling by a specialized robot that was developed by British scientists in 1998. There's a short delay between the command to tickle and the actual tickle, which is enough to make the contact seem like a surprise to the brain and induce fits of laughter.

Chapter 16

Unsolved Mysteries

Who Built Stonehenge?

Part of the enduring charm of Stonehenge—that curious structure of rocks located in Wiltshire County, southern England—is that it continues to defy explanation, baffling experts throughout the centuries.

✳   ✳   ✳   ✳

THOUGH NO ONE can definitively say who erected this massive monument, when and why they built it, and how they did so without the aid of modern machinery, there are no shortage of theories. So let's hear from the experts:

Archaeologists: Speculate that the site first took shape about 5,000 years ago, with the first stones being laid in 3000 B.C. The monument was finally completed in 1500 B.C., perhaps serving as a memorial to fallen warriors, as the burial mounds that surround the site might indicate.

Geologists: Claim that 80 of the four-ton rocks at Stonehenge, known as bluestones, were quarried from the Prescelly Mountains in Wales—240 miles away—and then transported by sled and barge to their current location.

Astronomers: Observe that builders placed the rocks in concentric circles, thus creating a massive solar observatory through which early man could predict the arrival of eclipses and follow the passage of the seasons. On the longest day of the year, the rising sun appears directly behind one of the main stones, the so-called "Heel Stone."

Historians: Think that the stones form the walls of an ancient temple—a place for people to worship the heavens. In later times, it was used by druids to celebrate their pagan festivals.

Conspiracy theorists: Believe Stonehenge was placed there by a UFO.

What Happened to the Roanoke Island Colony?

Twenty years before England established its first successful colony in the New World, an entire village of English colonists disappeared in what would later be known as North Carolina. Did these pioneers all perish? Did they join a friendly tribe? Could they have left descendants who live among us today?

✳ ✳ ✳ ✳

Timing Is Everything

TALK ABOUT BAD timing. As far as John White was concerned, England couldn't have picked a worse time to go to war. It was November 1587, and White had just arrived in England from the New World. He intended to gather relief supplies and immediately sail back to Roanoke Island, where he had left more than 100 colonists who were running short of food. Unfortunately, the English were gearing up to fight Spain. Every seaworthy ship, including White's, was pressed into naval service. Not a one could be spared for his return voyage to America.

Nobody Home

When John White finally returned to North America three years later, he was dismayed to discover that the colonists he had left behind were nowhere to be found. Instead, he stumbled upon a mystery—one that has never been solved.

The village that White and company had founded in 1587 on Roanoke Island lay completely deserted. Houses had been dismantled (as if someone planned to move them), but the pieces lay in the long grass along with iron tools and farming equipment. A stout stockade made of logs stood empty.

White found no sign of his daughter Eleanor, her husband Ananias, or their daughter Virginia Dare—the first English child born in America. None of the 87 men, 17 women, and 11 children remained. No bodies or obvious gravesites offered clues to their fate. The only clues—if they were clues—that White could find were the letters CRO carved into a tree trunk and the word CROATOAN carved into a log of the abandoned fort.

No Forwarding Address

All White could do was hope that the colonists had been taken in by friendly natives.

Croatoan—also spelled "Croatan"—was the name of a barrier island to the south and also the name of a tribe of Native Americans that lived on that island. Unlike other area tribes, the Croatoans had been friendly to English newcomers, and one of them, Manteo, had traveled to England with earlier explorers and returned to act as interpreter for the Roanoke colony. Had the colonists, with Manteo's help, moved to Croatoan? Were they safe among friends?

White tried to find out, but his timing was rotten once again. He had arrived on the Carolina coast as a hurricane bore down on the region. The storm hit before he could mount a search. His ship was blown past Croatoan Island and out to sea. Although the ship and crew survived the storm and made it back to England, White was stuck again. He tried repeatedly but failed to raise money for another search party.

No one has ever learned the fate of the Roanoke Island colonists, but there are no shortage of theories as to what happened to them. A small sailing vessel and other boats that White had left with them were gone when he returned. It's possible that the colonists used the vessels to travel to another island or to the mainland. White had talked with others before he left about possibly moving the settlement to a more secure location inland. It's even possible that the colonists tired of waiting for White's return and tried to sail back to England. If so, they would have perished at sea. Yet there are at least a few shreds of hearsay evidence that the colonists survived in America.

Rumors of Survivors

In 1607, Captain John Smith and company established the first successful English settlement in North America at Jamestown, Virginia. The colony's secretary, William Strachey, wrote four years later about hearing a report of four English men, two boys, and one young woman who had been sighted south of Jamestown at a settlement of the Eno tribe, where they were being used as slaves. If the report was true, who else could these English have been but Roanoke survivors?

For more than a century after the colonists' disappearance, stories emerged of gray-eyed Native Americans and English-speaking villages in North Carolina and Virginia. In 1709, an English surveyor said members of the Hatteras tribe living on North Carolina's Outer Banks—some of them with light-colored eyes—claimed to be descendants of white people. It's possible that the Hatteras were the same people that the 1587 colonists called Croatoan.

In the intervening centuries, many of the individual tribes of the region have disappeared. Some died out. Other tribes were absorbed into larger groups such as the Tuscarora. One surviving group, the Lumbee, has also been called Croatoan. The Lumbee, who still live in North Carolina, often have Caucasian features. Could they be descendants of Roanoke colonists? Many among the Lumbee dismiss the notion as fanciful, but the tribe has long been thought to be of mixed heritage and has been speaking English so long that none among them know what language preceded it.

Who Was the Castaway at Sandy Cove?

This mute amputee has a foothold in Nova Scotian folklore—nearly a century after his death.

✳ ✳ ✳ ✳

Who Is This Man?

ON SEPTEMBER 8, 1863, two fishermen in Sandy Cove, Nova Scotia, discovered an unusual treasure washed ashore: a lone man in his twenties with newly amputated legs, left with just a loaf of bread and jug of water.

There were a few clues, such as his manner of dress, that led the townspeople to speculate on whether the fellow was a gentleman, an aristocrat. But there was no point in asking him—he didn't speak. In fact, he was said to have uttered only three words after being found: "Jerome" (which the villagers came to call him), "Columbo" (perhaps the name of his ship), and "Trieste," an Italian village.

Based on these three words, the villagers theorized he was Italian and concocted various romantic stories about his fate: that he was an Italian nobleman captured and mutilated by pirates (or perhaps a pirate himself), a seaman punished for threatening mutiny, or maybe he was an heir to a fortune who had been crippled and cast away by a jealous rival.

Charity Case

Jerome was taken to the home of Jean and Juliette Nicholas, a French family who lived across the bay in Meteghan. There was still a chance Jerome could be French and Jean was fluent in five languages. (Although none of which proved successful in communicating with Jerome.)

In 1870, the Nicholases moved away. The town, enthralled with their mysterious nobleman, rallied together and paid the Comeau family $140 a year to take him in. On Sundays after mass, locals would stop by and pay a few cents for a look at the maimed mute. Jerome lived with the Comeaus for the next 52 years until his death on April 19, 1912.

Records suggest Jerome was no cool-headed castaway. Though he never spoke intelligibly, hearing certain words (specifically "pirate") would send him into a rage. It's also been said that he was particularly anxious about the cold, spending winters with his leg stumps shoved under the stove for warmth. Though in his younger days he enjoyed sitting in the sun, he allegedly spent the last 20 years of his life as a complete shut-in, huddled by the stove.

Mystery Revealed

Jerome's panic about the cold makes sense—if the latest hypotheses about him are true. Modern historians have posited a couple of different theories, both of which trace Jerome to New Brunswick.

One group of scholars uncovered a story in New Brunswick about a man who was behaving erratically and couldn't (or wouldn't) speak. To rid themselves of the weirdo, members of his community put him on a boat to New England—but not without first chopping off his legs. The man never made it to New England but instead wound up on the beach at Sandy Cove.

Another theory links Jerome to a man—believed to be European—who was found in 1861, pinned under a fallen tree in Chipman, New Brunswick, with frozen legs that had to be amputated. Without a doctor nearby, the man was sent down the St. John River to Gagetown and then shipped back to Chipman, where he was supported for two years by the parish and nicknamed "Gamby" by the locals (which means "legs" in Italian). At that point, the parish got tired of taking care of him and paid a captain to drop him across the bay in Nova Scotia. Another account suggests that after the surgery, the man wasn't returned to Gagetown but put directly on a boat.

Regardless of which theory is more accurate, all suggest that the reason for Jerome's arrival in Nova Scotia is that an entire town disowned him.

But New Brunswick's loss has been Nova Scotia's gain. There, Jerome is a local legend. He has been the subject of a movie (1994's *Le secret de Jérôme*), and a home for the handicapped bears his name. Tourists can even stop by his grave for a quick snapshot of the headstone, which reads, quite simply, "Jerome."

What Are Some Unexplained Mysteries of the Universe?

Unidentified flying objects are old hat compared with these popular supernatural mysteries, unexplained phenomena, and unsolved puzzles. Read on and see if we can make you a believer.

✳ ✳ ✳ ✳

Bermuda Triangle

THIS AREA IN the Atlantic Ocean between Bermuda, Miami, and San Juan is legendary as the site from which a great number of ships, small boats, and airplanes have allegedly disappeared. Although the United States Coast Guard does not officially recognize the Bermuda Triangle or maintain any data on the area, conspiracy theorists have spent countless hours documenting the mysteries of the region. Some researchers estimate that more than 2,000 boats and 125 planes have been lost there, including the famous Flight 19, and five Navy bombers that disappeared in 1945, followed by their search-and-rescue seaplane. Explanations for the disappearances include extraterrestrials that captured the boats and planes, deep-water earthquakes that caused freak waves, and time warps that took vessels to a different time or dimension.

Easter Island

One of the most remote areas on Earth, Easter Island is in the southern Pacific Ocean, 1,400 miles from any other island. So how is it that more than 800 giant, centuries-old stone statues line the island's coast? Who built them? How did they get there? These questions have baffled enthusiasts for decades. The island was discovered in 1722 by a Dutch explorer who found it uninhabited, except for the numerous *moai*, as the statues are known. The most popular explanation for the statues suggests that Polynesian seafarers arrived on the island between A.D. 400 and 1600 in canoes carried by ocean currents. Unable to paddle against the currents to leave the island, the new inhabitants carved the statues out of a volcanic wall and placed them around the island using simple machines. But when the island's resources began to give out, the people resorted to cannibalism, wiping out the population by the time the Dutch landed.

Area 51

Officially, Area 51 is a remote strip of land about 90 miles north of Las Vegas that the Air Force uses to test new military aircraft. Unofficially, it's a storage and examination site for crashed alien spaceships, a meeting spot for extraterrestrials, a breeding ground for weather control and time travel technology, and possibly the home of a one-world political group. Because the government won't discuss what goes on at Area 51, inquiring minds have had to develop their own theories. In 1989, Bob Lazar, a former government scientist, told a Las Vegas TV station that he worked on alien technology at a facility near Area 51. Millions believed Lazar's story and Area 51's mysterious reputation was sealed.

Nostradamus

Whether you believe his predictions or not, 16th-century French philosopher Nostradamus was an impressive guy. After all, how many authors' books are still in print over 460 years after their first editions? *Les Prophéties*, first published in 1555, is a series of poems that predict major world events in a vague, timeless manner that leaves much room for interpretation. Nostradamus's followers credit him with predicting the rise of both Napoleon and Hitler, the French Revolution, the Great Fire of London, both World Wars, the death of Princess Diana, the Apollo moon landings, and the terrorist attacks of September 11, 2001, among other things. Skeptics say the links between his prophecies and world events are the result of misinterpretations or mistranslations, or are so vague that they're laughable.

Crop Circles

Art exhibit, practical joke, or universal mystery, crop circles have been captivating observers for decades. They occur when crops are flattened to form geometric patterns most visible from the sky. Crop circles are usually found in England but have also been spotted in Australia, South Africa, China, Russia, and other countries. In 1991, two men admitted they had created a number of the crop circles identified in England since 1978 by marking out circles with a length of rope and flattening the crops with iron bars and wooden planks. But "croppies," a group of scientists and paranormal enthusiasts, argue that some of the designs are far too complex for humans to create with simple tools. Croppies believe that some of the circles are the result of flying saucers that land in fields, freak wind vortexes, or ball lightning—a brief flash of light usually the size and shape of a basketball that's not always associated with a thunderstorm.

What Caused the Tunguska Event?

What created an explosion 1,000 times greater than the atomic bomb at Hiroshima, destroyed 80 million trees, but left no hole in the ground?

✳ ✳ ✳ ✳

The Event

ON THE MORNING of June 30, 1908, a powerful explosion ripped through the remote Siberian wilderness near the Tunguska River. Witnesses, from nomadic herdsmen and passengers on a train to a group of people at the nearest trading post, reported seeing a bright object streak through the sky and explode into an enormous fireball. The resulting shockwave flattened approximately 830 square miles of forest. Seismographs in England recorded the event twice, once as the initial shockwave passed and then again after it had circled the planet. A huge cloud of ash reflected sunlight from over the horizon across Asia and Europe. People reported there being enough light in the night sky to facilitate reading.

A Wrathful God

Incredibly, nearly 20 years passed before anyone visited the site. Everyone had a theory of what happened, and none of it good. Outside Russia, however, the event itself was largely unknown. The English scientists who recorded the tremor, for instance, thought that it was simply an earthquake. Inside Russia, the unstable political climate of the time was not conducive to mounting an expedition. Subsequently, the economic and social upheaval created by World War I and the Russian Revolution made scientific expeditions impossible.

Looking for a Hole in the Ground

In 1921, mineralogist Leonid A. Kulik was charged by the Mineralogical Museum of St. Petersburg with locating meteorites that had fallen inside the Soviet Union. Having read old newspapers and eyewitness testimony from the Tunguska region, Kulik convinced the Academy of Sciences in 1927 to fund an expedition to locate the crater and meteorite he was certain existed.

The expedition was not going to be easy, as spring thaws turned the region into a morass. And when the team finally reached the area of destruction, their superstitious guides refused to go any further. Kulik, however, was encouraged by the sight of millions of trees splayed to the ground in a radial pattern pointing outward from an apparent impact point. Returning again, the team finally reached the epicenter where, to their surprise, they found neither a meteor nor a crater. Instead, they found a forest of what looked like telephone poles—trees stripped of their branches and reduced to vertical shafts. Scientists would not witness a similar sight until 1945 in the area below the Hiroshima blast.

Theories Abound

Here are some of the many theories of what happened at Tunguska.

Stony Asteroid: Traveling at a speed of about 33,500 miles per hour, a large space rock heated the air around it to 44,500 degrees Fahrenheit and exploded at an altitude of about 28,000 feet. This produced a fireball that utterly annihilated the asteroid.

Kimberlite Eruption: Formed nearly 2,000 miles below the Earth's surface, a shaft of heavy kimberlite rock carried a huge quantity of methane gas to Earth's surface where it exploded with great force.

Black Holes and Antimatter: As early as 1941, some scientists believed that a small antimatter asteroid exploded when it encountered the upper atmosphere. In 1973, several theorists proposed that the Tunguska event was the result of a tiny black hole passing through Earth's surface.

Alien Shipwreck: Noting the similarities between the Hiroshima atomic bomb blast and the Tunguska event, Russian novelist Alexander Kazantsev was the first to suggest that an atomic-powered UFO exploded over Siberia in 1908.

Tesla's Death Ray: Scientist Nikola Tesla is rumored to have test-fired a "death ray" on June 30, 1908, but he believed the experiment to be unsuccessful—until he learned of the Tunguska event.

Okay, but What Really Happened?

In June 2008, scientists from around the world marked the 100-year anniversary of the Tunguska event with conferences in Moscow. Yet scientists still cannot reach a consensus as to what caused the event. In fact, the anniversary gathering was split into two opposing factions—extraterrestrial versus terrestrial—who met at different sites in the city.

Who Downed the Red Baron?

He was the most successful flying ace of World War I—the conflict that introduced the airplane as a weapon of war. Yet, his demise has been credited to a number of likely opponents, both in the sky and on the ground.

✳ ✳ ✳ ✳

A Precious Little Prussian

MANFRED VON RICHTHOFEN was born in Silesia, Prussia (now part of Poland), in May 1892. Coming from a family steeped in nobility, the young von Richthofen decided he would follow in his father's footsteps and become a career soldier. At 11 years old, he enrolled in the cadet corps and, upon completion, became a member of a Prussian cavalry unit.

Up, Up, and Away

The Germans were at the forefront in using aircraft as offensive weapons against the British, French, and Russians during World War I. Von Richthofen was recruited into a flying unit as an "observer"—the second occupant of a two-seat plane who would direct the pilot over areas to gather intelligence. By 1915, von Richthofen decided to become a pilot himself, having already downed an enemy aircraft as an observer.

The young and green pilot joined a prestigious flying squad, one of the premier German jagdstaffeln—literally "hunting squadrons." In late 1916, von Richthofen's aggressive style brought him face-to-face with Britain's greatest fighter pilot, Major Lanoe Hawker. After a spirited battle in the sky, the German brought Hawker down in a tailspin, killing him. Von Richthofen called Hawker "a brave man and a sportsman." He later mounted the machine gun from the British plane over the door of his family home as a tribute to Hawker. The bold flying ace often showed a great deal of respect and affinity for his foes, once referring to his English dogfight opponents as "waltzing partners." Yet, he remained ruthless, even carrying with him a photograph of an Allied pilot he had viciously blown apart.

Creating an Identity

Von Richthofen quickly became the most feared, and respected, pilot in the skies. As he sought faster and more nimble aircraft, he decided he needed to be instantly recognizable. He ordered his plane to be painted bright red, with the German Iron Cross emblazoned on the fuselage. The "Red Baron" was born.

The End—But at Whose Hands?

By the spring of 1918, the Red Baron had shot down an amazing 80 Allied airplanes. This feat earned him the distinguished "Blue Max" award, and he assembled his own squadron of crack-shot pilots known as "the Flying Circus." But the celebrated pilot was not without his failures.

Von Richthofen suffered a head wound during an air battle in July 1917, which may have left an open wound exposing a small portion of his skull until his death. There are theories that this injury resulted in brain damage—if so, it would have caused the Red Baron to make some serious errors in judgment that may have led to his death on April 21, 1918.

On that day, von Richthofen was embroiled in a deadly dog-fight with British Royal Air Force Sopwith Camels. As the Red Baron trained his machine-gun sights on a young pilot, enemy fire came seemingly from nowhere, striking his red Fokker. Von Richthofen crashed in an area of France occupied by Australian and Canadian allies. He was buried with full military honors by a respectful British Royal Air Force (RAF).

However, questions remain to this day as to who exactly killed von Richthofen. He suffered a fatal bullet wound through his chest. The RAF credited one of their pilots, but another story tells of Canadian soldiers who pounced on the plane crash and literally murdered the Red Baron. Still other tales claim von Richthofen was shot from the ground by rifle or machine-gun fire as he flew overhead.

The answer remains lost, perhaps forever. But there is no question as to the identity of the greatest flying ace of the First World War. That honor belongs to the Red Baron.

Who Killed Thomas Ince?

Who's at the heart of the cloaked-in-secrets demise of Thomas Ince? Who, of the loads of lovelies and gallons of gents on the infamous Oneida yacht that night, was the killer? Curious minds demand to know.

✳   ✳   ✳   ✳

THE NIGHT IS November 15, 1924. The setting is the *Oneida* yacht. The principal players are: Thomas H. Ince, Marion Davies, Charlie Chaplin, and William Randolph Hearst.

The Facts

By 1924, William Randolph Hearst had built a huge newspaper empire; he dabbled in filmmaking and politics; he owned the *Oneida*. Thomas H. Ince was a prolific movie producer.

Charlie Chaplin was a star comedian. Marion Davies was an actor. The web of connections went like this: Hearst and Davies were lovers; Davies and Chaplin were rumored to be lovers; Hearst and Ince were locked in tense business negotiations; Ince was celebrating a birthday.

For Ince's birthday, Hearst planned a party on his yacht. It was a lavish one—champagne all around. In the era of Prohibition, this was not just extravagant, it was also illegal. But Hearst had ulterior motives: He'd heard rumors that his mistress, Davies, was secretly seeing Chaplin, and so he invited Chaplin to the party. The *Oneida* set sail from San Pedro, California, headed to San Diego on Saturday, November 15.

An unfortunate but persistent fog settled over the events once the cast of characters were onboard the yacht. What is known definitively is that Ince arrived at the party late, due to business, and that he did not depart the yacht under his own power. Whether he was sick or dead depends on which version you believe, but it's a fact that Ince left the yacht on a stretcher on Sunday, November 16. What happened? Various scenarios have been put forward over the years:

* Possibility 1: Hearst shoots Ince. Hearst invites Chaplin to the party to observe his behavior around Davies and to verify their affair. After catching the two in a compromising position, he flies off the handle, runs to his stateroom, grabs his gun, and comes back shooting. In this scenario, Ince tries to break up the trouble but gets shot by mistake.

* Possibility 2: Hearst shoots Ince. It's the same end result as possibility 1, but in this scenario, Davies and Ince are alone in the galley after Ince comes in to look for something to settle the queasiness caused by his notorious ulcers. Entering and seeing the two people together, Hearst assumes Chaplin—not Ince—is with Davies. He pulls his gun and shoots.

* Possibility 3: Chaplin shoots Ince. Chaplin, a week away from marrying a pregnant 16-year-old to avoid scandal and the law, is forlorn to the point where he considers suicide. While contemplating his gun, it accidentally goes off, and the bullet goes through the thin walls of the ship to hit Ince in the neighboring room.

* Possibility 4: An assassin shoots Ince. In this scenario, a hired assassin shoots Ince so Hearst can escape an unwanted business deal with the producer.

* Possibility 5: Ince dies of natural causes. Known for his shaky health, Ince succumbs to rabid indigestion and chronic heart problems. A development such as this would not surprise his friends and family.

Aftermath

Regardless of which of the various scenarios might be true, Ince was wheeled off Hearst's yacht. But what happened next?

That's not so clear, either. The facts of the aftermath of Ince's death are as hazy as the facts of the death itself. All reports agree that Ince did, in fact, die. There was no autopsy, and his body was cremated. After the cremation, Ince's wife, Nell, moved to Europe. But beyond those matters of record, there are simply conflicting stories.

The individuals involved had various reasons for wanting to protect themselves from whatever might have happened on the yacht. If an unlawful death did indeed take place, the motivation speaks for itself. But even if nothing untoward happened, Hearst was breaking the Prohibition laws. The damage an investigation could have caused was enough reason to make Hearst cover up any attention that could have come his way from Ince's death. As a result, he tried to hide all mention of any foul play. Although Hearst didn't own the *Los Angeles Times*, he was plenty powerful. Rumor has it that an early edition of the paper after Ince's death carried the screaming headline, "Movie Producer Shot on Hearst Yacht." By later in the day, the headline had disappeared.

For his part, Chaplin denied being on the *Oneida* in the first place. In his version of the story, he didn't attend the party for Ince at all. He did, however, claim to visit Ince—along with Hearst and Davies—later in the week. He also stated that Ince died two weeks after that visit. Most reports show that Ince was definitely dead within 48 hours of the yacht party.

Davies agreed that Chaplin was never aboard the *Oneida* that fateful night. In her version, Ince's wife called her the day after Ince left the yacht to inform her of Ince's death. Ince's doctor claimed that the producer didn't die until Tuesday, two days later.

So, what really happened? Who knows? Most of the people on the yacht never commented on their experience. Louella Parsons certainly didn't. The famed gossip columnist was reportedly aboard the *Oneida* that night (although she denied it as well). She had experienced some success writing for a Hearst newspaper, but shortly after this event, Hearst gave her a lifetime contract and wide syndication, allowing her to become a Hollywood power broker. Coincidence? No one can say for certain.

What Happened to Amelia Earhart?

Was Amelia Earhart the victim of some kind of conspiracy? Her choice not to keep up with technological knowhow is more likely to blame for her disappearance.

✳ ✳ ✳ ✳

PIONEERING AVIATOR AMELIA Earhart set records and made headlines because of her talent, courage, tireless work ethic, and willingness to craft her own image. But no one is perfect, of course. Earhart failed to keep up with the technologies that helped other pilots to call for help and made flying a much less dangerous job.

Opening the Books

After Orville and Wilbur Wright made the first powered airplane flight in 1903, an ugly patent war began among inventors in the United States. A huge number of researchers from all kinds of backgrounds—the Wrights themselves were bicycle mechanics, publishers, and journalists—had made incremental improvements on one another's work, brainstormed similar ideas, and generally squabbled over who was making the best progress. Think of it as a grade-school classroom where all the students are grown men, and they've propped up folders and textbooks to hide their tests from their classmates.

These aviation pioneers were out-pettying today's worst startup companies in Silicon Valley. They went to court over fine details of one aircraft versus another, citing their own notes and evidence that had largely been kept secret. But after a decade of brutal lawsuits and public fighting over who was first, who invented what, and where the credit was due, the United States entered World War I. Aviation companies were de facto forced to pour their proprietary research and patents into a large pool shared by all of America's aircraft industry.

Making their technology "open source" was part of the war effort, but as with software and other inventions today, the open industry led to better and more rapid developments. After World War I ended, pilots began to set records left and right using ingenious inventions like the artificial horizon—something pilots still use in cockpits today, in a modernized form of course. And some pilots made their livings in traveling airshows as airplanes became more and more familiar, but no less mesmerizing, to the American people. Amelia Earhart was one of these pilots, traveling to build buzz for her own career.

The Morse the Merrier

Earhart was a gifted and remarkable pilot, the first woman to *ride* in a plane (as a passenger) across the Atlantic and then to fly across it as the pilot. Earhart started a professional organization for women pilots and took a faculty position at Purdue University. She and fellow groundbreaking pilot Charles Lindbergh were like movie stars by the 1930s, and Earhart was witty and engaging when she spoke with the press or members of the public. Her career was at a perfect point for her to make an outsize gesture in the form of a trip around the world. She wasn't the first, but she was definitely the most famous.

Technology leapt ahead during her career, and Morse code was in wide use by the time Earhart began her trip around the world. The world's leading navigation instructor offered to teach Earhart radio operation, Morse code, and cutting-edge navigation, but she didn't have time before her trip, which had already been delayed by a failed first attempt. The navigator she chose also didn't know Morse code. When they grew disoriented in poor weather over the Pacific Ocean, they could not call for help in Morse code, and their radio reception was too poor to send or receive verbal messages from the Navy ships assigned to support the open water sections of their flight.

The "what ifs" of Earhart's failed final journey stoke pop culture across the decades, and who can say what could have happened if she and her navigator were able to get help? Without specific coordinates or landmarks, which Earhart likely could have relayed to her support team, even modern rescuers can't cover large swaths of open ocean with success. Morse code might have made the critical difference.

What Is Ohio's Greatest Unsolved Mystery?

From 1935 until 1938, a brutal madman roamed the Flats of Cleveland. The killer—known as the Mad Butcher of Kingsbury Run—is believed to have murdered 12 men and women. Despite a massive manhunt, the murderer was never apprehended.

✳ ✳ ✳ ✳

IN 1935, THE Depression had hit Cleveland hard, leaving large numbers of people homeless. Shantytowns sprang up on the eastern side of the city in Kingsbury Run—a popular place for transients—near the Erie and Nickel Plate railroads.

It is unclear who was the Butcher's first victim. Recent research suggests it may have been an unidentified woman found floating in Lake Erie—in pieces—on September 5, 1934; she would be known as Jane Doe I but dubbed by some as the "Lady of the Lake." The first official victim was found in the Jackass Hill area of Kingsbury Run on September 23, 1935. The unidentified body, labeled John Doe, had been dead for almost a month. A mere 30 feet away from the body was another victim, Edward Andrassy. Unlike John Doe, Andrassy had only been dead for days, indicating that the spot was a dumping ground. Police began staking out the area.

After a few months passed without another body, police thought the worst was over. Then on January 26, 1936, the partial remains of a new victim, a woman, were found in downtown Cleveland. On February 7, more remains were found at a separate location, and the deceased was identified as Florence Genevieve Polillo. Despite similarities among the three murders, authorities had yet to connect them.

Tattoo Man, Eliot Ness, and More Victims

On June 5, two young boys passing through Kingsbury Run discovered a severed head. The rest of the body was found near the Nickel Plate railroad police station. Despite six distinctive tattoos on the man's body (thus the nickname "Tattoo Man"), he was never identified and became John Doe II.

At this point, Cleveland's newly appointed director of public safety, Eliot Ness, was officially briefed on the case. While Ness and his men hunted down leads, the headless body of another unidentified male was found west of Cleveland on July 22, 1936. It appeared that the man, John Doe III, had been murdered several months earlier. On September 10, the headless body of a sixth victim, John Doe IV, was found in Kingsbury Run.

Ness officially started spearheading the investigation. Determined to bring the killer to justice, Ness's staff fanned out across the city, even going undercover in the Kingsbury Run area. As 1936 drew to a close, no suspects had been named nor new victims discovered. City residents believed that Ness's team had run the killer off. But future events would prove that the killer was back…with a vengeance.

The Body Count Climbs

A woman's mutilated torso washed up on the beach at 156th Street on February 23, 1937. The rest would wash ashore two months later. (Strangely, the body washed up in the same location as the "Lady of the Lake" had three years earlier.)

On June 6, 1937, a teenager found the decomposed body of a woman inside of a burlap sack under the Lorain-Carnegie Bridge in Cleveland. With the body was a newspaper from June of the previous year, suggesting a timeline for the murder. An investigation indicated the body might belong to one Rose Wallace; this was never confirmed, and the victim is sometimes referred to as Jane Doe II. Pieces of another man's body (the ninth victim) began washing ashore on July 6, just below

Kingsbury Run. Cleveland newspapers were having a field day with the case that the "great" Eliot Ness couldn't solve.

Burning of Kingsbury Run

The next nine months were quiet, and the public began to relax. When a woman's severed leg was found in the Cuyahoga River on April 8, 1938, however, people debated its connection to the Butcher. But the rest of Jane Doe III was soon found inside two burlap sacks floating in the river (*sans* head, of course).

On August 16, 1938, the last two confirmed victims of the Butcher were found together at the East 9th Street Lakeshore Dump. Jane Doe IV had apparently been dead for four to six months prior to discovery, while John Doe VI may have been dead for almost nine months.

Something snapped inside Eliot Ness. On the night of August 18, Ness and dozens of police officials raided the shantytowns in the Flats, ending up in Kingsbury Run. Along the way, they interrogated or arrested anyone they came across, and Ness ordered the shanties burned to the ground. There would be no more confirmed victims of the Mad Butcher of Kingsbury Run.

Who Was the Mad Butcher?

There were two prime suspects in the case, though no one was ever charged. The first was Dr. Francis Sweeney, a surgeon with the knowledge many believed necessary to mutilate the victims the way the killer did. (He was also a cousin of Congressman Martin L. Sweeney, a known political opponent of Ness.)

In August 1938, Dr. Sweeney was interrogated by Ness, two other men, and the inventor of the polygraph machine, Dr. Royal Grossman. By all accounts, Sweeney failed the polygraph test (several times), and Ness believed he had his man, but he was released due to lack of evidence. Two days after the interrogation, on August 25, 1938, Sweeney checked himself into the Sandusky Veterans Hospital. He remained institutionalized at various facilities until his death in 1965. Because Sweeney voluntarily checked himself in, he could have left at any time.

The other suspect was Frank Dolezal, who was arrested by private investigators on July 5, 1939, as a suspect in the murder of Florence Polillo, with whom he had lived for a time. While in custody, Dolezal confessed to killing Polillo, although some believe the confession was forced. Either way, Dolezal died under mysterious circumstances while incarcerated at the Cuyahoga County Jail before he could be charged.

As for Eliot Ness, some believe his inability to bring the Butcher to trial weighed on him for the rest of his life. Ness went to his grave without getting a conviction. To this day, the case remains open.

What Was the Dyatlov Pass Incident?

Nine experienced hikers and skiers trek into the Russian wilderness and promptly disappear. Weeks later, their mangled bodies are found among the ruins of the campsite, with no trace of evidence as to how they died. Read on for a closer look at one of the greatest unsolved mysteries of modern times.

✳ ✳ ✳ ✳

Off to the Otorten Mountain

IN EARLY 1959, a group of outdoor enthusiasts formed a skiing and hiking expedition to Otorten Mountain, which is part of the northern Ural Mountain range in Russia. The group, led by Igor Dyatlov, consisted of seven other men and two women: Yury Doroshenko, Georgy Krivonischenko, Alexander Kolevatov, Rustem Slobodin, Nicolas Thibeaux-Brignolle, Yuri Yudin, Alexander Zolotaryov, Lyudmila Dubinina, and Zinaida Kolmogorova.

The group's journey began on January 27. The following day, Yudin became ill and had to return home. It would be the last time he would see his friends alive. Using personal photographs and journals belonging to the members of the ski trip to piece together the chain of events, it appeared that on February 1, the group got disoriented making their way to Otorten Mountain and ended up heading too far to the west. Once they realized they were heading in the wrong direction, the decision was made to simply set up camp for the night. What happened next is a mystery to this day.

Mountain of the Dead

When no word had been heard from the group by February 20, eight days after their planned return, a group of volunteers organized a search. On February 26, they found the group's abandoned campsite on the east side of the mountain Kholat Syakhl. (As if the story were written by a horror novelist, *Kholat Syakhl* happens to mean "Mountain of the Dead" in the Mansi language.) The search team found a badly damaged tent that appeared to have been ripped open from the inside. They also found several sets of footprints. Following the trail of footprints, searchers discovered the bodies of Krivonischenko and Doroshenko, shoeless and dressed only in their underwear. Three more bodies—those belonging to Dyatlov, Kolmogorova and Slobodin—were found nearby. It was later determined that all five had died from hypothermia.

On May 4, the bodies of the four other hikers were recovered in the woods near where the bodies of Krivonischenko and Doroshenko had been found. The discovery of these four raised even more questions. To begin with, Thibeaux-Brignolle's skull had been crushed and both Dubunina and Zolotaryov had major chest fractures. The force needed to cause these wounds was compared to that of a high-speed car crash. Oddly, Dubinina's tongue appeared to have been ripped out.

Looking at the evidence, it appeared as though all nine group members had bedded down for the night, only to be woken up by something so frightening that they all quickly left the tent and ran into the freezing cold night. One by one, they either froze to death or else succumbed to their injuries, the cause of which was never determined.

Remains a Mystery

Things got even stranger at the funerals for the nine individuals. Family members would later remark that some of the deceased's skin had become orange and their hair had turned grey. Medical tests and a Geiger counter brought to the site showed some of the bodies had high levels of radiation.

So what happened to the hikers? Authorities eventually concluded that "an unknown compelling force" caused the deaths. The case would be officially closed in the spring of 1959 due to the "absence of a guilty party." Stories and theories still abound, pointing to everything from the Russian government covering up secret military exercises in the area to violent UFO encounters. Today, the area where the nine hikers met their untimely demise is known as Dyatlov Pass, after the leader of the ill-fated group.

What Happened to D. B. Cooper?

On the day before Thanksgiving, 1971, in Portland, Oregon, a man in his mid-forties who called himself Dan Cooper (news reports would later misidentify him as "D. B.") boarded a Northwest Orient Airlines 727 that was bound for Seattle. Dressed in a suit and tie and carrying a briefcase, Cooper was calm and polite when he handed a note to a flight attendant.

✳   ✳   ✳   ✳

THE NOTE SAID that his briefcase contained a bomb; he was hijacking the plane. Cooper told the crew that upon landing in Seattle, he wanted four parachutes and two hundred thousand dollars in twenty-dollar bills.

His demands were met, and Cooper released the other passengers. He ordered the pilots to fly to Mexico, but he gave specific instructions to keep the plane under ten thousand feet with the wing flaps at fifteen degrees, restricting the aircraft's speed. That night, in a cold rainstorm somewhere over Washington, Cooper donned the parachutes, and with the money packed in knapsacks that were tied to his body, he jumped from the 727's rear stairs.

For several months afterward, the FBI conducted an extensive manhunt of the rugged forest terrain, but the agents were unable to find even a shred of evidence. In 1972, a copycat hijacker named Richard McCoy successfully jumped from a flight over Utah with five hundred thousand dollars and was arrested days later. At first the FBI thought McCoy was Cooper, but he didn't match the description provided by the crew of Cooper's flight. Other suspects surfaced over the years, including a Florida antiques dealer with a shady past who confessed to his wife on his deathbed that he was Cooper—though he was later discredited by DNA testing.

Cooper hadn't hurt anybody, and he had no apparent political agenda. He became a folk hero of sorts—he was immortalized in books, in song, in television documentaries, and in a movie, *The Pursuit of D.B. Cooper*. In 1980, solid evidence surfaced: An eight-year-old boy found $5,800 in rotting twenty-dollar bills along the Columbia River, and the serial numbers matched those on the cash that was given to Cooper. But while thousands of leads have been investigated over the years, the case remains the only unsolved plane hijacking in U.S. history.

Late in 2007, the FBI's Seattle field office kickstarted the investigation, providing pictures on its website of some key evidence, including the money and Cooper's black clip-on tie.

Agent Larry Carr, leader of the investigative team, thinks he knows what happened to Cooper, who jumped into a wind of two hundred miles per hour in total darkness on a cold and rainy night. "Diving into the wilderness without a plan, without the right equipment, in such terrible conditions," Carr says, "he probably never even got his chute open."

What Really Killed John Wayne?

The Conqueror (1956) wasn't exactly John Wayne's masterpiece. The historical drama has been criticized for miscasting Wayne in the lead role. However, The Conqueror *has been connected to far worse things than box-office failure: Some say the movie is to blame for Wayne's death from stomach cancer two decades after its debut. What's more, Wayne isn't the only person believed to have died as a result of the project. Was the nearby nuclear testing site to blame?*

✳ ✳ ✳ ✳

Radiation Exposure

THE QUESTIONS SURROUNDING *The Conqueror* come as a result of its filming location: The movie was shot near St. George and Snow Canyon, Utah, an area in the vicinity of a nuclear testing site. In the early 1950s, the U.S. military set off nearly a dozen atomic bombs just miles away from the location, sending clouds of radioactive dust into St. George and Snow Canyon. Work on *The Conqueror* began just two years later, even though the film company and cast knew about the radiation. To make matters worse, after the location work had wrapped, the film's crew transported dirt from the area back to soundstages in Hollywood to help re-create the setting for in-studio shooting. (At the time, the effects of radiation exposure were not as well documented as they are today.)

In the years following the filming of *The Conqueror*, numerous members of the cast and crew developed cancer. Aside from Wayne, at least 45 people from the group died from causes related to the disease, including actress Agnes Moorehead, who died in 1974 from uterine cancer; actress Susan Hayward, who died from brain and skin cancer at age 57 in 1975; and director Dick Powell, who, in 1963, passed away at age 58 from lymphatic cancer. Actors Pedro Armendariz and John Hoyt and both took their own lives after learning of their diagnoses.

An article published in *People* magazine in 1980 stated that 41 percent of those who worked on the movie—91 out of 220 people—later developed cancer. That figure reportedly didn't include the hundreds of Utah-based actors who worked as extras. Still, the numbers far exceeded any statistical normality for a given group of individuals. A scientist with the Pentagon's Defense Nuclear Agency was quoted in the article as saying: "Please, God, don't let us have killed John Wayne."

Broader Findings

While many of the actors were heavy smokers—Wayne included—the strange circumstances surrounding the filming of *The Conqueror* have turned into an underground scandal of sorts. And the general findings from the city of St. George certainly don't help quell the concerns.

In 1997, a study by the National Cancer Institute found that children who lived in the St. George area during the 1950s were exposed to as much as 70 times the amount of radiation than was originally reported because of contaminated milk taken from exposed animals. Consequently, the study reported that the children had elevated risks for cancer development. The report further stated that the government "knew from the beginning that a Western test site would spread contamination across most of the country" and that the exposure could have easily been avoided.

The government eventually passed an act called the Radiation Exposure Compensation Act, which provided $50,000 to people who lived downwind of the nuclear testing site near St. George and had been exposed to radiation. At least 40,000 people are thought to have been exposed in Utah alone.

While John Wayne is the most famous of them, the true cause of his cancer may never be definitively known.

What Happened to Malaysia Airlines Flight 370?

On March 8, 2014, Malaysia Airlines Flight 370 (also known as MH370) mysteriously disappeared with 227 passengers and 12 crew members on board. The Boeing 777 jetliner departed Kuala Lumpur, Malaysia, but never reached its destination of Beijing, China. It completely dropped off the radar.

* * * *

THE PLANE TOOK off at 12:41 A.M. and soon reached its cruising altitude of 35,000 feet. At 1:07 A.M. the plane's communications system issued what would be its last transmission. The Aircraft Communications Addressing and Reporting System (ACARS), which transmitted data about the aircraft's performance, showed nothing unusual and normal routing to Beijing. At 1:19 A.M. the last voice check-in was made as the plane was entering Vietnamese airspace. Two minutes later, the plane's transponder, which communicated with air-traffic controllers on the ground, was curiously turned off.

Although there was no communication by ACARS or transponder, at 2:15 A.M. Malaysian military radar tracked the plane passing over the Strait of Malacca. This would indicate that Flight 370 had turned around and flown southwest over the Malay Peninsula. At 2:22 A.M., the last primary radar contact was made by the Malaysian military determining Flight 370 had flown out across the Andaman Sea. A final "ping" was detected by a satellite at 8:11 A.M. The aircraft responded electronically, providing evidence that Flight 370 ended somewhere in the southern Indian Ocean.

No crash site has ever been discovered, nor have any bodies been recovered. The first piece of debris from MH370 was found in 2015 on the French island of Reunion, east of Madagascar. It was part of a wing called a flaperon. In total, more than 30 pieces of debris have turned up in Tanzania, Mauritius, South Africa, Mozambique, and Madagascar. However, only three wing fragments have been confirmed to be from MH370.

Due to the nature of the plane's complete disappearance there have been no shortage of conspiracy theories over the years. Investigations have ruled out the pilot's mental state, aircraft malfunction, and remote control of operation systems as possible factors in the disappearance.

In January 2017, the official search for MH370 by Malaysia, China, and Australia was called off. An American company, Ocean Infinity, continued the search, sweeping 112,000 square kilometers of the ocean floor, but turned up nothing.

In what was billed as their "final" report on Flight 370 in July 2018, the Malaysian government declared they could not determine with any certainty why the Boeing 777 had disappeared. They did, however, concede that the critical turn made by the plane was done manually.

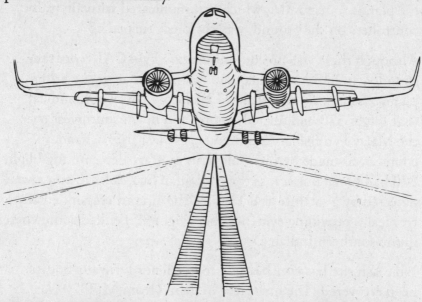

What Are the World's Greatest Missing Treasures?

They were fantastic examples of opulence, decadence, and splendor. People marveled at their beauty, drooled over their excess, and cowered at their power. And now they're gone. But where are they? And what happened to them?

✳   ✳   ✳   ✳

The Amber Room

DESCRIBED AS THE eighth wonder of the world by those who saw it, the Amber Room is certainly the most unique missing treasure in history. It was an 11-foot-square hall consisting of large wall panels inlaid with several tons of superbly designed amber, large gold-leaf-edged mirrors, and four magnificent Florentine mosaics. Arranged in three tiers, the amber was inlaid with precious jewels, and glass display cases housed one of the most valuable collections of Prussian and Russian artwork ever assembled. Created for Prussia's King Friedrich I, and given to Russian czar Peter the Great in 1716, it was located at Catherine Palace, near St. Petersburg. Today, the Amber Room would be valued at around $500 million.

When Adolf Hitler turned his Nazi war machine toward Russia, the keepers of the Amber Room got nervous. They tried to move it, but the amber began to crumble. Faced with probable destruction of one of Russia's greatest treasures or its abandonment to the Nazis, they attempted to hide the room's precious panels by covering them with gauze and wallpaper.

Although Leningrad (formerly called St. Petersburg) withstood a long, bloody siege, Nazi troops captured the city in October 1941. Soldiers discovered the treasure hidden behind the wallpaper, and German troops disassembled the room's panels over a 36-hour period, packed them in 27 crates, and shipped them back to Königsberg, in East Prussia.

The fabled Amber Room panels were put on display in Königsberg's castle museum during the remaining war years. But, when Königsberg surrendered in April 1945, the fabled treasure was nowhere to be found. The Amber Room was never seen again.

Did the Soviets unwittingly destroy their own treasure with bombs? Was it hidden in a now lost subterranean bunker outside the city? Or was it destroyed when Königsberg Castle burned shortly after the city surrendered? We will probably never know for sure.

Fortunately for lovers of opulence, the Amber Room has been painstakingly recreated at a cost exceeding $7 million. The reconstructed room was dedicated at a ceremony in 2003 marking the tricentennial of St. Petersburg's founding. The dazzling Amber Room is now on display in Catherine Palace.

Blackbeard's Treasure

The famous pirate Blackbeard only spent about two years (1716–1718) plundering the high seas. Within that time, however, he amassed some serious wealth. While the Spanish were busy obtaining all the gold and silver they could extract from Mexico and South America, Blackbeard and his mates waited patiently, then pounced on the treasure-laden ships as they sailed back to Spain.

Blackbeard developed a fearsome reputation as a cruel and vicious opportunist. His reign of terror centered around the West Indies and the Atlantic coast of North America, with headquarters in both the Bahamas and North Carolina. His end came in November 1718, when British Lieutenant Robert Maynard decapitated the pirate and hung his head from the bowsprit of his ship as a grisly trophy.

What happened to the vast treasure that Blackbeard had amassed? He acknowledged burying it but never disclosed the location. But that hasn't stopped countless treasure hunters from trying to get their hands on it. Blackbeard's sunken ship, *Queen Anne's Revenge*, is believed to have been discovered near Beaufort, North Carolina, in 1996, but the loot wasn't onboard. Possible locations for the hidden stash include the Caribbean Islands, Virginia's Chesapeake Bay, and the caves of the Cayman Islands.

Treasures of Lima

In 1820, Lima, Peru, was on the edge of revolt. As a preventative measure, the viceroy of Lima decided to transport the city's fabulous wealth to Mexico for safekeeping. The treasures included jeweled stones, candlesticks, and two life-size solid gold statues of Mary holding the baby Jesus. In all, the treasure filled 11 ships and was valued at around $60 million.

Captain William Thompson, commander of the *Mary Dear*, was put in charge of transporting the riches to Mexico. But the viceroy should have done some research on the man to whom he handed such fabulous wealth because Thompson was a pirate, and a ruthless one at that. Once the ships were well out to sea, he cut the throats of the Peruvian guards and threw their bodies overboard.

Thompson headed for the Cocos Islands, in the Indian Ocean, where he and his men allegedly buried the treasure. They then decided to split up and lay low until the situation had calmed down, at which time they would reconvene to divvy up the spoils. But the *Mary Dear* was captured, and the crew went on trial for piracy. All but Thompson and his first mate were hanged. To save their lives, the two agreed to lead the Spanish to the stolen treasure. They took them as far as the Cocos Islands and then managed to escape into the jungle. Thompson, the first mate, and the treasure were never seen again.

Since then over 300 expeditions have tried—unsuccessfully—to locate the treasures of Lima. The most recent theory is that the treasure wasn't buried on the Cocos Islands at all, but on an unknown island off the coast of Central America.

The Ark of the Covenant

To the ancient Israelites, the Ark of the Covenant was the most sacred thing on Earth. The central and paramount object of the Hebrew nation, this ornate chest was, according to the Bible, designed by God. Measuring 44 inches long, 26 inches wide, and 26 inches high, the chest was made of acacia wood, overlaid inside and out with pure gold, and surrounded by an artistic gold border. Mounted on the solid gold cover were two golden cherubs, one at each end of the cover facing each other, with heads bowed and wings extending upward.

The Ark served as a holy archive for the safekeeping of sacred relics, including the two stone tablets of the Ten Commandments. As a historical and religious treasure, the Ark and its contents were absolutely priceless.

In 607 B.C., Jerusalem, the capital city of the Israelite kingdom of Judah and home of Solomon's Temple, where the Ark was housed, was besieged and overthrown by the Babylonians. In a terrible slaughter, more than a million people were killed, with the survivors driven off into captivity. Seventy years later, when the Israelites returned to rebuild the city, the Ark of the Covenant was gone. The priceless relic's fate remains a mystery.

It is widely believed that the Ark was hidden by the Hebrews to keep it from the Babylonians. Possible locations for its hiding place range from Mount Nebo in Egypt to Ethiopia to a cave in the heart of Judah. Yet, if the Ark was hidden, why was it not recovered when the Israelites returned to Jerusalem and rebuilt the temple? Others believe that the Ark was destroyed by the rampaging Babylonians. Still another explanation put forth by the faithful is that God miraculously removed the Ark for safekeeping by means of divine intervention.

Montezuma's Treasure

The Spanish decimation of the Aztec empire in Mexico came to a head on July 1, 1520. After mortally wounding Emperor Montezuma, Hernando Cortés and his men were besieged by enraged Aztec warriors in the capital city of Tenochtitlán. After days of fierce fighting, Cortés ordered his men to pack up the vast treasures of Montezuma in preparation for a night flight, but they didn't get far before the Aztecs fell upon them. The ensuing carnage filled Lake Tezcuco with Spanish bodies and the stolen treasures of Montezuma. The terrified army had thrown the booty away in a vain attempt to escape with their lives. The hoard consisted of countless gold and silver ornaments, along with a huge array of jewels.

Cortés and a handful of his men got away with their lives and returned a year later to exact their revenge. When the inhabitants of Tenochtitlán got wind of the approaching invaders, they buried the remains of the city's treasure in and around Lake Tezcuco to prevent it from falling prey to the gold-crazed Spanish. Today, a vast treasure trove remains hidden beneath nearly five centuries of mud and sludge on the outskirts of Mexico City, the modern day incarnation of Tenochtitlán. Generations of treasure seekers have sought the lost hoard without success. A former president of Mexico even had the lake bed dredged, but no treasure was found.

Chapter 17

Odds and Ends

Why Did John Hancock Sign His Name So Big?

Take a look at the 56 signatures on the Declaration of Independence and you'll notice that one name stands out. It's written in large, flamboyant script in the center of the page directly below the main body of text. That signature, of course, belongs to John Hancock. Hancock's inscription is so well known that his name has become synonymous with the word signature, as in "put your John Hancock on the dotted line."

✳   ✳   ✳   ✳

ONE OF THE reasons Hancock's signature is so enormous is that he, as president of the Continental Congress, was the first to sign the Declaration of Independence. Hancock had plenty of real estate, and he used it. But goodness gracious, there were 55 other signatures that needed to be added. Leave some room for everyone else, guy.

Still, it wasn't necessarily a case of a man doing something simply because he could. Hancock felt that a big signature was important. Signing such a document did two things: First, it told American colonists and the rest of the world why the Congress felt it was necessary to break away from Great Britain. Second, by creating the Declaration of Independence, the congressional members were directly insulting England's

King George III, a treasonous act that could lead to hanging. Hancock believed that a bold sweep of his feathered quill would instill confidence and courage into his fellow colonial delegates, and into everyone else who read the document.

It's been said that after signing his name, Hancock defiantly exclaimed, "There, I guess King George will be able to read that!" or "The British ministry can read that name without spectacles; let them double the reward for my head!" Sure, and George Washington never told a lie. In all likelihood, Hancock never made such a boast—there simply wasn't the audience for it. Only one other person was present when Hancock signed the Declaration of Independence: Charles Thomson, the secretary of the Continental Congress, who claimed that Hancock never uttered such words. Besides, saying something that grandiose with just one other person in the room would have been, well, weird.

The delegates voted to ratify the Declaration of Independence on the night of July 4, 1776, but they did not sign it. (Now, go out and use that piece of info to win a bar bet!) The first version was printed, copied, signed by Hancock and Thomson, and distributed to political and military leaders for their review. On July 19, the Congress ordered that the document be "fairly engrossed on parchment," a fancy way of saying officially written. On August 2, the final version was ready to be signed. Hancock signed first, putting his John, er, his name in the middle of the document below the text. As was the custom, others started signing their names below Hancock's.

Not everyone whose name is on the Declaration of Independence was present that day. Signatures were added in the coming days, weeks, months, and years. The last person to sign was Thomas McKean, in 1781. And you just know that when McKean saw what little room there was for his signature, he thought, "[Bleeping] Hancock!"

How Did Murphy Get His Own Law?

Murphy's Law holds that if anything can go wrong, it will. It's a simple adage that seems to perfectly sum up so many situations in our topsy-turvy lives.

✳ ✳ ✳ ✳

Project M3981

IN 1949, CAPTAIN Edward A. Murphy, an engineer at Edwards Air Force Base in California, was working on Project M3981. The objective was to determine the level of sudden deceleration a pilot could withstand in the event of a crash. It involved sending a dummy or a human subject (possibly also a dummy) on a high-speed sled ride that came to a sudden stop and measuring the effects.

George E. Nichols, a civilian engineer with Northrop Aircraft, was the manager of the project. Nichols compiled a list of "laws" that presented themselves during the course of the team's work. For example, Nichols's Fourth Law is, "Avoid any action with an unacceptable outcome."

"If There Is Any Way to Do It Wrong . . ."

These sled runs were repeated at ever-increasing speeds, often with Dr. John Paul Stapp, an Air Force officer, in the passenger seat. After one otherwise-flawless run, Murphy discovered that one of his technicians had miswired the sled's transducer, so no data had been recorded. Cursing his subordinate, Murphy remarked, "If there is any way to do it wrong, he'll find it." Nichols added this little gem to his list, dubbing it Murphy's Law.

Not long after, Stapp endured a run that subjected him to 40 Gs of force during deceleration without substantive injury. Prior to Project M3981, the established acceptable standard had been 18 Gs, so the achievement merited a news conference.

Asked how the project had maintained such an impeccable safety record, Stapp cited the team's belief in Murphy's Law and its efforts to circumvent it. The law, which had been revised to its current language before the news conference, was quoted in a variety of aerospace articles and advertisements, and gradually found its way into the lexicon of the military and of pop culture.

Why Does a Seashell Sound Like the Ocean?

Is that big spiral conch you picked up during last year's trip to Hawaii still whispering sweet nothings in your ear? Well, that isn't the roar of the blue Pacific you hear—it's nothing more than the barrage of ambient noise around you.

✳ ✳ ✳ ✳

AH, SCIENCE CAN be so harshly unsentimental sometimes! Seashells don't really create any sound all by themselves. Inside, they're a labyrinth of hollow areas and hard, curved surfaces that happen to be really good reflectors of racket.

When you hold a seashell up to your ear, that shell is actually capturing and amplifying all the little noises occurring around you. These noises are usually so hushed that you don't even hear them unless you're paying very close attention. However, when they begin bouncing off the cavity of a shell, the echoes resonate more loudly into your ear. And what do you know? They sound a lot like ocean waves rolling up to shore.

It doesn't matter how far away you are from the sea, or even if you have a seashell. You can recreate the same "ocean sound" effect by simply cupping your hand, or a coffee mug, over your ear. Just be sure that mug is empty, or you'll really hear a splash.

How Does Glow-In-the-Dark Stuff Work?

Switch off the light in the bedroom of a typical eight-year-old and you might see a ceiling glowing with stars, planets, and dinosaurs. How does this work? First, let's review simple physics.

✳ ✳ ✳ ✳

ATOMS GAIN AND lose energy through the movement of electrons. Electrons are the tiny, negatively charged particles that orbit the atom's positively charged nucleus. When something energizes an atom, an electron jumps from a lower orbital (closer to the atom's nucleus) to a higher orbital (farther from the atom's nucleus).

Basically, the atom is storing energy that will be released in some form when the electron falls back to the lower orbital.

Light is one thing that can energize an atom in this way. When a light photon (an individual packet of light energy) hits the atom, that energy boosts an electron to a higher orbital. Some atoms can release energy as light: When the electron falls back to a lower orbital, the stored extra energy is emitted as a light photon.

Glow-in-the-dark stuff contains atoms that do just this; they're called phosphors. When you turn on the lights in your kid's room, the photons from the light excite these atoms and boost their electrons to higher orbitals. When you turn off the lights, the atoms release the stored energy. The electrons return to a lower level, emit photons, and the atoms glow. There's some energy loss in the process, so the glowing light of the little dinosaur will be of a different frequency (a different color) than the light that excited the atom in the first place.

Phosphors are everywhere. Your fingernails, teeth, and bodily fluids all contain natural phosphors. Your white clothes are phosphorescent too, thanks to whitening agents in laundry detergent. This is why all this stuff glows under a black light. The black light emits invisible ultraviolet light, which causes the phosphors to glow. (Dark clothes may contain phosphors, too, but the dark pigments absorb the UV light.)

Most phosphors have very short persistence—the atoms release the light energy immediately after they're charged, so they glow only when light is shining on them. By contrast, glow-in-the-dark stickers and the like are made of phosphors such as zinc sulfide and strontium aluminate that have unusually long persistence, so they keep glowing after you turn out the lights. Manufacturers mix these phosphors with plastic to make glow-in-the dark items in many shapes and sizes.

Other types of phosphors react to radiation from radioactive elements and compounds rather than from visible light radiation. This is how the hands on some watches glow with no charging required: They're coated with a radioactive isotope of hydrogen called tritium or promethium that's mixed with phosphors.

How Do Fireworks Form Different Shapes?

Fireworks have been delighting people for more than 700 years, and the design hasn't changed much in that time. Getting those fireworks to form complex shapes is a tricky challenge, but the basic idea is still fairly old-school.

✳   ✳   ✳   ✳

Fireworks Basics

To understand what's involved, it helps to know some fireworks basics. A fireworks shell is a heavy paper container that holds three sections of explosives. The first section is the "lift charge," a packet of black powder (a mixture of potassium nitrate, sulphur, and charcoal) at the bottom of the shell. To prepare the shell for launch, a pyrotechnician places the shell in a mortar (a tube that has the same diameter as the shell), with the lift charge facing downward. A quick-burning fuse runs from the lift charge to the top of the mortar. To fire the shell, an electric trigger lights the quick fuse. It burns down to ignite the black powder at the bottom of the shell, and the resulting explosion propels the shell out of the mortar and high into the air.

The second explosive section is the "bursting charge," a packet of black powder in the middle of the shell. When the electric trigger lights the quick-burning fuse, it also lights a time-delay fuse that runs to the bursting charge. As the shell is hurtling through the air, the time-delay fuse is burning down. Around the time the shell reaches its highest point, the fuse burns down to the bursting charge, and the black powder explodes.

Expanding black powder isn't exactly breathtaking to watch. The vibrant colors you see come from the third section of explosives, known as the "stars." Stars are simply solid clumps of explosive metals that emit colored light when they burn. For example, burning copper salts emit blue light and burning barium nitrate emits green light. The expanding black powder ignites the stars and propels them outward, creating colored streaks in the sky.

Determining Shape

The shape of the explosion depends on how the manufacturer positions the stars in the shell. To make a simple ring, it places the stars in a ring around the bursting charge; to make a heart, it positions the stars in a heart shape. Manufacturers can make more complex fireworks patterns, such as a smiley face, by combining multiple compartments with separate bursting charges and stars in a single shell. As the fuse burns, these different "breaks" go off in sequence. In a smiley face shell, the first break that explodes makes a ring, the second creates two dots for the eyes, and the third forms a crescent shape for the mouth.

It's hard to produce designs that are much more complex than that, since only a few breaks can be set off in quick succession. So if you're hoping to see a fireworks tribute to origami, you're out of luck.

Can You Beat a Lie Detector Test?

If you've been told that you'll need to take a polygraph test to be cleared of a crime, watch out—you're about to be duped. The polygraph or "lie detector" test is one of the most misunderstood tests used in law enforcement.

✳ ✳ ✳ ✳

MANY EXPERTS WILL tell you that lie detector tests are based on fallible data—there's no sure way a person can tell whether or not someone is lying. Since the test is so imperfect, be suspicious of anyone who makes your fate contingent upon the results of a polygraph test. Still, here are a few suggestions on how to beat one:

1. Unless you're applying for a job, refuse to take the polygraph test. There are no laws that can compel you to take it.

2. Keep your answers short and to the point. Most questions asked of you can be answered with a "yes" or "no."

3. During the polygraph test, you'll be asked three types of questions: irrelevant, relevant, and control questions. Irrelevant questions generally take the form of, "Is the color of this room white?" Relevant questions are the areas that get you into trouble. Control questions are designed to "calibrate" your responses during the test. See the next point.

4. Control questions are asked so that the technician can compare the responses to questions against a known entity. The easiest way to beat a lie detector test is to invalidate the control questions. Try these simple techniques when asked a control question:

* Change your breathing rate and depth from the normal 15 to 30 breaths per minute to anything faster or slower.

* Solve a math problem in your head, or count backward from 100 by 7.

* Bite the sides of your tongue until it begins to hurt.

How Does a Flak Jacket Stop a Bullet?

"Flak" is an abbreviation of Fliegerabwehrkanone, *a German word that looks rather silly (as many German words do). There's nothing silly, however, about its meaning: anti-aircraft cannon.*

* * * *

SERIOUS DEVELOPMENT OF flak jackets began during World War II, when Air Force gunners wore nylon vests with steel plates sewn into them as protection against shrapnel. After the war, manufacturers discovered that they could remove the steel plates and instead make the vests out of multiple layers of dense, heavily woven nylon.

Without the steel plates, the vests became a viable option for ground troops to wear during combat. Anywhere from 16 to 24 layers of this nylon fabric were stitched together into a thick quilt. In the 1960s, DuPont developed Kevlar, a lightweight fiber that is five times stronger than a piece of steel of the same weight. Kevlar was added to flak jackets in 1975.

It seems inconceivable that any cloth could withstand the force of a bullet. The key, however, is in the construction of the fabric. In a flak jacket, the fibers are interlaced to form a super strong net. The fibers are twisted as they are woven, which adds to their density. Modern flak jackets also incorporate a coating of resin on the fibers and layers of plastic film between the layers of fabric. The result is a series of nets that are designed to bend but not break.

A bullet that hits the outer layers of the vest's material is flattened into a mushroomlike shape. The remaining layers of the vest can then dissipate the misshapen bullet's energy and prevent it from penetrating. The impact of the offending bullet usually leaves a bruise or blunt trauma to internal organs, which is a minor injury compared to the type of devastation a bullet is meant to inflict.

While no body armor is 100 percent impenetrable, flak jackets offer different levels of protection depending on the construction and materials involved. At the higher levels of protection, plates of lightweight steel or special ceramic are still used. But all flak jackets incorporate this netlike fabric as a first line of defense. *Fliegerabwehrkanone*, indeed.

Are All Coffins Six Feet Under?

It's widely believed that the standard graveyard procedure is to put a coffin six feet under. But the truth is, burial depths vary considerably.

✳ ✳ ✳ ✳

Different Feet for Different Folks

WE'VE ALL HEARD the line in a cheesy movie that, against our better judgment, has sucked us in and stuck us to the couch: "One more move, and I'll put you six feet under." Whether the words are growled by a cowboy in a black hat or a mobster in pinstripes, everyone knows what those six feet represent: the depth where coffins reside after burial.

Or do they? The bad guy may well mean what he says, but the final resting place for someone unfortunate enough to be in a coffin varies depending on the site of the burial. These depths can range from 18 inches to 12 feet. There's no world council that has decreed that a person must be put to rest exactly six feet under. Think about it. Digging a six-foot grave in a region below sea level, such as New Orleans, would get pretty soggy.

Who Makes the Call?

Most grave depths are determined by local, state, or national governments. New Orleans has dealt with its topographical issues by placing most of its dead above ground in crypts. The area's gravesites in the ground are almost always less than two feet deep—and even that doesn't prevent the occasional floater.

The California requirement is a mere 18 inches. In Quebec, Canada, the law states that coffins "shall be deposited in a grave and covered with at least one meter of earth" (a little more than three feet). This is similar to New South Wales in Australia, which calls for 900 millimeters (slightly less than three feet). And the Institute of Cemetery and Crematorium Management in London says that "no body shall be buried in such a manner that any part of the coffin is less than three feet below the level of any ground adjoining the grave."

The Turn of a Phrase

If burial depths vary from place to place, how did the phrase "six feet under" come to life? (Sorry, couldn't resist.) Historians believe it originated in England. London's Great Plague of 1665 killed 75,000 to 100,000 people. In Daniel Defoe's book *A Journal of the Plague Year*, he writes that the city's lord mayor issued an edict that all graves had to be dug six feet deep to limit the spread of the plague outbreak. Other sources confirm Defoe's claim.

Of course, the plague is a scourge of the past, and today's world has no uniform burial depth. But who really cares? It still makes for a winning line in an otherwise schlocky movie.

Why Does It Take Longer to Fly West Than East?

If you've ever flown a long distance, you might have noticed that it takes more time to fly from east to west than west to east. Since there's no real traffic in the sky (apart from the occasional flock of birds), the delay seems inexplicable. It should take the same amount of time, regardless of direction.

✳ ✳ ✳ ✳

BUT THE BITTER truth is, the air up there isn't quite as wide open as it seems. At the high altitude that is required for commercial flights, there's a powerful and persistent horizontal wind known as the jet stream. Because of the differences in temperature and pressure between the equator and the earth's polar regions, the jet stream flows from west to east in the Northern Hemisphere. This jet stream is a lot like a current in a river: If you're moving with the current, you'll go faster; conversely, working against the current slows you down and makes you work harder to get where you're going.

The airlines, of course, know all about the wily ways of the jet stream. They take advantage of it, purposely flying within it on eastbound flights to allow planes to reach their destinations sooner and with less wear and tear. (Some airlines even offer cheaper fares on the eastbound leg of a journey.) But on a westbound flight, a pilot must fly against the jet stream, which obviously means that it takes more time.

A westerly cross-country flight lasts about a half-hour longer than its easterly counterpart. Though it's invisible to the naked eye, the jet stream is like a giant traffic jam in the sky.

Why Isn't the Whole Plane Made of the Same Stuff as the Black Box?

Planes, believe it or not, are pretty lightweight. They're built with light metals, such as aluminum. The newer ones are built with even lighter composite materials and plastics. This allows them to be fairly sturdy without adding too much weight.

* * * *

I F PLANES WERE made of the same stuff as the black box, they just wouldn't get off the ground. But let's backtrack a bit here. The term "black box" is a little misleading. What the media refer to as a "black box" is actually two boxes: the Flight Data Recorder (FDR), which records altitude, speed, magnetic heading, and so on; and the Cockpit Voice Recorder (CVR), which records the sounds in the cockpit (presumably ensuring that pilots are on their best behavior all the time). What's more, these boxes are generally bright orange, making them easier to find after a crash. "Black" box either comes from older models that were black or from the charred and/or damaged states of the boxes after a crash.

Whatever the reason behind the name, black boxes are sturdy little things. They carry a bunch of microchips and memory banks encased in protective stainless steel. The protective casing is about a quarter-inch thick, which makes the boxes really heavy. Furthermore, black boxes are not necessarily indestructible—they usually remain intact after a crash partially because they are well placed. They're generally put in the tail of the plane, which often doesn't bear the brunt of a crash.

Even with this extra protection, black boxes sometimes don't survive a plane crash. Still, they typically have been useful, though not so useful that you'd want to build an entire plane with their stainless steel casings.

Does Running Through the Rain Keep You Drier Than Walking?

It makes intuitive sense that running through the rain will keep you drier than walking. You will spend less time in the rain, after all. But there's a pervasive old wives' tale that says it won't do any good. So every time there's a downpour and you need to reach your car, you are faced with this confounding question: Should you walk or run?

✳   ✳   ✳   ✳

THE ARGUMENT AGAINST running is that more drops hit your chest and legs when you're moving at a quicker pace. If you're walking, the theory goes, the drops are mainly hitting your head. So the proponents of walking say that running exposes you to more drops, not fewer.

Several scientists have pondered this possibility (after finishing up their actual work for the day, we hope). In 1987, an Italian physicist determined that sprinting keeps you drier than walking, but only by about 10 percent, which might not be worth the effort and the risk of slipping. In 1995, a British researcher concluded that the increased front-drenching of running effectively cancels out the reduced rain exposure.

These findings didn't seem right to two climatologists at the National Climatic Data Center in Asheville, North Carolina, so they decided to put them to the test. In 1996, they put on identical outfits with plastic bags underneath to keep moisture from seeping out of the clothes and to keep their own sweat from adding to the drenching. One person ran about 330 feet in the rain; the other walked the same distance. They weighed the wet clothes, compared the weights to those when the clothes were dry, and determined that the climatologist who walked got 40 percent wetter than the one who ran.

In other words, run to your car.

Why Doesn't Water in a Water Tower Freeze?

Although our chemistry teacher more likely compared us to Linus Van Pelt than Linus Pauling, even we know that water freezes at 32 degrees Fahrenheit. So why doesn't the water in a water tower freeze during those long, cold winters?

✳ ✳ ✳ ✳

TO FULLY UNDERSTAND why you're able to turn on your faucet and have running water even on the coldest days, we need to look at how water towers work. Most towns get their water from wells or bodies of water such as lakes. This water is pumped to a water treatment plant, where it is disinfected before being delivered through a main pipeline to the rest of the area's delivery system. A water tower is hooked up to that system, drawing water into its reservoir as it is pumped through the main pipes. When the demand for water is too much for the system pump to handle, gravity and water pressure release water from the tower back into the main pipeline. During off-peak times, the water tower refills from the pipeline.

This is a simple, efficient system, and one that helps explain why water towers don't freeze solid in the winter. When a water tower pulls water from the pipeline to refill its reservoir, it is drawing somewhat warmer water from the pipes. Furthermore, water towers are drained and refilled fairly frequently, making it difficult for ice to form. The agitation of water molecules from the movement of draining and refilling slows down the freezing process, too. (To get an idea of the way this works, think of how long it takes waterfalls or rivers to freeze.)

However, in some parts of the country—such as the frozen tundra of North Dakota—water in water towers does freeze. Rarely, though, does it freeze solid. In climates where freezing is a danger, water towers are more heavily insulated, and some are even built with heating systems near their bases that prevent water from freezing on its way into the tower.

Of course, no precautions are foolproof. Just about anything can freeze over if it's cold enough for long enough: lakes, waterfalls, water towers, and, if our passing grade in high school chemistry is any indication, even hell.

How Do People Swallow Swords?

Verrry carefully. There are ways to fake it—such as using a trick sword with a plastic blade that collapses into the hilt—but authentic sword swallowing is no optical illusion. The blade isn't as sharp as that of a normal sword, but that doesn't change the fact that the swallower is pushing a hard metal shaft deep into his or her body.

✳   ✳   ✳   ✳

IRONICALLY, ONE OF the essential skills of sword swallowing is not swallowing. When you stand and face upward, your upper gastrointestinal tract—the passageway that's made up of your throat, pharynx, esophagus, and stomach—is straight and flexible enough that a sword can pass through it. When you swallow, muscles contract and expand along the passageway in order to move food down to your stomach. Two sphincters along this tract—the upper esophageal sphincter between your pharynx and esophagus and the lower esophageal sphincter between your esophagus and stomach—are normally closed; they open involuntarily as food moves past. To keep the passageway clear, the swallower must learn deep relaxation techniques to resist the urge to swallow.

Sword swallowers also have to suppress their gag reflex, an automatic muscle contraction triggered when nerve endings in the back of the throat sense a foreign object. To deactivate the gag reflex, a sword swallower crams progressively larger objects into the back of the throat while trying not to gag.

After hours of disgusting noises and periodic vomiting, the gag reflex is suitably numbed and the aspiring swallower can get down to business.

As the sword slides down the gastrointestinal tract all the way into the stomach, it straightens the various curves of the tract. Some swallowers coat their swords with a lubricant, such as olive oil, to help them along.

This mind-over-matter feat is one of the oldest stunts out there. Historians believe that the practice originated in India around 2000 B.C., as a part of rituals designed to demonstrate powerful connections to the gods. The ancient Romans, Greeks, and Chinese picked up the practice, but generally viewed it as entertainment rather than religious observance. Sword swallowers at the 1893 World's Fair in Chicago sparked America's interest in the spectacle, and it soon became a staple of traveling sideshows.

Did we mention that you shouldn't try this trick at home? It goes without saying that sword swallowing is a dangerous and generally ill-advised endeavor. Even master swallowers sustain injuries—cram a sword, even a dull one, down your throat enough times, and you're likely to nick something important. If you must impress your friends, stick with more manageable sharp objects, such as Doritos.

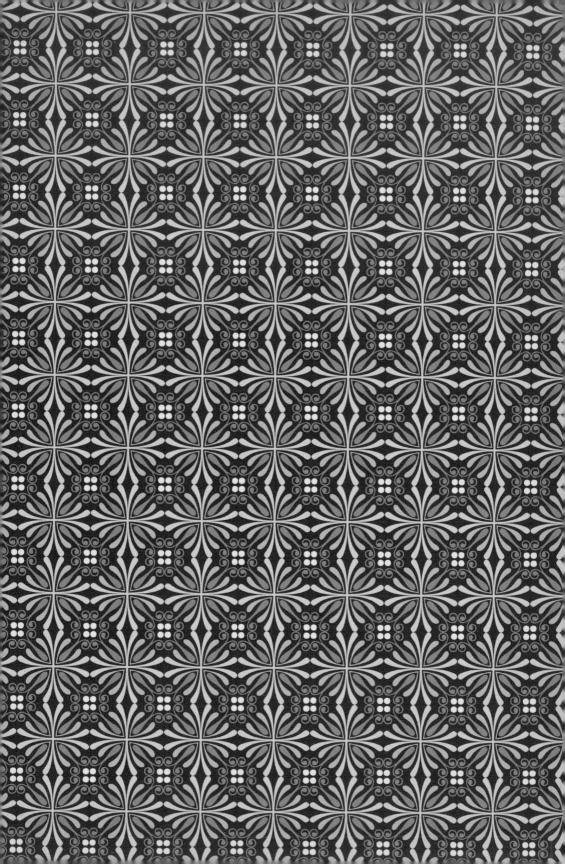